AF262863

The LOST FOUNDER

ALSO BY JESSE WEGMAN

Let the People Pick the President

The *The* LOST FOUNDER

*James Wilson
and the Forgotten Fight
for a People's Constitution*

JESSE WEGMAN

CELADON
BOOKS

NEW YORK

THE LOST FOUNDER. Copyright © 2026 by Jesse Wegman. All rights reserved. Printed in the United States of America. For information, address Celadon Books, a division of Macmillan Publishers, 120 Broadway, New York, NY 10271. EU Representative: Macmillan Publishers Ireland Ltd., 1st Floor, The Liffey Trust Centre, 117–126 Sheriff Street Upper, Dublin 1, D01 YC43.

www.celadonbooks.com

The Library of Congress Cataloging-in-Publication Data is available upon request.

ISBN 978-1-250-85107-9 (hardcover)
ISBN 978-1-250-85109-3 (ebook)

Our books may be purchased in bulk for specialty retail/wholesale, literacy, corporate/premium, educational, and subscription box use. Please contact MacmillanSpecialMarkets@macmillan.com.

First Edition: 2026

10 9 8 7 6 5 4 3 2 1

For Kyra, Sami, and Natalya

I'm different from you, John. I'm different from most of the men here. I don't want to be remembered.

—JAMES WILSON TO JOHN DICKINSON,
1776, the Broadway musical

Contents

The LOST FOUNDER

Prologue

LATE AUGUST WAS no time to be stuck on the Carolina coast. From Cape Fear north to Albemarle Sound, a dank foulness settled in by early summer and blanketed the region, not lifting until the first frost. The miasma, farmers and fishermen called it—a noxious, invisible presence that seemed to emanate from the stagnant swamps, pocosins, and millponds, the places where neither air nor water moved.

No one knew what caused it, not in the late 1700s, but they did know that the summer air made people terribly sick. In small towns and plantations up and down the eastern part of the state, victims were ravaged by a paroxysm of fevers, chills, and sweats that lasted for days before burning itself out, only to return and repeat the cycle. Infected children suffered seizures; adults collapsed in pools of vomit.

The disease's distinctive pattern gave it its common name at the time, the intermittent fever. Today it is known around the world as malaria—literally, "bad air."

Those who succumbed endured a grinding end, gasping for their last breaths. Those who survived were marked by their ordeal with the telltale signs: jaundiced eyes, a swollen belly, a withered constitution. Men and women throughout the region appeared "pale, decayed and prematurely old," a visitor from Germany observed in 1788. Carolina, he wrote, was "in the spring a paradise, in the summer a hell, and in the autumn a hospital." But the doctors in this hospital had little training and no cures for the pestilence. Instead, they burned frankincense, fed spiders to their desperate patients, or made them drink their own urine.

In Edenton, a once-bustling harbor town tucked into the corner of Albemarle Sound near the northern edge of the state, the miasma made the summer of 1798 seem endless. Deep into the fall, the fever tore through households and devastated neighborhoods.

It was the latest blow to a community that had prospered throughout the eighteenth century, first as the colonial capital and later as a global hub of shipbuilding, but whose prominence had faded as newer, more accessible ports had risen on the Atlantic, drawing most of the shipping traffic that used to navigate the shoals of the sound. In losing its prosperity, Edenton gained some rougher edges. Most of its 1,600 or so residents were poorer whites or enslaved Blacks. Town leaders complained of "the midnight revels of sailors" and of "fine fat hogs" roaming freely in the streets, which were "so thronged by clans of negroes, that the fair sex find it difficult to pass, without being jostled." A group of young men nicknamed the Witty Club loitered in the courtyards of local taverns, making crude jokes and gawking at women.

Edenton was not, in short, somewhere you would expect to find one of the richest and most powerful figures in the new nation—which is why it was appealing to someone who did not want to be found.

That summer of 1798, in the second-floor bedroom of John Horniblow's tavern on East King Street, lay a middle-aged man, many miles from home. James Wilson had been holed up there for months, refusing to leave even as the Carolina heat and signature fever had descended. He had no choice: He was a fugitive from the law.

He was also a sitting justice of the US Supreme Court.

For more than a year, Wilson had been absent from the court and on the run from authorities and creditors. He had been arrested and thrown into jail at least twice after failing to pay staggering debts from a string of land deals gone bad. He blamed everyone except himself for his predicament.

Upon his release from a New Jersey jail the previous year, Wilson had faced a stark choice: head back to his home in Philadelphia and almost certainly get arrested again or make a run for it. He chose the latter. Over hundreds of miles, Wilson eluded his pursuers, heading south through Maryland and Virginia and, finally, toward the North Carolina home of his friend and fellow justice James Iredell. Wilson thought he would find refuge there, but another creditor, to whom he owed nearly two hundred thousand dollars, tracked him down and sought to have him arrested and locked up at the county jail in Edenton, blocks from John Horniblow's tavern.

Wilson was determined to stay free, which meant staying hidden. "I have been hunted like a wild beast," he wrote to his lawyer in the spring.

Day after day in the small, dark room at Horniblow's, Wilson's young wife, Hannah, sat beside him, pleading with him to pay his debts and return home. He refused, although he didn't have the money anyway. By the end of July, his condition had worsened, and his lawyer had run off with the last of his funds. Hannah, who now spent days without break at his bedside, was selling her needlework to pay down the bills for the tavern's room and board. Her husband's bedclothes were ragged and stained; there was no money to replace them. His graying hair was untied and uncombed. His once-imposing frame had wasted away, and his belly was bloated even though he ate little. For days he had been battling a raging fever that would come and go and come again.

One sweltering afternoon, as Wilson tried to sleep off his latest bout of illness, his wife took up a quill and drafted a letter to her stepson back in Philadelphia. "He has sat up three hours today," she wrote. "He has had a violent attack; it will be some days before he recovers his strength, and the weather is very warm. He has not had a return of the fever since Monday. It takes back constantly; weakness is his chief complaint now. My friends advise me to be very careful as the sickly season is coming on, but I think I shall be proof against it. I am obliged to leave off every minute to wipe the perspiration from my face and hands."

The window to the room was propped open, in the hope of drawing a slight breeze to dry Wilson's sweats. As he slept fitfully, his wife continued her letter. "His clothes are all going to pieces, he has not had anything since he left home, which is fifteen months." She closed with a request: "Write me what people say to our not coming home. You need not be afraid of distressing me, as I can hear nothing worse than I expect."

No treatment eased Wilson's suffering. The few concoctions on offer could be found in jars lining the shop windows of local country doctors, most of whom had no formal medical education. The labels read like a wizard's poem: camphire, sweet mercury, rheubarb, jallap, Ipecacuanha, myrrh, gummastick, borax, saltpetre, brimstone, Peruvian bark. The last of these, made from the powdered bark of the Andean cinchona tree, contained quinine, which is still used to treat malaria today. Every morning, Hannah dissolved a spoonful of the bitter powder into a glass of water and helped her husband force it down. But the fever kept coming back, each time worse than before.

By the third week of August, Wilson was delirious and had stopped responding to Hannah, who had not left his side for days. She sat, vigilant, not able to accept that his health was declining rapidly and not ready to admit what anyone else could plainly see. Late in the afternoon on August 21, she allowed Iredell into the room and left to get some rest. In the still, blue darkness of the late summer evening, Iredell watched Wilson draw short, reflexive gasps of air, each one smaller than the last, until the gasps stopped.

"The illness of which he died was of short duration, tho' very sharp," Iredell wrote to Wilson's sister-in-law a few days later.

The following week, Hannah recounted Wilson's final moments in a letter to her stepson. "I had not my clothes off for three days and nights, nor left him till the evening of his death, when I could not bear the scene any longer. I am astonished at myself when I think of what I have gone through. They told me he died easy."

"What a miserable termination to such distinguished abilities," Jacob Rush wrote to his brother, Benjamin, upon learning of Wilson's death. "What a dark cloud overcast the last days of a life that had once been marked with uncommon lustre." Remarks like these were few and mostly in private. In the August 29 edition of the *State Gazette of North Carolina*, the newspaper published around the corner from Horniblow's, there was no mention of a death at the tavern. It was not until two months later that a careful reader, scanning the second-to-last page of the *Gazette*'s October 31 edition, might have come across a three-line item indirectly referencing Wilson's death and his position as a justice of the Supreme Court, but making no mention of his role in the nation's founding. The item read: "Bushrod Washington, of Virginia, is appointed Associate Justice of the Supreme Court of the United States, *vice* James Wilson, dec."

Introduction

IF YOU HAVE not heard of James Wilson—and most people have not—the story of his ruinous spending and anonymous death is a big part of the reason. It made no difference that he was a political visionary and legal colossus, a Supreme Court justice, signer of the Declaration of Independence and the Constitution, and one of the Constitution's most influential drafters. It did not matter that he was, by a long shot, the most democratic of all the founders—a man who believed that all power resides in the people themselves and who saw the future of America more clearly than any of his peers. His wretched demise, barely a decade after the Constitution became the law of the land, erased him from the story of America's birth with astonishing speed.

Little more than twenty-five years later, a biographer collecting the life stories of the Declaration of Independence's signers wrote in desperation to one of Wilson's former law apprentices. The biographer, Robert Waln, had been trying to locate anyone with information about Wilson, but had had little success beyond Wilson's only granddaughter and one of his oldest friends. "I know of no other living source," Waln wrote.

Another decade would pass before the American people finally got to read James Madison's copious notes of the Constitutional Convention, which he had ordered to be kept private until after his death. For the first time, it was clear to anyone who looked how central Wilson had been to the creation of our national charter and how radical and prescient his ideas were.

By then, the heroes of the founding had already been anointed. Acolytes of the leading founders promoted their legacies, preserved their records, and ensured that their names would be remembered through history. Today, the National Archives identifies seven of these founders as "major shapers of the United States": George Washington, Benjamin Franklin, John Adams, Thomas Jefferson, Alexander Hamilton, James Madison, and John Jay. James Wilson remains largely invisible, despite being their equal, at least, in shaping the American republic. Even his headstone in the courtyard of Philadelphia's Christ Church lists the wrong date for his death.

Inquiring into Wilson's absence from the narrative of the founding leads to a broader question: Why do we spend so much time thinking and talking and arguing about the creation of the United States and the people who led it? Why are we so transfixed by the stories of those who wrote the Declaration of Independence and the Constitution?

The answer lies, in part, in the audacity of what they and their fellow colonists pulled off: declaring that they would no longer live under the rule of a powerful despot; fighting and winning a war against a far superior military force; and, finally, designing a new nation based on political theories that had never been tested on such a large scale. In their hubris, they were convinced that their experiment in republican self-government would change the course of history. And they were right.

But our fascination is with not only what they did but why they did it. America was not founded on a shared ethnicity, religion, or geography, as have been most other countries. It was founded on a set of radical ideas—including the consent of the governed, the rule of law, the separation of powers, and human equality—that reflected the dawn of a new era in human history, one based on individual freedom and self-determination.

At the same time, the people who championed these ideas were full of contradictions. They claimed ownership of millions of acres of land that wasn't theirs. They kept humans in bondage for their own benefit, and they enshrined a system that resulted in the enslavement of millions of men, women, and children for decades after independence. Thomas Jefferson, who gets credit for writing "all men are created equal," held hundreds of humans as his personal property. The Constitution gave no rights to enslaved people, yet it counted them toward the congressional representation of the states that profited the most from slavery. These were affirmative choices, and they cannot be dismissed as necessary steps on the path to creating a "free" republic. Rather, they call into question the viability of the central ideas undergirding that republic.

All these elements—the history, the ideas, the contradictions—are part of the story of America. When a key part of that story is left out—when we erase someone like Wilson, who played such an influential role in the design of the nation even as he was so different from the other founders—it prevents us from more fully understanding our nation, its history, and its potential.

The great irony of Wilson's modern-day anonymity is that among his peers there was no question about his prominence. To those who attended the Constitutional Convention with him he was without equal.

"No man is more clear, copious, and comprehensive than Mr. Wilson," said William Pierce, a delegate from Georgia.

He was "as able, candid, and honest a member as any in convention," George Washington wrote in a letter after the delegates had completed their work.

Benjamin Rush, who also signed the Declaration of Independence, said of Wilson, "His mind, while he spoke, was one blaze of light."

These men knew it was impossible to separate the birth of the United States from the ideas of the Scottish immigrant who arrived on American shores as an ambitious twenty-three-year-old in 1765. Wilson's perceptive legal analysis was central to the push by the colonies for independence, and his political and moral arguments informed every major deal struck at the 1787 constitutional convention in Philadelphia. There is a good case to be made, as several scholars of the founding era have, that Wilson was as central to the architecture of the Constitution as James Madison.

Wilson seemed destined for greatness almost from the moment he stepped off the boat in New York Harbor. Within three years of his arrival, he drafted a lengthy essay arguing that the British Parliament had no authority at all over the colonies—a radical claim that went farther than any other political thinker was willing to go at the time. The essay laid the legal groundwork for the American Revolution and may have inspired the most celebrated passage in the Declaration of Independence: "We hold these truths to be self-evident, that all men are created equal."

This was Wilson's central principle, the one that illuminated his entire life—all people are equal, and all political authority resides in them alone. A self-governing republic could succeed only to the extent that it reflected this principle. "The truth is, that the supreme, absolute, and uncontrollable authority remains with the people," he said in 1787.

Earlier that year, Wilson had infused the debate over the new Constitution with his radical democratic vision, weighing in with his rough Scottish brogue more often than all but one other delegate. In his precise, balanced script, he wrote the Constitution's first draft. It was Wilson who coined its famous opening words, "We the People." He was one of only six men to sign his name to both of the nation's founding documents, the Declaration of Independence and the Constitution. He was the only one who insisted on the unbreakable bond between them. It would be many decades before an American president, Abraham Lincoln, made the same observation in public, standing on the smoldering battlefield at Gettysburg and invoking the Declaration's egalitarian principle as central to the survival of the American experiment.

Even before the Constitution was ratified, Wilson was widely regarded as the nation's best lawyer. George Washington hired Wilson to tutor his nephew Bushrod, and when Washington assumed the presidency in 1789 he appointed Wilson to be an associate justice on the first Supreme Court. (Following Wilson's death, Bushrod took his seat on the court.) Beginning in 1790, Wilson delivered a celebrated series of lectures on American law that shaped the nation's legal principles and jurisprudence for decades. All the pieces were in place for him to join Washington, Jefferson, Madison, and the rest in the canon of the American founding, but only eight years later, he died impoverished and disgraced and disappeared from the story of the nation's founding.

If James Wilson is going to be restored to his rightful place in history, then his own story needs to be told. It is the story of a brilliant, single-minded son of a farmer raised in a modest, deeply religious family on the windswept hills outside Edinburgh. As a young man, Wilson rejected his parents' desire that he enter the ministry and chose instead to study with the leading minds of the Scottish Enlightenment. All the founding fathers were well versed in Enlightenment ideas, but none had trained, as Wilson had, at the feet of the masters themselves.

It is also the story of a visionary who never fully understood what it took to be a leader, nor looked the part. He was tall, stout and ruddy, with reddish-brown hair and wire-rimmed glasses that perpetually slipped to the end of his nose, forcing him to tip his head back to keep them in place, a mannerism that was often misinterpreted as arrogance. He struggled to overcome that impression. Even around friends, he was stiff, stern, and rarely at ease. His political rivals took every chance to mock and attack him. They ridiculed him as "Jimmy de Caledonia" (the Latin word for what is now Scotland) and burned him in effigy.

Finally, it is the story of addiction and contradiction. Wilson's politics championed the common man, but his private life was consumed by a compulsion for speculating in frontier land that grew increasingly reckless, eventually landing him in debtors' prison. Well before then, his affinity for the perks of wealth cast him as suspicious in the eyes of revolutionary radicals, who considered him at best a conservative aristocrat and at worst a Loyalist to the British Crown.

One October day in 1779, an armed mob attacked Wilson's house in Philadelphia while he barricaded himself inside. That incident, which led to the deaths of seven people and became known as the Fort Wilson Riot, is in many ways the animating force behind this book. Unknown to the public today, the attack is seen by historians of the founding era as "perhaps the most dramatic riot of the revolutionary period." And it raises the obvious question of how someone like Wilson, whose life was devoted to the ideal of popular sovereignty—the rule of the people—could survive a near-death experience at the hands of a violent mob and come out the other side no less committed to that ideal.

Wilson's erasure from American history is even more perplexing when you consider how modern his ideas were for their time and how much they continue to drive our debates about politics and government. Consider popular sovereignty—the idea that in a self-governing society, the ultimate political authority resides in the people themselves and nowhere else. Throughout his life, Wilson advocated for this idea more fervently than did any other founder. "As our constitutions are superior to our legislatures, so the people are superior to our constitutions," he said. This brought him to a radical-sounding conclusion: "The people may change the constitutions whenever and however they please. This is a right of which no positive institution can ever deprive them." But to Wilson it wasn't radicalism; it was common sense.

It was also at odds with the views of most of his peers, many of whom were openly hostile to the idea that the people could or should govern themselves. Elbridge Gerry of Massachusetts derided the people as "the dupes of pretended patriots" and spoke of the evils that flowed from "the excess of democracy." Connecticut's Roger Sherman said "the people immediately should have as little to do as may be about the government." Benjamin Rush called democracy "the devil's own government."

Wilson could not disagree more, as he made clear throughout his life. The people, he argued, should have a direct hand in choosing their leaders at every level of government—and they should be represented according to their numbers. He was adamant not only that the people rule, but that they do so by majorities. "The majority of people wherever found ought in all questions to govern the minority," he said.

Coming from a man who was nearly killed by a mob, Wilson's insistence on the popular will and majority rule might appear strange. But these two things were, in his mind, the only way to ensure political equality. That is why he argued so strongly, if in vain, for a popularly elected president, House, and Senate, and it is why he was so mystified at his peers' insistence that their states should enjoy equal power in Congress regardless of their size. "It is strange that annexing the name of 'State' to ten thousand men should give them an equal right with forty thousand," Wilson said. "This must be the effect of magic, not of reason."

The other key component of Wilson's political philosophy was a powerful national government, one that was supreme over the states. To Wilson, the perils of not having such a government were clear: States were equipped to handle local matters, but in a republic as sprawling and diverse as America the most pressing issues were far bigger. What was the point of creating a federal constitution if not to solve the types of problems that are continental in scope?

This argument—that the federal government should have the powers it needs to confront the challenges it faces—has been invoked at moments of extreme crisis throughout American history, from the aftermath of the Civil War to the New Deal, from Lyndon Johnson's Great Society to Barack Obama's Affordable Care Act, and most recently through the Covid-19 pandemic.

Wilson, unlike any of his peers, saw these two components as inseparable: a supreme national government chosen by a sovereign people, all of whom are, or should be, political equals. He also intuited that the people would accept living under such a powerful government only to the extent that they understood its workings. Despite his extensive training in law, Wilson insisted that the Constitution and laws be easy to read and as free as possible from artifice and legalisms. "Simplicity and plainness and precision should mark the texture of a law," he wrote in 1791. "It claims the obedience—it should be level to the *understanding* of all."

The idea that the people should be able to see for themselves how government works was as radical as any political theory. One hundred and fifty years later, Franklin Roosevelt seemed to channel James Wilson in his 1937 Constitution Day speech, delivered at another moment when representative democracy faced an existential threat. "The Constitution of the United States was a layman's document, not a lawyer's contract," Roosevelt said.

Roosevelt wasn't alone in understanding the importance of Wilson's thought, even though he didn't name him. In the early 1960s, the Supreme Court issued a string of decisions that fundamentally altered American democracy by requiring that all congressional and state legislative districts contain roughly the same number of people, so that all people would have equal representation, no matter where they lived. It was a groundbreaking reform, this principle the court called "one person, one vote," and as their primary authority for it, the justices cited Wilson. "All elections ought to be equal," Wilson had said in a 1791 speech quoted by the majority. "Elections are equal, when a given number of citizens, in one part of the state, choose as many representatives, as are chosen by the same number of citizens, in any other part of the state. In this manner, the proportion of representatives and of the constituents will remain invariably the same." Today, "one person, one vote" is among the most revered principles of American democracy, more than two centuries after James Wilson fought for it to be the defining feature.

Indeed, no other founder foresaw more accurately where America was headed—a country more democratic, more inclusive, and more egalitarian than any of his contemporaries dared imagine. Wilson's expansive vision of democracy led him to support lenient immigration laws, which had special relevance to him as an immigrant. He spoke of women with the respect of a man from another era, which in many ways he seemed to be—a twenty-first-century man trapped in the eighteenth century.

Can Wilson's erasure be chalked up simply to his catastrophic final years and his pathetic final days? To the absence of any concerted effort to cement his legacy? Is it simply Wilson's "perennial tragedy" that "he was born too soon and his time was limited"? All these explanations play a part, but there are others.

There are Wilson's political failures—above all, his failure to convert his vision of America into reality, at least in his time. Compared to the founders whose names we know, Wilson did not get his way when it came to key pieces of our constitutional design and function, specifically a popularly elected president and a Senate based on population rather than states. Nor did he serve as president, a job that goes a long way toward cementing a legacy.

There are Wilson's personal failures—the crazed land speculation that led to the "deranged state of his affairs," in the words of his friend Benjamin Rush. Ironically, America's democratization in the early nineteenth century was accelerated by the financial collapse of founding era titans like Wilson and the financier Robert Morris, which created space for a new generation of leaders in business and government. These latter men were less educated than the founders; they were, in the words of the historian Gordon Wood, "very ordinary indeed."

There are Wilson's epistolary failures—his unfortunate aversion to putting things down on paper for future historians and archivists to comb through, as virtually all his fellow framers had the generosity and foresight to do. Wilson, by contrast, left comparatively little behind. His papers, most of which reside at the Historical Society of Pennsylvania, are "a disaster," in the words of his most meticulous scholar. When his granddaughter donated them to the society 150 years ago, she included a cover note saying that they could be thrown out if they were of no interest. (She did not notice, apparently, that among the small stash were original drafts of the Constitution.) Even in the letters of Wilson's that survive today, his ambivalence shines through. "I write this letter just to tell you that I am in a Hurry and have Nothing to say," reads one 1775 missive.

There is his actuarial failure—for an American founder, Wilson died relatively young, a few weeks shy of fifty-six. Many of his peers lived well into their eighties, impressive even by today's standards and even more so for a time when the average male lived to sixty-seven. Only Alexander Hamilton died in a similarly premature fashion to Wilson, and he could at least blame it on a bullet.

And on top of all these failures were Wilson's many contradictions. He fought for democracy but was scorned as an aristocrat. He argued for a popularly elected president but proposed the original concept of an electoral college. He publicly opposed slavery but probably kept a slave of his own for many years and was responsible for proposing the Three-Fifths Clause in the Constitution, locking in the slave-owning South's political power for generations.

At the same time, all the founders were flawed, complicated, and contradictory men, and many of them led lives filled with drama and discord, yet Washington, Jefferson, Hamilton, and the rest have been chiseled into our mountainsides, printed on our currency, studied in our classrooms. They are resurrected through bestsellers and blockbusters, hit TV series and smash Broadway musicals. Alone among them, James Wilson remains anonymous. There is no Mount Vernon or Montpelier to visit and learn about his life and work. There is no current biography of the nation's most visionary founder.

As America marks its 250th anniversary, Wilson remains at best a bit player in a story about more important men. He is overshadowed in Pennsylvania by Benjamin Franklin; he is overshadowed at the 1787 convention by James Madison; he is overshadowed in his advocacy of radical democracy by Thomas Jefferson—and yet, in each case, the more well-known founder depended on Wilson. In the rare instance when his name is uttered publicly today, it is met with a shrug. "The neglect of Wilson, the unsungest of the unsung heroes," one historian wrote in 1992, is so often "deplored in the retellings of the events of the American beginnings that in the select world of books his unsungness is sung."

Overshadowed for so long, James Wilson has become, in a sense, his own shadow, a ghost lurking in the darkness behind the conventional story of the American founding. Today, as the nation faces one of its deepest existential crises since that founding, it is trapped, like

Wilson himself was, between democracy and dissolution, between self-rule and self-enrichment. If we are to understand where we came from and where we might be headed, we need first to understand the man who saw it all so clearly 250 years ago.

1

A Scottish Childhood

THERE WAS NOTHING immediately remarkable about the boy born on a late summer day in 1742 inside William Wilson's squat stone farmhouse in the Scottish Lowlands.

The house, nestled among the misty, gently rolling hills of Fife and overlooking a fourteenth-century plot of fields called Carskerdo, was typical for a tenant farmer's family—low doors, small windows, and thick walls stuffed with divots to keep out the wind. In the spring, the divots sprouted grass, so that someone standing a hundred meters off could squint and imagine that the sheep, desperate for a taste of anything green, had crowded round to eat down the house.

Like most Scottish farmers of the time, William Wilson had been trained with methods that had evolved little since the Middle Ages. He managed wandering flocks of sheep and grew oats and barley, the only crops that would tolerate the soft, waterlogged earth at Carskerdo. Inside the house, a single fireplace strained to warm the central room. An iron cook pot hung from a hook over the bare-earth floor, the room's smoky darkness pierced only by candlelight. William and his wife, Alison Landales, lay in box beds padded with straw and slept on sackcloth pillows filled with chaff.

The Wilsons were prisoners of the land, and they ate like it. At breakfast, Alison would serve skink, a thin, watery gruel; at noon, there were dry oat cakes; and at supper, "knockit bear," stone-ground barley mixed with water and cabbage. In a place where "half-starved spiders prey'd on half-starved flies," famine was never more than a few seasons of bad weather away. From Edinburgh to Inverness, a tedious poverty was the defining feature of Scottish life. The British lexicographer Samuel Johnson defined *oats* in his 1755 dictionary as "a grain, which in England is generally given to horses, but in Scotland supports the people." Physically joined to the world's most powerful empire, Scotland in the 1700s might as well have been on the other side of the planet.

And yet the boy who entered that world on September 14—the fourth child and first son of the Wilsons, who named him James— would grow up to lead one of the more remarkable and consequential lives of the eighteenth century. This was a result both of James Wilson's inborn and doggedly persistent optimism about humanity and also of a bit of good timing. Wilson was born and raised in a time of revolutions—revolutions of the land, of the mind, of politics and religion—that would define his childhood and instill in him a conviction that all people were equal and that they were the only true source of political power. With this radically democratic vision of society in his head, he would cross an ocean and take a lead in founding a new nation based on principles that would change world history.

Wilson's worldview was taking shape before he knew it, when he and his cousin Robert Annan started making the daily hour-and-a-half trek to grammar school in Cupar, a bustling market town five miles north of Carskerdo. Like schools across Scotland, the Cupar grammar school was open to children of all backgrounds, the intentional design of what may have been the most developed public education system in the world at the time. "A school in every parish" was the slogan, advocated by Scottish adherents to Calvinism in the aftermath of the Reformation two centuries earlier. The purpose was to ensure that all Scots could read Scripture from a young age, but the effect was to instill a culture of reading and literacy that expanded over time to encompass people of all social and economic orders. Education came to be seen as a worthwhile, even desirable pursuit, and most children attended school for at least a few years, long enough to learn to read the Bible; those who studied for longer were generally headed for a life in law or business. Girls attended along with boys, although as they grew older, they left to help with housework and younger siblings.

Despite Scotland's widespread poverty, by the time Wilson was old enough to attend school in 1750, literacy rates in the country approached 75 percent, the highest in the Western world. On top of that, the Cupar grammar school was the best of the burgh schools in the region. Everything about the schoolhouse, which had been rebuilt from its foundations in 1729, reflected the importance Scots attached to education. Its exterior featured a cupola and a clock. Inside, the schoolroom was open and light, with high ceilings and large windows that ensured freshly circulating air. Seats and desks were made of quality wood, and in winter the room was warmed by sunlight or coal fires.

When Wilson and his cousin arrived at the school, the curriculum included programs in English and Latin, writing, arithmetic, geography, geometry, navigation, and bookkeeping. Before he was ten, Wilson was studying the Romans and Greeks, and Latin poets and writers including Cicero, Cato, Ovid, Horace, Virgil, and Juvenal. And he quickly made his mark. "He early gave proofs of a fine genius, a prompt capacity for learning and a steady application," Robert Annan recalled years later. Wilson's obvious intelligence compelled his parents to keep him in school, even though they could have used him at the farm. For both boys, the awareness that their education was as important as that of any other Scot, and the daily experience of studying alongside their neighbors from all walks of life, served as a powerful example of human equality in practice.

As Wilson grew into a young man, his hunger to learn only increased. The good news for him was that the University of St. Andrews, one of four universities in Scotland, was only a day's walk east from Carskerdo farm, on the wind-bitten Scottish coast. The problem was that university education, unlike grammar school, was not free. So, in 1757, at the age of fourteen, Wilson tested his way into St. Andrews on a bursary, a scholarship available to a handful of promising young men whose families could not afford tuition. In the matriculation rolls for 1757, he is listed as "Jacobus Wilson," the Latin version of James.

In Wilson's daily life as a student at St. Andrews, which was already more than three centuries old when he arrived, class divisions were more prominent than they had been in grammar school. With the other bursars, he performed menial chores, sat at a separate table, and ate a mix of bread, oats, fish, and broth. Students who could afford the tuition, known as boarders, sat at the High Table and ate better food, often accompanied by private tutors.

In class, however, Wilson could forget such distinctions. As in grammar school, he was an exceptionally good student, better than many of the boarders; that was no surprise, given that he had had to test his way in. His curriculum included Latin and Greek, math and rhetoric, metaphysics, logic, and natural philosophy. He took courses in English literature, Greek and Roman history, and ecclesiastical history. It was a better and more thorough education than he could have received anywhere else in the world, including England, which had only two universities, both of which functioned more as aristocratic finishing schools.

St. Andrews was also one of the homes of the intellectual movement that would become known as the Scottish Enlightenment, an extraordinary efflorescence of innovative political thought and moral philosophy that would soon echo around the world. The broader Enlightenment was already sweeping across Europe, changing how people thought about everything from society and government to human nature and their own inborn senses. Wilson's studies exposed him to thinkers like John Locke, Jean-Jacques Rousseau, and Charles-Louis de Secondat, baron de Montesquieu, and to concepts such as the consent of the governed, the separation of powers, and human equality—all of which would prove central to the American founding.

The Scots came at things from a different perspective. For the leading thinkers of their Enlightenment—Francis Hutcheson, David Hume, Adam Smith, Thomas Reid, and Adam Ferguson—deep poverty was within living memory. This prompted them to try to answer the vexing question of how a society progresses from poverty to wealth, from backwardness to civilization. From the science of farming to the building of roads and canals to the shape of the human mind, Scottish thinkers were consumed with what it meant to rise out of poverty, to improve as individuals and as a society—to adapt to the modern world. In doing so, they established a systematic approach to the dilemmas presented by the democratizing, increasingly egalitarian societies of the West.

For Wilson, one strand of Scottish Enlightenment thought would prove especially compelling: how to incorporate what the Scots called "commercial society" and what would later be called capitalism. This posed a dilemma because the classical republican understanding of Enlightenment thinkers was that the marketplace was the enemy of virtue. It involved self-interest, the age-old reasoning went, and virtue depended on the abnegation of self-interest, meaning that the market was where people went to get what they needed, not to become better people. Thus commerce was associated not with virtue but with vice, moral decline, and corruption. The Scots pushed back on this. Yes, they said, a citizenry had to be virtuous if it was to be self-governing. But having just emerged from the depths of poverty, they understood commerce as the ultimate and most advanced stage of human societies, not something that merely coexisted with virtue but enhanced it. Markets were not merely places to go for the necessities of life; they were places of economic and social diversity, forcing those who used them to expand their social connections and, thus, create more interdependence, and economic equality, within a society.

This linking of commerce and virtue soon became an article of faith among the Scots. David Hume argued that people were *more* virtuous in their private, commercial capacities than in their public, political ones. Francis Hutcheson wrote of a "moral sense"—those innate ideas of good and evil that exist in all people—that provided a natural and necessary balance between our public and private passions. "The road to virtue and that to fortune," Adam Smith wrote, "are, happily in most cases, very nearly the same."

Wilson would absorb these ideas in one of the most impressionable periods of his life. They would shape his vision for the design of a new American government. They would also come to dominate and warp his own behavior and, in the end, decide his fate.

For the time being, he remained happily at St. Andrews, where he was periodically exposed to people who would become central to his personal and political life in the years to come. In October 1759, when Wilson was beginning his third year, Benjamin Franklin rode into town to receive an honorary "doctor of laws" degree from the university, which described him as "famous for his writings on Electricity." Taking a break from his post in London, where he served as a colonial agent for the Pennsylvania Assembly, Franklin reciprocated by giving the school a copy of his latest book.

"I think the Time we spent there, was Six Weeks of the *densest* Happiness I have met with in any Part of my Life," Franklin wrote later to a friend about his travels through Scotland. "Did not strong Connections draw me elsewhere, I believe Scotland would be the Country I should chuse to spend the Remainder of my Days in."

Franklin could not have fully apprehended it at the time, but the ideas being birthed by the Scottish Enlightenment were soon going to resonate with a small group of men struggling with many of the same existential questions as the Scots—the future American founders, one of whom was a student at St. Andrews during Franklin's visit.

Did Franklin and Wilson meet that October day? There is no record of it, but it is very likely that, given the small size of the student body, Wilson was at least aware of the famous American's presence on school grounds. Either way, their proximity serves as a symbol of the growing connections between Scotland and America in the mid-eighteenth century.

At the same time, the conditions that would force both men to put their ideas about government to the test were falling into place. On October 25, 1760, just over a year after Franklin's visit to St. Andrews, King George II fell off his commode in Kensington Palace and died. He was succeeded by his twenty-two-year-old grandson,

George William Frederick, the Prince of Wales—known from then on as George III.

For the American founders, George III would come to represent everything they despised about life in the shadow of empire—as colonial citizens, they lacked sovereignty. But Wilson, like all Scots in the 1700s, grew up struggling with the nature of independence. Sovereignty had been a central part of the national culture for generations. Scotland had been its own kingdom going back centuries, and it fiercely guarded its independence. In 1320, for example, the Scottish barons wrote to the Pope in defense of the sovereignty of their king, Robert the Bruce. The Declaration of Arbroath, as it was known, located the source of the king's authority not in divine right but in "the due consent and assent of us all." This was an assertion by the barons of ancient prerogatives; if the king ever failed to protect Scotland's independence from England, they wrote, they were empowered to depose him "as a subverter of his own rights and ours."

This idea—that kings represented the people and could be deposed by them for serious violations of law—would develop and gather strength through the ages. It reached its pinnacle in the Glorious Revolution of 1688, when the Catholic James II (his British title; in Scotland, he was known as James VII) was deposed and replaced by his daughter Mary II and her husband, William III, both Protestants.

The 1688 revolution further weakened the monarchy's authority, elevating the Parliament as the ruling power and relegating the king to a position of subservience. A key feature of this revolution was the English Bill of Rights of 1689, which anchored power in the consent of the people, an idea popularized by John Locke, the English political philosopher. It also established individual rights, such as a prohibition on cruel and unusual punishment that would serve as a model for the American founders a century later.

What the revolution could not fully resolve was Scotland's relationship to England. The two countries warred repeatedly before settling into an uneasy coexistence in 1707, when they joined in a political union. For Scotland, the union came at the steep cost of independence, but it opened up global trade markets and other modernizing influences that benefited the rapidly growing nation, including a major reform of its agricultural practices.

The 1688 revolution also failed to end the violence that swirled around Wilson's early years and likely contributed to his desire to establish a powerful government in America. One steady source of bloodshed came from lingering tensions between Protestants and Catholics, who had never accepted what they saw as their unlawful removal from power (the 1689 Bill of Rights barred Catholics from the throne). At the time of Wilson's birth, the Scottish government was struggling to put down another wave of revolts by the defenders of James II, who were called Jacobites. The final uprising was extinguished in a brutal confrontation in the Scottish Highlands in 1746, when Wilson was not yet four.

Another kind of violence resulted from the country's rapid agricultural reform in the wake of the 1707 union—what became known as the clearances, the mass displacement of hundreds of thousands of Scots who worked on and, in some cases, owned land, but who were forced to relocate to growing cities like Edinburgh and Glasgow. Many, like Wilson, would venture much farther in search of a better life and, perhaps, wealth.

Like most Lowland families, Wilson's family was Presbyterian—a consequence of the Scottish Reformation. His parents, William and Alison, both devoutly religious, intended for their eldest son to enter the ministry. Had he followed their wishes, he would have joined a church that was notably democratic. Unlike Catholicism's papal hierarchy or the Anglican Church's parade of bishops and archbishops, Presbyterian leadership in Scotland consisted of elected elders, often chosen by the congregation and governing as a group, with equal votes. This unique structure, to which Wilson was exposed from birth, would help shape his democratic, egalitarian worldview no less than his later secular education. And yet the more time Wilson spent in the outside world, absorbing new ideas, the less he wanted to live as his parents wished.

Two events conspired to divert Wilson from his prescribed path. First, his father died in 1762 at the age of sixty-nine, forcing Wilson, then nineteen, to leave St. Andrews and return home to help his mother at Carskerdo, where he took a job as a tutor to earn money for the family. Around the same time, he became apprenticed to William Robertson, a lawyer and the town clerk of Cupar. Wilson's work for Robertson was significant not only because it was his first legal training but because that training was in Scots law, which was distinct from the English common law in ways that would turn out to matter a great deal to Wilson's own legal, political, and philosophical development.

The main difference between the two legal traditions was that the common law derived from decisions by the king's courts; it was rooted in precedent and taught by practitioners. Scots law, in contrast, derived from documents used in ancient Roman law that had been rediscovered in the twelfth century, and it took a more intellectual and philosophical approach to resolving legal questions. Where the common law drew its legitimacy from the authority of tradition and the accretion of judicial opinions, Scots law, also known as civil law, was more concerned with logic and reflection. Arguments were won not by reliance on prior case law but by appeal to first principles. Freed from the burden of history, Scots could range more broadly in their efforts to make sense of the modern world. This fit neatly with a well-educated population, one that relied on learning, empirical evidence, and the quality of its own reasoning and argumentation.

In short, the common law was a trade, while Scots law was more of an intellectual pursuit, even a science. Because it engaged with numerous other disciplines, including history, literature, and philosophy, it was ideally suited to Enlightenment-era Scotland. And because of the time in which Wilson began his own training, Scots law was paying more attention to the concerns of a modern, commercializing society.

All this was important to the American founding because the colonies were facing many of the same issues as eighteenth-century Scotland. Both were struggling with their relationship to England,

the nature of independence, and self-government (or the lack of it)—
Scotland as the weaker half of the 1707 union and America as an
increasingly neglected outpost of a vast, distracted empire. Both were
dealing with large areas of geographically isolated land, poor trans-
portation and communication networks, and regional violence. And
both faced tensions between, on the one hand, the elites, who tended
to live in cities and were mostly religious moderates, and on the other,
the commoners who lived in rural areas and practiced stricter, more
traditional forms of Christianity.

In other words, the Enlightenment Scots and the American
founders—particularly Wilson—were trying to solve similar problems. It was no surprise, then, that Americans would find inspiration
in the writings from Scotland. In his *Short Introduction to Moral Philosophy*, published posthumously in 1747, Francis Hutcheson wrote, "If
the mother-country attempts any thing oppressive toward a colony,
and the colony be able to subsist as a sovereign state by itself . . . the
colony is not bound to remain subject any longer: 'tis enough that it
remain a friendly state." These words weren't written about the American colonies—the war wouldn't start for three decades—but they
might as well have been.

Scots law also mattered to the American founding because most
of the leading founders were, like Wilson, trained as lawyers. And
while the English common law provided much of the basis for the
more concrete elements of American life, Scots law was at least as
influential when it came to higher-level constitutional thought. The
founders were familiar with English law, but none was as steeped in
Scots law as Wilson.

The other event that steered Wilson away from a religious life and
toward a future on American shores was his choice to leave Carskerdo
after a year of helping his mother and to continue his education at
the University of Glasgow. Glasgow in the mid-1760s, when Wilson
began his studies there, was an auspicious place and time, with a faculty that included Adam Smith, chair of the moral philosophy department, who was teaching the themes he would later elaborate on in
The Wealth of Nations. For Wilson, it was not Smith but his successor as

chairman of the department, Thomas Reid, whose teaching would account for many of the key political and philosophical differences Wilson had with his future peers in America. In 1764, Smith stepped down and was replaced by Reid, who had just published his own most famous work, *An Inquiry into the Human Mind on the Principles of Common Sense.* Given the timing of Wilson's enrollment at Glasgow, it is possible he studied directly with Reid; either way, Reid's influence would continue throughout Wilson's life in politics. Reid, however, did not teach political theory or philosophy. His subject was the mind, and his organizing principle was, as his book's title suggested, common sense. By Reid's definition, common sense referred to a human's capacity for moral judgment that resulted from "an imperceptible seed" planted by God, one that informs our understanding of, and reactions to, the world. It is enjoyed equally by all people, no matter their station in life.

"To judge of first principles, requires no more than a sound mind free from prejudice," Reid wrote. "The learned and the unlearned, the philosopher and the day-laborer, are upon a level, and will pass the same judgment, when they are not misled by some bias, or taught to renounce their understanding from some mistaken religious principle." Not only did all people have the capacity to come to these moral judgments, Reid said, but the judgments were correct.

It is easy to see the appeal of Reid's work to a poor farmer's son who had been primed from boyhood for an egalitarian approach to human problems. While moral skeptics like David Hume believed philosophers were better situated than ordinary people to understand the complexities of human perception and the moral rules that came out of it, Reid's common sense theory assumed a universally shared faculty of moral perception that enabled everyone to perceive moral truths directly. It was a "profoundly democratic" conception: The wealthy and the wellborn were no more able to discern truth than a simple plowman. For this reason, Reid believed the skeptics were not just wrong, but dangerously wrong. Moral skepticism and its denial of any shared reality brought "death and destruction to all science and common sense," he wrote.

Reid's writings (and those of the rest of the Scots) were well known to all the American founders—it wasn't a coincidence that Thomas Paine titled his famous revolutionary pamphlet *Common Sense*—but their experience of the Scottish Enlightenment was secondhand, through books and teachers. Only Wilson learned at the feet of these thinkers, in real time, as their theories and philosophies were evolving. No other founder would put Reid's ideas to work as Wilson would and, as a result, few had as optimistic a view of human nature. Wilson's exposure to common sense theory was, in the words of the historian Robert McCloskey, "a fortuitous meeting of man and idea."

"I despise Philosophy, and renounce its guidance," Reid wrote. "Let my soul dwell with Common Sense." Decades later, Wilson would paraphrase this quote in his law lectures at the University of Pennsylvania. In those lectures, he would rely on Reid's core precepts and quote him nearly word for word. He would reject the belief in people's inherent selfishness and desire for tyranny. The fact that people were able to live together in peace was, in Wilson's mind, evidence of their inborn sociability and sense of justice.

Contrast this with other leading founders' reliance on skepticism, which spoke more directly to their doubts about human nature. James Madison, for instance, was inclined in this direction; he would also turn to Hume to help him make his case in favor of larger republics, which had traditionally been seen as unworkable, but which Hume believed could be even stronger than small ones.

If Wilson harbored any doubts about the people, he seemed unburdened by them. A decade before the events that would redefine both his life and America's future, the essential elements of his worldview were already in place. His commitment to political equality and majoritarian democracy is remarkable not only for existing in the first place but for the single-minded tenacity with which he fought to turn those ideas into a political reality.

At the same time, given his childhood and education, that commitment seems foreordained. As McCloskey put it, "If intuitive insight is both dependable and evenly distributed among mankind, and if human motivations are largely social and benevolent, it follows that the 'right' judgment will be the one most people approve."

Consumed by these big, urgent ideas, Wilson was growing increasingly impatient for something more than the life he saw before him in Scotland. In June 1765, after the end of the school term in Glasgow, he apprenticed briefly as a bookkeeper in Edinburgh. The dullness of accounting and tutoring soon convinced him that it was time to go. "His genius being too sublime for such low drudgery he formed the resolution to try his fortune in America," his cousin Robert Annan recalled later. Annan had already made the journey across the ocean by then, settling in eastern Pennsylvania, so Wilson knew it could be done. Late that summer, he set sail for America and never returned.

And while he is not ranked as a thinker of the Scottish Enlightenment, he carried its ideas with him across the Atlantic—along with his experiences in school, in church, as a law clerk, and as the son of farmers who toiled on land owned by others. He brought all this to the forefront of the American Enlightenment—a movement in which his ideas, in their most innovative and destructive forms, would become reality.

2

New Life in America

"AN AMERICAN IN PRINCIPLE, IF NOT BY BIRTH"

EVEN FOR THOSE who made the trip of their own free will, the passage from the British Isles to North America in the eighteenth century was a grueling one. For two months or more on the open seas, desperate emigrants were stuffed in a dark, dank hold for the entire stomach-churning journey. Survival was not guaranteed. A smallpox outbreak killed dozens on one voyage; food ran out mid-crossing on another, leading survivors to eat the remains of their own family members.

Despite the risks, the demand for travel to the New World—"this epidemical fury of emigration," Samuel Johnson called it—rarely abated. Every year, thousands of Scots and Irish emigrants laid out most of their savings to secure a transatlantic berth. Between 1760 and 1775, the peak of the final Scottish wave, forty thousand Scots attempted the crossing. Most were from the Highlands in the mountainous northwest, which were still suffering the aftermath of the failed Jacobite uprisings. And most traveled as families, looking for opportunity in a land they had heard offered far more of it than the one they were leaving.

James Wilson fell into neither of these groups. In the late summer or early fall of 1765, an unattached young man from the Lowlands, he paid for a ticket across the Atlantic. The only account of his voyage, partial and secondhand, was in a letter from his brother-in-law several years later: John Balfour recalled the "bad wether" Wilson said he had endured.

Wilson was not escaping poverty like so many of his countrymen; rather, he was one of a "special restless breed," as McCloskey put it, electrified by the ideas he had absorbed at St. Andrews and Glasgow and eager to apply them to the real world. With this training, he could have chosen a relatively safe and predictable life in Scotland, as a scholar or, as his parents had wished, a minister. But he had wanted something bigger. "He was an American in principle, if not by birth," Robert Waln, the biographer of American founders, wrote in 1824. American principles did not exist in 1765. But over the next several decades, Wilson would be central in defining them for the generations to come.

He disembarked in New York City as a full-grown man, still lean after a lifetime of eating on the farm and in student mess halls. (The stoutness that would come with a more sedentary life was still years ahead of him.) He quickly made his way south to Philadelphia, the largest and most vibrant city in the colonies at the time. By the end of the year, or early in 1766, he applied for a post as a tutor in Latin at the College of Philadelphia, the city's preeminent school. Founded by Benjamin Franklin in 1749 as the Academy of Philadelphia, it trained many of America's future leaders. One of its trustees, Dr. Richard Peters, a rector and an ally of the Pennsylvania proprietors, had been alerted to Wilson's arrival—perhaps by one of his Scottish professors—and contacted him for an interview. Peters found Wilson to be "the best classical scholar" yet to seek the job, and hired him.

Wilson performed so well in his first term that the trustees granted him an honorary degree of master of arts, "in Consideration of his Merit, & his having had a regular Education in the Universities of Scotland." The Scottish pedigree was critical, given that less than one tenth of 1 percent of Americans at that time had attended college. Wilson had arrived on American shores as one of the best-educated people in the colonies.

As it happened, on the same day the college announced his honorary degree, news reached the colonies that Parliament had repealed the Stamp Act, a widely unpopular tax on paper products. The broad public uproar against the act had driven much of the pre-revolutionary sentiment that Wilson would latch on to as he sought to make his name in his adopted country.

But at this point, the next logical step for someone with Wilson's background and ambitions was a formal training in the law. He hadn't crossed an ocean to sit and watch over young men trying to conjugate their verbs, so it was only a matter of choosing the best mentor—and paying for the privilege. His choice was John Dickinson, an outspoken opponent of the Stamp Act, who had a thriving practice in Philadelphia. Wilson, however, had little in the way of cash to pay for his apprenticeship, and "John would do nothing without his fees," Wilson's cousin Robert Annan recalled. So Annan, who had come to America four years before Wilson and was one of his few acquaintances, offered to sell him a farm for five hundred pounds, for which Annan agreed to take payment "at easy installments, and when it was on his power." Wilson then sold the farm and used the proceeds to pay Dickinson and support himself during his apprenticeship. There is no record of when, or whether, Wilson paid Annan back, but according to Waln, Annan received satisfaction for the loan to his cousin "by assurances made good in Scotland."

This simple act of kindness from a relative marked Wilson's unwitting entry into the world of land purchases, sales, and profits—a world that would bless him with more money than he could have dreamed of and then curse him in ways he could never have imagined.

Wilson completed his studies with Dickinson in about a year—an unusually short time and likely the result of the former's familiarity with legal concepts, which he had acquired working for William Robertson when he was still in Scotland. In November 1767, Wilson was admitted to the Pennsylvania bar and moved to Reading, a largely German town near the state's western frontier, to open his first practice. It was perhaps not a coincidence that the frontier abounded with large tracts of unclaimed land.

As Wilson was getting established in Reading, the *Pennsylvania Chronicle* ran a front-page essay on the British Parliament's authority over the colonies. Signed by "A Farmer in Pennsylvania," the essay made a simple argument: Parliament had the authority to enact laws regulating international trade, but not those with the purpose of raising revenue, as the Stamp Act had done. The core issue, the "Farmer" wrote, was "whether the parliament can legally take money out of our pockets, without our consent. If they can, our boasted liberty is but . . . a sound and nothing else."

To anyone who knew him, the identity of the "Farmer" was no secret: He was John Dickinson, Wilson's mentor. Over the next several months, Dickinson would publish twelve essays under that pen name, focused on the powers of Parliament and the proper responses of the colonists. The essays were reprinted in almost every colonial newspaper and in England and France. They were the talk of the colonies and made Dickinson the most influential writer on the American political situation until Thomas Paine published *Common Sense* nearly a decade later.

This makes it even more notable that the tenth letter in the series, which was published on February 1, 1768, did not appear on the *Chronicle*'s front page. The piece of prose that replaced it, amid a growing public clamor for resistance, was not about politics at all. It was an eighteenth-century dating advice column. Signed by "The Visitant," who styled himself a sort of social philosopher, it was directed at younger readers, or at least those open to advice on how to live in the world as gentlemen or ladies. It touched on matters of morality, manners, sociability, gender relations, and philosophy.

"Our happiness," the Visitant wrote in his first column, "is the final end of our existence." Because a key component of happiness is understanding human nature, it was necessary to consider the ways we acquire that knowledge—first, through reading and study; and second, through talking to other people. Both are necessary, the Visitant wrote, but "I must own that I receive greater satisfaction from the latter than the former." That led him to the place he was trying to get to from the start: the unique qualities of women. "I am happiest in small companies," the Visitant professed, and especially those with a roughly equal ratio of men to women. In fact, he wrote in closing, "I prefer the conversation of a fine woman to that of a philosopher."

These were James Wilson's first published words. However affected the prose, he came off as a fundamentally happy guy who seemed pleasant enough to be around. "Though my reflections are sometimes abstracted, my disposition is easy. I am inclined to view everything in the most agreeable light," he wrote. "I conform myself to the temper of my company."

The Visitant's essay was in fact a two-person production: Wilson wrote it with his close friend Billy White, whom he had met at the College of Philadelphia. Billy would end up following the path Wilson had rejected, becoming the Reverend William White—the United States' leading Episcopalian, the first bishop of the Pennsylvania diocese and the second chaplain of the Senate.

In the 1760s, however, White was still a young man, eager to join Wilson, six years his senior, in the consideration of more earthly matters. While their columns give no indication, it appears Wilson and White took turns playing the Visitant, with Wilson writing the odd-numbered installments.

This arrangement seems clear enough in the difference in style and focus. The even-numbered installments, presumably by White, are written in a more formal tone, like somewhat tedious sermons. One essay undertook an extended study of the distinction between a "man" and a "fop"; another meditated on modesty and bashfulness. The odd-numbered essays, by Wilson, are looser, more free-ranging, and, most of all, attentive to the concerns of women.

"The fair sex were entitled to a principal share of my regard," Wilson's Visitant wrote in the third installment, referring to himself as a "humble servant of the ladies." He explained in greater detail the closing thought of the first installment—why he preferred conversing with women rather than philosophers: because their thought processes are derived more from direct observation than from long chains of reasoning, as men's are. It was a neat distillation of the common sense philosophy Wilson had learned in Scotland.

He went on to defend women's intellect from accusations of

inferiority, arguing that any shortcomings were the result of poor education. Throughout the column, Wilson as Visitant went to pains to demonstrate his sensitivity to the struggles of women, and the women responded in agreement. A later installment of the Visitant included a poem submitted by a "circle of ladies": "You, sir, with better sense, will justly fix / Our faults on education, not our sex."

In assuming a persona to offer reflections on life, love, and morality that was both entertaining and serious, Wilson was taking a page from writers like Joseph Addison, whose periodical *The Spectator* had played a similar role in early eighteenth-century England. Closer to home, a teenage Benjamin Franklin had made his debut in print with a series of irreverent letters to the editor of *The New-England Courant*, a paper published by his older brother James. The letters were written in the voice of a minister's widow, Silence Dogood.

The Visitant only rarely glanced at politics, and yet the column was as much a reflection of Wilson's mind and preoccupations as anything he would write over the next three decades. It also gave him his first chance to exercise his Scottish education in a public setting. "The most important moral truths are discovered not by reasoning, but by that act of the mind which I have called perception," Wilson wrote in one installment, closely echoing Thomas Reid's common sense philosophy. He also drew on Jean-Jacques Burlamaqui, the Swiss philosopher, in his emphasis on happiness, which Burlamaqui equated with morality and virtue.

The Visitant's sixteenth and final column ran in May 1768, with one more bit of advice to women on how to appeal to men. ("A lady should take care never to display her beauty at the expense of her delicacy and good sense," etc.) For all its youthful levity, the writing had whetted Wilson's appetite for speaking to the public on more political matters. Over the ensuing weeks, he followed in Dickinson's footsteps and sat down to write an essay about the most pressing issue of the day: the relationship between the colonies and Great Britain. What came pouring out was the product of his upbringing in the Scottish countryside, his training in common sense at Glasgow, his apprenticeship with Dickinson, and his own sharp intellect. In a matter of a couple of years,

Wilson had absorbed the essence of the legal debate over the colonies and recast it in terms no one had previously dared to do. The result was a thorough, deeply sourced legal analysis of Parliament's claim of authority over the colonies. And its radical conclusion went beyond Dickinson: Parliament, Wilson said, had no authority at all.

Wilson took the precaution of showing the essay to Francis Alison, a rector at the College of Philadelphia. Alison read the draft and urged him not to publish it.

"From what the doctor says, I judge he don't want it printed," Billy White wrote to Wilson in November 1768, conveying Alison's reaction. "I believe he likes the piece, though he says it is too long."

White then offered what he understood to be the reason for Alison's hesitation. "He spoke of the unjust envy Mr. Dickinson had incurred," following the publication of his "Farmer's Letters." "I urged that it might not be known who was the author," White wrote. "He said people would naturally be inquisitive; you were a young man just coming into the world and it might be a disadvantage to you." Wilson took the advice and put the essay away. He wouldn't take it out for another six years.

Around the same time, a smallpox epidemic swept through Reading. Wilson had been considering an invitation from a cousin who owned a farm just outside Carlisle, a town with a large Scots-Irish population eighty miles deeper into Pennsylvania's western frontier. But the trauma of the epidemic, which killed sixty children, may have compelled him to leave sooner. Before the end of the year, he had moved in with another cousin, also named James Wilson. In contrast to Reading, which was dominated by the "Pennsylvania Dutch" or descendants of German immigrants, Carlisle was a place where a native Scot could feel at home.

Still, as 1769 began, Wilson was finding himself pulled into the orbit of Philadelphia's intellectual elite. On January 2, he was admitted as a member of the newly formed American Philosophical Society, an outgrowth of a project Benjamin Franklin had begun a quarter century before. Wilson joined a distinguished group that included Franklin, Benjamin Rush, Thomas Mifflin, and Wilson's good friend

Billy White. The connections Wilson had made at the College of Philadelphia were beginning to pay off.

Wilson's legal practice was starting to pay off, too. In 1769, Carlisle had several well-established lawyers handling most of the legal business in town, but within weeks Wilson was appearing in court on behalf of a range of clients. Over the next five years, his practice would grow to be the biggest in the region—of 819 cases heard by the courts in that time, Wilson handled 346, more than 40 percent.

One of those cases, a 1773 land dispute involving the descendants of the commonwealth's founder, William Penn, cemented Wilson's status as one of the preeminent lawyers of the day. The dispute involved the ownership of seven thousand acres of land purchased by Samuel Wallis, a Quaker and one of the wealthiest and most aggressive land speculators of the time, known as the Susquehanna Land King. Pennsylvania's governor, John Penn, said some of those seven thousand acres were his, so Wallis, who had built his home on the land in dispute, hired Wilson to represent his interests in court. Penn was represented by Benjamin Chew, a highly regarded lawyer who had served as Pennsylvania's attorney general.

As soon as Wilson began his argument to the court, Chew "fixed his eyes on him with intense interest" and did not look away until Wilson had finished. Wallis ended up losing the case, but Wilson had made another powerful impression. Before the session of court ended, the Penns hired him to handle their future cases. But that wasn't the only result of the case. In his dealings with Wallis, Wilson was exposed to a man possessed by the same "land fever" that would eventually infect him.

The law was only one arena for Wilson's growing ambitions. Perhaps it was the result of the months he had spent as the Visitant counseling other young men on how to appeal to women, but by the time he had moved to Reading he was ready to settle down and start a family. In 1770, he was introduced to Rachel Bird, the sister of one of his clients and the daughter of William Bird, a wealthy ironmaster who had died some years earlier, leaving behind an estate consisting of mills, forges, and massive tracts of land worth more than ten million in today's dollars. Rachel and her brother Mark, who took over the ironworks, lived at a homestead they called the Furnace, in the seat of the iron industry, near Reading, an area known as Birdsboro.

Over the next year, Wilson tried repeatedly and unsuccessfully to win over Rachel, who was eight years his junior. At one point, he sent a melancholy note to Billy White, who was in more regular contact with her, and asked him to put in a few good words for his lovelorn friend. "I have a particular reason for asking this," Wilson added. "She will by and by become one of my friends: For husband and wife, you know, are, in the phrase of us lawyers, one person."

A few months later, Wilson wrote Billy again, this time in despair. "Is there a character more dear to you than that of a friend? Yes, Billy, there is—I have been and am in love." But Rachel would not budge, so Wilson did what spurned suitors have done across history: After requesting Billy's "most inviolable secrecy," he recounted, in detail, every painful interaction between him and the object of his affection.

He wrote for pages, describing how Rachel, with a "sweetness peculiarly hers," had told him that "she did not know a gentleman of whose friendship she would be more glad than she would of mine," but that "I must visit her in the character of a friend and not in that of a lover; for that she did not purpose ever to marry."

The rest of the letter had the air of the Visitant, only now the voice was not suave and confident, but stunned and uncomprehending. It is the longest letter of a personal nature that I have located in Wilson's surviving papers, and it reveals a great deal about the way he reconciled his intellectual precepts with the complexities of the real world. From behind the safety of the (pseudonymous) printed word, Wilson could muse all he liked about preferring the conversation of a fine woman. But now he had encountered an actual woman, and she was not behaving as his fantasies had promised. He could not accept this.

"I will still be convinced in my own mind that her professed aversion to marriage might be easily conquered," he wrote to Billy. "I told her that I would continue to visit her as a lover; but never would visit her in any other character. Her answer was that then she must not see me. . . . This I was not satisfied with. I solicited her express consent to be mine. This I could not obtain, but as she did not absolutely refuse it," he went on, "I pressed for an explicit declaration in my favor with a peculiar and perhaps imprudent ardor."

Once again, Rachel tried to make herself clear. "A denial ensued," Wilson admitted, "but attended with so much kindness and good nature that I could not forbear believing she meant yes when she said no." As a result, he could not let go of his obsession. "Write me as nearly as possible her very expressions on the subject," he pleaded with Billy. "To be tossed among contending passions is certainly of all things the most uneasy."

If there are other letters between Wilson and Rachel Bird, their whereabouts are unknown. What is known is that Rachel overcame her distaste for marriage; she and Wilson were wed on November 5, 1771, at St. Gabriel's Episcopal Church in Douglassville, a few miles up the road from Birdsboro, with a reception held at the Bird Mansion. *The Pennsylvania Gazette* reported that Rachel was "a very agreeable young lady, with a genteel fortune." Less than a year later, she gave birth to the couple's first child, Mary.

Two details stand out from this story. First, thanks to his new wife, Wilson was now flush with more cash than he had ever seen. Second, his success in wooing Rachel was more evidence for the new husband that if he only persisted long enough, he could shape the world to match his vision.

The cash he used almost immediately, as his legal practice and their family continued to grow. In December 1772, two months after Mary's birth, Wilson bought a 278-acre farm for seven hundred pounds. In 1775, he added another farm, 173 acres for two hundred pounds. Carlisle tax records show that Wilson was taxed as a citizen without property in 1770, but by 1773 he had "a lot, a negro, two horses and a cow," and by 1776 he had "two lots, two servants, three horses and a cow."

The Wilsons stayed in Carlisle until the summer of 1778, when the political and legal demands on Wilson would require a move back to Philadelphia. The month before they returned, they sold both farms for fifty-five hundred pounds—more than six times what they had paid a few years earlier.

While Wilson was beginning his new family in America, his old one, on the other side of the Atlantic, was becoming increasingly concerned about their prodigal son's prolonged silence. In a steady stream of letters, his relatives recounted the daily trials and tragedies of life in the Lowlands. Scotland was still a harsh and unforgiving place to be, worlds apart from pre-revolutionary Pennsylvania.

Death was a recurring theme of the correspondence from Fife. First, it was a cousin who succumbed to fever. Then one of Wilson's brothers drowned in a creek while walking home late one night. And in 1771, another brother, William, wrote to tell James that the family had at last sold their late father's effects, netting barely one hundred pounds.

More than anything else, the letters expressed frustration bordering on exasperation at Wilson's failure to write home more often. The only news they got, it appeared, was secondhand. "Last letter we heard of from you was dated 2d Januar 1770," John Balfour, Wilson's brother-in-law, wrote in July of that year. "A good whill Before and ever since I have been waiting with impatience to give you our Cuntrey news and particularly how our friends are." Beneath John's letter, Alison had a few stern words for her son. "Dear Jamie, the last letter I hade from you gives no account of any you have got from us and we have sent a good many since your last," she wrote. "It gives me great trouble that we get so Seldom word from you and it seems you get as Seldom word from us but it is not for want of writing."

Whether or not Wilson received the letters, he was too busy to respond. As the 1770s wore on, the central elements of his American life were taking root: a thriving legal practice, a growing family, the beginnings of a national political career. In each case, he plowed ahead with confidence and, it seemed, in total control. But there was another element at work, one that would bring out a different, less disciplined side of Wilson.

Land speculation—the game of investing in real estate by "monied individuals and companies, who will buy to sell again," as Alexander Hamilton put it—lured many of the men who would go on to found the new nation. It would make them wealthy and powerful and would shape the country they were creating. But none of them got hooked as fast or fell in as deep as Wilson, and none would suffer such drastic consequences to his life or legacy.

Maybe it was the 1766 deal with his cousin, which allowed Wilson to sell a farm and reap the proceeds without being immediately responsible for the debt. Maybe it was the firsthand exposure to clients like Samuel Wallis, the inveterate speculator. Or maybe it was the sudden access to large amounts of capital from Rachel's estate. Whatever the combination of factors, Wilson's early experiences dealing in American land were like an alcoholic's first drink: The addiction was inside him before he knew it.

He was intoxicated most of all by the prospect of what looked like endless opportunities to buy land across his adopted continent. He had happened to arrive from Scotland at just the right time. By the 1760s, land speculators in America had been pushing westward for years, envisioning all the profits that could be had on the backs of a rapidly growing population. Much of the land still belonged to indigenous tribes, but speculators had been acquiring deeds from those tribes for decades—sometimes honestly, more often through extortion or fraud. Then, in 1763, King George III prohibited colonists from settling west of the Appalachians and from privately purchasing any Native land. It was a strategic move, both to keep the colonies concentrated around the Eastern Seaboard and thus easier to manage and to avoid triggering hostilities with Native tribes over land disputes when Britain was already saddled with massive debts from the Seven Years' War.

The king's ban on buying Native lands outraged speculators and would play a key role in the colonists' arguments for independence. But Wilson got lucky: Carlisle was just far enough east of the king's prohibition line that speculators could scout around for property without running into trouble. That's what Wilson did, buying up unimproved plots around the region as he traveled for legal work. He sought out deals wherever they appeared and seemed to have no compunction about hitting up friends and colleagues for help.

"I have in view a purchase of land, which I think a very advantageous one," he wrote to Jasper Yeates, a fellow lawyer, in early December 1773. The catch: "I will not be well able to make [it] without commanding about £400. This sum I have not now by me. If you could advance, or if any of your acquaintance would be willing to advance it some either for a year or for four months, it would be laying me under a very particular obligation. If it be insisted upon, I can give any security for the money. . . . Please to let me know as soon as possible what it is likely you can do."

The letter's language tells half the story. Wilson's reliance on adverbs and contingencies—*well able, if, or if, would be, as soon as possible, likely*—makes him sound less like the smooth, self-assured Visitant and more like the anxious, beseeching suitor of Rachel Bird.

But there was something deeper at work, too. Wilson's upbringing and education at the feet of thinkers like Adam Smith and Thomas Reid had instilled in him the Scottish Enlightenment's merging of virtue and commerce. Those men had come of age in a time of profound poverty in Scotland and had, as a result, developed the notion that commerce, and economic development more broadly, not only was not corrupting, as had been generally accepted, but was "an engine of civilizing progress."

Through this lens, Wilson could gaze out across the vast lands of North America and see not only profit but the expansion of a happy and vibrant republic. Indeed, private profit and public good could go hand in hand. He would be a developer of real estate and democracy at the same time.

In this way, Wilson's speculation would be of a piece with his ventures in love and in politics. As always, he pushed the limits of his ideas, often going beyond where others were prepared to go. And when he encountered someone else's hesitation—whether about marriage or real estate or the design of a national government—he ignored it.

In August 1774, his old mentor John Dickinson wrote in response to Wilson's pestering him for cash for a land investment. "I have used all the industry I possibly could, in trying to procure you the money you desire, but have not been able," Dickinson wrote. "I have considered the proposal you made me of being concerned with you in the purchasing of lands, & if we could have an opportunity of meeting, think we might come to an agreement mutually advantageous."

Dickinson said he would be in Lancaster soon and asked if it would be possible to postpone any sale until then. At the bottom of the letter, he added, "Be so good as to excuse this hasty scrawl. I am a good deal indisposed." That postscript may have meant nothing, but it is worth pausing over it nonetheless. Along with the opening sentence, it suggests that Dickinson, a wealthy and established lawyer, felt enough pressure to answer his former apprentice's importunate requests that he did so from his sickbed. And it is easy to imagine Wilson sitting in his office in Carlisle when Dickinson's reply was delivered, skimming it with rising anxiety and immediately searching his mind for another well-off acquaintance to partner with.

On a shelf somewhere in that office, he had filed away a well-worn copy of Dickinson's "Letters from a Farmer"—the series that the Visitant had bumped off the front page six years before. The twelfth and final installment of that famous work had been published in the *Pennsylvania Chronicle* in 1768, on the same day the Visitant, on page one, referred to himself as a "humble servant of the ladies."

Had Wilson pulled that last Farmer's letter off the shelf, he might have been reminded of these words from his old teacher: "A people is travelling fast to destruction, when individuals consider their interests as distinct from those of the public. Such notions are fatal to their country, and to themselves. Yet how many are there, so weak and sordid as to think they perform all the offices of life, if they earnestly endeavor to encrease their own wealth, power, and credit, without the least regard for the society, under the protection of which they live."

Even as he was trying to wheedle money out of Dickinson, Wilson found himself tossed among contending passions, as he might put it—the temptations of land and wealth on the one hand, the duties of democratic self-rule on the other. He had decided to publish, at last, his six-year-old essay about parliamentary authority, and in that summer of 1774 he drafted a short introduction to the piece, explaining why he had held on to it for so long and how he had surprised himself at his own radical conclusion.

3

The "Considerations" Essay

"DENIED IN EVERY INSTANCE"

How DOES ONE make a legal case for a fundamentally illegal act?

American colonists in the early 1770s were on the cusp of violent revolution, but they may not have realized they needed an answer to that question. They got one anyway, or at least the readers of *Rivington's New-York Gazetteer* did, on October 20, 1774.

The *Gazetteer* was one of the most popular and influential papers in the colonies, claiming a circulation of 3,600, a strong number in a city of fewer than 25,000 people. It was a handsome production, with wide four-column pages smelling of fresh ink, every inch covered with broadsides, advertisements, announcements, and even, here and there, a little news. Every week, copies were stacked in chest-high bundles outside the entrance to James Rivington's small print shop on Hanover Square, at the southern tip of Manhattan.

In the October 20 edition, the front page featured two dense columns of an essay that opened with a daunting question to the colonists: "Does the legislative authority of the British Parliament extend over them?" The question wasn't new. To the contrary, the nature of Britain's control over the American colonies had become a subject of intense interest from Boston to Savannah since Britain surprised the colonists with a slew of new taxes Parliament said were needed to offset its massive wartime debt. The taxed, used to being left alone, were not at all happy with this sudden flexing of imperial muscle. They wrote broadsides against Parliament, attacked customs officers who tried to collect the taxes, and dumped forty-five tons of British tea into Boston Harbor.

Their central argument was straightforward: They could not be taxed by a legislature that refused to give them any representation. Still, nearly everyone acknowledged that Parliament had *some* authority over the 2.5 million British colonists in America. Virtually no one dared challenge the underlying premise—that Parliament was supreme. Which is why the unsigned essay James Rivington printed on October 20 was so shocking. Parliament's power, it said, is "denied in every instance."

This conclusion was not merely asserted; it was argued and proven with a methodical, legalistic rigor over seven consecutive editions and 11,000 words—not counting the copious footnotes citing the great thinkers on law, philosophy, and politics. In the decade of pre-revolutionary ferment that had swept the colonies, no one had seen anything quite like it.

During that time, the public debate over America's knotty relationship to the mother country had observed well-established boundaries that prevented any overly bold conclusions from being drawn. The essay in the *Gazetteer* rejected that approach, reframing the whole conversation in one short paragraph near the beginning.

> All men are, by nature, equal and free: no one has a right to any authority over another without his consent: all lawful government is founded on the consent of those who are subject to it: such consent was given with a view to ensure and to increase the happiness of the governed, above what they could enjoy in an independent and unconnected state of nature. The consequence is, that the happiness of the society is the *first* law of every government.

Less than two years later, these words would find their way, with slight alterations, into the heart of one of history's most transformational documents, a declaration by the American colonists that they were fully independent from Britain.

According to the *Gazetteer*, the author of the essay, which had made its way to Rivington after being circulated among delegates at the First Continental Congress, was "the celebrated Dr. Benjamin Franklin." But Franklin didn't write it, as an anonymous letter to the editor explained several weeks later.

"Mr. Rivington, you have been misinformed," the letter began. Franklin's "political principles are quite different, that Gentleman always acknowledged that Great Britain had a right to regulate our trade. The real author of that performance is Mr. Wilson, of this province, a native of Scotland, and a warm Patriot."

The author of the correction remains unknown, but it may well have been Franklin himself. He had been thinking along the essay's lines for years, but ever the diplomat, he had reserved such thoughts for private correspondence or notes to himself. In public, he zealously guarded his reputation as an incrementalist.

Wilson had his own incentive not to correct the error: As a relative unknown on the political stage, he was in no rush to broadcast his name at such a tense and uncertain moment. And beyond printing the letter to the editor, Rivington himself never publicly acknowledged the error.

Wilson need not have worried. In the six years since he had written the essay on Parliament, the colonists had grown increasingly comfortable with the idea of independence. Had Wilson published it at the time, it might have been too much, too soon. But in 1774, despite the unspoken rules about discussing independence, it landed with immense force, changing forever the terms of the debate about the issue at the heart of the American Revolution.

To place Wilson's essay in its proper context, it is necessary to rewind about a decade, to the early 1760s—the period when the American colonists began to struggle in earnest with the nature of their relationship to Great Britain.

They were unaccustomed to such a struggle. Throughout the eighteenth century, Americans were largely left to their own devices. The British Empire may have been the biggest and most powerful in world history, but the geographical fact of the Atlantic Ocean, along with the mother country's benign neglect of her colonies, allowed for a culture of political autonomy and local control.

As a result, generations of colonists grew up with the rituals and expectations of a self-governed people. They elected local officials, participated in town meetings, wrote letters to the editor. Neither side fully realized it at the time, but the Americans were practicing for independence.

This delicate arrangement collapsed following the French and Indian War, a brutal and bloody fight for control of vast tracts of North American territory that carried into the early 1760s. It was only one theater in the Seven Years' War, a far larger conflict that was playing out across multiple continents, stretching Britain's military perilously thin and saddling the country with massive national debt—nearly double the 72 million pounds of debt that existed before the conflict. Someone had to pay up.

Meanwhile, the Americans, whose economic output accounted for 40 percent of Britain's gross domestic product, were the beneficiaries of British protection while enjoying the perks of living under a distracted empire. One of those perks was being able to flout existing tax laws with impunity. In the 1760s, the Americans were technically required to pay customs duties on all sorts of goods, but in practice they paid almost nothing. Instead, royal customs collectors in London nursed their hefty salaries and looked the other way as their deputies in America accepted bribes from smugglers who, if they were caught at all, were usually let off the hook by sympathetic local juries.

The situation was untenable, so in 1764, Parliament resolved to collect the revenue it was entitled to. The Sugar Act, as it became known, updated duties on a range of imported goods—notably molasses, a cornerstone of the colonial economy—and made it far harder for Americans to avoid paying them. If there was any doubt among the colonists that Britain was serious, Parliament made sure to quash it. Even before the act took effect in April of that year, the prime minister, George Grenville, warned that more new taxes were around the corner.

The reaction to the Sugar Act was immediate and fierce. Up and down the Eastern Seaboard, the taxes were denounced. At a Boston town meeting in May, voters sent instructions to their assembly members to stand firm in opposition: "If taxes are laid upon us in any shape without ever having a legal representation where they are laid," a town meeting in Boston concluded, "are we not reduced from the character of free subjects to the miserable state of tributary slaves?"

Tying taxation to representation was the heart of the colonists' case, which was summed up best by James Otis Jr., the fiery and charismatic Boston lawyer. The colonists enjoyed all the same rights as their British counterparts, Otis wrote in 1764, rights that "no man or body of men . . . can take away." One of these rights was that Parliament "cannot take from any man any part of his property, without his consent in person, or by representation." In other words: no representation, no tax.

The slogan took hold in the colonies, but it failed to move Parliament, most of whose members were becoming increasingly fed up with the Americans' refusal to pay what they considered the reasonable costs of security.

"If America looks to Great Britain for protection, she must enable her to protect her. If she expects our fleets, she must assist our revenue," said Charles Townshend during a floor debate in the House of Commons. When another MP voiced sympathy with the Americans' resistance to the taxes, Townshend angrily responded, "And now will these Americans, children planted by our care, nourished up by our indulgence until they are grown to a degree of strength and opulence, and protected by our arms, will they grudge to contribute their mite to relieve us from the heavy weight of that burden which we lie under?"

Questions that had long been avoided on both sides of the Atlantic now broke into open view: What was the true scope of Britain's power? What rights did the Americans possess? As the answers started coming, the distance between the two sides was revealed to be as vast and deep as the ocean separating them.

To Britain, the most powerful justification was also the simplest: its sovereignty, embodied by Parliament, was, in the words of the great

British jurist William Blackstone, "supreme, irresistible, absolute, uncontrolled," such that what it does "no authority on earth can undo."

The colonists strongly disagreed, but they struggled to come up with a coherent legal argument for why. Some accepted Parliament's general claim of authority, but argued that taxes were a special case and could not be levied without the consent of those being taxed. Others drew a distinction between external taxes on the one hand, like those necessary to regulate trade, which they considered legitimate, and internal taxes, like those on molasses and other goods, which existed solely to raise revenue and were unacceptable.

The underlying dilemma was that most colonists still felt an allegiance to Britain and were not yet willing to throw off the yoke. James Otis, who argued for the colonists' right not to be taxed without consent, admitted in the same document that Parliament was, in fact, in charge. "The power of parliament is uncontrollable, but by themselves, and we must obey," he wrote in his 1764 tract.

How to square those two seemingly contradictory positions? Otis's solution—for America to be represented in Parliament—would have resolved the immediate problem, but not whether Parliament had any right to rule the colonies in the first place. One year later, in the early fall of 1765, Wilson, only twenty-three, disembarked from his weeks-long voyage from Glasgow to New York and began his quest to answer it.

The young immigrant did not have much time to get adjusted. The newest parliamentary tax, the Stamp Act, was taking effect on November 1, weeks after his arrival in America. The colonists would be required to print all manner of products—newspapers, pamphlets, leases, college diplomas, professional licenses, even playing cards—on officially stamped paper purchased directly from Britain. The payments had to be made in British money. And dispensing with juries, the law would be enforced by special admiralty courts.

Introducing the new law, Prime Minister Grenville expressed the hope "that the power and sovereignty of Parliament, over every part of the British dominions, for the purpose of raising or collecting any tax, would never be disputed."

If Grenville really believed this, he had not been paying attention. The blowback to the Stamp Act was even more intense than that to the Sugar Act. The cost of the stamped documents—cards would run a shilling per pack, newspapers one penny per sheet—was beside the point. The colonists understood that the true purpose of the law was not to raise revenue. It was, as the historian Edmund Morgan wrote, to put "the Americans in their place." Not for the last time, they refused.

Newspapers again took up the charge, running dozens of angry editorials and essays. One accused the new law of being designed "to strip us in a great measure of the means of knowledge" by saddling books and newspapers with taxes. Another decried "the most UNCONSTITUTIONAL ACT that ever these colonies could have imagined." Many more openly defied the law, printing on unstamped paper on the day that the law went into effect and for weeks after.

But what, exactly, was wrong with the law? No one could quite say.

Pamphlets published over the summer made the case that Americans were not being properly represented by Parliament, but they acknowledged that Parliament was supreme either way. In October, delegates from nine of the thirteen colonies gathered in New York for what became known as the Stamp Act Congress and drafted a fourteen-point response to the new law, repeating the argument that Americans had the same rights as British citizens. But the delegates professed their allegiance to the Crown and framed their appeal as "a loyal and dutiful address to his Majesty, and humble applications to both houses of Parliament."

Efforts like these exposed the colonies' primary weakness—the lack of a coherent legal case against the taxes—leaving them trapped between two unappealing alternatives: beseeching pleas and armed resistance. As the first path failed to lead anywhere, impatient colonists began to turn to the second.

In August, a mob in Boston set out in search of the customs officials in charge of distributing stamped paper. They hung one in effigy, then broke into his house and wrecked his furniture. Facing no consequences, they reconvened later in the month and vandalized the home of the widely despised lieutenant-governor, Thomas Hutchinson, hacking down trees, destroying windows and doors, slashing paintings, and stealing money, clothing, and silverware.

A third approach, mass boycotts of British goods, was more effective in forcing Britain's hand. In March, after months of open defiance of the new law, Britain relented and repealed the Stamp Act. But Parliament made sure to frame the repeal as a purely political decision that did not reflect at all on its authority over the colonies. In a law passed the same day as the repeal, the members reiterated their "full power and authority to make laws and statutes of sufficient force and validity to bind the colonies and people of America . . . in all cases whatsoever."

To win the fight for good, the Americans would need something more. They would need a bulletproof legal argument. They would need to speak the language of their oppressors.

Meanwhile, the British kept providing new material. In 1767, Parliament followed through on its promise to exercise its authority over the colonies "in all cases whatsoever" by enacting a string of new tax laws, the Townshend Acts. Named for the chancellor of the exchequer who spearheaded them (the same man who had described Americans as "children planted by our care, nourished up by our indulgence"), the acts imposed levies on glass, lead, tea, paper, and other goods that the colonists could get nowhere other than from Britain. Only, this time, with the Stamp Act brouhaha in mind, Parliament focused on taxing imported goods rather than those produced in the colonies. This internal-external distinction was dubious at best—indeed, James Otis had rejected it in his own pamphlet several years earlier—but Britain was tiring of all this nit-picking from its "children."

In 1768, John Dickinson published his Farmer's letters to international acclaim, but despite the stridency of his rejection of Parliament's taxing authority, he still was careful to perform the standard colonial dance of submission. "We are but parts of a whole; and therefore there must exist a power somewhere, to preside and preserve the connection in due order," he wrote in his second essay. "This power is lodged in the parliament; and we are as much dependent on Great Britain, as a perfectly free people can be on another." He neglected to explain how a people who are "perfectly free" could exist under the control of someone else.

By the first months of 1774, there was still no clear and coherent legal case for American sovereignty. And yet, in the six years since Wilson wrote his essay, Americans had become increasingly comfortable with the idea of resisting British authority. Revolutionary energy was everywhere—the Boston Tea Party had happened the previous December.

Britain would force the issue with the most punishing set of laws yet, enacted in undisguised contempt for American claims of liberty. The first bill, passed in late March, shut down the port of Boston to all ships, effectively eliminating trade in one of the colonies' largest and most important cities. The next moved all jury trials to Great Britain, forcing colonists to cross the Atlantic in search of justice. Another act reinstated royal governance in Massachusetts, gutting the elected colonial government and ending the local town meetings that colonists had come to cherish. The royal governors were then given the power to quarter British soldiers in colonists' homes without their consent.

Each law came with its own ostensible rationale, but as a package the laws had one clear purpose: to demonstrate to the Americans who was boss. Britain called them the Coercive Acts. The colonists called them the Intolerable Acts. Both terms were accurate.

And in their wake, a door seemed to open. The first to walk through it publicly was a thirty-one-year-old lawyer from Virginia named Thomas Jefferson. Jefferson, a member of the House of Burgesses, Virginia's elected assembly, was not well known outside the small community of lawyers and legislators with whom he worked. But he was a naturally gifted writer and had spent the early summer of 1774 drawing up a comprehensive list of complaints against the king and Parliament, which he accused of "many unwarrantable encroachments and usurpations" against the colonies. "Scarcely have our minds been able to emerge from the astonishment into which one stroke of parliamentary thunder has involved us, before another more heavy, and more alarming, is fallen on us," Jefferson wrote.

In a foreshadowing of the declaration he would draft two years later, Jefferson cataloged offenses large and small—one of the Intolerable Acts prohibited Americans from making hats from the fur of animals they captured on their own land—before getting to the heart of his case: "The true ground on which we declare these acts void is, that the British parliament has no right to exercise authority over us." It was a bracing conclusion—not just that Parliament could not levy taxes on the colonies, as Dickinson had argued, but that it had no authority over them at all. No one had previously dared go so far, and even Jefferson felt compelled to soften his rhetoric: "It is not our wish, nor our interest, to separate from her," he wrote.

Still, it was the strongest statement of its kind to date, and when Jefferson sought to persuade Virginia's newly chosen delegates to the First Continental Congress to take up his arguments, which he had styled as a set of instructions to Congress, it was not surprising they declined.

"Thought too bold for the present state of things," he later recalled. That might have been the end of it, but several friends who had taken Jefferson's side in the debates had his essay printed as a pamphlet and distributed publicly, without his permission. It carried the title *A Summary View of the Rights of British America*. Cocky, provocative, and brimming with self-assurance, in a matter of weeks it had reached Philadelphia, New York, and London.

Yet, for all its rhetorical muscle, *A Summary View* was just that: a summary. When it came to providing a logical, reasoned basis for the total denial of Parliament's authority, Jefferson's broadside was missing something essential: He had failed to make an actual *legal* argument. One might say that his conclusion was self-evident—not ideal if you were trying to convince an empire whose system of laws had just been mapped out in detail by William Blackstone, the world's most famous legal authority.

Three weeks later, on October 20, Wilson's misattributed essay "Considerations on the Nature and the Extent of the Legislative

Authority of the British Parliament" appeared on the front page of *Rivington's Gazetteer*. In a brief unsigned introduction, he noted that the essay had been written in 1768 but was "judged unfashionable to publish" at the time. He anticipated readers' surprise at his ultimate denial of all parliamentary authority, admitting that "when he began this piece, he would probably have been surprised at such an opinion himself." He had expected to be able to "trace some constitutional line" between cases in which Parliament had power and those in which it did not. But as he completed his inquiry, he wrote, "he became fully convinced that such a line does not exist."

Wilson's essay wasn't as easy a read as Jefferson's, but as the author had promised, it was a thorough and methodical analysis grounded in law, history, and political theory. Parliament lacks authority over the colonies, he argued, because its members have no obligation to represent Americans' interests and, thus, to ensure their happiness. The Americans can neither elect MPs to office nor remove them from it. Thus, there is a complete disconnect between the representatives and the people, from whom "all power is derived."

Speaking of this power, the essay continued, how is it that one group of people has less of it than another in the same situation? "By what title do they claim to be our masters?" it asked of the British public. "Is British freedom denominated from the *soil,* or from the *people* of Britain? If from the latter, do they lose it by quitting the soil? Do those who embark freemen in Great Britain disembark slaves in America?"

It was an ingenious argument. First, define all political power as deriving from the people themselves. Then, explain that they may confer this power only by their consent and only to representatives who are obligated to ensure their happiness. Finally, tie it together by pointing out that because the American people are unrepresented in Parliament, they are not bound by its rule.

Taken separately, these points were not original. But the essay was the first to synthesize them and to offer an accessible framework for the claim that the people, not Parliament, held ultimate sovereignty over their own lives. Amid the foggy equivocation that characterized so much of the writings of the previous decade, the essay shone a bright light in the direction of independence.

October 20, 1774, turned out to be an auspicious day for such an argument to reach the American public by way of Wilson's long-delayed essay. A hundred miles southwest of Hanover Square, more than four dozen delegates to the First Continental Congress gathered in Carpenters' Hall in Philadelphia to come up with an appropriate response to the Intolerable Acts.

As we have seen, what qualified as "appropriate" had been carefully circumscribed for years. Even the staunchest critics of the empire had felt forced to join in the colonies' delicate dance with Parliament, pushing back against taxes and other burdens while never fully denying its authority or their own allegiance to the Crown.

That decade-long dance ended with the Intolerable Acts, the combined effect of which could not have been more humiliating to the colonists. This, of course, was precisely the point. Britain meant to impress upon the Americans that they were not the masters of their own fate.

It was the most aggressive response yet, and some members of Parliament saw danger in it. "When you drive him hard, the boar will surely turn upon the hunters," said Edmund Burke, one of the most outspoken opponents of unfettered parliamentary sovereignty. "If that sovereignty and their freedom cannot be reconciled, which will they take? They will cast your sovereignty in your face. Nobody will be argued into slavery."

Meeting in Philadelphia, the Continental Congress adopted the Articles of Association, which reiterated the standard list of grievances over Parliament's "cruel and oppressive acts" and imposed a total boycott on the import and export of British goods, whether from the motherland or her other colonies around the world. No molasses, no sugar, no coffee. No Portuguese wine, no indigo, no East India tea. And, significantly, no slaves: "We will wholly discontinue the slave trade, and will neither be concerned in it ourselves, nor will we hire our vessels, nor sell our commodities or manufactures to those who are concerned in it," read the second article.

The Articles of Association also sketched out a vision of a unified social, political, and economic community—one in which farmers helped one another by redistributing goods and animals as needed; in which citizens practiced frugality by manufacturing their own goods and abstaining from "expensive diversions and entertainments"; and in which mourners at funerals expressed their grief with a simple black ribbon rather than a brand-new outfit. From one angle, this looked like the stirrings of a people preparing to join in political unity; from another, it looked like one preparing for the privations of war.

But like every other response to the British, the Articles were missing the key ingredient: a rationale. Congress was responsible for passing legislation for the colonies, and yet it had failed to explain why Parliament didn't have any authority over them. To the contrary, the Articles of Association conceded that Parliament *did* have at least some power. But sovereignty is, after all, indivisible. It cannot be split. So by conceding that Parliament had some power, the Articles acknowledged Parliament had total authority over the colonies.

Previous attempts to articulate a rationale for why it did not had fallen short, in part because the colonists could not conceive of full separation from Britain, or, if they could, they couldn't explain why. Wilson now presented a different argument. Sovereignty was indeed indivisible, he agreed, but it resided not in Parliament, as Blackstone had authoritatively stated; it resided in the people themselves. Here at last was the basis for a coherent, detailed, and compelling case against British rule. Wilson had produced "the most sophisticated legal analysis" of the dispute between America and Great Britain written before 1776. And he did so by speaking the oppressors' language. It took Wilson to say it out loud, with legal support: *If you say your power over us is all or nothing, then it's nothing.* Edmund Burke's boar had turned against its hunters.

The implications of Wilson's argument had indeed triggered an earthquake, as some of his friends pointed out. "Upon the Principles of Law, as far as I am capable of judging, you are certainly right, but how far, upon the Principles of *Temporary* Policy, such principles may be avowed, I will not venture to give my opinion," Thomas Smith wrote to Wilson in January 1775. "It will perhaps be the wisest System of Policy that the Colonies can adopt at present, to Temporize a little and not *now* to insist too peremptorily on *all* those rights, which Time will both *justify* and enable them to do."

It was too late. The engines of revolution, fueled by Wilson's essay, were now in full gear.

"All men are, by nature, equal and free," Wilson had written, "no one has a right to any authority over another without his consent: all lawful government is founded on the consent of those who are subject to it: such consent was given with a view to ensure and to increase the happiness of the governed."

Among the men with whom he would soon share the responsibility for creating a new government, Wilson's essay drew attention and praise. John Adams wrote to his wife, Abigail, "There is a young Gentleman from Pennsylvania whose Name is Wilson, whose Fortitude, Rectitude, and Abilities too, greatly outshine his Master's."

Another admirer was Jefferson, who cut out several long sections of the *Gazetteer* essay and pasted them into his commonplace book, where he collected quotes and writings he wanted to remember. The paragraph beginning "All men are, by nature, equal and free" was not among them, but less than two years later, Jefferson would include in his draft of the Declaration of Independence the passage that is considered today the most famous of all:

> We hold these truths to be self-evident, that all men are created equal, that they are endowed by their Creator with certain unalienable Rights, that among these are Life, Liberty and the pursuit of Happiness.

Was Jefferson knowingly paraphrasing Wilson? Numerous historians have come to that conclusion over the years. The case is strengthened by the fact that Jefferson had not used language like this in his *Summary View* or anywhere else.

Wilson's essay would continue to echo over the years in service of the profound idea that the people were the ultimate sovereign. As the 1770s progressed, Americans increasingly warmed to that notion. Wilson wasn't just speaking the language of law; he was speaking the language of revolution.

With the "Considerations" essay, Wilson made his name in American politics and marked himself as a leading political thinker. His peers noticed, inviting him to give an address at a provincial convention that was called to express support for the Continental Congress's work. He attended as a representative of Cumberland County, although he was increasingly absent from home as the conflict with Britain reached a boiling point. Rachel had recently given birth to their first son, William, who joined his older sister, Mary (who went by Polly), on the farm in Carlisle. They would grow up hearing about their father from family friends more than seeing his face themselves.

The provincial convention, held in January 1775, would be Wilson's first opportunity to prove his public speaking abilities and his political instincts. At that time, before Lexington and Concord, before the Battle of Bunker Hill, the colonists were still making a show of allegiance to the mother country. Even as the convention debated provisions for a possible war, it expressed an "earnest wish and desire . . . to see harmony restored between Great Britain and the colonies." Wilson had to thread the same needle in his oration.

"Whence, Sir, proceeds all the invidious and ill-grounded clamor against the colonists of America?" he began. It was a seductively innocent opening for what was to follow: an overlong, legally dense yet erudite dismantling of the Intolerable Acts and a justification of the colonists' defiance of them.

Wilson then articulated a key distinction between the letter and the spirit of the law. "Our counsels, our deliberations, our resolutions, if not authorized by the forms, because that was rendered impossible by our enemies, are nevertheless authorized by that which weighs more in the scale of reason—by the spirit of our constitutions."

Anticipating a raised eyebrow from those colonists who might balk at what sounded like a call to violate the law, Wilson had come prepared with a provocative history lesson. He asked whether the signing of the Magna Carta—the foundational text of the British constitutional system and the origin of the concept that the king was subject to the rule of law—was "authorized by the forms of the constitution?" What about the Parliament that restored the monarchy and put King Charles II on the throne? Or the one that offered the job to King William? "The objections of our adversaries cannot be urged against us," he concluded, without acknowledging these antecedents. In other words, if you British don't like the sound of what we are saying, you did it first.

But Wilson was invoking the more profound idea that the people have natural, God-given rights of which no law or constitution can deprive them. Certainly not one that denies them representation in government.

He then warned of the specter of violent resistance. Would Britain's repeated violations of the colonists' rights, and its rejections of their grievances, drive them to such extreme measures? he asked. "The fate of us; the fate of millions now alive; the fate of millions yet unborn depends upon the answer."

He had already disclaimed any parliamentary authority over the colonies, but like many of his fellow Americans, he was not yet prepared to reject the king. He offered him another chance to do right by his subjects. "Are we enemies to the power of the crown? No, sir, we are its best friends," Wilson said. "We know—for our constitution tells us—that oppression can never spring from the throne," only from the ministers in Parliament. But when the king, "forgetting his character and his dignity," takes part in Parliament's unconstitutional schemes, there will be consequences. "The distinction between him and his ministers has been lost: but they have not been raised to his situation: he has sunk to theirs."

By spring, the Continental Congress was preparing to convene for a second session, this time in the shadow of the all-out war that had begun at Lexington and Concord. Wilson did not fight himself, although he was made a colonel and put in charge of one of four Cumberland battalions of associators, or volunteer military men. He had also made enough connections in the Pennsylvania Assembly that he was named to the Pennsylvania delegation for the new Congress, alongside Thomas Willing and Benjamin Franklin, who had just returned from his years in London.

The Continental Congress was a noble attempt at self-government, but it soon became clear that it was barely up to the task of managing the affairs of the colonies or of funding the army for the fight ahead. Much of its work happened in committee—committees on printing paper currency, on war acquisitions, on Indian affairs, and more. Wilson, like many delegates, was named to a seemingly endless string of them. But the experience acquainted him with delegates like John Adams, Samuel Adams, Thomas Jefferson, Patrick Henry, John Hancock, Roger Sherman, John Rutledge, and John Jay—soon-to-be revolutionary leaders with whom he would one day build a country.

Wilson spent much of his first year in Congress negotiating treaties with Indian nations, including the Lenape (whom colonists called the Delaware), the Shawnee, and the Wyandot. This involved a degree of diplomacy that did not come naturally, but Wilson made the effort, learning specific traditions and protocols—such as the presentation of belts of wampum beads that were an essential part of any official meeting. He soon took the lead in shaping Congress's relations with the Indian nations. "We are anxious to take every Step which will have a Tendency to preserve Peace with the Indians," he wrote in July to John Montgomery, a well-off friend from Carlisle who served in the state assembly and had helped steer him into Congress. "We have not yet determined upon the Time or Place of holding a Treaty. But Speeches are prepared, and the Belts are getting ready." Closing on a wistful note, Wilson the absent father added, "Give little Polly a kiss for me."

Wilson's deep involvement in Indian affairs would turn out to be helpful to his growing interest in land purchases—and, perhaps unsurprisingly, would become the source of some of the earliest suspicions of his motives. Later in 1775, as Wilson attempted to mediate a long-running land dispute between Pennsylvania and Virginia that included dealings with Native nations, several Virginians complained in a letter to their colleague Thomas Jefferson about what they believed was Wilson's unseemly investment in the outcome. "A certain eminent Gentleman" has "greatly interested himself in this affair," they wrote, implying that Wilson was taking advantage of his relations with Natives to navigate the land dispute to Pennsylvania's benefit and to his own.

Wilson's time in Congress provided other foreshadowings of his future. In December 1775, shortly after he was reappointed as a Pennsylvania delegate, he was appointed to a committee to respond to a complaint from Lord Stirling, a New Jersey colonel, whose soldiers were being arrested and imprisoned for failing to pay "very triffling" debts. The committee returned with a rebuke of the "pernicious" practice of locking up debtors and recommended that all colonies prohibit the arrest of any soldier for debts under thirty-five dollars.

4

The Declaration

"THE SACRED AUTHORITY OF THE PEOPLE"

WILSON HAD PRODUCED the best legal argument against parliamentary authority over the colonies that anyone had ever read. And yet he would find himself trapped between his ideals and his instincts—on the one hand, his desire to create a powerful new American government founded on popular sovereignty and, on the other, his wariness of the rash approach of some of the strongest advocates of separation from Britain, who he felt risked getting too far ahead of a public not yet certain about independence.

Wilson's attempt to balance these concerns was evident in his January 1775 speech to the provincial convention, a valiant argument that there was a fundamental difference between George III and Parliament. But however much he still believed in that distinction, he greatly underestimated the king's disregard for it.

Later that year, George III, thoroughly fed up with his insolent colonial subjects, accused them of seeking to establish "an independent Empire." Wilson was appointed to a committee to respond to the charge, and in early 1776 he drafted yet another lengthy speech in which he denied that America sought independence but warned the king that the ball was now in his court. "Though an independent Empire is not our *Wish*; it may—let your Oppressors attend—it may be the *Fate* of our Countrymen and ourselves," the speech read. In case the point was not clear, he added, "We are *desirous* to continue subjects; But we are *determined* to continue freemen." He again invoked his foundational principle, noting with pride that America's colonial governments were based on the "*sacred Authority of the People, from* whom *all* legitimate Authority *proceeds*."

He never got to deliver the speech. As James Madison explained in a note years later, Wilson had written it "to lead the public mind into the idea of Independence," but it was dropped when it became clear that the public didn't need to be led there anymore. They were ready, as evidenced by the massive popularity of a pamphlet published around the same time: Thomas Paine's *Common Sense.*

Paine, an Englishman with minimal education, had arrived in America just over a year earlier, around the time that Wilson's "Considerations" essay was helping to make the legal and intellectual case for revolution. But Paine's work—angry, eloquent, and a pleasure to read—hit the colonists in the gut.

Mocking the king as the "Royal Brute of England," Paine called the very concept of hereditary monarchy "exceedingly ridiculous." And, he wrote, "though we have been wise enough to shut and lock a door against absolute Monarchy, we at the same time have been foolish enough to put the Crown in possession of the key."

Paine offered a vision of an egalitarian, republican society that he said the American people were well on the way to creating themselves, if only they would throw off the fetters of empire. "We have it in our power to begin the world over again," Paine wrote. It was a stirring call to action, one that helped lead the public mind into the idea of independence, as Madison had intended Wilson's speech to do.

Paine was more of a polemicist than a policymaker, or as John Adams put it to his wife, Abigail, he "has a better hand at pulling down than building." In early 1776, however, a polemic was exactly what people needed. Paine's pamphlet became an instant hit, with more than one thousand copies selling out in a matter of weeks and distribution throughout the English-speaking world.

Meanwhile, the pressure to declare independence was only growing. Benjamin Franklin, who had recently returned from a decade in

London, was now among its strongest advocates, along with the radicals who had long had enough of the Crown's insults. On the other side were Tories who would stand with the king until the end and even some moderate Whigs like John Dickinson. Wilson was stuck in the middle, having made the case for independence and yet wary of a headlong rush into an unknown future.

When Congress reconvened on May 10, 1776, John Adams introduced a resolution that would force the issue. "Resolved," it read, "That it be recommended to the respective Assemblies and Conventions of the United Colonies, where no Government sufficient to the Exigencies of their affairs hath been hitherto established, to adopt such Government as shall in the Opinion of the Representatives of the People best conduce to the happiness and Safety of their Constituents in particular and America in General."

In short, Adams was calling for the colonies to reject British rule and establish their own governments. It was jarring to see the words on paper, and yet the call for local governments to be set up was not particularly controversial, because most colonists understood that some sort of government was needed. What really brought matters to a head was the preamble, which Adams spearheaded and which was adopted five days later.

Longer than the resolution itself, the preamble announced that it was "absolutely irreconcilable" for colonists to swear oaths to the Crown, and that "every kind of authority under the said crown should be totally suppressed [by the colonists] . . . against the hostile invasions and cruel depredations of their enemies."

This preamble was clearly directed at Pennsylvania, where the Quaker-led political establishment stood by the Crown. In their eyes, they already had a government "sufficient to the Exigencies of their affairs," and they had held power for too long to give it up without a struggle. This made Pennsylvania the colony most resistant to a separation from Britain. Indeed, the previous fall the Assembly had forbidden its congressional delegates from voting in favor of independence. But a declaration of independence was precisely what the preamble amounted to. Adams—who by his own account had been pushing for something along these lines for at least a year and who was anxious to secure his own legacy—later wrote that it was "considered by men of understanding as equivalent." On the day of its passage, he called it "the most important Resolution that ever was taken in America."

Wilson, trapped between the warring factions of his state, got the job of arguing Pennsylvania's case against the preamble. At least his argument aligned with his cautious tendencies. "In this Province, if that preamble passes, there will be an immediate dissolution of every kind of authority; the people will be instantly in a state of nature," he warned. "Why then precipitate this measure? Before we are prepared to build a new house, why should we pull down the old one, and expose ourselves to all the inclemencies of the season?"

Adams's resolution, along with the preamble, was adopted the next day, with Pennsylvania abstaining. It would have voted nay, but a series of artillery attacks by British forces had echoed across Philadelphia in the previous week, unsettling even the most ardent Loyalists.

Within weeks, the colonies found themselves at the doorstep of declaring their independence. On June 7, Virginia's Richard Henry Lee submitted to Congress a resolution that had been in the works since early May: "These United colonies are & of right ought to be free & independent states, that they are absolved from all allegiance to the British crown, and that all political connection between them and the state of Great Britain is & ought to be totally dissolved."

Still, Wilson held back. On June 8, he and a group of moderates responded that "tho' they were friends to the measures themselves, and saw the impossibility that we should ever again be united with Great Britain, yet they were against adopting them at this time." They defended their hesitation on the ground that it was improper to take such a monumental step "till the voice of the people drove us into it: That they were our power, & without them our declarations could not be carried into effect."

Popular sovereignty, in other words. The people were the deciders, and they were "not yet ripe for bidding adieu to British connection but that they were fast ripening & in a short time would join in the general voice of America." On the same day, however, the Pennsylvania

Assembly lifted its prohibition on its congressional delegates voting for independence, removing what had been Wilson's most reasonable fallback for not voting.

Whatever his public position, Wilson knew as well as anyone what was coming. "Our Affairs have been in such a fluctuating and disordered Situation, that it has been almost impossible to form any Accurate Judgment concerning the Transactions as they were passing," he wrote a few days later to William Thompson, a Carlisle friend. "Matters are, however, now, in all Likelihood, approaching to a Crisis."

If the story had stopped there, Wilson's reputation as a waffling temporizer might seem deserved. But it didn't stop there.

On July 1, a muggy summer day, Congress began the debate over Lee's resolution. The advocates of independence knew they were close to having support from the required 9 colonies. A few, most notably Pennsylvania, were still unknowns, but when it came time to vote, John Dickinson, Wilson's old mentor, stood and offered his last best case against separation, warning of the perils of a protracted war with the world's superpower and the risks of moving forward without unanimity. His pleas won out—the Pennsylvanians' first vote was 4 to 3 against independence. Dickinson was joined in his "no" vote by the more conservative delegates, Robert Morris, Thomas Willing, and Charles Humphreys. On the other side were John Morton, Benjamin Franklin, and James Wilson.

South Carolina also voted no, while Delaware split its vote, and New York abstained. Nine colonies now were in favor of independence—enough, Wilson might have said, for the letter of the law, but not enough for its spirit. If unanimity was necessary to take such a monumental step, the colonies were not there yet.

Pennsylvania's assent was the most important of all. By virtue of its size, location, and the scope of its commerce, it was "what the heart is to the human body in circulating the blood," as Robert Morris put it. Any move in the direction of independence could not happen until Pennsylvania joined in.

There are no records of whatever private conversations Wilson engaged in that night, but it is possible that, as a trusted friend of both

Dickinson and Morris, he prevailed on them to stand down, to let Pennsylvania cast its vote for independence and allow history to take its course.

The next morning, July 2, all seven members of the Pennsylvania delegation appeared in Congress, but only five took their seats at their assigned table. Dickinson and Morris stayed "behind the bar," standing alongside the visitors who had come to watch the proceedings. Humphreys and Willing stuck to their guns, voting no. Wilson, sitting in his usual seat, voted yes, along with Franklin and Morton. By a vote of 3 to 2, Pennsylvania was on board. With the exception of New York, which continued to abstain, the colonies were now unanimous.

Two days later, Congress adopted the Declaration of Independence. Reading over the document he had helped inspire, Wilson must have felt a wash of conflicting emotions—anxiety and relief, vindication and resentment, pride and ambivalence. Without Pennsylvania's support, the Declaration most likely would not have come together, or at least not have landed with the impact it did. And Wilson was a key factor in pushing Pennsylvania across the line.

Six days after its adoption, the Declaration was read aloud in public for the first time, in the State House Yard in Philadelphia. The king's arms were pulled down from over the State House door, as they were from buildings in colonies up and down the coast, then paraded through the streets and burned. The world Wilson had dreamed of was coming into view, and he had played a central role in bringing it into being.

As a piece of writing, the Declaration of Independence was not particularly original. It was, as Thomas Jefferson described it in a letter decades later, a collection of the most resonant ideas in the air at that pre-revolutionary moment, including the social contract theory of John Locke. "All American Whigs thought alike on these subjects," Jefferson wrote to Henry Lee in 1825. The purpose of the Declaration was "not to find out new principles, or new arguments, never before thought of, not merely to say things which had never been said before; but to place before mankind the common sense of the subject." He went on: "Neither aiming at originality of principle or sentiment, nor yet copied from any particular and previous writing, it was intended to be an expression of the American mind, and to give to that expression the proper tone and spirit called for by the occasion. All its authority rests then on the harmonizing sentiments of the day."

Still, certain tracts have long been associated with the core ideas and language of the Declaration, including *Common Sense*, which had been published the previous January and praised by John Adams to his wife, Abigail, as "good sense delivered in clear, simple, concise and nervous style."

A few months later, another significant piece of writing appeared—the Virginia Declaration of Rights, written by George Mason. Mason had drafted it in May in response to Congress's call for states to establish their own governments. It was enormously influential; most of the state constitutions that followed would mirror the structure outlined by Mason—a declaration of rights followed by a design of government.

The Virginia Declaration's opening provision—"that all men are by nature equally free and independent and have certain inherent rights, of which, when they enter into a state of society, they cannot, by any compact, deprive or divest their posterity; namely, the enjoyment of life and liberty, with the means of acquiring and possessing property, and pursuing and obtaining happiness and safety"—has powerful echoes in the Declaration of Independence. This fact, along with its wide popularity, accounts for its common association with the Declaration, though Wilson's essay was published and widely distributed two years earlier, and both Mason and Jefferson had clearly read it.

We cannot know which essays were arrayed on Jefferson's desk when he drafted the Declaration, or how much Paine's or Mason's or Wilson's language ("All men are, by nature, equal and free: no one has a right to any authority over another without his consent") made its way into the final text. What we do know is that the passages of that document that matter most to us today went unnoticed by virtually everyone at the time—everyone with the exception of Wilson.

"We hold these truths to be self-evident, that all men are created equal," Jefferson had written—"the most soaring line of all," as the scholar and historian Akhil Reed Amar writes, "whose contested meaning has structured much of America's constitutional conversation ever since."

Two and a half centuries later, we still understand and invoke the words "created equal" (along with the entire preamble) for the revolutionary concept they embody, for their upending of moral, social, and legal systems that had endured for millennia. So we should expect the founders to have made regular reference to it in their speeches and writings as the country was rising on the foundations set down in that document.

They almost never did. In a meticulous review of Jefferson's letters, speeches, diaries, and essays from July 4, 1776, until his death precisely fifty years later, William Ewald, a professor of law and philosophy at the University of Pennsylvania Law School, found that he did not use the phrase "created equal" a single time. Neither did George Washington. Or John Adams. Or Benjamin Franklin, or James Madison, or Alexander Hamilton, or John Jay. Nor did any of them use "self-evident," "inalienable," or "pursuit of happiness"—the other key phrases of the Declaration's preamble.

Ewald, startled, then consulted all twenty-six volumes of *Letters of Congress* between 1774 and 1789, when the first government under the Constitution began. Again, he found nothing. He searched one other source: *The Documentary History of the Ratification of the Constitution*, a thirty-volume set cataloging the ratifying debates in every state. In all those volumes, Ewald located only two relevant references to the phrase "created equal." They were both spoken on the same day, December 4, 1787; in the same place, Philadelphia; and by the same person, James Wilson.

The context of these mentions, Ewald points out, was the pivotal speech in favor of the Constitution that Wilson delivered at Pennsylvania's ratifying convention. The Declaration's preamble and its words "created equal" were, Wilson said, "the broad basis on which our independence was placed; on the same certain and solid foundation this system [the Constitution] is erected."

In other words, Wilson, alone among America's founders, invoked the Declaration of Independence—specifically its preamble about human equality—as central to the nation-building project they were all engaged in. For someone whose entire political world was rooted in the authority of the people, that should come as no surprise.

Throughout the 1780s and '90s, in fact, Wilson made the Declaration's text central to his politics, as Harvard University's Danielle Allen has documented. For example, in a 1786 article in *The Pennsylvania Gazette*, Wilson (writing under a pseudonym) envisioned a copy of the Declaration, complete with golden lettering, adorning the walls of the Bank of North America.

In his essay of the previous year defending the bank's charter from attack, Wilson articulated a view that the nation's first constitution was not the Articles of Confederation, with their overemphasis on state sovereignty, but the Declaration itself. "The act of independence was made before the articles of confederation," he wrote. "This act declares, that '*these United Colonies*,' (not enumerating them separately) 'are free and independent states; and that, as free and independent states, they have the full power to do all acts and things which independent states may, of right, do.'"

Wilson also appears to have been the only delegate to the Constitutional Convention to mention the Declaration. In response to a complaint by Maryland's Luther Martin that treating states as unequal to each other—that is, in proportion to how many people lived in them—would be unfair to the smaller states, Wilson said that he "could not admit the doctrine that when the Colonies became independent of G. Britain, they became independent also of each other." He proceeded to quote the Declaration out loud to the delegates, inferring from its text that the states "were independent, not *Individually* but *Unitedly*."

This is the only reference to the Declaration that appears in all the records of the federal convention. A few weeks later, Wilson coined the Constitution's opening phrase, "We the People," to define it forever as a document based, like the Declaration itself, on popular sovereignty. But it was not until the middle of the nineteenth century that the Declaration, and its principle of "created equal," began to be invoked more regularly. The most famous example comes from the Gettysburg Address, which Abraham Lincoln began with a reference to 1776—that, and not 1787, was the year "our fathers brought forth" this nation, he was saying, a nation "dedicated to the proposition that all men are created equal."

Lincoln was invoking those words very intentionally, of course—in the aftermath of a key battle in a war being fought over the essential contradiction at the heart of the Declaration: slavery. Even though slavery had been a fact of societies through history, the colonists' fight against their own subjugation by Britain brought the practice's moral profanity to the fore. It was no coincidence that in their attacks on the mother country, the colonists often described themselves as "slaves." And yet, as the day of independence arrived, there were still nearly half a million enslaved people living in the colonies, a hypocrisy that did not go unnoticed. "How is it that we hear the loudest yelps for liberty among the drivers of Negroes?" the English essayist Samuel Johnson wrote in 1774.

He was right to ask. It's not easy to square a proclamation of equality and self-determination with a thriving industry of human bondage. And yet, even before the Declaration's signing, some founders were becoming uneasy with the discrepancy between their egalitarian ideals and their far less egalitarian reality. In April 1775, the Society for the Relief of Free Negroes Unlawfully Held in Bondage was founded in Philadelphia, the first anti-slavery society in the world. Two of its early leaders were Benjamin Franklin and Benjamin Rush—both close associates of Wilson.

Others were also questioning the new nation's commitment to its founding premise. In his survey of founding-era writings, Ewald turned up one reference to the phrase "all men are created equal" in a 1791 letter to Jefferson from a free Black man named Benjamin Banneker. Banneker asked Jefferson how he reconciled slavery with the Declaration's preamble. Jefferson, who had inveighed against the slave trade in the past, wrote a brief note back. He expressed a general sympathy to "our black brethren," but he didn't have an answer for Banneker's question.

5

The Pennsylvania Constitution of 1776

"KNOW YE, THAT WE DESPISE YOU"

THE CHOICES WILSON made in the lead-up to July 4, 1776, were in large part the result of his temperamental caution. He was not a radical firebreather like Samuel Adams or Tom Paine, nor was he a conciliating conservative like his mentor John Dickinson or his friend Robert Morris. Nor, crucially, was he a very skilled politician. He was a political thinker who relied on his innate moral sense and on his faculties of logic and reason, often with a rigid self-assurance that could infuriate both his friends and his foes.

Especially his foes. Pennsylvania's debate over independence, and the meaning of democratic self-government that would flow from it, was as pitched as in any colony. Wilson was confident that he had stayed true to his principles, and yet, for many of the state's radicals, the halting path he took to voting in favor of independence left a stain he was never fully able to erase. Within a few years, he would pay dearly for it.

That price was becoming evident even before the final vote on the Declaration. On the morning of June 20, 1776, the Continental Congress paused briefly for the reading of an unusual letter rebutting "misrepresentations" about Wilson's views on independence. It was signed by twenty-two of his fellow delegates in Congress, including John and Samuel Adams, Robert Morris, John Hancock, and Thomas Jefferson.

Lawmakers were not in the habit of offering certified excuses for one another's behavior. But a few weeks earlier, Robert Whitehill, a strong supporter of independence who had recently been elected to the Assembly, had warned of Wilson's "danger" to the revolutionary cause, based on what he claimed was Wilson's unwillingness to vote in favor of independence. "I will never trust a Scotchman again," Whitehill wrote. "They cannot be honest when liberty is in question."

The June 20 letter rebuffed Whitehill's attack. Wilson did not oppose independence, it said, but his hands were tied because the Pennsylvania Assembly had forbidden him and his fellow delegates from voting for it, and so he had sought to postpone the matter until the people could express themselves more directly.

Then, the writers reminded the public, the Assembly had reversed itself, freeing the delegates to vote their conscience. "He thought the People ought to have an opportunity given them to signify their opinion in a regular way upon a matter of such Importance," the letter read.

Wilson was no stranger to the verbal combat and harsh personal attacks of pre-revolutionary writing, but he took particular offense at the imputation that he was a secret Loyalist. He wasn't alone. Congress's concerted reaction to Whitehill's letter—in a setting where the accused could easily have spoken for himself—illustrated how central Wilson was to the entire project of independence and how eager his allies were to protect his name and reputation.

This would not be an easy task. Despite more than a decade in America, despite having made the most legally sophisticated case for independence from Britain, Wilson remained untrustworthy in the eyes of many radicals.

At almost the same time that Wilson and his fellow delegates in Congress were debating the nation's independence, Pennsylvania was engaged in its own debate over a new state constitution. By the end of the summer, a radical wave across the state produced what remains the most democratic state constitution in American history.

Wilson, however, had almost nothing to do with it. His time was occupied by the debate over independence and his growing responsibilities in a Congress left severely short-staffed by the war. Still, he soon emerged as one of the Pennsylvania constitution's strongest critics and learned lessons that would influence his own drafting of the US Constitution a decade later.

The fight over the Pennsylvania constitution would play out primarily as a political and class battle between an old regime and a new one. On one side were the old-line conservatives, mostly pacifist Quakers and landed aristocrats like the Penns, who lived in the eastern half of the state. They represented an "elected oligarchy" that had dominated Pennsylvania's government for more than a century. They were conciliatory toward Britain, desiring neither separation nor military conflict, and when the Continental Congress, at the urging of John Adams, passed a resolution calling on the colonies to establish their own governments, these leaders were unmoved. They had a functional government already, and they were in charge of it. Why would they change?

On the other side were the radicals or, as they preferred to call themselves, the constitutionalists—small farmers and Scots-Irish backcountry men from the western frontier who chafed at decades of living under a system that devalued their voices and their votes. Joined by laborers who lived in the city, these were the people firebrands like Thomas Paine were speaking most directly to, and they were listening.

Unlike the conservatives, the radicals were not politically experienced; to the contrary, many were uneducated and, by the standards of the old guard, uncouth. "They were mostly honest, well meaning country men, who are employed; but entirely unacquainted with such high matters," recalled the Rev. Francis Alison, Wilson's old mentor who had advised him to hold off on publishing his essay on parliamentary authority. "They seem hardly equal to the Task to form a new plan of Government." Others were blunter on the abilities of the radicals. "Numsculs," a businessman from Lancaster called them.

In the radicals' eyes, assessments like these were to their credit. "Our principle seems to be this: that any man, even the most illiterate[,] is as capable of any office as a person who has had the benefit of education," wrote Thomas Smith in a letter to Arthur St. Clair, a veteran politician and brigadier general in Washington's army. "Education perverts the understanding, eradicates common honesty, and has been productive of all the evils that have happened in the world."

Smith, who had legal training himself, went on: "We are resolved to clear every part of the old rubbish out of the way and begin upon a clean foundation. . . . You learned fellows who have warped your understanding by poring over musty old books, will perhaps laugh at us; but, know ye, that we despise you."

The radicals understood that being experienced in the political arts was not the same as reading the political moment, and they had been warning with increasing urgency of British incursions on their liberties, to no avail. The old guard of elected leaders refused to provide the necessary protections to their citizens, even as the signs of imminent war appeared everywhere. When Congress pleaded with the colony to send 4,500 troops to New Jersey, the Assembly couldn't even gather a quorum to vote on the request.

The radicals' challenge was how to wrest power from the state's elected leaders and, more important, convince the people at large that such a coup was both necessary and legitimate. As the Assembly dithered, the radicals grabbed the momentum, calling for a convention to establish a new government that could better serve Pennsylvania's needs. To organize that convention, the radicals held a provincial conference in June that was dominated by the backcountry Germans and Scots-Irish—classes of citizens who had long been excluded from Pennsylvania's politics. Suffused with an urgency that the Assembly could never muster, the conference quickly and formally approved Adams's resolution of May 10, finding that the current government was not "competent to the exigencies of our affairs" and that it must be replaced by one founded *"on the authority of the people only."*

The resolve couldn't have come sooner. British forces were attacking New York and heading for New Jersey. Pennsylvania would be next. That meant a new government had to be established fast, and forcefully.

The Assembly was still the legitimate elected government in Pennsylvania, but in practice, its members realized their power was coming to an end. The revolution was under way at every level.

Setting rules for the upcoming convention, the radicals expanded the right to vote and instituted an oath that any convention delegate could be forced to take, denying allegiance to the Crown and swearing to support a government "on the authority of the people only." This would weed out any monarchist Tories or moderate Whigs, like John Dickinson, who were disinclined to separate from Britain. More controversially, they instituted a requirement that convention members profess their faith in Jesus Christ, which would further ensure the absence of Quakers, who refused to swear oaths and had until then dominated Pennsylvania's political power structure.

The convention ran from the middle of July to the end of September, and when it was done, it had created a document that was rooted like none before it in the authority of the people. At its start, a Declaration of Rights referred to "all power being originally inherent in, and consequently derived from, the people."

That democratic spirit pervaded from start to finish. The Pennsylvania constitution eliminated property qualifications, expanding the right to vote and hold office to include almost the entire adult white male population. It established annual elections for its one-chamber legislature, which held far more power than either the executive (a toothless twelve-member council chosen by the legislature) or the judiciary (appointed for seven-year terms and removable by the legislature). It mandated subsidized public education, abolished imprisonment for debt, and created a unique institution, the Council of Censors, to ensure the government stayed faithful to the constitution.

Only a few months earlier, Pennsylvania had remained a stubborn, elitist holdout from independence. Now, at the end of 1776, it had become, in the words of one historian, "perhaps the most vital participatory democracy in the world."

It was a dramatic political transformation, as a letter to *The Pennsylvania Evening Post* in late July described it: "In those colonies where the government has, from the beginning, been in the hands of a very few rich men, the ideas of government both in the minds of those rich men, and of the common people, are rather aristocratical than popular. The rich having been used to govern, seem to think it is their right; and the poorer commonality, having hitherto had little or no hand in government, seem to think it does not belong to them to have any."

The constitutionalists did not prevail in every instance. Their draft Declaration of Rights had established, in Section 16, "That, an enormous Proportion of Property vested in a few Individuals is dangerous to the Rights, and destructive of the Common Happiness, of mankind; and therefore every free State hath a Right by its Laws to discourage the possession of such Property." It was a direct shot at land speculators like Wilson, and (possibly at the gentle urging of Benjamin Franklin, who was assisting the drafters) it was cut.

Nor did the constitutionalists get to savor their victory for long. As soon as the first draft of the Pennsylvania constitution was published in the *Evening Post* on September 10, it triggered an intense backlash. Some of it came from the conservatives so recently in charge, who violently opposed the ascension of a new class that had never been allowed to hold any power, especially recent immigrants.

But opposition also came from others who saw in the new constitution the embodiment of the "leveling spirit" that so many of them sought to quash. Pennsylvanians who had previously sided with the radical movement came to reject its overly democratic emphasis. In 1789, Benjamin Rush called the government created by the 1776 constitution a "mobocracy." He recounted a warning from John Adams: that "the people of your state will sooner or later fall upon their knees to the King of Great Britain to take them again under his protection, in order to deliver them from the tyranny of their own government."

Other colonies, scrambling to pass their own constitutions and watching events in Pennsylvania closely, lined up either for or (more often) against the "democratical order." A delegate from North Carolina called Pennsylvania's new government a "motley mixture of limited monarchy and an execrable democracy—a beast without a head." A New York congressional delegate wrote, "We ardently wish that in our own state the utmost caution may be used to avoid a like calamity."

What about Wilson? Going by the language of Pennsylvania's 1776 constitution, it is not hard to imagine the radicals winning his heart. "Any man, even the most illiterate, is as capable of any office as a person who has had the benefit of education" (as Thomas Smith put it) sounds like an Americanized version of Thomas Reid. And in important ways, the new Pennsylvania charter did embody the essence of Wilson's Reidian political vision: a relatively egalitarian franchise; broad and direct popular participation in government; proportional representation in the legislature.

At the very same time the radicals were shaping their constitution along these lines, in fact, Wilson was making identical arguments in Congress, where he fought strenuously against giving states equal voting power in the early debates over the Articles of Confederation. "It has been said that Congress is a representation of states; not of individuals," he said in late July. "It is strange that annexing the name of 'State' to ten thousand men, should give them an equal right with forty thousand. This must be the effect of magic, not of reason."

For him, it was simple: People were the only proper measure of power, and majority rule was the only fair way to decide. "Shall two millions of people put it in the power of one million to govern them as they please?" Wilson asked. "It is pretended too that the smaller colonies will be in danger from the greater. Speak in honest language and say the minority will be in danger from the majority. And is there an assembly on earth where this danger may not be equally pretended?"

It wasn't only the substance of the Pennsylvania constitution that was Wilsonian but also the process—a real-life demonstration of the "revolution principle": All power resides in the people, and if they become unhappy with their government, they may alter it when and how they please.

So why wasn't Wilson cheering on the radicals? This was exactly how he believed self-government should work—in theory, at least. In practice, he believed, the constitutionalists had gone overboard, indulging their zeal for unfettered democracy by disregarding the structures that Wilson insisted were necessary to a functional government. Over the coming years, he would become a leading critic of the Pennsylvania constitution, organizing opposition around the state and writing to friends that it was "high Time that those who think the Constitution a bad one should rouse themselves."

It would be more than two years before he laid out the basis of his criticisms in full—in a letter addressed "To the Citizens of Pennsylvania" that ran on the front page of the March 24, 1779, edition of *The Pennsylvania Gazette*, signed by the eighty-two members of the Republican Society.

The Republicans were not a formal political party so much as a faction that had formed among the upper classes of Philadelphia as a response to what they saw as the evils the new constitution had introduced into Pennsylvanian life and government.

Their letter was among the fiercest public indictments yet of the Pennsylvania constitution. And this time, in contrast to 1774, there was no mistaking the voice behind the words. Wilson, as was his style, wasted no time getting to the point. The Pennsylvania government established by the 1776 constitution, he argued, was little better than the one across the ocean that the Americans had just rejected. "While we oppose tyranny from a foreign power," it would be wrong "tamely to acquiesce in a system of government which, in our opinion, will introduce the same monster, so destructive of humanity, among ourselves."

The new constitution combined "the qualities of the different extremes of bad government," Wilson wrote. "It will produce general weakness, inactivity and confusion; intermixed with sudden and violent fits of despotism, injustice and cruelty."

He then ran through a list of specific objections. First and most important was the lack of any check against the legislature, "a single body, without any control." This meant there was no way to prevent the legislature from abusing its power or becoming corrupt. "If the

Assembly choose to disregard [attempts to check] them, to whom shall we apply for relief? To the Assembly? Shall the lamb, upon whom the devouring jaws of the wolf are opened, apply to the wolf for protection?"

In all other states but Georgia, Wilson noted, bicameral legislatures were in use, and while those states "enjoy happiness and tranquility under their governments, Pennsylvania exhibits mournful scenes of weakness and distraction." The two houses may not always agree, he said, but that wasn't a bad thing.

Next, Wilson took on the state judiciary, whose judges were appointed to seven-year terms but could be removed by the legislature. "No state can enjoy internal peace and security, unless the administration of justice is able and impartial," he wrote, but that is impossible if judges are "tossed about by every veering gale of politics."

He rounded this out with an attack on the Council of Censors ("a jubilee of tyranny") and the mandated oath, "which the convention had no authority to make" yet "was extorted from *all the citizens* of Pennsylvania, before they could exercise the first right of freemen— that of choosing their legislators."

He then leveled a pointed attack on the radicals who had prevailed in pushing the constitution through: "a set of men, chosen by not a tenth part of the inhabitants of the state, met at Philadelphia, and called themselves representatives of the freemen of Pennsylvania," even though they were "conscious that they did not stand on the broad and firm basis of the affection of the people." Coming from someone who had staked his entire political career on the idea of the authority of the people, it was an understandable complaint. And yet it would be equally applicable to Wilson himself, who eight years later would join with dozens of other men in the same building as the radicals had, elected by no one yet working in secret to write a constitution for all Americans.

Indeed, Pennsylvania's radicals in 1776 behaved in remarkably similar ways to the fifty-five people who would draft the US Constitution in 1787. Both groups established conventions of questionable legality to write their charters, disregarding the existing political bodies that were tasked by law with making large-scale changes to the government. Both strong-armed their opponents and manipulated voting systems to favor their side. Both considered themselves the true representatives of the people and employed brute political force to get around existing legal and constitutional requirements in the name of emergency. The resulting documents in both cases—the 1776 Pennsylvania constitution and the 1787 US Constitution—were literally extralegal. The Pennsylvania radicals' ad hoc convention in 1776 was a revolutionary body because "it had to be." As the historian Richard Alan Ryerson explained, "only a revolution could save Pennsylvania from subjection to Britain, war with her neighbors, and internal violence." This was the same rationale Wilson and his allies used in 1787.

Still, it is not accurate to lump Wilson in with the founders who railed against the "excess of democracy." Some of those men genuinely mistrusted the common people or were driven by personal financial interests, but Wilson's criticisms stood on principle alone—and were largely borne out by the verdict of history. Given all the ways in which he believed the 1776 Pennsylvania constitution fell short—poorly designed, never submitted for popular ratification, and requiring an oath that replaced one type of inequality with another—it wasn't hard for him to oppose it while holding fast to his commitment to the people's rule.

Nor did he forget these lessons in 1787, when he fought to include key features in the US Constitution—like meaningful checks on the legislature and an independent judiciary—that were missing from Pennsylvania's. Together with Gouverneur Morris, Wilson would design a federal executive far more powerful, and singular, than the weak twelve-member council of Pennsylvania. To him, a true separation of powers with checks and balances was the only reliable guard against abuse. As he wrote in the closing lines of the Republican Society letter, "Trust not us—trust no man—trust no body of men with uncontrolled power."

6

The Fort Wilson Riot

"STAINED WITH FRATERNAL BLOOD"

DURING THE EVENTFUL summer of 1776, James Wilson had been central to the passage of the Declaration of Independence, and by rights, he should have been celebrated for it. As 1777 began, it was clear he would be punished instead.

The radicals who now controlled the Pennsylvania legislature would never forgive him for what they saw as his two major sins: delaying the state's vote on independence and opposing the state constitution. It did not matter that they misrepresented his motivations regarding the first, casting him as a secret Loyalist who sought to undermine the vote rather than a canny operator who ultimately ensured its success. Nor did it matter that they misunderstood his rationale regarding the second, which was grounded in his certainty that a democracy without checks and balances was not much better than tyranny.

The bottom line was that the radicals in the Assembly, at that time the only statewide legislative body, held the power to appoint delegates to the Continental Congress, and they were going to use it. In late January 1777, Robert Morris wrote Wilson to tell him that after his one term, the Assembly had crossed him off the list of new delegates, along with two other opponents of the state constitution, Benjamin Rush and George Clymer.

Wilson took his expulsion in stride. "I retire without Disgust," he wrote to his friend Arthur St. Clair in February, "and with the conscious Reflection of having done my Duty to the Public, and to the State which I represented."

With no apparent prospects of political office in the near future, Wilson returned to Carlisle to be with Rachel, who had just given birth to their third child, a "fine young boy" they named Bird. Wilson stayed at home for nine days as Rachel recuperated, a long stretch for him at a time when he was constantly on the road, meeting with prospective legal clients or scoping out land deals and investing as his cash flow allowed. Even with a war under way, Wilson found the temptation of quick profits irresistible.

At the same time, he didn't want to disappear from the world of politics. It would never bring in the sort of money his speculating demanded, but he was transfixed by the ideas he had fleshed out in his essay on Parliament's authority, and he wasn't ready to put them aside.

"The situation of public affairs is so interesting that I find myself incapable of fixing upon those tranquil pleasures in my library," Wilson wrote to St. Clair from Carlisle in January. As it turned out, his excommunication from the Continental Congress was postponed briefly when one of the Assembly's picks for a new delegate dropped out, forcing them to reappoint Wilson for a few months. "What in the name of Wonder, has induced the Assembly to reappoint me?" Wilson wrote to Morris. "I am undetermined how to act; I really think I could be more useful to the Public in another Character." Still, he accepted the job, knowing it was temporary. "If at *any* time I can be useful to my country, I can at *this*," he wrote to St. Clair. "Pennsylvania is in the greatest confusion; perhaps order may, at last, arise from it."

When the next round of appointments came up in September, Wilson was again removed from the list of delegates; he would not serve in Congress again if the radicals had anything to say about it. It was the first time he would pay a concrete price for his efforts to construct a democracy that fit the vision in his head. It would not be the last.

Meanwhile, life in Carlisle had gradually lost its attraction. Wilson's appetite for land acquisition was outgrowing the frontier town, which was something of a hotbed for radicals. So, in June 1778, he and Rachel sold their property, packed up the children, and headed back to Philadelphia.

They returned to a city in ruins. The British Army had only just abandoned its nine-month siege, and the defilement and destruction wrought by 15,000 royal troops was everywhere: fetid piles of trash and excrement filled the streets; and throughout northern Philadelphia, shops were boarded up while hundreds of private houses had been razed or stripped clean of doors, windows, and roofs and any valuables stolen or sold off. (Benjamin Franklin lost his books, paintings, and a printing press.)

Church congregations returned to find windows shattered, pews stripped, walls and floors desecrated. The State House on Chestnut Street, where two years earlier James Wilson and his fellow founders had signed their names to the Declaration of Independence, was in especially poor shape. It had been used as a military hospital, and a large pit in the yard held the rotting bodies of dead soldiers and horses. The British occupation had driven out the Continental Congress, the state government, and one in three Philadelphians, about 12,000 people in all. Among those who stayed behind were hundreds of Loyalists, and now it was their turn to face consequences. The new Pennsylvania government, whose constitution had passed barely a year before the invasion, was under intense pressure to prove that it could reassert control over the city.

The hostility toward the Loyalists from the returning citizens was fierce and quick. "A Hint to the Traitors and those Tories who have taken an active part with the enemy, during their stay in this city," read one letter in *The Pennsylvania Evening Post* of July 16. "You are desired, before it is too late, to lower your heads, and not stare down your betters with angry faces. For you may be assured the day of trial is close at hand when you shall be called upon, to answer for your impertinence to the Whigs, and your treachery to this country."

In other words, treason had been committed, and those responsible had to be held to account.

The Pennsylvania Assembly had passed a treason statute the year before, with seven separate grounds for conviction, including making war, aiding the enemy, and spying. The state supreme court was in no position to hear cases, however—a consequence of the governmental paralysis brought on by the battles between those in favor of the new constitution and those against it—and thus the law had not yet been applied in a prosecution.

That was about to change. Philadelphians were furious, and they were pressing for quick revenge. But in a government based on the rule of law, any prosecution had to be countered by a defense—especially in treason cases, where a conviction was punishable by death. Pennsylvania's Supreme Executive Council, wanting to ensure the success of any prosecutions, asked the Assembly to pay the state attorney general a higher fee and provide him with a legal assistant. "There is every reason to suppose that some of the persons charged with treasonable practices will endeavour to obtain, at any expense, the most experienced [counsel] in this and the neighboring states," the Executive Council wrote to the Assembly.

One man fit that job description above all: James Wilson. He and Rachel and the children had come along with the thousands of refugees streaming back in to Philadelphia to rebuild their broken city. Unlike most of them, Wilson had not lost anything. The remuneration for this particular job, however, was not going to be primarily in cash.

Wilson agreed to take up the defense of the accused traitors as a matter of principle, just as John Adams had done following the Boston Massacre several years earlier. "Those who are acquainted with legal history," Wilson wrote later, "know what dreadful engines of tyranny prosecutions have been, when the accused have not been allowed [counsel] to instruct and assist them in their defense."

The twenty-three trials held that fall and into the spring of 1779, taking place in the largest and most influential city in America with a cast of characters that included the fledgling nation's leading lawyers and revolutionary figures, was not just a spectacle but also a test of revolutionary justice. And even with the help of a lawyer as brilliant as Wilson, a defendant charged with treason had good reason to fear for his life.

One of the first defendants to face a judge and jury was John Roberts, a well-off Quaker miller and one of Philadelphia's more prominent citizens. Before the war, he donated money toward founding the Pennsylvania Hospital, was named by the state assembly to help make Philadelphia's roads and rivers easier to pass, served on the city's Committee of Correspondence, and was a representative at the January 1775 provincial convention.

But once the British invaded Philadelphia in the fall of 1777, Roberts left his wife and children behind at the family farm, in Lower Merion Township, and rode south into the city, the opposite direction of the hordes scrambling to escape. Wilson, along with another lawyer, George Ross, took the case.

Much of the evidence against Roberts was debatable, but key parts of it appeared damning. He had been seen in the company of British forces entering Philadelphia—enough by itself for a conviction. Friends claimed they had heard him say in a tavern that he was trying to help some of his Quaker friends who had been arrested.

Roberts's trial began on September 30, at the College of Philadelphia, the only option given that the court's normal location, at the State House, was still in unusable condition.

According to the grand jury's indictment, Roberts had aided and abetted the enemy by joining the British Army, persuading others to enlist, and gathering intelligence on American troop movements. Wilson and Ross did their best with what they had, fighting for strict rules of evidence. When prosecutors called one witness to testify that Roberts had attempted to enroll him in the British Army, Wilson objected. If there was an attempt, he argued, it had not succeeded, and thus could not be introduced as evidence. "Where no actual inlisting," he said, "there can be no persuasion to inlist." The judge accepted this argument but allowed the testimony anyway as evidence of motive.

Wilson and Ross called at least twenty-nine witnesses, compared to seven for the prosecution. Under skilled questioning, the witnesses testified that Roberts had been coerced into serving the British, had voluntarily alerted the Americans that records of the Continental Congress were hidden at his farm for safekeeping, and that the prosecution's witnesses were not reliable.

The trial lasted two days, lengthy for a trial at the time, and after twenty-four hours of jury deliberation Roberts was convicted. Two weeks later he was sentenced to death. Despite pleas for clemency from his family, his friends, and even from the judge and jury that convicted him, Roberts and another Quaker convicted of treason, Abraham Carlisle, were marched by a militia guard to the outskirts of town, following a cart carrying their coffins, and hanged.

Both men had been Wilson's clients, but they were not his only ones. Wilson, along with three other top lawyers, defended nearly all the defendants charged with treason that fall—artisans, millers, blacksmiths, and a baker accused of collecting arms for the British, guiding their troops, keeping bridges, and conducting wagons—in short, "with attempting to undo the very revolution to which Wilson had pledged his life, his fortune, and his sacred honor." Only four defendants were sent to the gallows. The rest were acquitted, an astonishing record of success—or, if you were a radical, failure.

The trials raised profound questions about the meaning of treason and the scope of the government's power to prosecute it. Those questions stayed with Wilson, as did his experiences in the trials; eight years later, at the Constitutional Convention, he would lead the successful push to include a treason clause that required the government to meet a far higher standard of proof than did the state law he litigated under in 1778 and 1779.

First, though, he would have to contend with the anger his representation had provoked in a city only recently freed of British occupiers. Because the four trials that ended in guilty verdicts all came relatively early in the process, the most fervent advocates of revenge against collaborators may have felt confident that the rest of the cases would turn out the same. When that didn't happen, they were furious.

The April 1779 acquittal of David Franks, a well-known Jewish merchant who had been prosecuted for sending a letter to his son-in-law with the help of British forces, was the last straw. The case against Franks was poor from the start—the first grand jury to consider it refused even to indict him—but that didn't matter to the radicals. In *The Pennsylvania Packet*, the radicals' favored newspaper, an anonymous writer attacked the unnamed jurors in the trial, arguing that a juror "is a public character" whose name and conduct should be "open to the public eye." The writer of the letter turned out to be Timothy Matlack, secretary of the Supreme Executive Council, the ruling body established by Pennsylvania's 1776 constitution. It triggered a wave of further attacks on the juries. Someone was going to pay, and if it wasn't the alleged traitors themselves, it would be the people who exonerated—or defended—them.

Watching one Loyalist after another escape punishment only intensified the rage of Philadelphians, particularly those in the lower economic classes, who were suffering on a daily basis the skyrocketing costs of bread, flour, salt, sugar, molasses, and coffee caused by wartime shortages and devalued Continental currency. "You can't think how much worse the money is since you left this [city]," Sarah Bache wrote to her husband in mid-May. "Many families yesterday went without bread; not a bit to be bought." The state assembly made weak efforts to stem the spiraling prices, with no success.

"We have turned out against the enemy," one broadside warned, "and we will not be eaten up by monopolizers and forestallers"— the terms for merchants who bought up all of a product in order to demand whatever price they wanted. James Wilson was neither of these, but he was nevertheless regarded as a friend to the mercantile class.

By June, threats of force were becoming more common. "We have arms in our hands and know the use of them," one militia member said in a public statement. "We wish not to have the preeminence; but we will no longer be trampled upon."

A general committee formed by the radicals attempted to force prices down, but the merchants pushed back, and by fall a confrontation seemed inevitable. One morning in October, a large crowd gathered at Paddy Burns's Tavern on Tenth Street, not far from the State House. They were hungry, angry, and out of patience. It was time to take action, and broadsides posted around town the previous evening had included a list of targets, including some of Philadelphia's wealthiest citizens: John Drinker, Buckridge Sims, and Thomas Story.

The militias that had summoned the crowd had also sent word to leading radicals, including Charles Willson Peale, a member of the state assembly and also a militia captain, in the hope of getting some institutional support for what they intended to do. Peale was sympathetic to the militia's ends but not to its means, and on the morning of October 4, he went to Burns's Tavern to reason with the radicals once again. But at noon, the crowd—armed and, in many cases, inebriated—marched out of the tavern in search of the price gougers, the monopolizers, the forestallers, or anyone who might arguably be connected to them.

They found John Drinker, a prominent Quaker and Tory, coming out of the meetinghouse and promptly took him into their custody. They grabbed three more men and then broke in and ransacked the house of a fourth, Joseph Wirt, who had been tried and acquitted of treason. Wirt was not home at the time. James Wilson, a few blocks away, was not so lucky.

The house he had moved into upon his return from Carlisle was as grand as one might expect of a successful lawyer—a solid four-story brick structure with two wings and a private garden on the corner of Walnut and Third Streets. It would have stood out for its ostentatiousness at any time, but especially at a moment of citywide desperation. Wilson had gotten word that the militia had him in its sights, and he rounded up as many as thirty men to protect his house after dispatching Rachel and their children to Robert Morris's house to wait out the storm.

Around three o'clock that afternoon, a passerby noticed six or eight men huddled with Wilson around his front door and asked what was going on. Wilson replied that a mob was coming and that "he was determined to defend himself."

Meanwhile, the crowd, now numbering as many as two hundred men, marched east on Arch Street, playing "The Rogue's March" on drums and fife. When a bystander asked if the crowd was headed for Wilson's, the leaders denied it, saying "their object was to support the constitution, the laws and the Committee of Trade." But the marchers quickly arrived in front of Wilson's house, and when one of the men holed up inside the house, Captain Robert Campbell, stuck his head out a second-floor window and told the crowd to move along, he was struck immediately by a bullet. The wound was fatal, and the fight erupted.

Inside the house, Wilson and the others were gathered in an upstairs room, according to one account, as "a number of desperate-looking men in their shirt sleeves" moved toward them "armed with bars of iron, and large hammers." An attacker swung his sledgehammer against the front door, and the men entered, only to be met by shots from the top of the stairs. With at least one of them hit, others dragged one of Wilson's defenders down the stairs by his hair and bayoneted him, and Wilson's crew barricaded the door.

Whether Wilson could have held out much longer is doubtful; the militia had sent for reinforcements, and a cannon was being hauled over from the arsenal. But before it could be loaded, Joseph Reed— the president of the Executive Council, who had been laid up sick in bed when a frantic Charles Willson Peale alerted him to what was going on—arrived on horseback with the City Light Horse Cavalry in tow, scattering the crowd with the help of Peale and, ironically, Timothy Matlack, whose letter to *The Pennsylvania Packet* had helped fuel the riot.

When it was all over, one member of Wilson's crew, Captain Campbell, and at least six of the radicals were dead, as was a young Black boy who had been standing nearby on Walnut Street and was caught in the crossfire. The exact number of militiamen killed was never determined, but at least seventeen were wounded.

After the City Light Horse Cavalry hauled away the last of the militant stragglers, Wilson left as quickly and quietly as he could, taking up Robert Morris's offer to join his family and hide out at the

Hills, Morris's country estate on the Schuylkill River. As night fell, the city quieted at last, but not for long. In the morning, militia officers marched on the city jail and demanded the immediate release of their men, and after that was done, they insisted that Wilson and his friends spend a night in jail "as a kind of retaliation."

Meanwhile, Morris and Wilson kept up a daily correspondence through secret channels. "The storm is over for this day," Morris wrote on Tuesday morning. Still, he said, it wasn't safe for Wilson to come back home. "As the ferment is particularly high against you, it may be best to keep out of the way for a day or two," Morris said, pleading with him to go to New Jersey, because "where you are cannot be deemed secure or anywhere in that neighborhood."

Like a diligent lawyer, Wilson had already prepared a defense of his actions. "It will be of use to prove that we called upon them from the windows <u>not</u> to fire," he wrote to Morris that afternoon, listing a string of witnesses who could testify to the fact. "The manner too of their appearances forming before the house, and firing into it without any previous demand or complaint should be shown."

Wilson added that he wanted to return to the city as soon as possible. "My absence, I'm afraid, only makes matters worse." Morris wrote back as soon as he received the letter that evening. "Perhaps it may be best if you don't come in tomorrow," he urged. "I will let you know whether to venture it at night or not."

But Wilson, anxiously pacing the halls of Morris's vast home, was already plotting how to eliminate any future attacks. He proposed creating an association to give "some Stability to our Defense of the first Rights of Men," which he thought would "produce a mutual Confidence in each other." Send a petition from house to house to be signed, he said, and then present it to Joseph Reed in his capacity as president. "This Appears to me to be the only Measure, by which we can expect to live in any tolerable Degree of Quiet."

The violence of October 4, which soon became known as the Fort Wilson Riot, would echo through Philadelphia society and across the nation. Only hours after the attack, Henry Laurens, a former president of the Continental Congress, wrote to John Adams: "We are at this moment on a precipice, and what I have long dreaded and often intimated to my friends, seems to be breaking forth—a convulsion among the people." Benjamin Rush, Wilson's friend and fellow signer of the Declaration, sent his own warning to Adams a week later. "Our streets for the first time were stained with fraternal blood."

From the perspective of men like these, Wilson was blameless. "It surprises me exceedingly that Mr. Wilson could have been pointed out as an enemy to his country, as his conduct has from a very early period been uniformly friendly," Arthur St. Clair, an army general, wrote to Reed a few days after October 4. Admitting that Wilson had perhaps been overly critical of the state constitution, St. Clair added, "his advocating the causes of the accused persons should certainly not have been considered as a crime, as it is both a part and a consequence of that liberty we have been struggling to establish."

The radicals saw Wilson very differently. He had been one of their primary targets because, no matter the insult to their finances or their dignity, his name always seemed to be involved. They believed that as a core member of the city's elite and a friend to the merchant class, he was responsible, even if indirectly, for the price gouging that had immiserated so many poorer Philadelphians. What's more, he had fought against the adoption of a state constitution that many of those citizens felt included them in government for the first time. Perhaps worst of all, he had led the legal defense of the accused traitors in the fight for independence. Days after the riot, a coalition of militias released a statement blaming it on "the exceeding lenity which has been shown to persons notoriously disaffected to the Independence of the United States."

And even though Joseph Reed had come to Wilson's rescue that day, he and the Supreme Executive Council issued a proclamation that "the principal cause of the present Commotion" had been the "encouragement" of suspected traitors to America by those "whose rank and character in other respects gave weight to their conduct."

The council ordered everyone involved—militia members and those who had barricaded themselves in Wilson's house—to surrender to authorities. Wilson paid a ten-thousand-dollar bond, double the amount of any of the others in his house, to appear before the next session of court.

Still, the horror of the attack had exposed a rift among the constitutionalists, with leaders like Reed and Matlack shrinking from the crowd violence of the "lower sort." Pennsylvania's 1776 constitution may have been radical, but it was still a constitution, one premised on the rule of law and concerned above all with establishing a stable, predictable society. Such a project could not coexist with political violence, even toward sympathetic ends. That this sentiment prevailed was evident in the virtual disappearance after the riot of any verbal attacks on juries.

It also resulted in the election of the less fervent radical Charles Willson Peale to an Assembly seat one week after the riot, in a vote that threw out several leading republicans and members of the merchant class, including Robert Morris. Wilson certainly had grounds to complain about the violence directed at him and his friends, but it was harder to reject the same sentiments when they were expressed at the ballot box.

Thomas Paine, no friend of Tories, also spoke up against the violence, which he believed had achieved nothing and had hurt the larger cause. "Those whose talent it is to act, are seldom much devoted to deliberate thinking," he wrote in *The Pennsylvania Packet* of October 16. "That Mr. Wilson is not a favourite in the State, is a matter which, I presume, he is fully sensible of," Paine continued, "yet the difference is exceedingly great, between not being in favor and being considered as an enemy."

Demands for a "moral economy" in which wealthy elites could no longer profit off the backs of the working poor and in which the state ensured that all people had fair access to the necessities of life was one enduring legacy of the Fort Wilson Riot. But such demands would have to compete with countervailing demands in favor of property rights and societal order, and the former would often lose.

The riot likely played a role as well in the public's increased acceptance of powerful, centralized governments at both the state and national levels. This trend would culminate in the Constitutional

Convention of 1787 and the revision of the Pennsylvania constitution in 1790. Both resulting documents established strong governments characterized by separated powers and checks and balances—the brand of republicanism favored by elites. Wilson, with all his contradictory impulses, would be at the center of both.

In the end, no one would face prosecution for the events of October 4, 1779. Within weeks, the state assembly introduced an "Act of Free and General Pardon and Indemnity," passing it the following spring and foreclosing any criminal action against Wilson, his friends, or the radicals.

As a matter of law, the Fort Wilson Riot was over. As a matter of lore and culture, it would never be forgotten. A few years later, a visitor to Philadelphia brought his flute to an artisan for repair. When he gave the artisan the address, the artisan replied, "Oh, you live opposed that damned Wilson that defended the Tory Hamilton, that house where the damned Tories were sheltered. We were near breaking in and making short work of them."

It would have been easy, and understandable, for Wilson to have responded to the attack by joining in his peers' distrust of the crowd. Instead, he doubled down on his commitment to popular self-rule. What did such perseverance say about him? What did it say about the values at the core of his life's work? Was it that, as the historian Robert McCloskey surmised, "his confidence in the good judgment of a free electorate insulated him against the fears of popular rapacity"?

If that is correct, then the same confidence is part of what was leading, inexorably, to Wilson's ultimate ruin. He existed so much in the land of theory and ideas—what another historian called "the Panglossian excesses of Enlightenment optimism"—that even a deadly attack couldn't shake his faith. Whether that is to his credit or not, it does suggest a refusal, or at least an inability, to fully comprehend the darker sides and rougher edges of humanity—including his own.

For if Wilson emerged from 1779 undeterred from his commitment to rule by the people, he was similarly undeterred from his commitment to increasing his own wealth. His attachment to its trappings may not have dimmed his belief in popular sovereignty, but it was a main source of the radicals' suspicion of him. As the money from his legal clients continued to pour in, he reinvested it into ever more "extravagant and daring business schemes."

In August, weeks before the attack on his house, Wilson had become the chairman of the Illinois and Wabash Company, one of the largest land ventures of the founding era. The company, of which he was also a major shareholder, claimed rights to about thirty million acres throughout modern-day Illinois, Ohio, and Indiana. Wilson's financial entanglements with it would continue through the rest of his life and pose conflicts he never fully resolved. The company's land claims held up passage of the Articles of Confederation, resulted in Supreme Court cases, and triggered congressional investigations.

To make enough money to invest in schemes of this size, Wilson was constantly on the lookout for clients. Within a few months of the attack, he managed to get himself an appointment representing France in its dealings with the United States, opening the door to a big payday as trade between the two countries expanded. Assuming the appointment was in hand, Wilson sent word to John Adams, then in Paris to negotiate peace with Great Britain, asking him to purchase a couple hundred pounds of books on French law and history. But before Adams could get the books, the French balked at the fee Wilson was demanding for his services and revoked the offer. After a drawn-out negotiation, Wilson at last succeeded in getting his money—ten thousand livres. As it turned out, no amount would ever be enough.

7
Prosperity, Speculation, and Crisis

A LESS RESOLUTE man might have been chastened by a near-fatal mob attack on his home and family. He might have withdrawn into a quieter, less ostentatious lifestyle that would not call as much attention to his wealth and political views.

James Wilson did not choose that path. By 1782, he was forty, and his life was expanding in every direction. In the fall, he was reelected to Congress for the first time in five years. Several months earlier, Rachel had given birth to Emily, their second daughter and fifth child. She joined Polly, eleven; William, nine; Bird, five; and James, three, in the family's comfortable Philadelphia home.

Bird had become a particular favorite of Wilson's. A quiet and bookish boy who preferred the comfort of being near his parents over roughhousing with friends, he showed early signs of being a reliable confidant despite his young age, leading Wilson to allow him to keep his books and toys in his office, and to accompany him on legal and business trips around the city.

Stern and stiff-backed, Wilson must have cut an amusing figure as he marched through the fetid streets of Philadelphia in hat and coattails, his sandy hair tied back with a ribbon, his nose in the air to keep his spectacles from slipping off, and a small boy weighed down by a bag of books scrambling to keep up in his wake.

Meanwhile, Wilson's family in Scotland kept sending letters to Philadelphia, sharing news of their trials back home and hoping for even a little news from abroad. In 1783, his mother, Alison, wrote to inform him that another of his brothers had died; this time it was Andrew, in a sudden attack of cholera. At the end of her sad account, almost in passing, she wrote, "We saw your name sometimes in the publick, particularly in the Address to the King in 1775, which we took to be you." She then reminded him, as she always did, to be dutiful to God and thus ensure his protection. It was for the best that she remained unaware of the Fort Wilson Riot.

Wilson had not forgotten, but he had moved on. He was one of the most respected members of the city's political and legal elite. He was also one of its wealthiest and best connected, thanks to his service in Congress, his work for high-end clients like Robert Morris, and his burgeoning land investments—not to mention his marriage to a daughter of high Philadelphia society and the old money that came with her. Rachel knew what was expected of someone of her station. When she wasn't managing their growing household, she was going door-to-door collecting donations for revolutionary soldiers.

Wilson's social discomfort didn't keep him from periodic fly-fishing excursions on the Schuylkill, or from joining fraternal organizations like Benjamin Franklin's Society for Political Inquiries, the American Philosophical Society, and the Saint Andrew's Society, a philanthropic organization that raised money for impoverished Scots. When the society named Wilson its president, he was tasked with replacing its long-standing motto, proposing *ubi libertas ibi patria,* or "where there is liberty, there is my country"—a fitting choice for someone who had crossed an ocean to build a free nation.

Even with a packed professional and personal calendar, Wilson spent hours in his own study, reading, thinking, and writing. "He has in his library all our best authors on public law and jurisprudence," wrote the Marquis de Chastellux, a French general who recorded his travels around the young country, "and he makes them his daily study." Chastellux's translator added that Wilson was "making a fortune rapidly in the profession of the law at Philadelphia."

The money was rolling in thanks to the volume of work, and to Wilson's fees, which were a good deal higher than those of almost any other lawyer in town. His rates gave pause not only to the French government but also to Bushrod Washington, a promising nineteen-year-old law student who arrived at Wilson's door in the spring of 1782 at his uncle George's urging. When Wilson informed the young man of his tutoring fee of one hundred guineas, Bushrod balked. It was an enormous sum; there was no way he or his father, John Washington, could pay it. But Wilson's reputation was great enough that George Washington agreed to underwrite the cost, asking Wilson to take his nephew on "not only as a student requiring your instruction—but to your attentions as a friend." General Washington was somewhat distracted at the time. Having led the Continental Army to victory at the Battle of Yorktown a few months before, he was in the middle of negotiating the terms of the British surrender and was short on cash, so he sent Wilson a promissory note for the fee.

With his ever-growing fortune, Wilson was investing in more land deals and borrowing more money to finance them. His need for cash was endless. Writing to William Bingham, one of the wealthiest men in Philadelphia, he proposed "an adventure in lands" in the frontier regions of New York and Pennsylvania that would require up to one hundred thousand pounds of capital, and in which Wilson would be a one-fourth owner. From a group of Dutch businessmen, he sought at least ten thousand pounds for "a very extensive System of Works," including sawmills and iron forges, that he and his brother-in-law Mark Bird were building along the Delaware River. "We have already expended a very considerable sum of money," Wilson wrote the Dutch, but "it will be absolutely necessary for us to be in possession of still larger sums."

One of his biggest lenders was the Bank of North America, the brainchild of Robert Morris, the superintendent of finance and Wilson's regular client and friend. The bank—chartered by Congress in 1781 as America's first national bank and chartered in the state of Pennsylvania the following year—had become a particular sore spot for the radicals in the Assembly. If the American Revolution had been about anything, they believed, it was political and social equality, but to them, this bank epitomized the opposite: It was a sop to the wealthy like Wilson, who were its primary investors and directors and were already making enormous profits from their investments. Farmers in the western part of the state, meanwhile, were being driven toward bankruptcy. The bank's opponents were also upset about its growing power. "We have nothing in our free and equal government capable of balancing the influence which this bank must create," the Assembly wrote in a committee report.

As the young American economy faltered once again, popular anger at the bank only increased. In 1784 and 1785, the radical-dominated Assembly pushed repeatedly to revoke the bank's state charter. Newspapers published screeds against "merciless creditors" and the "insatiable leeches," landlords who kept "the honest mechanic and hardworking laborer" in permanent debt. A public defense of the bank was needed quickly, and the bank's board of directors turned to Wilson to make it. He was busy enough with his other commitments and with his home life—Rachel had just given birth to Charles, their sixth child, in August—but he took the job anyway. He was the obvious choice: In addition to his abundant legal, political, and financial acumen, he was the bank's lead counsel and served on its board of directors. He would get four hundred dollars for the assignment, a piddling sum for a wealthy man. Yet the success of his land investments depended on a political and financial regime where credit was easy and money could flow freely. More to the point, he had been able to make those investments largely thanks to the Bank of North America, which had loaned him close to one hundred thousand dollars—and unlike the farmers and workingmen in the western part of the state, Wilson kept managing to get extra time to pay his debts.

The essay Wilson produced in defense of the bank would be a prime example of how his political commitments and his personal interests were becoming increasingly intertwined. He genuinely believed in the need for a powerful central government. He also believed, as a student of the Scottish Enlightenment, that there was no conflict between virtue and commerce, and defending the bank offered the perfect way to make his case.

First, he wrote, Congress unquestionably had the power to charter the Bank of North America, even though the Articles of Confederation did not explicitly grant it. The bank's opponents claimed that this omission meant any such power remained in the states. Wrong, Wilson replied. The states never had any power to charter a national bank in the first place. Therefore, Congress does not need an express delegation of that power to use it. "The United States are to be considered as one undivided, independent nation," he wrote, and as a nation, it has "general rights, general powers, and general obligations . . . resulting from the union of the whole." If a necessary task is beyond the competence of individual states—and the establishment of a national bank falls into that category—then the national government may do it, even if it received no express grant of power.

This brought him to the heart of his case, the one he had been making from the beginning—that the sovereignty on which America was founded resides not in the states or in the nation, but in the people themselves. And the Declaration of Independence is the ultimate expression of this fact; through it, the people created their nation, and therefore it supersedes any subsequent law or constitution. "The act of independence was made before the Articles of Confederation," Wilson wrote. "This act declares, that '*these United Colonies*,' (not enumerating them separately) 'are free and independent states; and that, as free and independent states, *they* have full power to do *all* acts and things which independent states may, of right, do.'"

Wilson went on to explain why it would be a bad idea, politically and financially, for Pennsylvania to revoke the bank's charter, including the damage it would do to the country's credit and to its trade prospects. This argument did not change the final vote; in September, the Assembly revoked the bank's state charter. Still, Wilson's essay had served a deeper purpose. In making an eloquent case for the importance of national power, he was laying the groundwork for the implied powers that a functional American government would need to have to survive. Two years before the 1787 convention, Wilson was sketching out the case to rebuild, and salvage, America.

Arguments for a stronger central government could not have come at a better time. Americans' first attempt at collective government, the Articles of Confederation, was only a few years old and already nearing collapse. The Articles had been drafted and ratified over the course of several years amid the Revolutionary War, and it had become clear that fighting a common enemy was easier than governing together in the absence of one.

Like many first drafts, the Articles read as hesitant and overwritten. "To all to whom these Presents shall come, we, the undersigned Delegates of the States affixed to our Names send greeting," they began. Nothing to see here, only an awkward hand wave to the rest of the world. The Articles continued in that vein, the work of a nation still finding its footing, still unsure of the nature of its sovereignty.

"Remember," Benjamin Rush, the physician and Declaration signer, said in arguing for their revision, "we assumed these forms of government in a hurry, before we were prepared for them." As he pointed out: "We had just emerged from a corrupted monarchy. Although we understood perfectly the principles of liberty, yet most of us were ignorant of the forms and combinations of power in republics."

By the mid-1780s, the young nation was facing two concurrent crises, one political and one economic, that would soon come crashing into each other, forcing the leading figures of the Revolution to contemplate drastic steps to save the country they had fought so hard to create.

The political crisis was the direct result of the failure of the Articles, which operated less like the charter for a national government than like a treaty among independent states, each equal in power and jealous of its own interests. Article II put it simply: "Each state retains its sovereignty, freedom and independence"—a more politic way of saying "Don't tread on me."

The farthest the states were willing to go in permitting centralized power was the Congress of the Confederation, a single-chamber body where delegates from each state debated and passed laws. But this congress, which grew out of the Continental Congress that had been meeting since 1774, reflected the ambivalence of the whole project. Operating like "an international assemblage of ambassadors," it was not really a legislature at all. Its member states each got one vote, regardless of size. It could ask states to pay into the treasury, but it had no enforcement mechanism if they refused, as many did. It often struggled to achieve a quorum, going weeks or longer without being able to conduct the basic business of government. Even when the bare minimum of delegates showed up, they had no power to levy taxes directly and so could not raise the revenue needed to fund an army for self-defense or to provide for the welfare of the people—tasks that any functional legislature must be able to perform.

Making matters worse, this Congress was the only game in town. The Articles of Confederation provided for no president to serve as the nation's leader, nor any judiciary to resolve disputes among states or between citizens of different states. The states employed their own judges and their own governors or (like Pennsylvania) executive councils, but without a common baseline of laws or governmental bodies to pass and enforce them, the state-by-state differences— whether over trade, taxation, or the practice of human bondage—grew only sharper.

The biggest single obstacle to the new government's functioning, however, was the Articles' provision that any amendment had to be approved by all 13 states of the confederation. By requiring unanimity, the charter had bulletproofed itself against change. No matter how many people might agree on the need for an update to improve the functioning of the system, any one state could find something to object to. At least one always did. In 1781, shortly after the Articles took effect, Congress proposed an amendment giving itself the power to impose a 5 percent tax on foreign imports, a clear way to raise desperately needed revenue. Every state agreed—except for Rhode Island, which represented one sixtieth of the country's population.

In the seven years that the Articles were in operation, not a single amendment was adopted.

As a national government, it was a catastrophe. And yet, for a good number of politicians and power brokers, this arrangement was ideal. The ineffectiveness of the national government was, in their eyes, a feature and not a flaw. If they had drawn one lesson from the war for independence, it was that, in the words of one historian, "government should be small, weak, and, wherever possible, local." The problem was that these "local" governments, ostensibly bound under the Articles of Confederation in a "firm league of friendship," were increasingly coming into conflict and competition with one another—over territory, river navigation rights, commerce, and more. The subject matter of the dispute was beside the point; what mattered was that no superior authority existed to resolve it.

Almost from the moment the Articles were ratified, calls for reform came. George Washington, who knew firsthand how damaging it was when Congress could not raise the funds to properly arm and clothe its military, spoke up in favor of a strong central government. "We are either a united people under one head, or we are thirteen independent sovereignties, eternally counteracting each other." As early as 1783, members of Congress were talking about calling a convention to revise the confederation and strengthen the powers of the union.

This political crisis was calamitous enough on its own. But it was compounded by an economic crisis that threatened to tear the young country apart. The Revolutionary War and its aftermath had plunged the states deep into debt, and to pay it down, they imposed harsh new taxes. These taxes were far higher than the British taxes on the colonists of the 1760s and '70s—taxes that had also been levied in response to war debt and that had triggered the revolution in the first place. These newer taxes fell especially hard on farmers, who had more land than money; tens of thousands lost their farms to foreclosure, and many ended up in debtors' prison.

The farmers pleaded with state legislatures for help. Some lawmakers, as in Massachusetts, chose to protect the farmers' creditors first, insisting on prompt repayment even if it meant driving many debtors into bankruptcy and ruin. Other states were more sympathetic to the farmers, printing paper money to help ease trade and allow the payment of debts. Rhode Island required creditors to accept paper money or relinquish their claims.

It was class warfare. Defenders of the farmers disparaged opponents of paper money as "flint-hearted misers" and called on the government to "help the feeble against the mighty." The creditors, meanwhile, had little patience for what they considered the "lazy, lounging, lubberly" masses who lived beyond their means. Among this group were many of the nation's top political actors, including James Madison, who fervently opposed paper money. "Nothing but evil springs from this imaginary money," he wrote to Thomas Jefferson.

To the elites—bankers, lawyers, and other merchants—debtor relief measures like these were an ominous sign that state governments had fallen too much under the influence of the popular will. Some feared for their property rights, believing that the ultimate goal of the debtors was that all property be held in common. Others were concerned that Britain, which was already punishing its former colonies by blocking the importation of American goods, would take advantage of the chaos to further destabilize the wobbly young nation.

These twin crises, the political and the economic, came crashing into each other in the summer of 1786, when tax collectors in western Massachusetts found themselves facing down armed resistance. Entire communities were prepared to take up arms rather than pay the government another penny. The uprising spread and became known as Shays's Rebellion, after Daniel Shays, a farmer and Revolutionary War veteran, led a march on the federal arsenal in Springfield. Over the fall and winter of 1786, neither the Massachusetts government nor Congress had the money or organization to put down the rebels. In the end, a private militia had to do the job in late January 1787.

Shays's Rebellion taught the elites two things: One, the American people, abetted by excessively democratic state governments, were out of control. Two, the government under the Articles of Confederation wasn't strong enough to stop them. As one member of the Continental Congress wrote at the time, America's situation was "indeed wretched—our funds exhausted, our credit lost, our confidence in the federal government destroyed."

Even steadfast defenders of the Articles could see they were working with a defective product. More than a few were beginning to wonder if they had it in their power, as Thomas Paine had written a decade earlier, "to begin the world over again." So, on September 11, 1786, twelve men gathered in Annapolis, Maryland, to discuss amendments to the Articles of Confederation. Congress had called the meeting the previous winter, but only five of the thirteen states sent delegates—nowhere near enough to give them authority to take any action.

Still, those present included James Madison, Alexander Hamilton, and Edmund Randolph, all strong critics of the current system and proponents of a more powerful national government. They were prepared to move forward with major revisions to the Articles, but they knew that any real fix would require the buy-in of all member states. This meant organizing a meeting that people would feel compelled to attend. They drafted a letter to Congress requesting a formal convention "to devise such further provisions as should appear to them necessary to render the constitution of the Federal Government adequate to the exigencies of the Union."

Wilson might have added even more weight to the request, but he was not there: Rachel had died in April, at just thirty-nine—she had never fully recovered from Charles's birth and had fallen seriously ill in late winter—leaving her husband to manage a household bursting with children, one of whom was not yet on his feet. Wilson was bereft; Rachel was the only woman who had won his heart, although she would have been justified in wondering what that was worth. Over fifteen years, half a dozen children, and Wilson's punishing work commitments, the couple had had little time for each other. Now, as the cold weather approached, Wilson was alone, faced with existential crises in both his country and his family.

Meanwhile, weeks passed before the Congress considered even the idea of a convention. In part that was because several lawmakers doubted they had the power to authorize such a meeting in the first place. The main reason for the delay, however, was that Congress lacked a quorum from November through the middle of January 1787, during which time it could conduct no business.

At the same time, the uprising in Massachusetts was getting worse by the day. In mid-October, Henry Lee wrote a plea to his friend George Washington, who insisted he was done with public life and was looking forward to spending his remaining days at Mount Vernon, his Virginia farm. "We are all in dire apprehension that a beginning of anarchy with all its calamitys has approached," Lee wrote, begging Washington to intervene in Massachusetts. Washington responded with uncharacteristic pessimism, writing that the conflict was "melancholy proof of what our trans-Atlantic foe have predicted . . . that mankind, left to themselves are unfit for their own government."

With each passing week, the convention proposed by the Annapolis delegates seemed increasingly like the last chance Americans would have to prove that prediction wrong.

8

Philadelphia 1787

"LOST IN THE MAGNITUDE OF THE OBJECT"

ON DECEMBER 29, 1786, a group of Pennsylvania lawmakers met at a tavern across the street from the State House in Philadelphia to nominate delegates to the convention being called to ensure there was a constitution "adequate to the exigencies of the Union." They chose seven men—all Philadelphians, to keep travel costs down. Among them were Robert Morris, the powerful financier; Gouverneur Morris, the towering, one-legged ladies' man; and James Wilson. (Benjamin Franklin would be added in March.) When the full assembly voted on the nominees the next day, it took three ballots to elect Wilson, who won just 35 of 63 votes, fewer than anyone except Gouverneur Morris, who squeaked by with one more than a bare majority. Morris, only recently relocated to Philadelphia from New York City, likely got his spot because the Pennsylvania delegation was the largest of any state's. Wilson's difficulties were a product of his role in the fight over the Pennsylvania constitution of 1776, as well as the Fort Wilson Riot and his essay defending the Bank of North America, all of which had contributed to his being cast as an anti-democratic aristocrat. Still, within months, he and Morris would be helping to lead the drafting of the Constitution.

By February, seven states—a majority—had appointed their own delegates, but the convention wasn't a done deal. The Confederation

Congress remained without a quorum until February 21, nearly half a year after the Annapolis petition had been submitted. When it finally met, it voted to approve a convention "for the sole and express purpose of revising the Articles of Confederation," set to open on May 14 in Philadelphia—an emergency response to a nation on life support.

America was barely a decade old, but the State House where the delegates would meet had already earned eternal fame. It was there in the assembly room that fifty-six delegates had gathered in 1776 to sign the Declaration of Independence. The building then hosted the Continental Congress and, after the Articles of Confederation were ratified, the Confederation Congress. By 1787, it had attained the status of a civic church, complete with wooden steeple.

But at eleven o'clock on the morning of May 14, the assembly room of the State House was mostly empty. James Wilson was there, along with Benjamin Franklin and the other Pennsylvania delegates, which was no surprise. They lived in town and could have rolled out of bed and into their seats. Two Virginians, George Washington and James Madison, had arrived together, Madison from the boardinghouse around the corner and Washington from Robert Morris's mansion, where he had reluctantly agreed to stay at Morris's insistence.

Other than a smattering of delegates from Delaware and North Carolina, the rest—seventy in all had been chosen by the states—were delayed by bad weather, muddy spring roads, or poor health. Beginning the world over again would take some time, as it turned out.

The story was the same on Tuesday. One by one, delegates trickled into town, but the convention still lacked a quorum. Madison was growing frustrated. He had served in both Congress and the Virginia legislature and was well acquainted with the perils of weak government. Short, sickly, and bookish, he possessed neither Washington's charisma nor Gouverneur Morris's gift for oratory, but he would come to be regarded as among the most informed and thoughtful delegates at the convention.

"The number as yet assembled is but small," Madison wrote to Thomas Jefferson that night. "There is a prospect of a pretty full meeting on the whole, though there is less punctuality in the outset than was to be wished." He blamed the weather, but he was wary. He had seen the same lack of urgency before: It afflicted the Congress that had called the convention into existence.

Good thing, then, that Benjamin Franklin was around. Franklin, the nation's elder statesman and president of Pennsylvania's Executive Council, served as the de facto host of the convention. By 1787, he vied with Washington for the unofficial title of most beloved American; certainly he was the most famous worldwide, having spent a decade in London on behalf of the Pennsylvania Assembly, then serving as minister to France, where he mustered support for the Revolution. He no longer had the vigor to hold forth in front of a crowd, but he had a lifetime of wisdom to draw from. And if the old diplomat had learned anything about politics, it was that it never hurt to throw a good dinner party. On Wednesday evening, Franklin welcomed more than a dozen delegates to a feast in his new dining room. Washington, Madison, Randolph, Robert Morris, Gouverneur Morris, and Wilson were all there. It was "what the French call *une assemblée des notables*," Franklin recounted to a friend a few days later, in a note of gratitude for a cask of porter the friend had sent over. "The cask was broached, and its contents met with the most cordial reception and universal approbation," Franklin wrote. "In short, the company agreed unanimously, that it was the best porter they had ever tasted."

What Franklin did not say, what even he may not have fully realized in the moment, was that his dinner party was the true launch of the Philadelphia convention. By bringing together the most incisive and broad-ranging minds—men who happened to be, like him, strongly committed to building a powerful national government—and by plying them with food and his cask of beer, Franklin had helped set the course of the summer and, thus, of American history.

Over the following week, the Virginians and the Pennsylvanians met every day at 3 P.M., first gathering at the State House for a couple of hours of informal debate and then, in the late afternoon, shifting to a nearby tavern to continue over supper and drinks. Because those meetings were not official, no minutes were kept, but they were as significant as any that took place over the next four months. That is because the delegates were not planning to abide by the limits that Congress had explicitly placed on the convention—to only propose revisions to the Articles of Confederation and nothing more. Rather, they were preparing to rip the whole thing up and start over.

Madison had been in town since May 3, largely by himself, spending his time mapping out the plan. The fundamental flaw in the Articles of Confederation, by his estimate, was that they were ineffective. The states, all equal players, answered to no one and did as they pleased. Their refusal to pay their Revolutionary War debts, for instance, made it impossible for Congress to raise money to do anything a government should be able to do. It was an "evil," Madison wrote, that was "fatal to the object of the present system."

In a long letter to Washington in April, Madison had proposed that "a change be made in the principle of representation"; in other words, the states could no longer share an equal and independent status. "The lesser States must in every event yield to the predominant will," he wrote. "The national government should be armed with positive and complete authority in all cases which require uniformity," with the powers to tax and regulate trade being the most obvious examples.

The new plan would be "a total alteration of the present federal system," George Mason, Madison's fellow Virginian, wrote to his son after getting wind of the plan.

In the days following Franklin's dinner party, Madison gravitated to the two Pennsylvanians who would become his staunchest allies over the summer: James Wilson and Gouverneur Morris. In some instances, Wilson and Morris wanted to go even farther than Madison did, such as by applying this new principle of representation to voting in the convention itself. "The large states should unite in firmly refusing to the small states an equal vote" during the convention, they argued, since any "good system of government" must "be founded on a violation of that equality." Otherwise, they reasoned, the smaller states would do as they had done for the past six years and exploit their disproportionate voting power to block any measure they saw as threatening that power.

For all his eagerness, Madison rejected that idea as too far, too fast. "Such an attempt might beget fatal altercations between the large and small states," he wrote in his notes. The small states were more likely to accept a diminution of power slowly, over the course of the convention, he believed, than "to disarm themselves" at the out-set "and thereby throw themselves on the mercy of the large states."

It was an early illustration of the gap between Madison's political savvy and Wilson's—a gap that would reappear in various forms over the summer. Both men had served in Congress, and both were socially awkward in their own way, but Madison had instincts for achieving his desired goals that Wilson could never quite grasp. In this case, Madison's hesitation was well placed. As more delegates arrived, they were getting their hands on drafts of the new plan and were alarmed at what they saw.

George Read, recently arrived from Delaware, sent an urgent letter to his still-absent fellow delegate John Dickinson, now also a delegate from Delaware after representing Pennsylvania in Congress. "I wish you were here," Read wrote. "I am in possession of a copied draft of a federal system intended to be proposed." The small states "should keep a strict watch upon the movements and propositions from the larger states, who will probably combine to swallow up the smaller ones by addition, division, or impoverishment; and, if you have any wish to assist in guarding against such attempts," Read warned Dick-inson, "you will be speedy in your attendance."

Three days later, as the convention was on the verge of achieving its quorum, Rufus King of Massachusetts wrote to Jeremiah Wads-worth, a delegate from Connecticut. "I am mortified that I alone am from New England," King wrote. "Pray hurry on your delegates. . . . Believe me it may prove most unfortunate if they do not attend within a few days."

Only weeks earlier, the Virginians and Pennsylvanians had been fretting about the slow pace of the delegates' arrival. Now it was be-coming clear that the delay had been a blessing. During those cool, quiet days in the middle of May, Madison, Wilson, Gouverneur Morris, and the other nationalists had gotten a big head start, and they had made the most of it. As the rest of the delegates would soon discover, they were walking into a trap.

On Friday, May 25, almost two weeks after the convention was supposed to begin, seven states—a bare majority—were finally able to announce that they had enough delegates present to achieve a quorum.

Wilson was there, as he would be every day of the summer, weighing in more than any other delegate except his fellow Pennsylvanian Gouverneur Morris, who took pleasure in unleashing bursts of fiery rhetoric at his opponents.

Over the next several months, Wilson's prominence among the other delegates would be indisputable. "Mr. Wilson ranks among the foremost in legal and political knowledge," William Pierce, a Georgia delegate, observed. "He is well acquainted with Man, and understands all the passions that influence him. Government seems to have been his peculiar Study, all the political institutions of the World he knows in detail, and can trace the causes and effects of every revolution from the earliest stages of the Grecian commonwealth down to the present time. No man is more clear, copious, and comprehensive than Mr. Wilson, yet he is no great Orator. He draws the attention not by the charm of his eloquence, but by the force of his reasoning."

For the first few days, however, Wilson drew little if any attention, speaking almost not a word, according to Madison's recorded notes of the convention.

Perhaps that was because there was nothing yet to fight about. The first order of business that Friday morning was a relatively simple one: choosing a president of the convention. The only plausible options were George Washington and Benjamin Franklin. Franklin was feeling unwell that day, so he asked Robert Morris to nominate Washington in his stead. The outcome was unanimous and preordained; the Revolutionary War hero, stern and obsessed with protocol, was the most revered man in America. Washington was escorted to the front of the room by Morris and John Rutledge, of South Carolina. In his usual, overly formal manner, the general thanked the convention for the honor, apologized in advance for his lack of qualifications, and begged their indulgence for any errors he might make.

At least Washington's selection had been unanimous. Immediately afterward, there was an omen of the fault lines that would cut through the entire summer. As the credentials of each delegate were read aloud into the record, it was pointed out that the Delawareans had been expressly prohibited by their legislature from agreeing to any proposal that would eliminate the equal voting rights of states in Congress—a central plank of what the nationalists were about to put forward. George Read was clearly not alone in his suspicions.

All told, fifty-five delegates attended the convention at one point or another from May through September—not a bad showing when compared with the anemic turnout in Annapolis. They were a select and elite body of men—all white, most wealthy, and more than a third slaveholders. Averaging forty-two years old, the majority of the delegates had served in Congress, and virtually all of them had held some position in government. One in three had fought in the Revolutionary War. Seven had been governors. Six, including James Wilson, had signed the Declaration of Independence. And they were disproportionately well educated. More than half had graduated college, and thirty-four were trained as lawyers, Wilson foremost among them.

Another pertinent qualification was held by the fifteen delegates who had helped draft their state constitutions and brought with them the accumulated and hard-earned wisdom of those experiences. They had created governors, judiciaries, and two-chamber legislatures that could check and balance one another. They had drafted bills of rights. What they had not done was build a governing document together with states of different sizes or with states that disagreed about the practice of human slavery.

The following Monday, the delegates agreed to ground rules for the rest of the convention. Most important of all was a vow of secrecy regarding all deliberations. This meant no copying of documents that the delegates used in the assembly room and no communication between delegates and outsiders about what was being discussed. To ward off curious passersby, the large windows on either side of the room were shut. Such a degree of secrecy was essential if the delegates were to feel free to debate sensitive political topics and work through multiple changes toward a final product without the fear of public blowback. It would also be a major reason for Wilson's own erasure from the standard narratives of the American founding.

Some delegates grumbled at the restriction—it was not, after all, a very republican way to go about adopting a republican charter. Others, including Washington and Franklin, honored it in the breach, stealing moments in their boardinghouse or in the back of a tavern to write to friends and colleagues about what was happening in the assembly room. Nevertheless, the vow set the tone for the rest of the summer. The convention had been called to address an existential crisis, and as such, it represented extremely serious business.

On Tuesday, the delegates were at last ready to get down to that business. Edmund Randolph rose first, to present the outlines of what would become known as the Virginia Plan—which had been occupying Madison, Wilson, and Morris for the past few weeks.

Randolph prefaced his remarks with a reminder of the stakes, which were nothing less than "preventing the fulfillment of the prophecies of the American downfall." He made sure to pay due respect to the authors of the Articles of Confederation, who had "done all that patriots could do" given their lack of experience constituting large republics. He added, with more than a small hint, "Perhaps nothing better could be obtained from the jealousy of the states with regard to their sovereignty."

Randolph then introduced the plan itself: There would be a central government composed of three branches, legislative, executive, and judiciary. The national legislature would comprise two houses, both apportioned by population. The lower house, the House of Representatives, would be elected by the people directly; the upper house, the Senate, would be elected by the members of the lower house. Overall, the proposed government would possess far more expansive powers than it had under the Articles of Confederation, including a veto over any state laws that might contradict the union's.

As the session ended and the delegates filed out of the assembly room, many of the latecomers were starting to wonder what was going on. They got the answer the next morning, May 30, when Randolph rose again, this time to read off three resolutions proposed by Gouverneur Morris. First, that the existing arrangement under the Articles of Confederation was untenable. Second, that treaties among states would not be enough to fix the problem. And, finally, "that a *national* Government ought to be established consisting of a *supreme* Legislative, Executive & Judiciary."

What, exactly, did the words *national* and *supreme* mean in this context? Before an answer could be given, Charles Pinckney of South Carolina asked whether the nationalists "meant to abolish the state governments altogether." Pinckney, the son of a wealthy planter, was not yet thirty and had a tendency to exaggeration, claiming that he had been the youngest member of the convention (not true, by several years) and that he had drafted an alternative plan of government that he had presented at the beginning of the summer, but that had not gotten full consideration. (The story behind the "Pinckney Plan" is long and convoluted, but suffice it to say that in his later years he took far more credit for the final Constitution than he deserved.)

In response to Pinckney's question, Randolph tried to backpedal, saying the resolutions were only summarizing the main themes of the broader plan. Too late: It was all out in the open.

Pinckney's fellow delegate and cousin General Charles Cotesworth Pinckney rose and delivered a contender for understatement of the summer when he noted that Randolph's plan appeared to be "founded on different principles" than the Articles of Confederation. He said it was not clear that Congress even had the power to authorize such a sweeping change—a solid point the general carried to its inevitable conclusion: Were the convention to agree to Morris's resolutions, he said, it appeared "that their business was at an end."

Wilson was shifting in his seat. He knew as well as anyone that the Confederation Congress had not given the convention anything like the power to re-create American government from scratch. And yet, having served in Congress three separate times by 1787, he also knew that it had neither the political nor the institutional will to get behind meaningful reform of the Articles of Confederation. To Wilson, none of that mattered. What mattered was the "revolution principle"—the people are the only sovereign, and they retain the right to change their form of government whenever and however they please. They don't need the permission of Congress or anyone else. But he wasn't prepared to stand and say all that just yet.

Gouverneur Morris stepped into the silence and explained that by "supreme," the plan was referring to the power that rules over all others and that there could be only one such power in any society—so that if there were a conflict between the national government and a state government, the national government would prevail. George Read and General Pinckney didn't like that. How about instead of "a *supreme* legislative executive and judiciary," they proposed, we say a "*more effective* legislative executive and judiciary"? The motion failed.

The convention jumped from one land mine to another: Randolph's second resolution, which called for eliminating the equality of the states in Congress and, instead, giving them power in proportion to their size. But how to measure a state's size—by population or by wealth? Once again, everything was moving too fast. George Read, the tall, thin, elegant Delawarean, stood and reminded his colleagues of the constraint under which he and his fellow delegates were operating. If the equality of states in the new Congress were tinkered with in any way, he warned, "it might become their duty to retire from the convention."

Read's threat was only the latest small-state headache for the convention. Four days into the proceedings, New Hampshire's table remained empty; it had chosen its delegates, but the state professed to have no money to send them to Philadelphia. Meanwhile, Rhode Island, the smallest state in the union, flatly refused to attend—the only one of the thirteen states that never showed up that summer.

Madison responded to Read's threat, arguing that "whatever reason might have existed" for state equality at the nation's founding, there was no good rationale for it to continue once a truly national government was in place. As Madison recounted in his notes, this "did not appear to satisfy Mr. Read."

Outside the State House, there was skepticism that the delegates could accomplish anything significant. "I hardly think much good can come of it: The people of America don't appear to me to be ripe for any great innovations," William Grayson, a congressman from Virginia, wrote to James Monroe.

The clearest assessment came from George Washington, the delegate whose presence was most important to the convention's success, even if he was the one who least wanted to be there. "The business of this convention is as yet too much in embryo to form any opinion of the conclusion," Washington wrote to Thomas Jefferson on the evening of May 30. "Much is expected from it by some; not much by others; and nothing by a few. That something is necessary, none will deny; for the situation of the general government, if it can be called a government, is shaken to its foundation, and liable to be overturned by every blast. In a word, it is at an end; and, unless a remedy is soon applied, anarchy and confusion will inevitably ensue."

Through all the back-and-forth, James Wilson had yet to speak a single substantive word, a surprise given that he had been preparing for this moment all his life. From his boyhood indoctrination in the Scottish Enlightenment to his legal apprenticeship with John Dickinson, from his groundbreaking essay on Parliament's authority to his defense of the Bank of North America, he had been weaving together the threads of his worldview for decades. Now forty-four, he was the most respected and sought-after lawyer in the country and certainly one of the wealthiest. The 1787 convention was his opportunity to apply his complex and radical theory of government to the real world. Perhaps that is why he waited to speak; he was looking for the right opening. The next day's debate would give it to him.

For the People

The morning of May 31 began with a topic close to Wilson's heart: the role of the people in choosing their government. Resolution 4 of the Virginia Plan proposed that the lower house of Congress, what would be called the House of Representatives, "ought to be elected by the people of the states." Immediately the objections began.

"The people should have as little to do as may be about the government," Roger Sherman of Connecticut said. He believed members of Congress should be chosen by state legislators, a job he had held in Connecticut. The people, in contrast, "want information and are constantly liable to be misled."

Elbridge Gerry of Massachusetts, a "hesitating and laborious speaker" with a twitchy eye, echoed Sherman and added his own warning, which was suffused with the memory of Shays's Rebellion. "The evils we experience flow from the excess of democracy," Gerry said. "The people do not want virtue; but are the dupes of pretended patriots." As his state's experience had shown, regular people "are daily misled into the most baneful measures and opinions by the false reports circulated by designing men, and which no one on the spot can refute." Gerry still believed in republican government, he assured the room, but he warned of "the danger of the leveling spirit."

George Mason of Virginia pushed back. He was for a direct vote of representatives to the House, which he called "the grand depository of the democratic principle of the government." Like Britain's House of Commons, "it ought to know and sympathize with every part of the community."

Wilson sensed his moment had come, and he stood to speak. In his assertive Scottish brogue, he called for direct popular elections in Congress. He was, as he put it, "for raising the federal pyramid to a considerable altitude, and for that reason wished to give it as broad a basis as possible." It was a powerful metaphor, evoking both structural solidity and ancient wisdom. "No government could long subsist without the confidence of the people," Wilson continued, pointing out that this confidence was "peculiarly essential" in a republican government. He then opposed Sherman's pitch to give the power to state legislatures, which he saw as meddling in the relationship between the people and the national government.

Wilson's first real comment of the convention was brief, but it managed to embody the essence of his theory of government, that all power begins and ends with the people themselves. It was the idea he had articulated in his "Considerations" essay more than a decade before. In the intervening years, he had witnessed up close the dangers of putting power directly into the people's hands; his old house on Walnut Street had the bullet holes to prove it. And yet that experience had failed to strip him of his faith. Once he decided on the right way to think about something, whether it was the affections of Rachel Bird or the design of a new government, he refused to let go.

Over the next three and a half months Wilson would not miss a day of the convention. He would speak, by Madison's account, 168 different times, more than any delegate but Gouverneur Morris, who spoke 173 times. Wilson's commitment to the power of regular people—popular sovereignty—would guide him through constant battles with other delegates on the key points of contention: first, the number of seats each state would get in Congress; second, the power of the national government compared to the states; and third, the design and powers of the presidency. On the last two, Wilson's vision would largely prevail, shaping the American government as we know it today. But on the first point—how to allocate congressional seats—he struggled to win support, despite arguing himself hoarse. In the end, he would have to swallow a deal that violated his deepest convictions and then sell it to the very people in whose name he had struck it.

For the time being, his only audience was the several dozen men sitting around him in the assembly room of the State House. Among them, Wilson had no more consistent ally than James Madison, who immediately joined in to agree with him that people were the proper source of power and that direct election of the House, at least, was "essential to every plan of free government." Unlike Wilson,

Madison was in favor of using different methods of choosing the other branches—what he called "successive filtrations"—but he feared that the principle could be taken "too far" and that "the people would be lost sight of altogether."

This triggered a response from the delegates who wanted as little direct involvement from the people as possible. Elbridge Gerry agreed that generating confidence in one's leaders was a worthy goal, but the experience of the states showed that this wasn't guaranteed by letting the people vote directly for them. Pierce Butler, from South Carolina, added that a popular vote was "impracticable."

After the first round, however, Wilson and the popular-vote side prevailed. The vote went in favor of direct elections to the House 6 states to 2, with 2 divided.

The convention then moved on to the Senate, whose members the Virginia Plan proposed to be chosen by the House of Representatives after being nominated by their state legislatures.

Some delegates objected, arguing that the states were being unfairly cut out of the process and should have the power to fill the Senate by themselves. Others debated what the proper size of the Senate should be. Wilson had heard enough. The Senate should be independent both of the House and of the states, he said. The only way to ensure that? "Both branches of the national legislature ought to be chosen by the people." It was the most democratic position of anyone at the convention, and Wilson knew it, which is why he wasn't surprised when no one rose to support him. The issue was tabled for another day. Wilson, however, was just warming up.

The next morning, Friday, June 1, shortly after 10 A.M., Nathaniel Gorham, a thickset, easygoing Boston merchant picked to chair the convention, moved to begin the day with Resolution 7, regarding the executive, the political head of the country. America desperately needed national leadership; on this much the delegates could agree. But what should that leadership look like? What powers should it hold and for how long? How should it be chosen? Would it be one person or a council, as in Pennsylvania? These were all critical questions, and none had yet been answered. Resolution 7 stated only that the national executive was "to be chosen by the National legislature for the term of __ years" and would not be eligible for reappointment.

Wilson was eager to fill in the blanks. As soon as the debate began, he rose to speak. The executive should "consist of a single person," he proposed. Charles Pinckney of South Carolina seconded the motion. And then there followed, as James Madison recorded in his daily notes, "a considerable pause." Hunched over their clothbound desks, the delegates glanced around at one another or doodled on their notepads, waiting for someone to say something.

There were two explanations for the awkward silence—one absent, one present, both named George. The first: George III, by the Grace of God, King of Great Britain, France and Ireland, Defender of the Faith and so forth. Many of the delegates had personally taken up arms against the king in a bloody yearslong war for their independence, and they were in no mood to replace his transatlantic tyranny with a homegrown version.

But at least that George wasn't in the room. The other one—the revered general, hero of the Revolution, and the most admired man in America—was parked in a tall wooden chair by the imposing marble fireplace, directly in front of the delegates. He had been the natural choice as president of the convention, and no one doubted that he would be the unquestionable front-runner for any position of leadership the convention might establish. Tact was required.

Still, someone had to speak. Nathaniel Gorham at last broke the silence and asked gently if he should put Wilson's call for a single executive to a vote. Benjamin Franklin, sitting next to Wilson at Pennsylvania's table, told Gorham to wait. At eighty-one, Franklin was easily the oldest man in the assembly room, and the only person in America who could lay claim to as much public affection as Washington. Wilson's proposal was "a point of great importance," Franklin said, and he wanted to hear the range of opinions on it before any votes were cast.

First up was John Rutledge, of South Carolina. In his rapid-fire cadence, he admonished the other delegates for their timidity. It seemed, he said, that their reluctance to express any opinion on the matter was based on the fear that they could not later change their minds. Rutledge himself favored Wilson's proposal for a single executive, although he didn't think it was wise to give that person the power to make war.

Roger Sherman, a stocky Connecticut judge and former shoemaker with a thick New England accent, spoke next. Throughout the convention, Sherman would rise frequently on behalf of the smaller states. Although his manner was "awkward, unmeaning, and unaccountably strange," in the words of delegate William Pierce, "no Man has a better Heart or a clearer Head." The executive, Sherman said, is "nothing more than an institution for carrying the will of the legislature into effect." For that reason, he believed, it should be up to the legislature to decide how many people make up that office, and for how long.

Wilson, confident as always that he had thought through these issues more fully than anyone else, was irritated at the pushback. In fact, only a single person would have the "energy, dispatch and responsibility" needed to do the job, he said. Still, he was aware that some delegates feared creating a replica of "the royal brute," and so he emphasized that the powers wielded by George III were not a "proper guide" in designing the American executive.

Edmund Randolph was not persuaded. The tall, imposing, and smooth-talking governor of Virginia warned that a single executive would be "the fetus of monarchy." He added, in a dig at Wilson, that the convention "had no motive to be governed by the British government as our prototype."

To the contrary, Wilson shot back. A single executive would in fact be America's best defense against tyranny. And how could he be sure? After all, as he himself acknowledged, the sheer size of the country they were trying to create appeared to demand the "vigor" of a monarch. Not to fear, he assured the delegates: The American people's manners were "purely republican," and they would never accept an unelected king as their ruler. At the same time, he said, he believed the people would prefer a single leader to an executive council, such as the twelve-person body that led Pennsylvania's government. Wilson reminded his colleagues that Americans "did not oppose the British

King but the parliament," echoing his own groundbreaking essay published thirteen years earlier. "The opposition was not against an unity but a corrupt multitude."

Ben Franklin had been right to slow things down. There was no use holding a vote when the delegates couldn't even agree on what they were arguing about. Wilson's motion for a single executive was postponed, and the convention moved on to the next clause in Resolution 7—the method of choosing the executive.

Undeterred by his failure to win over his colleagues, Wilson again seized the floor. This time, aware that he might be pushing too far too fast, he tried some humility, saying he was "almost unwilling to declare the mode" he preferred, "being apprehensive that it might appear chimerical." "In theory," at least, he "was for an election by the people." It was "both a convenient and successful mode," he said, noting that voters in New York and Massachusetts already elected their governors directly and had chosen well. Roger Sherman from Connecticut again shook his head. The choice of the executive should be for the legislature alone, he repeated, not for average voters.

The convention tried to move on to the next topic, the length of the executive term, but Wilson was not ready to let the last question go. It was a central element of his vision for the national government, which he believed should be as close as possible to the people it served. This is why the people should vote directly for *all* national offices—both branches of the legislature as well as the executive—"in order to make them as independent as possible of each other, as well as of the States."

Wilson was dominating the debate and yet standing alone. At last, someone came to his defense. George Mason said he liked the idea of a direct election in principle, but he feared it would be "impracticable." He suggested that Wilson take a step back, give himself some time to "digest" the issue, and return with more developed proposals.

So Wilson did that. The next day, June 2, he returned to the State House with a new proposal: Divide the states into districts and allow the eligible voters in each district to pick one or more "electors." Those electors would then meet and elect by ballot the person (or people) "in whom the executive authority of the national government shall be vested."

Before anyone could respond, Wilson made sure to remind the delegates that this was not his preferred method for choosing the executive. He repeated his arguments in favor of "an election without the intervention of the states"—that is, a direct popular vote—which, he said, "would produce more confidence among the people."

Still, with his June 2 proposal Wilson had described with remarkable accuracy the system that would eventually be written into the final draft of the Constitution later that summer and that describes the Electoral College we still use more than two centuries later. It was a metaphor for his role throughout the convention—bold, visionary, deeply democratic, and, as throughout his life, far ahead of the game. Too far, it appeared. The delegates voted down his elector proposal 8 to 2.

Only a few days in, Wilson's hard-charging approach was threatening to backfire. By the following week, the delegates' skepticism of popular votes had bled back into the question of House elections, too. On June 6, Charles Pinckney of South Carolina opened the morning by pushing to reconsider the matter, arguing that the people were "less fit judges" of whom to elect than state legislatures would be. He was fixed on this point, so much so that two years later he was still unwilling to let the matter go, writing angry letters to Madison and other delegates denouncing the "theoretical nonsense" of direct election, which he called "the greatest blot in the Constitution."

Then Elbridge Gerry saw an opening to voice again his own dislike of popular voting. "In Massachusetts, the worst men get into the legislature," he complained, pointing out that several lawmakers in his home state—"men of indigence, ignorance and baseness"—had recently been convicted of crimes.

Wilson, alarmed that his early victory on direct elections in the

House appeared to be in jeopardy, was quick to defend the principle. A legislature is necessary, he pointed out, only because it is impossible for a large society like America to act collectively. But if the legislature is to be accepted by the people, it must be chosen by the people—"the legitimate source of all authority." That way it could express the "mind or sense of the people at large." It could be, in other words, "the most exact transcript of the whole society."

Piece by piece, as though rolling the blocks of the pyramid into place, Wilson was building out his vision of a government based on popular sovereignty—one in which the ultimate power belonged to the people themselves and in which they chose when, how, and to whom to delegate it. "The people had already parted with as much of their power as was necessary, to form on its basis a perfect government," Wilson said. If this new government was to succeed, the states now had to part with their own measure of power.

This was far from an accepted idea. Opposition came not only from Wilson's obvious antagonists but also from allies like Benjamin Rush, who was not even a delegate to the convention. As a signer of the Declaration of Independence, Rush could speak with earned authority on the principles of government, and he was not a fan of unfettered democracy. In a speech earlier that year, he seemed to reject the more expansive, democratic vision that Wilson was now advocating. "It is often said that 'the sovereign and all other power is seated *in* the people,'" he said. "This idea is unhappily expressed. It should be—'all power is derived *from* the people.' They possess it only on the days of their elections. After this, it is the property of their rulers, nor can they exercise or resume it, unless it is abused."

Wilson was uncowed by such criticism, no matter the corner from which it emerged. Over the next months, no one in the State House matched his devotion to the power of the people, which is perhaps why he felt compelled to keep hammering at it.

On June 7, when the debate returned to the selection of the Senate, John Dickinson, Wilson's old law mentor, joined the call to keep the choice away from the people. The upper house was upper for a reason; it should consist of "the most distinguished characters," Dickinson said, like the British House of Lords, and he did not trust the people to make that choice.

Wilson refused to budge. "If we are to establish a national government, that government ought to flow from the people at large." Returning to his pyramid, he said, "If one branch of it should be chosen by the Legislatures, and the other by the people, the two branches will rest on different foundations, and dissensions will naturally arise between them."

Wilson also rejected Dickinson's reference to the House of Lords. "The British government cannot be our model," he said. "Our manners, our laws" are very different. For example, Americans had not adopted the British practice of hereditary land ownership that ensured property stayed in the same family for generations. "The whole genius of the people are opposed to it," he said.

But Wilson was struggling to make headway. Elbridge Gerry argued that resting the two branches of Congress on different foundations was not only inevitable but preferable. Businessmen—the "commercial and monied interest," in his words—could not count on being protected by the farmers and other landowners who made up most of the people eligible to vote at that time. Only the state legislatures would provide the necessary check.

This made no sense to Wilson. He was a "monied interest" himself and had personally experienced the violence of a mob, yet he could not understand the impulse to keep the people away from the reins of power.

He was also an immigrant with no local allegiances, and he was mystified by the delegates' insistence on protecting the power of their own states—or on thinking in terms of states at all. States were abstractions, arbitrary lines drawn on paper, Wilson believed. Why should they receive any special treatment? What mattered to him was the people—and all people, wherever they lived, should be treated the same for political purposes. A few other delegates, notably Madison, agreed that this was a fundamental principle of republican government, although no one was as deeply devoted to or aggressively defensive of it as Wilson.

As the debates over the design of Congress played out through June and into the middle of July, Wilson remained at the center. He was confident in himself—in the depth of his erudition and the clarity of his vision of what America could be—and he argued doggedly throughout these weeks for a people-based government. That doggedness, however, tended to alienate him from other delegates, who tired of his sometimes overly pedantic and scholarly disquisitions.

The debates would center on a key question: Should Congress consist of two houses, apportioned according to population, as Wilson wanted, or just one, with equal votes for each state?

On June 9, a calm and warm Saturday, "very fine haymaking weather," two of the strongest advocates for the latter position, William Paterson and David Brearley, both of New Jersey, came prepared. Brearley, a supreme court judge back home, claimed that without state equality, New Jersey and the other smaller states "must have been destroyed instead of being saved." He pointed out that Virginia, the biggest state, paid roughly sixteen times as much in taxes as Georgia, the smallest. If votes in Congress were apportioned based on that measure, Virginia and the other big states, like Pennsylvania and Massachusetts, would win every time. "Virginia with her sixteen votes will be a solid column indeed, a formidable phalanx," Brearley said.

Paterson, a short, small, articulate man who had served as New Jersey's attorney general, was a stickler for rules and among the convention's fiercest defenders of the smaller states. He reminded his colleagues that they were bound by what Congress had authorized: to revise the Articles only. "We have no power to go beyond the federal scheme," he said. "We ought to keep within its limits, or we should be charged by our constituents with usurpation."

There it was again: the charge that in considering an entirely new form of government, the convention was exceeding its authority. The delegates who resisted a powerful central government would make this point repeatedly throughout the summer, and it was a fair one—but it was not gaining purchase. The severity of the crisis had convinced many, if not most, of the delegates that they had to do what was necessary to save the country, congressional authorization be damned.

Very well, then, Paterson suggested calmly but sharply: As long as we're talking about existential threats, let's talk about *all* of them. "If we are to be considered as a nation, all state distinctions must be abolished," he warned. "There was no more reason that a great individual state contributing much, should have more votes than a small one contributing little, than that a rich individual citizen should have more votes than an indigent one." Putting aside the irony of this particular analogy (voting had long been restricted to white men who owned property), it illuminated the central dispute: The argument in favor of proportional representation was precisely that states are *not* the same as people.

But Paterson was on a roll, and he was furious. "New Jersey will never confederate on the plan before the Committee," he said. "She would be swallowed up. He had rather submit to a monarch, to a despot, than to such a fate."

Threats by delegates to leave the convention if they didn't get their way would be a familiar theme throughout the summer, a weapon wielded mostly by those from smaller states, who feared losing the disproportionate power they enjoyed under the old system.

Wilson could give as good as he got. The principle that people are political equals, no matter where they live, seemed blindingly obvious to him. He could not understand why it was taking so long to get the message across. Speaking slowly and forcefully, as though to a class of schoolchildren, he reminded Brearley and Paterson that the Articles of Confederation had given the states equal votes only because of "the urgent circumstances of the time"—that is, the newly independent nation was scrambling to establish a functioning government in the midst of fighting a war and without any clear model to work from. He then reiterated the core principle: "As all authority was derived from the people, equal numbers of people ought to have an equal number of representatives, and different numbers of people different numbers of representatives."

Finally, he turned the New Jerseyans' numbers game—and their threats to abandon the convention—back on them. "Let us see how this rule will apply to the present question," Wilson said. "Pennsylvania, from its numbers, has a right to 12 votes, when on the same principle New Jersey is entitled to 5 votes. Shall New Jersey have the same right or influence in the councils of the nation with Pennsylvania? I say no. It is unjust—I never will confederate on this plan. The gentleman from New Jersey is candid in declaring his opinion—I commend him for it—I am equally so. I say again I never will confederate on his principles. If no state will part with any of its sovereignty, it is in vain to talk of a national government."

Paterson and Brearley were, for the moment, without words. Given the high stakes involved, Paterson suggested, it would be best to postpone the debate and take the weekend to cool down.

But the next week brought no respite. To the contrary, the New Jerseyans raised the stakes even higher by offering their own competing scheme of national government. The New Jersey Plan, which Paterson introduced on June 15, proposed three branches—legislative, executive, and judiciary—but its similarities to the Virginia Plan ended there. The legislature would remain a single house, and the states would keep the equal vote they enjoyed under the Articles of Confederation. The executive would consist of a council, not a single president, and its members would be removable from office by the vote of a majority of states. (By one measure, the small states outnumbered the large ten to three.) And enslaved people would count as three-fifths of a free person for the purposes of taxation. (Wilson would play a central role in this particular debate, which will be discussed in chapter 11.)

In short, it was a big gift to the smaller states. It was also not a serious proposal. By the middle of June, the delegates had voted enough times in favor of making population the measure of representation, at least in one house of Congress, that it was hard to imagine they would now go backward.

Still, the New Jerseyans were spoiling for this fight, and they were prepared to drag it out as long as necessary. On June 16, the day after he introduced the new plan, Paterson raised a cheeky question: "If a proportional representation be right, why do we not vote so here?" Whether or not he was aware that Wilson and Gouverneur Morris had proposed doing precisely this in the days before the convention began, he was shrewd to bring it up now. After all, as Madison had rightly feared when he shot the idea down, under those terms, the small states might well have refused to participate in the convention at all.

Paterson then twisted the knife. Perhaps, as Wilson had lectured them the week before, the larger states had agreed to equal state power only under extreme pressure and not out of any belief that it was a fair way to constitute a government. "Be it so," Paterson said, "are they for that reason at liberty to take it back? Can the donor resume his gift without the consent of the donee?"

It was a telling analogy; Paterson was characterizing the state-equality provision of the existing government as the result not of negotiation but of donation—and a forced donation at that. In other words, possession is nine-tenths of the law. *We have our equality. Come and take it.*

After Paterson had finished, Wilson stood up. He was exasperated at the jealousy with which so many of his fellow delegates guarded power they never should have had in the first place. He also failed to understand their resistance to a national government. "Why should a national government be unpopular?" he asked. "Has it less dignity? Will each citizen enjoy under it less liberty or protection? Will a Citizen of Delaware be degraded by becoming a Citizen of the United States?"

Wilson then proceeded to take apart the elements of the New Jersey Plan one by one. In particular, its lack of true political equality—that is, equality among people, not among states—"has ever been a poison contaminating every branch of government." He pointed to the example of Great Britain, whose unequal representation had placed political liberty "at the mercy of its rulers." Oh, and by the way, he added with a wink, "the smallest bodies in Great Britain are notoriously the most corrupt."

So it went for the rest of June. The convention rejected the New

Jersey Plan four days after it was introduced, and yet the debate over how to allocate power in Congress grew only more rancorous. On the one side were Wilson, Madison, Gouverneur Morris, and the other nationalists, who were adamant that people were the proper measure of representation. On the other were the small-state representatives, who refused to yield an inch. The gap between the two factions was not closing.

On June 25, Wilson reiterated the central point of the nationalists. "The general government is not an assemblage of states, but of individuals, for certain political purposes; it is not meant for the state, but for the individuals composing them: the *individuals* therefore not the *States*, ought to be represented in it."

This was a matter of global significance. When he considered "the amazing extent of country"—not just the size of its population but the influence its government would have across the planet, he said—he was "lost in the magnitude of the object."

For Wilson, it was always about the big picture—a functional government had to be founded on proper principles, or it would not survive. He returned to the pyramid metaphor he had used to open his remarks a month earlier. "We are laying the foundation of a building, which is to last for ages, and in which millions are interested," he said. "In laying the stone amiss we may injure the superstructure; and what will be the consequence if the cornerstone should be loosely placed?"

Wilson felt secure that the delegates would sign off on both a direct vote and proportional representation for the House of Representatives; the Senate was another matter. His calls for both houses to adhere to these same principles were not gaining the support he had enjoyed when the discussion was only about the lower house. The convention was at an impasse.

Maybe God could help? That was the idea Benjamin Franklin proposed on June 28. "How has it happened, Sir, that we have not hitherto once thought of humbly applying to the Father of lights to illuminate our understandings?" he asked. Coming from a man whom "the very heavens obey," in the words of delegate William Pierce, it was hard to say no. The delegates agreed to begin every morning session with a benediction, starting on July 4, the anniversary of independence.

Before the prayers began, New Jersey's delegates moved to appeal to a more earthly power—New Hampshire. The state was still absent, and David Brearley wanted to send word to them that they were needed immediately. This was an obvious ploy, as everyone in the assembly room knew. Tiny New Hampshire could be expected to side with the other small states, giving them a much-needed vote in favor of protecting their equality in at least one house of Congress. The motion was rejected.

The debate returned to the Senate. Wilson knew his grip was slipping, but that only seemed to make his appeals more urgent. He was prepared to lose, he said, although he would know he stood "supported by stronger and better principles."

In one of his longer speeches of the entire summer, he laid out the central flaw of state equality: its violation of majority rule. A Senate in which each state had one vote would replace the tyranny of the majority with that of the minority. It would, he said, "enable the minority to control in all cases whatsoever, the sentiments and interests of the majority. Seven states will control six." Because the seven smallest states together contained less than one-third of the population, "it would be in the power then of less than one-third to overrule two-thirds whenever a question should happen to divide the States in that manner."

And that, Wilson insisted, was flatly incompatible with the republican project. "Can we forget for whom we are forming a Government? Is it for *men*, or for the imaginary beings called *states*? Will our honest constituents be satisfied with metaphysical distinctions? Will they, ought they, to be satisfied with being told that the one-third compose the greater number of states?" It was as simple and strong a defense of majority rule as any at the convention. Even though he knew the odds were against him, he pressed on. "It is all a mere illusion of names. We talk of states, till we forget what they are composed of."

If Wilson had lost patience with the small-state delegates, the feeling was mutual. One by one, they stood and angrily denounced the nationalists. Jonathan Dayton of New Jersey called the plan for proportional representation "an amphibious monster" that the American people would reject. Luther Martin of Maryland said he would never agree to this new union "if it could not be done on just principles"—by which he meant equality among the states. Finally, Gunning Bedford of Delaware mocked Wilson's "dictatorial air" in suggesting this was the convention's last chance to establish a government on good principles. "The large states dare not dissolve the confederation," Bedford said. "If they do the small ones will find some foreign ally of more honor and good faith, who will take them by the hand and do them justice."

That was a step too far, and Rufus King admonished Bedford, saying he was "grieved that such a thought had entered into his heart." But Bedford knew he had hit on an uncomfortable truth: Wilson could prattle on about holding the moral high ground, but in the end, he would need to convince the small states to buy in. So far, he was failing.

When the convention gathered the following Monday, tempers had cooled, but moods had soured. Increasingly, a sense of futility pervaded the morning's discussion. "We are now at a full stop," Connecticut's Roger Sherman said. Hugh Williamson of North Carolina added, "If we do not concede on both sides, our business must be at an end." Yet no one was ready to go quite so far. As Elbridge Gerry reminded his colleagues, "Something must be done, or we shall disappoint not only America, but the whole world."

The one thing everyone wanted to avoid, after years of war, was more bloodshed. But that didn't stop Gouverneur Morris, the nationalists' most hotheaded ally, from darkly warning of the risk. "This country must be united. If persuasion does not unite it, the sword will." Morris had returned to the convention only a few days earlier, after a month away tending to various business matters. He was always ready for a fight, and particularly so now, given that he had not been worn down by weeks of circular debate. He seemed almost to relish the opportunity to play out his violent fantasy. "The scenes of horror attending civil commotion cannot be described," he said. "The stronger party will then make traitors of the weaker; and the gallows and halter will finish the work of the sword."

The last bit was too much for Gunning Bedford, who had just been rebuked for issuing his own threat. Standing and offering an apology for his intemperate words, Bedford called on Morris to do the same. "To hear such language without emotion," he said, "would be to renounce the feelings of a man and the duty of a citizen." Morris did not apologize.

Behind all the bluster and the chest-beating, however, it was becoming clear that Bedford and the other small-state delegates were going to prevail in their demand for equal power in at least one house of Congress. Whether or not those delegates were prepared to follow through on the threat to join with a foreign power, the nationalists didn't have the nerve to call their bluff. The entire convention was a highly delicate, arguably illegal venture, and the group didn't have endless time to hash out a final product. Given the pressure, and the small states' absolute refusal to negotiate on the issue of state equality, someone was going to have to blink.

The final showdown over the shape of Congress played out over a few days in the middle of July.

On July 13—the same day that the Confederation Congress, sitting in New York City, agreed to the Northwest Ordinance, which would pave the way for the introduction of several new states to the union—the delegates returned to the question of power and what it would mean if some states grew far bigger than others. Wilson took the opportunity to make one more plea for the basic principle of majority rule. "All men wherever placed have equal rights and are equally entitled to confidence," he said. Was he not concerned at the likelihood that a few of these new states would one day contain many more people than his own? No, he wasn't. "The majority of people wherever found ought in all questions to govern the minority," Wilson said. "If numbers be not a proper rule, why is not some better rule pointed out? No one has yet ventured to attempt it." For this reason, he rejected the argument that because the delegates had agreed to this principle in the House of Representatives, they should dispense with it in favor of state equality in the Senate.

He then broadened his point to include his Enlightenment education, saying he did not agree "that property was the sole or the primary object of government and society. The cultivation and improvement of the human mind was the most noble object. With respect to this object, as well as to other *personal* rights, numbers were surely the natural and precise measure of representation."

To Wilson, the whole scheme was intolerable. A convention in which each state, no matter its size, enjoyed a single vote—a rule he had tried to block—was about to adopt a Senate based on the same "vicious principle." The game was rigged from the start. Wilson pointed out with increasing frustration that if you measured support for state equality by counting people instead of states, two-thirds were opposed to it. "This fact would ere long be known, and it will appear that this fundamental point has been carried by one-third against two-thirds. What hopes will our constituents entertain when they find that the essential principles of justice have been violated in the outset of the government?" This was "a point of such critical importance," he said, that the convention should continue debating it as long as necessary. But the convention *had* debated it; Wilson had lost.

Luther Martin of Maryland, one of the strongest opponents of Wilson's proposal, rubbed salt in the wound by denying that two-thirds of the people actually opposed giving states an equal vote in the Senate. "The states that please to call themselves large are the weakest in the Union," he said. "Look at Massachusetts. Look at Virginia. Are they efficient states?" Go ahead, Martin suggested, take your toys and leave if you don't like it. He would prefer "two confederacies than one founded on any other principle than an equality of votes" in the Senate.

Wilson, too disillusioned now to fight back with any vigor, offered a withering response. He was "not surprised that those who say that a minority does more than the majority should say that that minority is stronger than the majority." He imagined "the next assertion will be that they are richer also," although he doubted they would keep saying that "when the states shall be called on for taxes and troops."

As the day wound down, Wilson could offer only words of warning. A Senate based on equal state power, he said, was "a fundamental and a perpetual error," and as such, "it ought by all means to be avoided. A vice in the representation, like an error in the first concoction, must be followed by disease, convulsions, and finally death itself."

In the end, this was Wilson's greatest frustration: He had come to Philadelphia on the understanding that the American government was on the verge of collapse because of a failure of design and that to save it, that design had to be changed fundamentally. Instead, one of the worst parts was being preserved. "It has never been a complaint against Congress that they governed overmuch," Wilson said at last. "The complaint has been that they have governed too little. To remedy this defect we were sent here. Shall we effect the cure by establishing an equality of votes, as is proposed? No; this very equality carries us directly to Congress, to the system which it is our duty to rectify."

Speaking in the voice of the people, he went on: "We sent you to form an efficient government and you have given us one more complex indeed, but having all the weakness of the former government."

On July 16, the final details of what would become known as the Great Compromise were ironed out: a lower house in which representatives were apportioned by population and an upper house in which each state retained equal voting power.

The following morning, before the convention got under way, several delegates from the larger states gathered to discuss whether it was worth fighting any longer. Some, Wilson surely among them, were convinced that "no good government could or would be built" on top of such a bad foundation. They even suggested proposing a separate constitution directly to the states, on the assumption that a majority of people would be on their side. Others were inclined to let the small states have their way and ensure that the entire convention agreed on one plan—even if, as Madison recorded with a touch of pique, that plan had been "decided by a bare majority of states and by a minority of the people of the United States."

On one, less noticed point, however, Wilson's push for popular sovereignty had prevailed—and it would turn out to be the single most significant element in the final adoption of the Constitution. Whatever document they produced, the delegates agreed, would have to be ratified in the states in order to take effect. But that ratification would not be done by state legislatures. It would fall to state-based conventions composed of the people themselves.

9
The Real Work Begins

AFTER ALMOST TWO months of tense debate inside the airless assembly room, for at least five hours a day six days a week, the delegates had settled only one major element of the proposed new government. They were weary and dispirited. They were also increasingly uncomfortable as summer in Philadelphia grew hotter and more humid.

Wilson was despondent. He'd held his own in the fight over Congress, making the best case he could in favor of the power of regular people, and still it wasn't enough. The smaller states would have a Senate based on equal votes for every state, thus smuggling the ghost of the confederation into the new government. And the slave-owning states would expand their power under the Three-Fifths Clause, which treated each enslaved person as three-fifths of a free person for the purposes of taxation and representation, rather than not counting them at all toward representation, as the northern states wanted. This pumped up the South's population numbers, giving its states extra members in the House and more influence over the federal government. Both deals infuriated Wilson (even though, as we will see in chapter 11, he was instrumental in making the latter a reality), but those battles were over. If Wilson and his allies were going to establish the sort of government they knew America needed, they would have to do it another way.

That opportunity arrived on July 24, when the delegates agreed to take a midsummer break. Before leaving, they appointed five men to make some sense of the back-and-forth of the preceding weeks and produce a working first draft of the new Constitution. This Committee of Detail had a clear task: to assemble a document incorporating the debates and votes on the various topics of the Virginia Plan. The delegates on the committee were chosen with what appeared to be an eye toward geographic distribution. From the North, Nathaniel Gorham of Massachusetts and Oliver Ellsworth of Connecticut. From the South, Virginia's Edmund Randolph and South Carolina's John Rutledge. And from the middle states, James Wilson.

As the rest of the delegates left the State House to catch their breath and attend to family, business, and political matters, these five stayed behind, hashing out what would become the first draft of the Constitution. For them, there would be no respite. Crucially, there would also be no oversight. For Wilson, the committee would be the perfect vehicle—small, relatively agile, and, for more than a week, free to shape the Constitution in private.

Beyond the draft itself, the committee kept no record of its conversations between July 27 and August 5. (It did not include James Madison or any of the convention's other reliable notetakers.) There is no account of where the five members met or for how long each day. That lack of documentation has led previous historians of the founding to downplay the Committee of Detail's work, treating it as an interlude between more consequential periods at the beginning and end of the summer. And yet the work produced by the Committee of Detail represented "the most creative period of constitutional drafting of the entire summer," in the words of William Ewald, the University of Pennsylvania professor who has conducted extensive analyses of that ten-day period. The initial Virginia Plan clocked in at three pages, and had grown to six by the time the delegates took their break. The Committee of Detail returned with double that— twelve pages, nearly as long as the eventual final product. As Ewald wrote of the committee, "in certain respects, and for certain fundamental issues, it was the main event."

Throughout its deliberations, Wilson was at the center. As the neatest scribe among the group, he ended up with the assignment to put the draft to paper, starting with a large sheet folded in half and writing on the right side only, to leave room for edits and comments.

The draft was not simply in his hand; it was in large part the product of his specific political vision. With the fight for fair representation in Congress now over, Wilson shifted his efforts to the other key part of his plan: national supremacy.

When the committee began, the delegates were still sharply divided over how strong the federal government should be. What Wilson and the other four committee members delivered to the delegates upon their return in early August was a document establishing an astonishingly powerful national government, different in all ways from the existing one, vested with both the authority and the means to act aggressively in the interests of the nation. The Committee of Detail's draft was, in short, a document that "altered the course of the Convention."

Among its most important provisions were two lists, one including specific powers granted to Congress, such as the power to tax, regulate trade, and make war; the other of powers prohibited to the states. The committee's draft also specified the jurisdiction of the federal courts and clarified the powers of the executive. It added the Privileges and Immunities Clause, which requires states to treat all citizens the same, whether they are from out of state or in state; the Full Faith and Credit Clause, which requires states to honor the court judgments of other states; and the Guarantee Clause, which guarantees a "republican form of government" in every state and protection against invasion. And it introduced what would become two of the most significant clauses in the Constitution: the Necessary and Proper Clause, which gives Congress the authority to make any law needed to carry out its enumerated powers and, critically, "all other powers vested in this Constitution"; and the Supremacy Clause, which says that federal laws and the Constitution trump conflicting state laws. Together, these components comprise "the very core of American federalism: the distinctive contribution of the Philadelphia Convention to western constitutional governance."

Because the committee preserved no records of its work, there is no firsthand evidence that Wilson himself was the originator of these last two clauses, although the circumstantial evidence suggests that he was. And while he may not have been able to achieve his goal of a single, overarching political community in America, in the Committee of Detail he managed to pull the Constitution much closer to that vision. Without him, American government as we know it today would not exist.

In this regard, the Committee of Detail was the entire convention in miniature. A body given one clearly defined job instead went well beyond its mandate, then had to convince the broader group to ratify its work. One delegate above all was key to both these arrogations of power: James Wilson.

Wilson, of course, did not see it as an arrogation. To his mind, the colonists had already created a single, supreme national government eleven years earlier—at the moment they signed the Declaration of Independence.

"It has been said that Congress is a representation of states, not of individuals. I say that the objects of its care are all the individuals of the states," Wilson had said in Congress on August 1, 1776, the day before he joined in the official signing of the Declaration. "As to those matters which are referred to Congress, we are not so many states, we are one large state. We lay aside our individuality whenever we come here."

By the time of the Philadelphia convention, Wilson, foremost among the delegates, had come to see the Declaration as the "first constitution" of a *united* America. That's why he was so perplexed by the other delegates' attachment to, and protectiveness of, their own states. What had been the point of the fight for independence if not to establish a united central government—the absence of which had prevented the individual colonies from mounting an effective defense against British tyranny? He was confident that the American people would become more attached to a national government, which he believed was "more important in itself, and more flattering to their pride," than state governments. But for the first two months of the convention, before the Committee of Detail met, he struggled to convince enough of his colleagues to agree.

Perhaps it was easier for him, an immigrant with no particular affection for any state, to reach that conclusion. The bottom line, as he said on June 6, is that the people don't care who governs them as long as they are governed well.

Connecticut's Roger Sherman took great exception to this. "The people are more happy in small than large states," he said. It was a theme the small-state delegates would return to throughout the summer. Sherman later said small states had more "vigor" than large ones, where it was "most difficult to collect the real and fair sense of the people." Oliver Ellsworth, Sherman's fellow Connecticut delegate, called the large states "the worst governed."

But the deepest fear among the delegates of the smaller states was expressed by George Read, who had already threatened to pack up and leave if the convention made any attempt to lessen Delaware's power. Soon enough, he predicted, the small states would exist for no reason except to choose the Senate. A national government would "swallow all of them up."

Wilson tried to assuage him. There's no reason a new national government can't coexist peacefully with the states, he said, "provided the latter were restrained to certain local purposes." In any case, it was more likely the states that would be doing the swallowing up. Wilson, who had prepared for the convention as thoroughly as anyone besides Madison, took the opportunity to show off his erudition. "In all confederated systems, ancient and modern," he said, the national government "was destroyed gradually by the usurpations of the parts composing it."

But Read wasn't alone in his fear. The next day, his colleague and Wilson's old mentor John Dickinson compared the proposed national government to the solar system, "in which the States were the planets, and ought to be left to move freely in their proper orbits." Wilson, he said, wished "to extinguish these planets."

Not so, Wilson shot back. He did not want to extinguish any planets. Still, he did not "believe that they would warm or enlighten the

Sun. Within their proper orbits they must still be suffered to act for subordinate purposes for which their existence is made essential by the great extent of our Country."

His point was that the convention had been called precisely because the states had not stayed "within their proper orbits." "No sooner were the state governments formed than their jealousy and ambition began to display themselves," Wilson said on June 8. "Each endeavored to cut a slice from the common loaf, to add to its own morsel, till at length the confederation became frittered down to the impotent condition in which it now stands." The fact that he was right didn't help his cause.

Nevertheless, Wilson went to lengths throughout the convention to show respect for states as political units integral to the larger system of government. "A citizen of America may be considered in two points of view—as a citizen of the general government, and as a citizen of the particular State in which he may reside," he said later in June. "We ought to consider in what character he acts in forming a general government. I am both a citizen of Pennsylvania and of the United States." So far so good, from the small-staters' perspective—although Wilson's conclusion was not as comforting. "I must therefore lay aside my State connections and act for the general good of the whole. We must forget our local habits and attachments."

For all his self-certainty, however, Wilson wasn't a bomb thrower like his nationalist ally Gouverneur Morris. Morris, who had been absent all of June, returned ready to take up the fight. He unleashed a diatribe at the small states' refusal to budge. He had come to Philadelphia "as a representative of America," he said, or even "in some degree as a representative of the whole human race, for the whole human race will be affected by the proceedings of this Convention." Morris wished certain delegates would "extend their views beyond the present moment of time, beyond the narrow limits of place from which they derive their political origin." Sensing that this might be too gentle, he drove home the central point. "State attachments and state importance have been the bane of this country. We cannot annihilate the states," he said, "but we may perhaps take out the teeth of the serpents."

In the end, Wilson returned to his lodestar, the Declaration of Independence, rejecting the idea that "when the colonies became independent of Great Britain, they became independent also of each other." Madison's notes then described how Wilson went on to read the Declaration out loud to the assembled delegates. When "the United Colonies were declared to be free and independent States," Wilson said, he inferred from this "that they were independent, not individually but unitedly."

Still, while Wilson may have preferred lawyerly persuasion to blustering threats, it had become clear by late July that neither approach was persuading anyone. That is why the Committee of Detail's work was so crucial—it allowed Wilson to torque the Constitution more to his liking, and without the tedious back-and-forth that had characterized the open sessions of the previous weeks.

As we've just seen, the committee drafted the constitutional provisions that make up the essence of American federalism. But it is likely that Wilson alone was responsible for writing the committee's final drafts of two of the most important provisions, the Necessary and Proper Clause and the preamble. It is worth considering each in turn, because together they embody Wilson's overarching plan for a government that was both all-powerful and rooted in the consent of the people.

First, how much power should a national government have? And should that power be limited to what could be written down on paper, or could it extend further, to include all powers "necessary and proper" to do the jobs a government is expected to do? This was a matter of intense debate throughout the summer of 1787. Everyone agreed the national government needed more power than it currently had. But many of the delegates insisted that any new powers be clearly defined and limited.

Wilson, along with the other nationalists, had long insisted that the national government not be restricted to a short list of prescribed powers. If Congress were to carry out its responsibilities—not only to wage war but to manage public funds, conduct foreign affairs, and oversee new lands in the west—it would have to be vested with as much power as it needed, whether or not that power was expressly granted by the constitution under construction in the summer of 1787. As Wilson made clear on May 30, the day he first spoke up at the convention, "it would be impossible to enumerate the powers which the federal Legislature ought to have." He had been making this point for years, including in his 1785 essay arguing that Congress had the authority to incorporate a national bank. The Committee of Detail was his opportunity to lock in the principle.

In fact, that 1785 essay was itself the likely basis for Resolution 6 of the Virginia Plan, which dealt with the scope of Congress's power and would eventually lead to the Necessary and Proper Clause. Resolution 6 stated that Congress should have the power to legislate "in all cases to which the separate States are incompetent, or in which the harmony of the United States may be interrupted by the exercise of individual Legislation." The breadth of that language—*in all cases*—tracks closely with the bank essay and points toward Wilson's having a direct hand in shaping the Virginia Plan earlier in May.

Wilson didn't get to incorporate those words right away. Edmund Randolph, the Virginia governor and his fellow committee member, took the first stab at drafting the provision on Congress's power. Randolph was a nationalist but a cautious one. He kept things narrow, limiting those powers to a clearly defined list, including those already in the Articles of Confederation plus a few key new ones, like the power to tax, to regulate trade, and to establish lower federal courts.

At the end of Randolph's list, an extra line was inserted—apparently by John Rutledge of South Carolina—giving Congress "a right to make all laws necessary to carry the foregoing powers into execution." This formulation was broadly accepted, even by those delegates most skeptical of centralized power. At the same time, it was as far as many of them were prepared to go.

For others, Wilson and Madison foremost, Resolution 6 represented the bare minimum of what a functional Congress would need.

"Without the substance of this power, the whole Constitution would be a dead letter," Madison would later write in *Federalist* no. 44. As he and Wilson saw it, any workable government must have the power to fulfill the purposes for which it was established, including the protection of its citizens' natural rights and providing for their common defense and general welfare.

Had Randolph's draft stood without significant alteration, it would have changed the course of American history. But at some point in the last days of July or the first days of August, Wilson took the lead in the drafting process. It is easy to imagine him sitting alone in the quiet, low-lighted study of his new house on Chestnut Street, across from the State House, rewriting the key lines to include "and proper" after "necessary." Then, critically, he added what is known as a "sweeping clause." Congress would have the power, Wilson's final draft read, "to make all laws that shall be necessary and proper for carrying into execution the foregoing powers, and *all other powers* vested, by this Constitution, in the government of the United States, or in any department or officer thereof."

With those three words—*all other powers*—Wilson sought to transform the Congress into the body he had always envisioned. This sweeping clause functioned, as sweeping clauses have done from the founding era to our own, by clarifying that a previous list of powers is not exhaustive. Now Congress could be more than a barely updated version of the hamstrung legislature that flailed under the Articles of Confederation; it could be a fully functional national institution with the power to act as needed to promote the general welfare of the country, however it might grow and evolve. As Wilson had said on July 26, the day the convention adjourned and left the Committee of Detail to its work, "We should consider that we are providing a Constitution for future generations, and not merely for the peculiar circumstances of the moment."

Wilson's draft would become a flashpoint throughout the ratification process, a blaring warning for those who did not want to give Congress such an open-ended grant of power. And while it was broadly accepted during the convention itself, all three delegates who refused to sign the final draft of the Constitution pointed to Wilson's sweeping clause as a major reason. One of them, Elbridge Gerry of Massachusetts, opposed it on the grounds that it would give Congress the authority "to make any laws they please." Later, during the state ratification debates, the clause was a primary target of the Constitution's opponents. Still, in the quiet early days of August, Wilson had taken his chance and framed the terms of the debate in a way that was hard to resist. Everyone knew Congress could achieve almost nothing under the existing system. Enough of them were open to Wilson's insistence that more power was the only answer.

If there was any question about the clause's utility, it was answered soon after the Constitution took effect, when Benjamin Franklin implicitly referred to it (and explicitly cited the preamble) to urge Congress to abolish slavery, though his plea was ignored. The Supreme Court has relied on it for multiple landmark decisions, most notably *McCulloch v. Maryland* in 1819, which confirmed Congress's power to establish a national bank. In short, Wilson's draft, which would survive with only minor changes to style and punctuation, has helped define the powers of Congress and the federal government for more than two centuries.

If Wilson's first innovation in the committee involved dry legal terminology, his second has become the most famous of America's civic poetry. In late July, he sat before one of his large folio sheets, folded it in half as was his style, and began to take some notes.

> The People of the States of New Hampshire etc, ^already confederated united and known by the Stile of the "United States of America"^ do agree upon ordain ^declare^ and establish the following Frame of Gov.t as the Constitution of the said United States.

He stopped, went back to the beginning of the sentence, and added "We" and then "We the People"—the three most resonant words in the history of democracy. Later that week, as his draft took shape, he flipped over the folio section on which he had scratched those words with his quill and started fresh. As a result, the first appearance of

"We the People" appears upside down on the last page of the last folio in his draft of the Constitution.

Wilson knew how important those words were as soon as he wrote them, which is why he insisted on their prominent placement—at the very beginning of the preamble to the charter that would establish a new government. The preamble itself is not a technical legal grant of power. In a sense, it's even more important. It states in a few simple phrases the purposes for which the entire Constitution was created, and thus can be referred to constantly as a way of understanding the document as a whole.

Wilson made sure to emphasize the preamble's significance at Pennsylvania's ratifying convention a few months later, once his words were locked down and the only question was whether the state would adopt them in full. "This single sentence in the Preamble is tantamount to a volume," he said, "and contains the essence of all the bills of rights that have been or can be devised; for, it establishes, at once, that in the great article of government, the people have a right to do what they please."

In early August, though, he was still fighting for every word. When the committee was preparing its draft to present to the convention, Wilson's preamble got recast: "We the People *and* the States of New Hampshire etc. . . ." It was a small but significant change, and Wilson eventually changed it back to "We the People *of* the States . . ."

In his last tweaks, Wilson tried to rename the country itself—the "United People and States of America"—invoking the ancient Latin phrase *Senatus Populusque Romanus*, or "the Senate and People of Rome," commonly abbreviated as SPQR. It was an intentional nod to the republican society that the framers revered, but for Wilson, the Romans had not gone far enough. He reversed the order of the phrase to make it more democratic—to put the people first.

For two months, Wilson had been repeating this very point in the assembly room—that the entire edifice must be built on the power of the people themselves. Often he did so from a defensive crouch, parrying one or another delegate's efforts to protect his own state. Now, in the privacy and silence of his study, Wilson could build his edifice of popular sovereignty simply by his choice and placement of words.

In this case, he added one brick too many. The final committee draft restored the nation's name to "the United States of America."

On August 5, a local Philadelphia printer named John Dunlap secretly printed about sixty copies of the draft Constitution to be distributed to the returning delegates. The convention would take up the committee's report the next day.

In the last moments before work resumed, Wilson could stand back and consider what he had accomplished. For two months he had fought to anchor this new America on the people themselves; in key respects, notably a Senate based on states rather than people, he lost that fight. Now, in a matter of days, he had prevailed in a different one—national power. It had not played out as he had imagined, perhaps, but the result was the same: The United States government would have more power than it had ever had, and the means to wield it. His task now was to justify to the larger group the changes he and the committee had made and, in the remaining weeks, push the Constitution over the finish line. To do that, he would need to tackle the project that had loomed, unfinished, over the convention from day one: the presidency.

The Presidency

Wilson had already tried to resolve the issue of the chief executive back in early June. He had not gotten very far.

That was frustrating, because what he had proposed then—a single, powerful leader elected directly by the people—was key to his vision of the American republic. That vision, unique among the delegates, combined a strong, unified central government with democratic self-rule. A leader of the type he imagined could act quickly and decisively; would be empowered with an absolute veto to counteract (or at least threaten) Congress; and, crucially, would be accountable to the people through direct election. This would eliminate the central problem with an unelected, and unaccountable, monarch. If the president does a good job, the voters will reward him with reelection; if he doesn't, they can kick him out.

It was the clearest and most consistent vision of the presidency of any of the delegates in Philadelphia. Why was it so hard for everyone else? For starters, no one other than Wilson had given the topic much thought, not even James Madison. In a letter to George Washington before the convention began, Madison laid out in detail the various components of the new proposed government. But when it came to the executive, he wrote, he had drawn a blank. "I have scarcely ventured as yet to form my own opinion either of the manner in which it ought to be constituted or of the authorities with which it ought to be clothed."

There were other, more practical concerns. During one of the early debates over the executive, Benjamin Franklin warned of the risks that would come with instituting a single leader. For instance, who would replace him if he were to become sick or die? Franklin's deeper ambivalence, though, had to do with the character of the officeholder himself. "The first man put at the helm will be a good one," he said, in an obligatory but genuine nod to Washington. "Nobody knows what sort may come afterwards."

Looming behind all these fears was the darkest of all—the fear of re-creating an unaccountable tyrant and thus undermining the whole point of independence. A tyrant in the rearview mirror; chaos and uncertainty ahead. The founders were trapped between their past and their future.

Which is why Wilson's initial proposal for a single executive back in June had been met with that uncomfortable silence and with Edmund Randolph's charge that it would be the "fetus of monarchy." Such a leader, John Dickinson had added, perhaps with a dubious glance toward his former student, "was not consistent with a republic" and "could only exist in a limited monarchy."

Wilson dismissed these criticisms. "All know that a single magistrate is not a King," he said. And yet he couldn't have been surprised at the negative reaction to his call for "a single person," a term whose historical resonance traced back to the seventeenth-century British monarchy. By the time of the Philadelphia convention, the term still echoed in that context, as John Adams illustrated in writing that "by kings, and kingly power, is meant . . . the executive power in a single person." Wilson, the most celebrated legal mind in the country and a diligent student of history, cannot have failed to hear the monarchical echoes of his own words.

At the same time, Americans had never fully worked out their feelings about the king. As recently as the early 1770s, many had unhesitatingly defended his honor and reaffirmed their deference to him. But even after the king violated the central bargain of monarchy (his protection in return for his subjects' obedience) and the colonists declared their independence, calling him "unfit to be the ruler of a free people," there remained an undercurrent of support for a strong, even king-like executive. This support grew stronger whenever the shortcomings of representative democracy revealed themselves most starkly, as they did in the years leading up to the 1787 convention. The privations of war, the persistent economic crises, the insurrections that no state or federal authority seemed able to put down—all of it left the American people without a clear sense of who would take care of them. They could point to only one previous example, and at times like this, it held an undeniable appeal. Whatever his other demerits, a king got things done.

By the winter before the convention, the voices in favor of a return to monarchy were louder than they had been in years. "I would sooner be subject to the caprice of one man, than to the ignorance and passions of a multitude," Noah Webster wrote in *The Connecticut Courant*. Even though such sentiments remained unacceptable to voice in polite society—Webster published his anonymously—they were common enough that the delegates were constantly on guard against charges that they were concocting a new king.

The fact that the convention insisted on secrecy only helped fuel suspicions. In July, newspapers around the country reported on a supposed scheme by the delegates to make the Bishop of Osnaburg, George III's second son, king of America. There was no evidence for such a plot, but the delegates were alarmed enough to issue a rapid (if carefully worded) response in *The Pennsylvania Herald*: "Tho' we cannot, affirmatively, tell you what we are doing; we can, negatively, tell you what we are not doing—we never once thought of a king."

And yet more than a few delegates were as uncertain as the general public about what they were creating. Following an afternoon break on August 6, the day the delegates came back from their recess, James McHenry of Maryland returned to his delegation's table to find his colleague John Mercer scribbling something on his copy of the Committee of Detail's report. On closer inspection, McHenry, who had worked as a surgeon during the war and later became one of George Washington's top advisers, saw that Mercer was "taking down the names of the members on a blank side of his report and affixing to most of them the word 'for' or 'against.'" The "for" column had more than twenty names in it, including that of their fellow Marylander Daniel Carroll. McHenry inquired what question had led Mercer to make such a careful accounting of the delegates' views.

Mercer laughed. "Those marked with a 'for' were for a king," he said.

"How do you learn that?" McHenry asked—a reasonable question, as it was Mercer's first day at the convention.

"No matter," Mercer replied. "The thing is so."

McHenry asked Mercer if he could copy the list, and Mercer allowed him to. McHenry took the liberty of adding his own name, along with Mercer's, to the "against" column. As he was doing so, a fourth member of their delegation, the irascible, insufferable Luther Martin, saw McHenry's version of the list and asked to borrow it to make his own copy. Martin was among the most vocal of the anti-monarchists, infamous among the delegates and his peers for his "tavern harangues" and his tendency to show up to court inebriated.

The scene evokes less a caucus of the greatest political minds in America than a crew of schoolboys passing notes behind the teacher's back. But Wilson did not share his colleagues' anxiety or ambivalence about the country's leader. He understood the fear of an unaccountable monarch that had led to the faulty design of the Articles of Confederation, but to him the cure had been worse than the disease. "We neglected to establish among ourselves a government that would ensure domestic vigor and stability," he would explain during Pennsylvania's ratifying convention. He was confident that a powerful executive was perfectly compatible with republican government—as long as that executive was elected by the people, not installed by heredity.

In achieving the first half of this equation, Wilson was very successful. The final Constitution established the president as a single person vested with broad executive powers and a veto over Congress, despite the many calls for a weak chief executive or even an executive council. It set a four-year term, even though delegates proposed anywhere from six to twenty years. (Wilson wanted three years, to increase accountability, but he gladly accepted this compromise.) And it made the president eligible for reelection, even though many delegates argued for ineligibility to reduce the risk of corruption.

How did Wilson win these fights? In some cases, by avoiding them. Much of the presidency, like the expansion of national power, would take shape in the Committee of Detail, where Wilson was unencumbered by the wearisome back-and-forth of open debate. The delegates still had to agree to what came out of the committee—but in the end, they did, whether because of Wilson's powers of persuasion or simply due to the sheer exhaustion of late summer.

It is why historians of the founding regularly describe Wilson as the "architect" or "intellectual father" of the presidency. On this topic, the standard Madison-centric narrative of the convention does not hold up. Wilson "nearly always takes the lead in framing the discussion" of the executive, one historian observed, with Madison following a few steps behind.

And yet Wilson failed to achieve the second half of the equation, popular election, which he considered essential to the whole plan. For republican government to work, the people, the source of all power, must exercise that power themselves. It was not a coincidence that when he first proposed his plan for a national executive, in early June, he specifically highlighted the experience of New York and Massachusetts—two states with unusually powerful, and popularly elected, governors.

Wilson would emphasize this point again and again over the years. The president would take office as the leader of "the whole Union, and will be chosen in such a manner that he may be justly styled THE MAN OF THE PEOPLE," he said during Pennsylvania's ratifying debates. "Being elected by the different parts of the United States, he will consider himself not particularly interested for any one of them, but will watch over the whole with paternal care and affection."

In his mind, the point of a popular vote wasn't merely to choose a better president but to create a better and more virtuous citizenry. Voting for their leaders, he said, will "naturally" turn the attention of voters "to the contemplation of public men and public measures." That sort of sustained attention to public matters creates virtue. Voting "has a powerful tendency to open, to enlighten, to enlarge, and to exalt the mind," he would say in a 1789 speech. Here was Wilson the Scot, suffused with the glow of Enlightenment values, imploring his fellow delegates to open their eyes and see the light.

At times he believed he was close to winning over enough delegates, but in the end, he would never secure the support of more than one state—his own.

When the matter came up for a second time, in mid-July, Wilson had gained a few allies, among them James Madison and Gouverneur Morris. On July 17, the day after the convention had settled the Connecticut Compromise, Morris briefly took charge of the fight and called for electing the president "by the people at large." He qualified this by adding "by the Freeholders of the country"—in other words, Morris, the wealthy elitist, was not speaking for *all* the people. He also admitted that there would be practical difficulties to this method, but contended that it was better than the alternative. "If the people should elect, they will never fail to prefer some man of distinguished character, or services"—a man "of continental reputation," Morris said. "If the Legislature elect, it will be the work of intrigue, of cabal, and of faction."

Roger Sherman of Connecticut disagreed. The "sense of the nation," he argued, would be expressed better by Congress than by the people themselves, who "will never be sufficiently informed of characters." Besides, Sherman added in his customary defense of the smaller states, the people "will never give a majority of votes to any one man. They will generally vote for some man in their own State, and the largest State will have the best chance for the appointment."

And so what if they do? Wilson shot back. "The concurrence of a majority of people is not a necessary principle of election," he pointed out, "nor required as such in any of the states." Wilson offered a compromise: Let the people vote, and if no candidate wins a majority, Congress can choose among the top vote-getters. "This would restrain the choice to a good nomination at least, and prevent in a great degree intrigue and cabal," he said.

Charles Pinckney of South Carolina came to Sherman's defense. The people, he said, "will be led by a few active & designing men. The most populous states by combining in favor of the same individual will be able to carry their points."

"Just the reverse," Morris said, jumping back in. "The people of such states cannot combine. If [there] be any combination it must be among their representatives in the Legislature." He then took up the other claims and rejected them in turn: The people would be uninformed? Perhaps of the proceedings in Congress, but not of the "great and illustrious characters" who would run for president. The people would be tricked by designing men? In a small district, maybe, but not across the entire country.

George Mason sided with the doubters, at least as far as the limits of the public's knowledge went. "It would be as unnatural to refer the choice of a proper character for chief magistrate to the people," he said, "as it would to refer a trial of colors to a blind man."

Finally, Hugh Williamson of North Carolina spoke up. He agreed with Morris that the public would often be aware of the candidates running for national office. Still, he shared Sherman's and Pinckney's apprehension about their state allegiances. "The people will be sure to vote for some man in their own State, and the largest State will be sure to succeed," he said, before tacking on a brief but perceptive point. "This will not be Virginia however. Her slaves will have no suffrage."

Williamson had, perhaps without realizing it, sounded the death knell for a popularly elected president. Virginia, after all, was by far the largest state by population, but only if you included its slaves, who accounted for 40 percent of the total. (Without slaves, its population was about the same as Pennsylvania's.) Of course slaves couldn't vote, and so Virginia would have no advantage in a direct election—a scenario that applied in varying degrees to every slaveholding state. Moments after Williamson's remark, the delegates took their first vote on the matter. It was defeated 9–1, with Pennsylvania the only state in favor. A second vote, on a system of electors similar to Wilson's proposal in June, lost 8–2, as it had the first time. At last, a vote on leaving the choice with Congress, the only method so far to have won majority support—it passed unanimously.

Wilson and his allies were not ready to give up. Two days later, Morris came back with a more developed argument on the need for directly electing a powerful executive. The country was large, he reminded the delegates, bigger than any republic in history, and so it required a leader with "sufficient vigor to pervade every part of it." That leader must also act as "the guardian of the people," Morris added, to protect them from the transgressions of the legislature. The conclusion was obvious: "If he is to be the guardian of the people let him be appointed by the people." Morris rejected the delegates' concerns of cabals, arguing that any cabal would fail not in spite of the vastness of the electorate, but because of it. "An election by the people at large throughout so great an extent of country could not be influenced by those little combinations and those momentary lies which often decide popular elections within a narrow sphere."

Rufus King joined Morris to agree that the people could be

trusted to make the choice, although he personally believed a system of electors "would be liable to fewest objections."

At this, Wilson permitted himself a ray of hope. He "perceived with pleasure that the idea was gaining ground, of an election mediately or immediately by the people."

James Madison spoke up, first to agree with Wilson that a popularly elected president would be best. "The people at large was in his opinion the fittest in itself," he said. "It would be as likely as any that could be devised to produce an Executive Magistrate of distinguished Character." But Madison, a slaveholding southerner himself, then drove home the point Hugh Williamson had made two days before. "There was one difficulty however of a serious nature attending an immediate choice by the people," he said. "The right of suffrage was much more diffusive in the Northern than the Southern States; and the latter could have no influence in the election on the score of the Negroes."

There it was, plain as day. Just as the small states had successfully held the convention hostage to their demands for equal voting in the Senate, the slave states were quite pleased with their newly enshrined political influence. Possessing such outsize power in Congress, why would they ever agree to a popular vote for president? As Madison's fellow Virginian George Mason had put it a week earlier, in one of the last debates on representation in Congress, "From the nature of man we may be sure, that those who have power in their hands will not give it up while they can retain it. On the contrary we know they will always when they can rather increase it."

Madison ended with a small but significant concession. The southern states may refuse to give their slaves a vote, he said, but "the substitution of electors obviated this difficulty and seemed on the whole to be liable to the fewest objections." He would turn out to be right.

As the convention lurched toward its midsummer recess, Wilson had grown resigned to the fact that there would be no popular election for president. Still, he remained adamant that Congress should have no role in the choice. On July 24, as the delegates once again seemed to warm to congressional selection, he pleaded with them not to go down that road. If they insisted on it, he said, he would support a presidential term of "almost any length of time," for no other reason than to prevent any president from becoming dependent on Congress.

The debate had stalled. "We seem to be entirely at a loss on this head," Elbridge Gerry said. But Wilson had one more idea up his sleeve. Increasingly desperate to salvage at least one component of his plan, and despairing that he could keep the choice away from Congress, he suggested "a mode which had not been mentioned." What if future Congresses drew lots? he said: Pick up to fifteen members of Congress at random, send them off immediately to a room, and let them make the choice. That way, they would have no opportunity to create cabals, and no real power over the president. "This was not," Wilson admitted, "a digested idea and might be liable to strong objections."

It certainly was. Rufus King, generally a strong Wilson ally, pointed out the obvious risk of a lottery: It could name a majority of delegates from the same state, ensuring the president came from that state, regardless of his merits. "We ought to be governed by reason, not by chance," King said.

Wilson was surely miffed. He knew the lottery idea was a bad one. But what other option was there? He still believed popular election was the way to go—on this, he said, his "opinion remained unshaken"—but once again, he had failed to convince enough of the delegates.

The next day, Madison made a final attempt to sell a popular election. "With all its imperfections," he said, he "liked this best." As for the disadvantage it would impose on the southern states, he added, "local considerations must give way to the general interest. As an individual from the southern states, he was willing to make the sacrifice." Alas, few if any others were.

The convention had now debated the presidency for more than two months, yet the delegates seemed no closer to agreement on most of the fundamental terms. By late August, time was running out. If all the delegates' work was going to have a chance at success, they needed to get the document finished and sent to the states for ratification soon.

Still, they could not come to agreement on the key question of selecting the president. They had considered giving the choice to Congress, to state legislatures, to the people directly, to state governors, and to others. On August 24 alone, the delegates rejected at least three different methods—including popular election (9–2 against), election by the state legislatures (6–5 against), and election by presidential electors "chosen by the people of the several states" (6–5 against). The question was narrowed down to whether there should be presidential electors, period, and this time the states were evenly split, 4–4, with two divided and Massachusetts absent. If only because no other method was drawing enough support, the elector proposal seemed to be gaining.

On the last day of the month, the convention formed a committee to resolve the presidency and other outstanding issues. Led by David Brearley of New Jersey and containing one representative from each state—Pennsylvania chose Gouverneur Morris, not Wilson—it became known as the Committee on Postponed Parts.

The committee issued its report on September 4. Its proposal for choosing the president was a system of electors, with each state having a number of electors equal to its two senators plus its members in the House of Representatives. The candidate winning a majority of electoral votes would be president, and the second-place finisher would be vice president. If no candidate received a majority of electoral votes, the Senate would choose from among the top five finishers.

Wilson had made his own uneasy peace with this outcome, but he didn't want anyone to forget how fraught the process had been. "This subject has greatly divided the House, and will also divide people out of doors," he said following the announcement of the committee's report. "It is in truth the most difficult of all on which we have had to decide."

The proposed plan, he added, was "a valuable improvement on the former"—that is, allowing Congress to make the choice. "It gets rid of one great evil, that of cabal and corruption; and continental characters will multiply as we more and more coalesce, so as to enable the electors in every part of the union to know and judge of them." It was a characteristically optimistic prediction from Wilson but, once again, it would be proven accurate in time.

For now, however, he knew as well as anyone that "continental characters" were hard to come by. Presidential electors might be expected to know more about candidates than the average citizen, but they still faced the same limits on information and communication. Most would probably support their state or regional candidate, with the result that votes for president would be spread so widely that no one candidate would win a majority. George Mason assumed this would happen "nineteen times in twenty."

Given such odds, Wilson proposed shifting the final choice for president away from the Senate—"the senate was not a favorite of mine," he would say, with remarkable self-restraint, during the Pennsylvania ratifying convention later that fall—and into the House of Representatives, where shorter term limits would reduce the chance of corruption. He also proposed limiting the choice to a smaller number than the committee's top five.

He got his way, but at a price he may have failed to anticipate. On September 6, the convention took up for the last time the question of how to choose a president in case the electors failed to give a majority to any one candidate. The delegates agreed to Wilson's proposal to shift the final choice from the Senate to the House—but only after Hugh Williamson and Roger Sherman proposed that each state delegation get a single vote. It was an equality even worse than the Senate itself, which at least gave two votes to each state, allowing senators from the same state to split their votes. Under the proposal by Williamson and Sherman, tiny Delaware would have as much influence in choosing the president as Pennsylvania. It was as significant a violation of majority rule as any that had been considered that summer.

Wilson found it difficult to protest, as he had been the one to request a last-minute change. Still, he could have seen it coming. Once again, state attachments proved to be the bane of the convention.

Either way, it was done. Three months after Wilson had first proposed a system of presidential electors, the convention had at last agreed to one. It was not rooted in the people, as he wanted, but it was, in one historian's words, "the second-most democratic idea of the day."

Almost forty years after that summer in Philadelphia, Thomas Hart Benton, a young senator from the new state of Missouri, sought out a meeting with one of the elders of the institution, Rufus King. King, near seventy and in failing health, was retiring from the Senate after a long career in government. Benton was curious about King's experience serving as a delegate to the 1787 convention, where he had represented Massachusetts. Recalling their conversation in his memoir, Benton wrote, "He said some things to me which I think ought to be remembered by future generations, to enable them to appreciate justly those founders of our government who were in favor of a stronger organization than was adopted."

> He said: "You young men who have been born since the Revolution, look with horror upon the name of a King, and upon all propositions for a strong government. It was not so with us. We were born the subjects of a King, and were accustomed to subscribe ourselves 'His Majesty's most faithful subjects;' and we began the quarrel which ended in the Revolution, not against the King, but against his parliament."

This was the identical argument that Wilson had made on June 1, 1787, the day he introduced his proposal for a powerful single executive. "The people of America did not oppose the British King but the parliament," he had said then, according to King's convention notes. "The opposition was not against an unity but a corrupt multitude." That remark was in turn a restatement of what Wilson had written in his 1774 essay arguing against the authority of Parliament over the colonies.

In other words, Wilson held a consistent vision of the executive for at least two decades before the Philadelphia convention. That vision was rooted in an understanding that the Revolution had begun in opposition to a tyrannical legislature, not the king himself. Other founders, including John Adams and Alexander Hamilton, agreed with Wilson, but they never linked a powerful leader to the popular will as expressed in a direct election. Wilson, perhaps alone among his peers, saw no contradiction between a near-monarchical conception of executive power and his own faith in the sovereignty and wisdom of regular people. For him the two were not only compatible; they were inseparable.

Thus we arrive at the Wilsonian synthesis: an immensely powerful executive who would be elected by, and thus accountable to, the people themselves. Such a leader would never turn into a tyrant, he felt certain—because if he attempted to, he would be thrown out of office. It was easy for Wilson's antagonists to smear him with charges of monarchism, but for all its surface similarities, Wilson saw his model as fundamentally different. It was the distinction between reigning over a people and ruling under them.

Other founders came to appreciate this distinction in time. Thomas Jefferson discussed it in an 1816 letter to his friend Samuel Kercheval, as he explained why the founding generation struggled with their relationship to the Crown. "In truth, the abuses of monarchy had so much filled all the space of political contemplation, that we imagined everything republican which was not monarchy. We had not yet penetrated to the mother principle, that 'governments are republican only in proportion as they embody the will of their people, and execute it.' Hence, our first constitutions had really no leading principles in them. But experience and reflection have but more and more confirmed me in the particular importance of the equal representation then proposed."

Wilson, of course, had penetrated to the "mother principle" decades earlier; most of his colleagues just weren't ready to join him there. And that is the enduring problem for him and for us—while he saw the two components of his presidential vision as inseparable, he would achieve only one of them. The presidency that emerged out of the 1787 convention was as powerful as anything Wilson or the other nationalists could have dreamed—akin to a "limited monarchy," as John Adams reflected in a 1789 letter to Roger Sherman. "I know of no first magistrate in any republican government, excepting England and Neuchatel, who possesses a constitutional dignity, authority, and power comparable to his," Adams wrote.

Earlier that year, just after Washington was elected, James McHenry—the Marylander who had spied the for-or-against-a-king list drawn up by one of his fellow delegates—wrote to congratulate the incoming president: "You are now a king, under a different name."

Whatever he was called, the American magistrate would not be chosen directly by the people over whom he ruled, severing the link between power and consent that Wilson considered essential to the functioning of a free society.

10

The Signing

ON SEPTEMBER 17, 1787, for the second time in eleven years, a group of several dozen men gathered around a low table at the front of the assembly room of the Pennsylvania State House to sign what would become, along with the Declaration of Independence, one of the most cherished covenants in the history of democracy. In all, eighty-nine delegates put their names to the Constitution and the Declaration. Of those eighty-nine, only six signed both documents. And of those six, only one understood the two documents as inextricably linked.

"All men are, by nature, equal and free: no one has a right to any authority over another without his consent." These were the words James Wilson had written in his 1768 essay published in 1774, and he never stopped trying to carve them into the foundation of a truly democratic America. They were the words Thomas Jefferson adopted, with only slight alterations, in the preamble to the Declaration—"We hold these truths to be self-evident, that all men are created equal."

Today, the lines of that preamble are sacred, chiseled into our collective political consciousness. But for nearly all the founders, the preamble, like the Declaration as a whole, was an afterthought. With one exception, none of them—not Madison, not Adams, not Washington, not Hamilton, not even Jefferson, its primary author—cited its words in public through the end of the eighteenth century. The exception was Wilson.

Recall that on June 19, one of the most contentious days of the summer of 1787, Wilson quoted the Declaration aloud to his fellow delegates. What occasioned this outburst was Luther Martin's claim that the states had entered the confederation as free and independent equals and wanted to maintain that equality in whatever new government would be formed. Not so, Wilson responded. The Declaration of Independence made no reference to individual states, he pointed out, only to "*United Colonies*," and therefore "that they were independent, not *Individually* but *Unitedly*." In other words, independence and unity were two sides of the same coin.

To the extent that the Articles of Confederation seemed to contradict this idea, Wilson had a ready rejoinder: The Declaration came first. While the drafting of the Articles of Confederation began in 1776, the Articles were not ratified until five years later. Even putting aside their numerous flaws, they did not negate what the Declaration had created—a single, unified country in which all *people*, as opposed to *states*, were equal and reserved all political power to themselves.

Wilson would invoke the Declaration once again at the height of the ratification debates later that fall. "I consider the people of the United States as forming one great community; and I consider the people of the different states as forming communities, again, on a lesser scale," he said during a daylong speech at Pennsylvania's ratifying convention, before quoting the Declaration's preamble. "This is the broad basis on which our independence was placed," he said. "On the same certain and solid foundation this system"—referring to the Constitution—"is erected."

Considering the two documents together, as Wilson did, helps us better comprehend what he accomplished, and what he failed to accomplish, in bringing America's governing charter into line with his grand political vision. That vision had many elements, and throughout the summer, Wilson cultivated allies in support of them. Some, like Madison and Morris, were with him on proportional representation in Congress. Others, like George Mason, were on board with direct election of the president. Still others, like Charles Pinckney, agreed on the need for a powerful national government. All had their own reasons for supporting one or another element, but no one shared Wilson's fervent commitment to all of them.

Of course, the document that emerged from the convention, riddled as it was with compromises and concessions, could not possibly reflect anyone's vision in full. But it must have seemed particularly wanting to Wilson, who was acutely aware of every instance in which he had allowed his carefully thought-out principles to take a back seat to political horse-trading.

In the final days of the convention, however, the Constitution would undergo one last, critical tweak that Wilson surely approved of and possibly inserted by himself. It happened in the Committee of Style, which was appointed in early September to go through the document once more, word by word, smoothing and polishing the language, giving it clarity, simplicity, and coherence.

Recall that several weeks earlier, in the Committee of Detail, Wilson had altered the preamble from "We the People *and* the States of New Hampshire, Massachusetts . . ." to "We the People *of* the States . . ." This put the people not on a par with the states but ahead of them. In the Committee of Style, those opening words were changed further. The final document read, "We the People of *the United States of America* . . ." The union was now paramount; the states had been erased entirely.

The style committee included leading nationalists—Madison, Hamilton, King, William Samuel Johnson, and Gouverneur Morris, the last of whom generally gets credit for the lion's share of the committee's work. For that reason, it is assumed that Morris made that final change to the opening words of the preamble. And yet the evidence for that proposition came from correspondence written decades after the convention. Another account, from immediately after the convention, placed Wilson at the center of the edit, as does a later one. In his comprehensive history of the convention, Charles Warren writes that these accounts suggest Wilson was "equally, if not more, entitled to the honor of making this final draft."

Whatever the nature of Wilson's involvement in the final draft, "We the People of the United States" is the ultimate Wilsonian gloss—seven words that Americans have committed to memory, most without realizing it, for more than two centuries.

That's why it is important to consider his influence on the nation's founding documents from the perspective of what his words accomplished not solely in 1787 but also in the years since, given the degree to which the country has come to share his vision. Today the sobriquet "father of the Constitution" refers almost exclusively to James Madison, yet that exaggerates Madison's influence and minimizes those arguably more attuned to the struggles confronting a modern democracy—both then and in the future. Madison, for example, was much more skeptical of the people and their wisdom than Wilson was, supporting stricter rules both for voting and for holding office. Wilson opposed voting restrictions, property qualifications, and lengthy residency requirements for immigrants who, like him, wished to serve in government.

Now consider the many ways the Constitution and American government have evolved since the founding—the expansion of the franchise to include Black former slaves, women, and virtually all adults eighteen and older; the elimination of property qualifications for voting and holding office; the right of the people to elect their senators directly; the Supreme Court's adoption of the principle of one person, one vote. In all these ways and more, modern America is remarkably aligned with what Wilson envisioned in 1787.

This doesn't demonstrate that Wilson is the "father" of the Constitution. But neither is anyone else. Assigning a single paternity to the document is impossible, given the complexity of the debate that summer and the cross-cutting motives and rationales of dozens of delegates. If Wilson deserves any moniker for his role, it is probably the one suggested by the constitutional scholar Akhil Reed Amar—"spiritual adviser." He did not enter the ministry as his parents had wished, but like no other delegate in Philadelphia that summer, he served as an evangelist for political equality and popular sovereignty. He understood these as the essential principles underlying any fair and functional self-government, and he spoke of them with the persistence and convictions of a true believer—not, as so many others did, in the temporizing language of political compromise.

On that cool Monday morning in the middle of September, as the delegates prepared to sign the product of the last four months of their efforts, Wilson stood to deliver some final words. Only, they weren't his; they were those of the man sitting next to him, Benjamin Franklin. Franklin, in his ninth decade, still had plenty to say, but he no longer had the energy to stand and say it in front of a crowd. Throughout the summer, he had relied on Wilson to read out his longer written remarks, and on this day he was doing that again.

Wilson's delivery of Franklin's words was a neat bookend to the revolutionary era, and to the lifelong connection between the two men. Almost three decades earlier, a seventeen-year-old Wilson had likely seen Franklin speak under his own power, during his visit to St. Andrews to collect an honorary degree. Fifteen years after that, a bracing argument on parliamentary authority was attributed to Franklin and not to its true author, a then-little-known lawyer and immigrant living in Pennsylvania. Now, thirteen years later, as the two prepared to sign their charter for a new nation, they stood on more even ground.

"I confess that there are several parts of this constitution which I do not at present approve," Wilson, speaking Franklin's words, said to the Assembly. "But I am not sure I shall never approve them: For having lived long, I have experienced many instances of being obliged by better information or fuller consideration, to change opinions even on important subjects, which I once thought right, but found to be otherwise. It is therefore that the older I grow, the more apt I am to doubt my own judgment, and to pay more respect to the judgment of others."

Wilson continued reading from Franklin's notes: "I doubt too whether any other Convention we can obtain may be able to make a better Constitution. For when you assemble a number of men to have the advantage of their joint wisdom, you inevitably assemble with those men, all their prejudices, their passions, their errors of opinion, their local interests, and their selfish views. From such an

Assembly can a perfect production be expected? . . . Thus I consent, Sir, to this Constitution because I expect no better, and because I am not sure that it is not the best."

In closing, Franklin asked "that every member of the Convention who may still have objections to it, would with me on this occasion doubt a little of his own infallibility—and to make manifest our unanimity, put his name to this instrument."

There would be no unanimity, but that was perhaps a fitting outcome. After all, the Constitution had been drafted specifically in reaction to the Articles of Confederation, which were failing in large part because they required unanimity, and thus could accomplish almost nothing. In any case, Franklin would get what he, and the country, needed. Of the fifty-five delegates who attended the convention at one point or another during the summer, forty-two remained. In the end, thirty-nine delegates would sign, representing all twelve states in attendance that summer.

Three delegates—George Mason, Elbridge Gerry, and Edmund Randolph—refused to sign. Mason, who had entered the convention strongly in support of a new national government, had soured on the enterprise by late summer. On August 31, he told his colleagues, he would "sooner chop off his right hand than put it to the Constitution as it now stands." He objected to many features of the charter, most of all its lack of a bill of rights, which would become a central point of contention during the ratification process.

Randolph, the Virginia governor, declined to sign with many apologies and prevarications, all centered on his concerns that the people would reject a document that had been drafted without a proper mandate. Two days before the close of the convention, he had pitched a solution: Send the Constitution to the states, let them offer any amendments they choose, and then hold a second convention to vote on those amendments. If the convention rejected this, it would "be impossible for him to put his name to the instrument." Mason agreed. "This Constitution had been formed without the knowledge or idea of the people," he said. "It was improper to say to the people, take this or nothing." The other delegates, exhausted and eager to go home, were in no mood to consider doing the whole thing over again in a few months. Not a single delegation endorsed Randolph's proposal.

But Randolph followed through on his threat. On September 17, moments before the delegates began to sign, he stood to speak. "Notwithstanding the vast majority and venerable names" who were lining up to take the quill, he said, he could not sign a document that might not be ratified by the people in the end. He wasn't saying that he personally would object to it at Virginia's convention; he only wanted to keep his options open. It was a feeble gesture from the man who had introduced the Virginia Plan, made even more so by the fact that more than three dozen of his colleagues were willing to sign despite their awareness of the risks.

Franklin was peeved. In writing his speech, he said, he had not anticipated such refusals. Still, he was a diplomat at heart, and so he expressed gratitude for the role Randolph had played so far before imploring him to reconsider his decision in order to "prevent the great mischief which the refusal of his name might produce." Randolph wouldn't budge, even though he admitted he was taking "a step which might be the most awful of his life."

Elbridge Gerry, meanwhile, had decided weeks earlier to withhold his signature, as he explained in an August 21 letter to his wife, Ann, back in Massachusetts. "I am as sick of being here as you can conceive," he wrote her. "Entre nous, I do not expect to give my voice to the measure." Gerry, among the delegates most mistrustful of the people, had been uneasy with the new plan from the start. With Shays's Rebellion never far from his mind, he feared the country was on the verge of civil war. In his own state, he explained, there were two factions that would collide during the ratification process, "one devoted to democracy, the worst of all political evils, the other as violent in the opposite extreme." The delegates had failed to produce a "more mediating" document that would reduce these passions, he said. He took some offense at Franklin's speech, which he believed (despite Franklin's claim) had unfairly targeted him and the other two dissenters. At least, Gerry promised, he would not go public with his refusal.

The defectors had dampened the mood in the room, but as Wilson and the rest of the delegates lined up to sign their names, it became clear that the losses would be confined to three. Seeing this, Franklin permitted himself a moment of optimism. He glanced over at the tall wooden chair that George Washington had occupied for the last four months, the back of which was decorated with a painted sun half submerged below the horizon, its rays extending outward in all directions. "Painters had found it difficult to distinguish in their art a rising from a setting sun," Franklin mused. Throughout the summer, he had looked at the sun on Washington's chair "without being able to tell whether it was rising or setting. But now at length I have the happiness to know that it is a rising and not a setting sun."

Still, nothing could be left to chance. Almost immediately after the convention ended, a group of delegates rushed upstairs to request a formal meeting with the Pennsylvania Assembly to begin the ratification process. They chose their target in part because it was so conveniently located, but they also saw Pennsylvania as friendly territory, and in many ways it was. The Assembly, which had long been in the hands of the radicals, was now dominated by members of the moneyed elite from the eastern half of the state. These men came from Philadelphia and its surroundings, moved in the same circles as Wilson and Franklin, and were similarly eager for a new constitution that would stabilize the national economy and prevent the violent uprisings that had haunted the country over the last several years. The next morning, the delegates, led by Franklin, read the new constitution to a "large crowd of citizens" who had gathered around the sides of the assembly room.

Outside Philadelphia, most Americans didn't know anything yet. "Reports and conjectures abound concerning the nature of the plan which is to be proposed," Madison wrote to Jefferson a few days before the convention ended. "The public however is certainly in the dark with regard to it. The Convention is equally in the dark as to the reception which may be given to it on its publication."

On the last page of his personal journal, dated September 18, 1787, James McHenry of Maryland wrote down two exchanges he had recently overheard. The first has become one of the most famous anecdotes of the American founding. As McHenry recorded it, Elizabeth Willing Powel, a prominent Philadelphian who was close with George Washington and other framers, inquired of Franklin, "Well, Doctor, what have we got, a republic or a monarchy?"

"A republic," Franklin replied, "if you can keep it."

The quote serves today as a pithy, solemn reminder of the inherent fragility of self-government. But in the days following the end of the convention, the departing delegates had more pressing concerns than how future Americans might reflect on what they had done. Perhaps the biggest anxiety triggered by the impending plebiscite was illustrated by the second, lesser-known anecdote in McHenry's journal. It involved two of his fellow delegates, Luther Martin and Daniel St. Thomas Jenifer. Speaking of the ratification conventions to come, Martin said, "I'll be hanged if the people of Maryland agree to it." Jenifer replied, "I advise you to stay in Philadelphia lest you should be hanged."

Martin didn't heed the advice; he left the convention in a huff on September 4, one of thirteen of the original fifty-five delegates to depart early, and one of sixteen who did not put their name to the Constitution. A few departed for health reasons, or to attend to family or business matters. William Pierce, of Georgia, left to take part in a duel. But most, like Martin, left because of fundamental disagreements over the final product. These disagreements had been kept under wraps for the entire summer, but as the Constitution began to be printed and distributed, they were about to explode into public view.

Even the nationalists, who had achieved many of the goals they had set out for themselves at the start of the summer, were dissatisfied with the final product. James Madison wrote to Thomas Jefferson in Paris that the new Constitution "will neither effectually *answer* its *national object* nor prevent the local *mischiefs* which everywhere *excite disgusts* against the *state governments*." Alexander Hamilton was unhappy that the new charter failed to emulate Britain's government, which gave far more power to the executive. Gouverneur Morris said he would sign the Constitution despite "all its faults." Benjamin Franklin said, in his closing speech to the delegates on September 17, that "there are several parts of this constitution which I do not at present approve."

At the same time, they were all aware that the country's survival depended on the Constitution's ratification. As George Washington had said, the alternative was "anarchy."

Wilson was the only major nationalist who expressed no public or private misgivings about the Constitution. He had as much reason to demur as his colleagues; indeed, he had expressed his frustrations over the course of the convention itself. But through his work on the Committee of Detail, he had also managed to shape the document in ways that other delegates, even the most influential, had not. From the powers of the presidency to the supremacy of federal law to the opening, definitional words "We the People," Wilson had won battles that other delegates may not have realized they were fighting. Now that the document was signed and being distributed to the public, he seemed to be taking extra care not to say anything that could undermine the fragile consensus that had created it.

As he would soon find out, that consensus had already begun to fracture.

11

Slavery and the Three-Fifths Clause

"THE CURSE OF HEAVEN"

THERE IS A deep and troubling contradiction at the heart of James Wilson's role in the federal convention of 1787: his approach toward slavery.

It would not have been hard for Wilson to become one of early America's most ardent and eloquent voices against the practice of human bondage, which violated every element of his worldview—from natural law to common sense to political equality and majority rule. His education, his religious upbringing, his political experiences, his principles, and his temperament all pointed in the same direction, toward abolition. And yet, throughout the summer of 1787, he said little on the subject. When he did engage with it, he helped usher in what would become the most notorious provision of the entire Constitution, the Three-Fifths Clause, which counted each slave as three-fifths of a free person for the purposes of taxation and representation in Congress. It was an outrageous giveaway to the southern states; in the end, it would take a war resulting in the deaths of more than six hundred thousand American soldiers to expunge this clause from the Constitution, along with other protections for slave owners that Wilson and his fellow delegates had blessed.

This is not an application of modern values to another era. Long before the American founding, the morality of slavery was a common topic of debate. For example, as Wilson was surely aware, Sir William Blackstone, the great British jurist and legal commentator, had described the practice as "repugnant to reason and the principles of natural law" in 1765. Wilson was also aware of the opinions of his American peers like Patrick Henry, who, despite owning more than fifty slaves himself (and criticizing the Constitution for not being sufficiently protective of slavers' rights), was clear-eyed about the moral obscenity of slavery, referring to it in 1771 as "abominable" and "a principle as repugnant to humanity as it is inconsistent with the bible and destructive to Liberty."

In 1774, the year Wilson published his transformative essay on the legal independence of the American colonies, Abigail Adams wrote to her husband, John, to say that it had "always appeared a most iniquitous scheme to me—fight ourselves for what we are daily robbing and plundering from those who have as good a right to freedom as we have."

By the time of the 1787 convention, slavery was declining in the North but exploding in the South, and the battle lines were clear. Several of the leading delegates—most notably Gouverneur Morris, who worked alongside Wilson in the final shaping of the Constitution— condemned the practice repeatedly in the strongest terms, calling it the "curse of heaven." The slavers themselves were as aware as anyone of the evil they were perpetrating. "Every master of slaves is born a petty tyrant," George Mason (who owned three hundred slaves throughout his life) said. "They bring the judgment of heaven on a country." The Constitution's protections for slavery were "inconsistent with the principles of the revolution and dishonorable to the American character," Luther Martin (six slaves) said.

Martin even cofounded the Maryland Society for the Abolition of Slavery following the convention. He was one of several founders who joined or formed abolition organizations, including Benjamin Franklin, who owned slaves for most of his life yet became, in 1787, the president of the Philadelphia Society for the Relief of Free Negroes Unlawfully Held in Bondage. Franklin spent his last years advocating not only for the abolition of slavery but also for the integration of freed slaves into American society. In February 1790, shortly before his death, he petitioned Congress to end slavery. "Mankind are all formed by the same Almighty being," the petition read, "and equally designed for the enjoyment of happiness." This was the message of Christianity as well as "the political creed of America," he said.

Hypocrites or not, these men were openly and honestly discussing the topic. By comparison, Wilson said almost nothing. So far ahead of his time on so many matters, he barely kept up with the present on this one. In a life otherwise defined by prescience, egalitarianism, and humanism, it was by far his biggest blind spot.

This near-total silence is even more glaring when we consider how central the issue of slavery was to the shaping of the Constitution. Twenty-five of the fifty-five men who initially attended the convention kept slaves. Even if they did not debate slavery as frequently as other topics, the entrenched dispute over the practice of owning other human beings was never far from the surface; it influenced every significant decision the delegates made that summer.

You would not know this by reading Wilson's hundreds of contributions to the convention. Contrast that with James Madison, who came from a slave-owning state and enslaved more than one hundred Black people himself.

"The great danger to our general government is the great southern and northern interests of the continent, being opposed to each other," Madison said euphemistically to the delegates on June 29. "Look to the votes in congress, and most of them stand divided by the geography of the country, not according to the size of the States."

The next day, Madison became more explicit. "The States were divided into different interests not by their difference of size, but by other circumstances; the most material of which resulted partly from climate, but principally from the effects of their having or not having slaves. These two causes concurred in forming the great division of interests in the United States. It did not lie between the large & small states: It lay between the Northern and Southern."

If Wilson or any of the other founders disputed this characterization,

Madison made no record of it. To the contrary, they appeared to be in general agreement.

Madison knew that the southerners' interest in their "peculiar species of property" was twofold: not merely the protection of their ownership of slaves but the chance to count those slaves toward their total population, and thus to increase their political power. And that was entirely rational: By 1787, enslaved people comprised about 40 percent of the population of the five southern states. If slaves were included in those states' representation, those states would get credit for roughly the same number of people as the eight northern states. If they weren't included, the North, where slave populations were a fraction of what they were in the South, would be dominant.

Madison gets no special credit for his transparency on this issue. As a slave owner himself, he was thinking mainly in terms of political strategy and was eager to appease everyone if it meant a successful convention.

In the end, however, it would be Wilson who took the lead in appeasing the slavers, by proposing what became the Three-Fifths Clause. As the delegates debated the proper measure of representation in Congress, they found themselves at an impasse. While most agreed that both wealth and population should play a role, delegates from the eight northern states generally favored using wealth. Those from the five southern states, for the most part, wanted to focus on population, with full credit for their slaves. For weeks, various proposals were considered and rejected. The winning formula, it turned out, had been on the table almost from the start: to allocate representatives to each state "in proportion to the whole number of white & other free citizens and inhabitants of every age, sex, and condition including those bound to servitude for a term of years, and three-fifths of all other persons." The proposal had been made on June 11, by James Wilson.

He hadn't invented the ratio, which had been floating around for a few years, first in an amendment to the Articles of Confederation that Madison proposed in 1783 as a means to calculate what each state owed the national government in requisitions. Nor had Wilson been the first to propose it at the Philadelphia convention. That distinction goes to Charles Pinckney, the South Carolina delegate, who had included it in his own draft plan for the new government, which never came up for debate. Wilson had seen Pinckney's plan, which perhaps reminded him of the idea.

Why three-fifths? It was a decidedly unscientific estimate of the worth of a slave's labor compared to that of a free person. As the reasoning went, slaves had no interest in their labor, and so they did not work as hard. No one pointed out that the source of this problem was not the people who were enslaved but those doing the enslaving.

The first vote on Wilson's proposal passed easily, 9 states to 2.

As the weeks wore on, however, the disputes among the states grew more fractious, and support for the three-fifths plan foundered. By mid-July, Wilson himself appeared to have grown uncomfortable with its implications. "Are slaves to be admitted as citizens?" he asked on July 11. "Then why are they not admitted on an equality with white citizens? Are they admitted as property? Then why is not other property admitted into the computation?"

It was a logical question. And Wilson wasn't alone in his misgivings. At the end of the day, only 4 states were still on board with the three-fifths plan, with 6 voting against.

Yet there was no workable alternative on the horizon. A majority of states would never accept counting slaves fully, and the South would never agree to not counting them at all.

The southerners continued to threaten to leave the convention at any hint that they would not enjoy political power from their enslaved population. On the next day, July 12, William Davie of North Carolina said he thought it was "meant by some gentlemen to deprive the Southern states of any representation for their Blacks." If that was the case, he warned, "the business was at an end."

In the same breath, however, Davie pointed the way out. Of the slaves, he said, his state "would never confederate on any terms that did not rate them at least as three-fifths." It was an opening, and the exhausted delegates took it. On July 13, the convention adopted the three-fifths provision. Nine states voted in favor, with one state,

Delaware, divided. It was almost precisely the proposal Wilson had put forward more than a month earlier.

In the end, and despite the fulminations of a few delegates, the debate turned not on the morality of slavery but on the same thing as almost everything else at the convention: the allocation of power and the protection of property. For the non-slaveholders, slavery represented an economic threat first and foremost.

Meanwhile, Wilson's reluctance to acknowledge the gap between slavery and his own values is hard to ignore. Recall that just before the vote on the Three-Fifths Clause, he stood to deliver one of the more powerful speeches of his time at the convention. Responding to concerns that the southern or new western states would soon have larger populations and thus more national power than the northern states, Wilson did not budge from his majoritarian principles. "All men wherever placed have equal rights and are equally entitled to confidence," he said. And what if most Americans ended up living in only a few states? No matter, according to Wilson. "The majority of people wherever found ought in all questions to govern the minority. If the interior country [i.e., the West] should acquire this majority, they will not only have the right, but will avail themselves of it whether we will or no."

To Wilson, the premise of the revolution—that all people were equal, and the majority rules—wasn't simply a nice idea; it was the essence of a republic. After all, what other measure could possibly work? "If numbers [that is, counting people rather than states as equals] be not a proper rule, why is not some better rule pointed out? No one has yet ventured to attempt it. Congress have never been able to discover a better. No State as far as he had heard, has suggested any other."

If he could hear the contradiction in his own words, he didn't mention it. Nor did his assist to the slavers end with the Three-Fifths Clause. The Committee of Detail's report that he had a lead role in drafting included not only the Three-Fifths Clause but also a blanket prohibition against Congress taxing or banning the slave trade, another against export taxes, and a requirement of a supermajority of both houses of Congress to enact navigation laws, which some of the southern delegates feared the northerners would use to undermine the slave trade and cripple the South's economy.

Wilson was not the author of these provisions—they were the work of the southerners Edmund Randolph and John Rutledge—and he likely objected to them on principle. Still, he had consented to their inclusion, knowing that there would be no Constitution without appeasing the slave states. This point had been reiterated just before the committee met. "If the committee should fail to insert some security to the southern states against an emancipation of slaves, and taxes on exports," Charles Cotesworth Pinckney warned on July 23, he would be "bound by duty to his state to vote against their report."

Wilson's fellow northerners were less conciliatory than he was. Two days after the convention got back under way, Rufus King of Massachusetts tried to reopen the debate over the Three-Fifths Clause itself, which he called "a most grating circumstance," adding that most Americans would agree with him. At the very least, he had expected that particular concession to be in exchange for southern support for a stronger central government. Instead, the committee report not only granted southern states full protection for the slave trade but the North would now be obligated to defend them from slave insurrections and have no extra funds for the purpose. It was a "monument to Southern craft and gall."

"There was so much inequality and unreasonableness in all this," King said, "that the people of the northern states could never be reconciled to it."

Gouverneur Morris was equally furious. What concession, he wanted to know, would northerners get in return "for a sacrifice of every principle of right, of every impulse of humanity?" Domestic slavery "was the curse of heaven on the States where it prevailed," he thundered, then echoed the observation Wilson had made several weeks before. "Upon what principle is it that the slaves shall be computed in the representation? Are they men? Then make them citizens and let them vote. Are they property? Why then is no other property included? The houses in this city are worth more than all the wretched slaves which cover the rice swamps of South Carolina."

He returned to the attack on the Three-Fifths Clause. "The admission of slaves into the representation when fairly explained comes to this: that the inhabitant of Georgia and South Carolina who goes to the coast of Africa, and in defiance of the most sacred laws of humanity tears away his fellow creatures from their dearest connections and damns them to the most cruel bondages, shall have more votes in a government instituted for protection of the rights of mankind, than the citizen of Pennsylvania or New Jersey who views with a laudable horror, so nefarious a practice."

Morris concluded that he "would sooner submit himself to a tax for paying for all the Negroes in the United States than saddle posterity with such a Constitution."

But the delegates of the South were unmoved. Indeed, such challenges made them only more defensive of their "nefarious institution." "The true question," South Carolina's John Rutledge said later in August, "is whether the southern states shall or shall not be parties to the union." He continued: "If the Convention thinks that North Carolina, South Carolina and Georgia will ever agree to the plan, unless their right to import slaves be untouched, the expectation is vain. The people of those States will never be such fools as to give up so important an interest."

The southerners were also aware that, despite the northern states' professed aversion to slavery within their borders, they had a soft spot—their reliance on the shipping industry. This led to one of the most significant quid pro quos of the summer: a deal struck in private between delegates from South Carolina and Connecticut, allowing the slave trade to continue uninterrupted for at least twenty more years. The point of leverage was the proposed supermajority requirement for Congress to enact navigation laws—which would grant monopolies to northern shippers—that had been proposed by the Committee of Detail. The southerners generally supported the requirement, as noted before, out of a fear that the North would use such laws to hurt the South's economy. Meanwhile, the northern states were opposed to anything that would make passing such laws more difficult, because they controlled the shipping industry and did not want the southern states blocking federal laws that would benefit that industry. In James Madison's notes for August 29, he recorded Charles Cotesworth Pinckney of South Carolina coming out against the requirement. Why the break with his fellow southerners? As a concession to the New England states and their "liberal conduct toward the views of South Carolina."

"He meant the permission to import slaves," Madison added in a clarifying footnote. "An understanding on the two subjects of *navigation* and *slavery* had taken place between those parts of the Union."

Through all this, Wilson stood by, mostly silent. When he did speak up, it was not to attack slavery in the righteous terms that King and Morris had. During debate over the Fugitive Slave Clause, which would require northern states to deliver escaped slaves to their owners, Wilson's main concern was that the clause "would oblige the executive of the state to do it, at the public expense." His problem with returning escaped slaves to their owners, in other words, was less moral than fiscal. Immediately after Wilson's comment, the Fugitive Slave Clause was adopted with no recorded debate or dissent. It was little more than an afterthought by then, but in forcing northern states to act affirmatively to protect slavery, rather than simply to tolerate its existence, it served as a bitter reminder of the immorality and the imbalance at the heart of the slavers' deals—an insult to the northerners that grew with time and set the stage for the Civil War.

From the comfortable distance of more than two centuries, it is easy to wonder why Wilson declined to join with his fellow Pennsylvanian and go on record as a fervent opponent of human bondage. Had enough influential northerners spoken up along with Morris, perhaps they could have negotiated terms more beneficial to the anti-slavery position and to the future of a country premised on the notion of human equality.

It is important to point out that, unlike Morris, who refused to keep slaves on principle, Wilson appears to have kept one Black man—Thomas Pursel—as either a domestic slave or indentured servant before freeing him in early 1794, months after marrying his second wife, Hannah, who was a Quaker. The historical evidence for Wilson's relationship to Pursel is equivocal. On the one hand, there is a clear record of Wilson freeing Pursel: a document signed by him on January 2, 1794, stating, "The Bearer Thomas Pursel has been emancipated by me." (The outside of the document refers to Wilson's "manumission" of Pursel.) This document, which was kept in the files of the Pennsylvania Abolition Society, is the sole source regarding Pursel cited by Charles Page Smith in his 1956 biography of Wilson. On the other hand, the first census, taken in 1790, lists no slaves in the Wilson household. There are several potential reasons for this discrepancy: the census takers or printers made a clerical error; Wilson was dishonest about who lived in his house; or Pursel was an indentured servant rather than a slave. Indentured servants were technically contract workers and, unlike slaves, could gain their freedom at the end of the contract. That might have been a distinction Wilson made in leaving Pursel off the list, although indentured servants were not manumitted or "emancipated," in Wilson's words— both actions applying only to enslaved people.

Whatever the explanation for the census omission, Wilson's relationship to Pursel is not necessarily relevant to his approach to slavery at the Constitutional Convention—after all, Ben Franklin and other anti-slavery founders also owned slaves at one time or another, albeit far fewer than the southern slavelords. By the same token, Gouverneur Morris's signature is right there on the last page of the Constitution, directly beneath Wilson's. That is because, like Wilson, Morris desired above all a strong union, and he knew that tolerating slavery was the only way to get it.

A few months after the convention, Wilson did at last speak out on the subject. During a lengthy speech at Pennsylvania's ratifying convention, he responded to the criticisms of the slavery-protecting features of the Constitution, specifically the provision barring Congress from regulating the slave trade until 1808, which some had interpreted to mean Congress could affirmatively approve the importation of slaves. Not true, Wilson said. Only the states would have the power to import. "I consider this as laying the foundation for banishing slavery out of this country," he said, "and though the period is more distant than I could wish, yet it will produce the same kind, gradual change, which was pursued in Pennsylvania." And that, he said, "was all that could be obtained. I am sorry it was no more; but from this I think there is reason to hope that, yet a few years, and it will be prohibited altogether."

Wilson's optimism was quickly overtaken by events on the ground. In the "few years" he referred to—the two decades between the Constitution's ratification and 1808—southern states would import more than two hundred thousand enslaved Africans, nearly as many as had been imported in the previous two centuries combined. The consequences were profound, not only for the people held in bondage but also for the political and geographic development of the United States.

It soon became clear that the South had gotten the far better deal in Philadelphia. With the 1787 Constitution in hand, they were able to expand their slavocracy and their political power at the same time.

Thanks to the Three-Fifths Clause, southern states enjoyed extra representatives in Congress based on their slave populations. While Virginia and Pennsylvania had almost the same number of free white men in 1790, Virginia was awarded six more House seats thanks to its slaves. By 1820, the southern states had at least eighteen extra representatives in Congress, all because of slaves.

That windfall translated directly to gains in the Electoral College, which allocates electors based on a state's combined number of House and Senate seats. Virginia's six "slave" seats in the House meant it also had six more electors than Pennsylvania. Referred to by northerners as "Negro electors," they provided the margin of victory in the 1800 presidential election for Thomas Jefferson, the Virginian and favored candidate in the slaveholding states. *The Mercury and New-England Palladium* in Boston wrote that Jefferson made his "ride into the TEMPLE OF LIBERTY, on the shoulders of slaves."

Philadelphia's *Gazette of the United States* put it more bluntly. "There are above 500,000 negro slaves in the United States, who have not more voice in the Election of President and Vice-President . . . than 500,000 New-England horses, hogs, and oxen. Yet," the *Gazette* wrote, "their masters for them choose 15 Electors!"

For nearly four decades, every president but one (John Adams) was a Virginia slaveholder. Eighteen of the first justices were at some point slaveholders, including a majority of those who decided the court's 1857 opinion in *Dred Scott v. Sandford*, which held that Black people could never be American citizens.

How could a nation premised on human equality adopt such blatant violations of that principle in its governing charter? In a word, leverage: The southerners cared more about keeping slavery than the northerners did about abolishing it. For the latter, the main concern was preserving the union and establishing a functional central government. This discrepancy gave the southern states the upper hand throughout the negotiations at the convention. Whenever their delegates felt that their power to enslave other humans was even slightly in question, they threatened to abandon the convention or even to make war against their own country. It worked. As Connecticut's Roger Sherman, no friend of slavery, put it succinctly, "it was better to let the southern states import slaves than to part with them, if they made that a sine qua non."

And yet the slaveholders made one small concession that ended up being a key factor in the push toward abolition: The word *slavery* appears nowhere in the Constitution. "Free persons" are mentioned in Article I, and then another group distinct from them—"all other persons."

Leaving out the term itself made no difference to the millions of enslaved people or to the legality of the practice, of course. As Luther Martin later explained, the convention had "anxiously sought to avoid the admission of expressions which might be odious in the ears of Americans, although they were willing to admit into their system those things which the expressions signified." Wilson's law mentor, John Dickinson, wrote in his private journal that the omission would rightly "be regarded as an endeavor to conceal a principle of which we are ashamed."

But there is another way to look at it: that the delegates were effectively writing two different constitutions in the summer of 1787. One accepted current political constraints in the service of winning enough support to be ratified. The other lay in wait, a silent promise that might one day, in the hands of more enlightened generations, be made good.

Wilson would not live to see any of this play out. How might he have responded to it? The practice of human slavery was "repugnant to the principles of natural law," he said in the years after the convention, and yet when it came to drafting the Constitution, he likely would have defended his actions on the same grounds as the other nationalists: We had no choice; it was the price of a union.

12

The Speech in the State House Yard

"THE SEEDS OF REFORMATION"

EXHAUSTED BY THE efforts of the previous four months, Wilson kept a low profile in the two weeks after the signing of the Constitution. If he was hoping for a moment of peace and quiet in which to savor his triumph, however, he wouldn't find it. The next and most critical stage of the entire process, ratification, was already under way.

Ratification would be the ultimate embodiment of Wilson's decades-long vision of popular sovereignty, the most important test yet of his radical theory of democratic government. Instead of a secret conclave behind closed doors and locked windows, Americans would now decide for themselves, in open and local conventions, whether to authorize this new charter as the supreme law of the land.

The importance of this step, both to the beginnings of the nation and to the understanding of James Wilson's life, cannot be overstated. Virtually all American governing charters to that point—state constitutions, amendments to those constitutions, the Articles of Confederation themselves—had been voted on by state legislatures, not regular citizens. (The Massachusetts constitution of 1780 was the notable exception, and became a model for the framers of the federal constitution.) Now those citizens—the white male ones, anyway—would be the deciders. It was the heart of Wilson's transformative philosophy of government. "The streams of power" run in all different directions, Wilson would say at the Pennsylvania ratifying convention, but "they all originally flow from one abundant fountain. In this constitution, all authority is derived from the People."

"We the People"—it was Wilson's phrase and his ideal; and as the process began, he was positioned to play one of the most important roles of anyone in the country. Convincing his fellow delegates over the previous four months had been trying enough; now he had to take his case directly to the public, and put proof to his entire theory of humanity, society, and government.

For Wilson, this generated an undercurrent of anxiety. Opposition to the new Constitution was growing as more Americans got their hands on it, creating battle lines that tracked many of the disputes that had played out all summer behind closed doors. Now those battles burst into the open, driving people into one of two camps: the Federalists, who were in favor of a powerful national government and sought a quick and unqualified ratification, and their opponents, referred to as Anti-Federalists, who brought a range of criticisms to the debate. Many of these critics agreed that the government needed a major overhaul, but they took issue with specific features of the new Constitution, such as its broad grant of power to the federal government and its lack of a bill of rights.

Wilson felt confident that the Federalists would prevail in Pennsylvania, at least, but he also knew any stumble would delay or even derail the entire project. Time was of the essence. Over the next few months, he had two contradictory tasks: declaring his allegiance to the people's voice while countenancing the efforts of his fellow Federalists to prevent Anti-Federalist voices from being fully heard—by force if necessary.

The most notorious example of this happened in late September, when the Pennsylvania Assembly took up the question of whether to hold a ratifying convention. Even though the Assembly now had a pro-Constitution majority, the Federalists were on edge. What happened in Pennsylvania, the country's biggest state, would be hugely significant to the fortunes of the ratification process. The Assembly members who opposed the Constitution knew this, too. When the debate was set to begin, several of them, knowing they were outnumbered, disappeared from the State House, preventing a quorum and stalling the vote. In response, a mob of Federalists went searching for the absconding members. They found them hiding in a nearby boardinghouse, dragged them through the streets back to the State House, and locked the doors to keep them from leaving.

The incident would soon be national news, after the seceding Assembly members published a detailed account of their abduction by the Federalists ("their lodgings were violently broken open, their clothes torn, and after much abuse and insult, they were forcibly dragged through the streets of Philadelphia to the State House, and there detained by force"). "The Federal Mania at present rages in this city with great violence," the *New York Morning Post* reported. It was not the sort of public relations the Federalists needed. But they had acted out of genuine fear. Had Pennsylvania failed even to call a ratifying convention, it would have emboldened the Constitution's opponents around the country and endangered the entire project almost before it could begin.

Wilson's absence from the scene ended on the cool early fall evening of October 6, when a large crowd, tense and excited, gathered in the State House Yard, the block-long shaded park next to which the convention delegates had spent the summer locked indoors. It was a Saturday night and Philadelphians were out in force. The purpose of the gathering was to select candidates for Philadelphia's seats in the Assembly, but many in the crowd were there to see one man: Wilson. He could be spotted sitting on a stage at one end of the yard, his nose in the air, a sheaf of notes clenched in his hands. For the assembled masses, it was a chance to hear one of the city's leading citizens, and one of the Constitution's framers, make the case for it for the first time.

Wilson would be playing defense as much as offense. The previous day, *The Independent Gazetteer* published a long essay condemning the Constitution as the product of "wealthy and ambitious" elites who "think they have a right to lord it over their fellow creatures." The essay was signed by Centinel, the pen name of Samuel Bryan, the son of a Pennsylvania supreme court justice who would become one of the Constitution's most eloquent and well-known critics.

Centinel accused the framers of ramming through a document that demanded close attention and deliberation and of hiding behind the eminence of "the two men in whom America has the highest confidence," meaning George Washington and Benjamin Franklin. Alas, neither man's approbation could be fully trusted in this case, he said. In a string of insults, Centinel mocked the revered Washington as "unsuspecting" and "inexperienced," suggesting he was distracted by "his other arduous engagements." He dismissed the eighty-one-year-old Franklin as a doddering old man afflicted with "the weakness and indecision attendant on old age."

Centinel's broadside would eventually be republished in nineteen newspapers, from the northern states down to Richmond, Virginia. It was one of the first extended critiques of the Constitution to find wide circulation, and it did an effective job of articulating most of the key concerns of its opponents.

Wilson may not have been the ideal person to defend the Constitution from these charges. He was, after all, the epitome of the wealthy elite—awkward, aloof, and unable to connect on an emotional level even with close friends. He had been nearly assassinated for, among other things, his suspected disloyalty to the revolution. And yet perhaps no one other than Wilson could have done it. He was defending a document he had largely authored and that in key respects represented the essence of his political vision. He now had to act not only as a political thinker but also as a salesman. He had paid close attention to the arguments of the Constitution's critics, keeping lists of them so as to answer them in turn. With those lists in hand, he made his way to the podium.

"I confess that I am unprepared for so extensive and so important a disquisition," he said, with a brief nod to Centinel's critique, which many in the crowd had likely already read. He then took up Centinel's most damning charge against the document: its failure to include a bill of rights. Without such a provision, the argument went, the federal constitution was less protective of Americans' liberty than the constitutions already enacted in many states, an argument Wilson now rejected out of hand. State constitutions, he pointed out, protect only those rights that they explicitly name. "Everything which is not reserved is given" to the state legislature, he said. In the federal constitution, however, the opposite is the case: "Everything which is not given, is reserved." A bill of rights makes sense in the first situation, but not the second.

To illustrate the point, he brought up freedom of the press, which Centinel had claimed would cease to exist under the new constitution. Not true, Wilson explained. The government had no power over the press in the first place, so it would be "superfluous and absurd" to make reference to it. "Nay, that very declaration might have been construed to imply that some degree of power was given, since we undertook to define its extent," he said. This was the key dispute between the Federalists and the Anti-Federalists, and Wilson defined its terms. In short, the baseline assumption is that a right exists. Any attempt to enumerate rights would only raise questions about why others were not included—increasing the risk that the government could decide that unenumerated rights didn't exist at all.

It was an argument that Wilson would make repeatedly in the coming months, but the Anti-Federalists were not convinced. They believed that a government, especially a large, centralized one, tends to hoard power and restrict rights where it can, and so it is essential to protect the most precious of those rights in writing. Contrary to Wilson's claim, they pointed out that the Constitution *did* contain certain explicit individual rights—for example, the right to a trial by jury in criminal cases. Under Wilson's logic, why would that right need to be included if the federal government had no power to withhold it in the first place?

One by one, Wilson batted away the other challenges as the pro-Federalist crowd roared in approval. An aristocratic Senate carrying out its own agenda? No, because it can't do anything without the agreement of the House of Representatives and the president. The annihilation of state governments? To the contrary, states play an indispensable role in the selection of all federal elected officials. Direct taxation? A necessary cost of having a Congress that, unlike the current one, can actually "provide for the national safety."

To this point, Wilson had remained studiously technical in explaining the convention's work product. Now, nearing the end, he got personal. "It is the nature of man to pursue his own interest, in preference to the public good," he said, aiming unmistakably at sitting members of the Confederation Congress. Opposition to major reforms like the Constitution was to be expected from anyone who enjoys "a place of profit" under the existing system, he added—"not, in truth, because it is injurious to the liberties of his country, but because it affects his schemes of wealth and consequence." If any Anti-Federalists were mixed in with the enthusiastic crowd, they were fuming.

In the end, Wilson admitted a certain degree of ambivalence about the document he had had a direct hand in drafting, acknowledging his disappointment in the process in which he had been so intimately involved. "I will confess indeed, that I am not a blind admirer of this plan of government, and that there are some parts of it, which if my wish had prevailed, would certainly have been altered," he said, without identifying what they were. Still, he emphasized the final product's capacity for change. "I am satisfied that anything nearer to perfection could not have been accomplished. If there are errors, it should be remembered that the seeds of reformation are sown in the work itself, and the concurrence of two-thirds of the congress may at any time introduce alterations and amendments."

With this evocation of popular sovereignty—if you, the people, don't like our work, you have the power to change it—he drew cascading applause. The Constitution, he concluded, "is the best form of government which has ever been offered to the world."

As it turned out, Wilson's speech was exactly what the Constitution's advocates needed. Most of them hadn't spent the previous four months in constant debate over the new Constitution, and they needed help to argue in its favor. Wilson's habit of keeping lists of opposing arguments and responding to them point by point—the result of a temperamental attention to detail as well as years of legal practice—had the effect of making his speech easy to digest and easy to share in smaller chunks.

Within days, the speech was printed in a special edition of *The Pennsylvania Herald*, whose editor, Alexander Dallas, introduced it as "excellent." "It is the first authoritative explanation of the principles of the NEW FEDERAL CONSTITUTION," Dallas wrote, "and as it may serve to obviate some objections, which have been raised to that system."

In the following weeks, the speech was reprinted in dozens of newspapers around the country, quickly becoming the primary source of arguments for Federalists in the ratification debates taking place in every state.

When George Washington got his copy of the speech at Mount Vernon, he quickly sent it along to David Stuart, one of his friends in the state legislature, as ammunition to use in responding to the criticisms of George Mason, the Virginia delegate who had backed out of signing the Constitution. In his cover note, Washington said Wilson was "as able, candid, & honest a member as any in Convention."

Today, the State House Yard speech has been largely lost to history. When it comes to constitutional advocacy, most Americans learn, nothing is more important than *The Federalist Papers*, the essays and articles written by Hamilton, Madison, and John Jay that were published around the same time. Yet, for all their insight, *The Federalist Papers* had nothing like the influence that Wilson's State House Yard speech did during the ratification period.

Also unlike *The Federalist Papers*, which were published to relatively little fanfare at the time, the State House Yard speech triggered an avalanche of angry and detailed refutations. Many critics took issue with the degree of power proposed for the national government. "The new constitution vests Congress with such unlimited powers as ought never to be entrusted to any men or body of men," one wrote, adding that "the possession of sovereign power is a temptation too great for human nature to resist." Another called Wilson's speech "the best that could be adduced in support of so bad a cause."

Others directed their criticisms at Wilson personally. A writer calling himself "An Officer of the Late Continental Army" (most likely William Findley, who had helped draft Pennsylvania's state constitution in 1776) questioned Wilson's patriotism and, recalling the Fort Wilson Riot, added that "the whole tenor of his political conduct has always been strongly tainted with the spirit of *high aristocracy*."

Centinel derided Wilson's explanation for the lack of a bill of rights as "an insult on the understanding of the people." Like many Anti-Federalists, he had contempt not only for the new Constitution but also for Wilson himself. While the nationalists were broadly disliked by their opponents, Wilson's stiff self-regard had always made him an especially easy target, and Centinel didn't hold back, mocking him as possessing the "transcendent merit" of "Revelation."

For the most part, the critics were not opposed to the Constitution outright; they wanted to slow the process down, debate the document and add amendments to it before voting to ratify it. Robert Whitehill, a drafter of Pennsylvania's 1776 constitution, complained, "I don't know any reason there can be for driving it down our throats, without an hour's preparation."

In a series of six essays that ran in *The New York Journal* through the fall, "Cincinnatus," whom some contemporaries identified as Richard Henry Lee or his brother Arthur, was barely able to contain his anger at Wilson. Quoting Wilson's complaint that the opponents of the Constitution were trying to undermine it through "insidious and clandestine attempts," he responded, "Perhaps these clandestine attempts might have been owing to the terror of *your mob*, which so nobly endeavored to prevent all freedom of action and of speech?"

Cincinnatus derided Wilson's defense of the lack of a bill of rights—specifically, Wilson's memorable line that in the state constitutions, whatever rights are not reserved are given away, but in the new federal constitution, whatever rights are not given away are reserved. "This has more the quaintness of a conundrum, than the dignity of an argument," Cincinnatus wrote.

But what most angered Cincinnatus was Wilson's imputation of self-interest to the Constitution's opponents. This accusation engendered one of the most brutal rhetorical attacks against Wilson of the entire ratification period. It was aimed directly at the central weakness in Wilson's character and his life—his own compulsive speculation in land and the financial ruin he was bringing on himself by engaging in that speculation. So, when Wilson had the nerve to accuse others in politics of being motivated by greed, Cincinnatus pulled no punches. "How could it escape you that this was a two-edged argument, and might cut its inventor," he wrote. "Perhaps these very violent gentlemen for the new establishment may be actuated by the same undue motives. Perhaps some of its framers might have had its honors and emoluments in view. When you have let loose suspicion, Mr. Wilson, there is no knowing where it will end."

Then Cincinnatus went in for the kill. "Perhaps some may be audacious enough to suspect even—*you*. They may think that the emoluments of an attorney generalship, or of a chief justice largely provided for under a government gifted with almost chemic powers to extract gold from the people, might happily repair your shattered fortunes. Let us, Sir, suppose a man fallen from opulence into the most gloomy depths of monied distress, by an unsatiable love of wealth and as unwise a pursuit of it; would not such a man be a fit instrument in the hands of others to agitate the introduction of the new constitution."

13
Ratification

FOR ALL THAT the framers accomplished in the summer of 1787, the convention was only the beginning. They had created a radically new government, yet the Constitution was still a proposal, and an unauthorized one at that. Now it would go to the states, where regular Americans would read it, debate it, and ultimately vote on whether to adopt its powerful national system in what amounted to America's first national election.

This was all part of Wilson's design. As he led the drafting of the Constitution over the summer, he was also setting the stage for its ratification. He avoided the Articles of Confederation's unanimity requirement by pushing for the Constitution to take effect with the support of just 7 states, a bare majority. It was the most extreme position of any delegate, and Wilson fought for it with a degree of urgency matching the proposal. "We must . . . in this case go to the original powers of Society," he said. "The House on fire must be extinguished, without a scrupulous regard to ordinary rights."

In the end, he settled for 9 of 13, which could at least be justified as being the same number required for Congress to exercise its most important powers under the Articles. After the convention, his speech in the State House Yard had launched the Federalist case for the Constitution. Now the ratifying conventions made up of the regular citizens he had championed would be put to the test.

But placing the power in the hands of the people meant letting all voices be heard, even those who vehemently opposed the Constitution. The imbroglio that ensued in the Pennsylvania Assembly suggested that the Federalists were not necessarily prepared to let that happen.

The way the Federalists "are attempting to force the new government upon the people betrays their consciousness of its not bearing the test of impartial examination," George Mason wrote. "They dread a thorough knowledge & public discussion of the subject." Mason had a point. Wilson had insisted on the importance of direct public participation in the adoption of this new Constitution, and yet at the first opportunity to demonstrate their commitment to that principle, his allies had used physical force to ensure that they would get to hold a ratifying convention quickly and on their terms.

As Wilson and the other Federalists were discovering, popular sovereignty was a double-edged sword. It involved listening to the people and accepting the decisions they made. That was not how the Constitution had been created. For all the fierce battles at the convention, the delegates were men of the same station—a few dozen wealthy, highly educated, landowning (and slaveholding) elites who shared a deep interest in the workings of power and the functions of government. They were hardly representative of the mass of Americans at the time, especially those in the more remote reaches of the country, who were far less educated and, for the most part, unaware of the heated debates shaping the nation's new government. Many of those people had "the wildest ideas of government in the world," as Elbridge Gerry put it in opposing popular ratifying conventions.

Some framers foresaw the dangers in the Federalists' strong-arm approach. Edmund Randolph of Virginia, who had refused to sign the Constitution because it had been drafted without public input, wrote that it "ought to have the hearts of the people on its side" and should not be "forced upon them." This, then, was the dilemma that Wilson faced. The popular ratification of the Constitution was the essence of his worldview. It was the people's document, and it was theirs to affirm directly, without the mediating forces of self-interested lawmakers.

And yet, if this was really being done by and for the people, why had the entire process to this point been kept secret from them? Why was it now being pushed through without time for debate? Why were its supporters resorting to violence to pass it? Wilson would find it was harder to reconcile these things than he had expected.

Even before Wilson's State House Yard speech, the public battle over the Constitution was under way; it grew far more heated in the days and weeks to follow, not only in Pennsylvania but throughout the states. The debates ranged from substantive and respectful to petty and insulting. Friends, neighbors, and family members could argue about the finer points of constitutional design or spew the crudest invective. An Anti-Federalist from Pennsylvania asserted that ratification supporters were "half-pay officers, Cincinnati [an elite hereditary society that consisted largely of high-ranking military men], attorneys-at-law, public defaulters, and Jews," while a New York Federalist compared opponents of the Constitution to Yahoos, the apelike creatures in Jonathan Swift's *Gulliver's Travels* who climb into trees and throw their excrement on passersby below.

Newspapers, almost all of which had published the text of the Constitution, were now filled with letters and essays making lengthy arguments on one side or the other. Most publishers were of the same class as the Federalists, and so most of what appeared in their pages was pro-Federalist. In Pennsylvania, newspapers rejected many submissions critical of the Constitution, making it appear as though there was essentially no opposition to the new government. "The newspapers with few exceptions have been devoted to the cause of despotism," wrote Centinel. Even moderate criticisms came in for attack from Federalists, who insisted that a national crisis was no time to be picking nits. "The fate of America depends on the unanimity of all classes of citizens," one Federalist wrote in response to what he called "trivial" challenges. He warned the writer to "choose some other subject" or risk being tarred and feathered.

In early November, on the eve of the vote for the delegates to Pennsylvania's ratifying convention—a vote that would almost certainly determine the final result—the Federalists were getting anxious again. They enjoyed advantages both in the press and in the location of the convention, which was set to be held in Philadelphia, where public sentiment was overwhelmingly in favor of the new Constitution and where people could more easily assemble than in the more remote western counties.

Still, there was no assurance that the document that emerged from months of debate in Philadelphia would be ratified. "I am far from being decided in my opinion that they will consent," Gouverneur Morris wrote to George Washington on October 30. "The city and its neighborhood are enthusiastic in the cause, but I dread the cold and sour temper of the back counties." Madison believed the convention would be "divided," and others predicted that any Federalist victory would be narrow.

As it turned out, the vote for convention delegates on November 6 wasn't close. The Federalists secured a two-to-one majority among the sixty-nine delegates chosen. Anti-Federalists complained that they had lost because their supporters were still in shock at the Constitution and had not yet figured out how to respond. On both sides, emotions were running high. Late on the night of the vote, a mob attacked the Philadelphia homes of several Anti-Federalist leaders as well as Alexander Boyd's boardinghouse, where the sergeant at arms had tracked down the dissenting assemblymen weeks before.

"The windows [were] broken with large stones," William Shippen wrote to his son Thomas Lee Shippen shortly after. Anti-Federalist houses "were attacked by a violent noise and they abused, their wives frightened, etc. Does not this give us a foretaste of this blessed Constitution?"

No newspaper reported on the riot, although three days later the state's Supreme Executive Council directed that a proclamation be issued ordering the apprehension and punishment of the rioters. None was ever caught.

Wilson would be accused by multiple Anti-Federalists of having fomented the riot—"the midnight mob headed by Jemey the

Caledonian," one writer described it—although no evidence that he did ever came to light.

Pennsylvania's ratifying convention opened a short time later, on November 20, making Pennsylvania the first large state to test the public's reaction to the Constitution. It would be in many ways a proxy for the state's politics, which had been bitterly contested for more than a decade. The 1776 Pennsylvania constitution was the most radically democratic in the country and had come under persistent attack from Wilson and his allies, who never stopped pushing for a version with more checks and balances. Meanwhile, its advocates strongly opposed what they saw as the imposition of a far less democratic federal version.

Over the three weeks of the ratifying convention, the proceedings were dominated by one man—James Wilson, who also happened to be the only delegate to have participated in writing the document at issue. Wilson's primary ally was Thomas McKean, the state's chief justice and, to the Anti-Federalists' great consternation, a onetime champion of Pennsylvania's 1776 constitution who came to side with the Federalists once he saw how much it weakened the judiciary.

Wilson and McKean's main antagonists were the same ones who had fought to delay calling the convention in September—William Findley, Robert Whitehill, and John Smilie, a fiery frontiersman from Ireland just two days younger than Wilson. All three had been members of the state assembly and had strongly supported the 1776 constitution; Findley and Whitehill remained in the Assembly, although Smilie had moved on to Pennsylvania's Supreme Executive Council. They agreed that a new, stronger federal constitution was needed, but they were skeptical that they would enjoy the same freedoms under the proposed one; they also resisted the accelerated timeline and all-or-nothing approach of Wilson and the other Federalists.

The Federalists' strategy extended to the recordkeeping of the convention itself. The official journal left out much of the criticism by the Constitution's opponents. The first "full" publication of the debates, by the shorthand reporter Thomas Lloyd, nearly erased the opponents altogether. "A reader might think only Federalists were present," the historian Pauline Maier wrote. "Wilson and McKean seem to be arguing with ghosts."

However successful the Federalists had been in keeping their opponents' arguments out of wide circulation, Wilson was well aware that many Anti-Federalists despised him and his constitution. By the time the ratifying convention officially began, Wilson had seen enough of his opponents' persistence to know that he couldn't leave anything to chance. Even with a two-to-one majority of delegates, he insisted on controlling the debate and responding to objections. "Nothing was done or said" without Wilson's direction, one Federalist delegate recounted in a letter published in *The Independent Gazetteer* a few days after the ratification vote. "None of our party attempted to argue except him," the delegate added. "If we had not put him in our Convention, the business would have been lost."

The opposition centered on a few basic themes: the alarming speed with which the Federalists were trying to push the Constitution through, the vast expansion of the federal government's powers compared to the Articles of Confederation, the elimination of annual elections, the lack of an enumerated right to a jury in civil cases, and, above all, the absence of a bill of rights. Wilson was confident he could parry all these criticisms by focusing on his paramount theme—the power of the people that the new document enshrined.

Government "has hitherto been the result of force, fraud, or accident," he said in his opening speech, but the constitution under debate represented the first time in the history of the world that a people had been "assembled to weigh deliberately and calmly, and to decide leisurely and peaceably, upon the form of government by which they will bind themselves and their posterity."

While there were many different governmental designs to choose from, Wilson pointed out, the key question was who held the ultimate power. "There necessarily exists in every government a power from which there is no appeal; and which, for that reason, may be termed supreme, absolute, and uncontrollable. Where does this power reside?"

"The truth is," he said, "that, in our governments, the supreme, absolute, and uncontrollable power remains in the people. As our constitutions are superior to our legislatures; so the people are superior to our constitutions," with the consequence "that the people may change the constitutions whenever and however they please. This is a right, of which no positive institution can ever deprive them."

Without accepting the great truth of popular sovereignty, Wilson said, "we shall never be able to understand the principle on which this system was constructed."

Those who watched Wilson in action that day resorted to classical allusions to describe the "astonishment" that followed his speech. "The powers of Demosthenes and Cicero seemed to be united in this able orator," Francis Hopkinson wrote to Thomas Jefferson.

Wilson's opponents had a different perspective. Centinel called Wilson and his allies "aspiring despots" who hoped "to gull" the people out of their liberties. Responding to a claim that the state governments would still exist in a meaningful way under the new government, he accused Wilson of constructing "mazes of sophistry . . . that exist only in his own fertile imagination."

What really angered the Anti-Federalists was the apparent hypocrisy of Wilson's commitment to popular rule. What, exactly, did he mean when he said the people can change the constitution whenever they please, when the people were now finding themselves forced to weigh in on the proposed one on the terms and timing set by its proponents?

"We were repeatedly told of the peculiar advantages which we enjoy in being able deliberately and peaceably to decide upon a government for ourselves and our posterity," John Smilie said. So why was it that "every measure that is proposed leads to defeat those advantages and to preclude all argument and deliberation?" The federal convention had "consumed four months in framing" the Constitution, he reminded the assembled crowd. "Shall we not employ a few days in deciding upon it?"

Robert Whitehill was no happier with the Federalists' "precipitancy," as Smilie had put it. He proposed dissolving into a committee of the whole, which would allow for extended debate on every part of the Constitution, without the convention's rules or speeches being recorded in the minutes. The proposal was shot down 44–24, on a party-line vote.

Smilie then warned the Federalists that even if they ratified the Constitution, Pennsylvanians would not be obliged to accept it, especially if it had not been properly and thoroughly vetted. Indeed, the citizens of the state had the right to call "another body to consult upon other measures and either in the whole, or in part, to abrogate this federal work so ratified." Wasn't this exactly what James Wilson had told them they had the right to do? Yes, but the Federalists weren't about to concede the point.

Soon the debate turned to the absence of a bill of rights—the one complaint that virtually all opponents of the Constitution agreed on. Wilson was adamant, as he had been from the beginning, that a bill of rights was not only unnecessary but dangerous, given that all powers that were not explicitly given to the federal government were implicitly withheld from it.

To illustrate the point, Wilson drew the convention's attention to the words he had placed so deliberately at the beginning of the Constitution: "We the People of the United States." "It is announced in their name. It receives its political existence from their authority," he said. He then reached out for what he knew would be an emotionally laden comparison—"the striking difference," he said, between the written American Constitution and the unwritten British one, which was based on the rights and liberties outlined in the Magna Carta.

"From what source does that instrument derive the liberties of the inhabitants of that kingdom?" he asked. "Let it speak for itself. The king says, '*We* have *given* and *granted* to all archbishops, bishops, abbots, priors, earls, barons, and to all the freemen of this our realm, these liberties following, to be kept in our kingdom of England forever.'" But those rights, however grandly they were proclaimed, were still given by a superior power—and anything that is given can be taken back. "No wonder," Wilson went on, "that the people were anxious to obtain bills of rights, and to take every opportunity of enlarging and securing their liberties!" In contrast, Americans' rights are not given to them, but inherent in them; the federal government established by the Constitution could never take those rights away.

Once again, the Anti-Federalists were less than convinced. Robert Whitehill pointed out that the words "We the People," far from ensuring any rights, in fact destroyed "the old foundation of the Union," which was the sovereignty and independence of the thirteen states. When the convention proposed to move forward, John Smilie objected. He "had not yet got over the first six words of the Preamble," he said.

Undeterred, Wilson turned to the next phrase of the preamble, "do ordain and establish"—which was as important to him as any part of the Constitution. "Those who can ordain and establish may certainly repeal or annul the work of government, which, in the hands of the people, is like clay in the hands of the potter and may be molded into any shape they please." It was a curious metaphor—like his imagery of the streams of power, it evoked pliancy. That was not how the Anti-Federalists saw it. To them, the Constitution was a hard, immovable object. "If the people are jealous of their rights, where will be the harm in declaring them?" asked "A Federal Republican" in a pamphlet published the same day.

This was a fair question. Why was Wilson so unwilling to compromise on a bill of rights, if that was what the people demanded? Did he truly believe that one was not necessary? Or was he afflicted with tunnel vision after spending a summer hashing out every last detail of the Constitution? Either way, his attitude did not evince the sort of trust in the people that he spoke of so earnestly.

On December 1, Wilson took up another major charge by the Anti-Federalists: that there was no way for a "supreme" federal government to coexist with the states. "The secret is now disclosed," he said mockingly. Then, more seriously, he asked, "Upon what principle is it contended that the sovereign power resides in the state governments?"

William Findley, he pointed out, had said there is no such thing as "subordinate sovereignty," which gave him the chance to reiterate his core point. "My position is that the sovereignty resides in the people. They have not parted with it; they have only dispensed such portions of power as were conceived necessary for the public welfare. This Constitution stands upon this broad principle."

In other words, he was saying, stop worrying about whether the power resides in the states or in the national government; it resides in one place only: the people. A few days later, on December 4, he tied it all together. "I consider the people of the United States, as forming one great community; and I consider the people of the different states, as forming communities again on a lesser scale," he said. Then, as he had during the Constitutional Convention, he pulled out a copy of the Declaration of Independence and began reading from its opening lines—lines he had inspired a dozen years earlier. Emphasizing the words "it is the *right* of the people to alter or to abolish" any government that doesn't work, Wilson concluded, "This is the broad basis on which our independence was placed; on the same certain and solid foundation this system is erected." Linking the Declaration and the Constitution was something Wilson would persist in doing through the rest of his life, and to a degree unmatched by any of his peers. To him, the documents were inseparable. Both were based on the power of the people to decide their own fate.

But Wilson's commitment to popular sovereignty was not as simple as he made it sound. He still believed that certain people were inherently suited to lead. In the afternoon session of December 4, he responded to a comment made earlier in the day by John Smilie, who was concerned that a "natural aristocracy" would inevitably rule America.

"What is meant by a natural aristocracy?" Wilson began. "When we trace it to the language from which it is derived, an aristocracy means nothing more or less than a government of the best men in the community"—that is, "those most noted for wisdom and virtue." He asked, "Is there any danger in such representation?"

To Wilson, a "natural" aristocracy was indeed distinct from the

old-fashioned kind, the one in which "the supreme power is not retained by the people but resides in a select body of men" who "succeed
on the principle of descent, or by virtue of territorial possessions, or
some other qualifications that are not the result of personal proper-
ties." Of course the lowborn son of a farmer, one who came to America and achieved legal, political, and financial glory through his wits
alone, would see the world in this way. But it also fit nicely with Wilson's fellow Federalists' conception of self-government, which they
believed depended on the leadership of only the best men.

This perspective also allowed him to justify his own actions as a
"natural" aristocrat who professed to speak on behalf of the people.
"I apprehend it is of more consequence to be able to know the true
interest of the people than their faces," Wilson said. For a man who
lived so much in the realm of the mind, who so rarely looked into
the eyes of the real-life people he championed, it would have been a
fitting epitaph.

Throughout the first two weeks of December, Wilson spoke constantly
and insistently in defense of the Constitution. He defended its allowance of slavery by pointing to the provision that gave Congress the
authority to ban the importation of slaves in 1808. He defended its
convoluted mechanism for selecting the president, a system of electors positioned between the people and the presidency. And he admitted that it had not been a smooth process. "The Convention, sir,
were perplexed with no part of this plan so much as with the mode
of choosing the President of the United States." He said he thought a
direct popular vote was "the most unexceptionable mode, next after
the one prescribed in this Constitution." This was a minor fib: Wilson
did not in fact prefer the mode in the Constitution, and supported
it only when the popular vote failed to gain backers. But now he was
selling the package as a whole, and it was no time to revisit old gripes.
Either way, he concluded, "it was the opinion of a great majority in
convention that the thing was impracticable." He added, in a subtle
dig at the southerners, "other embarrassments presented themselves."

As the convention neared its end, Wilson, exhausted from weeks of leading the charge, began to make uncharacteristic mistakes. When he and McKean made a factual error about the history of jury trials in Sweden, the Anti-Federalists gleefully corrected them. "What a stroke to the pride of two men who think themselves the greatest in the United States!" one wrote. The Anti-Federalists would take their victories where they could get them.

"I do not pretend to remember everything I read," Wilson said the next day in defending himself, before quoting the famous line "'Young man, I have forgotten more law than ever you learned.'"

Shaking off the embarrassment, he then offered his most fulsome tribute to the document he had just created. "By adopting this system, we become a NATION," he said. "At present we are not one. Can we perform a single national act? Can we do anything to procure us dignity or to preserve peace and tranquility? Can we relieve the distress of our citizens? Can we provide for their welfare or happiness?" Wilson asked.

"As we shall become a nation," he continued, "I trust that we shall also form a national character, and that this character will be adapted to the principles and genius of our system of government."

The Anti-Federalists were shifting in their seats, but Wilson was already dreaming of a future in which American democracy became the model for the entire world, a future that in so many ways he anticipated more accurately than any of his peers.

He concluded with what was, for him, a stab at humility. "I feel myself lost in the contemplation of its magnitude. By adopting this system, we shall probably lay a foundation for erecting temples of liberty in every part of the earth. It has been thought by many, that on the success of the struggle America has made for freedom will depend the exertions of the brave and enlightened of other nations."

The next day, the Anti-Federalists tried once more to adjourn the convention, hoping to buy some time in which they (and their allies in other states) might be able to introduce amendments for consideration. The Federalists quickly rejected this, and the vote on ratification was held. It passed 46 to 23. Pennsylvania had become the first large state to adopt the new Constitution.

14
Aftermath

"THESE DOMINEERING DESPOTS"

THE DECISIVE VICTORY for ratification in Philadelphia should have been James Wilson's crowning achievement. He had guided the first big state to endorse the Constitution; had the Pennsylvania effort failed, it is hard to say what would have happened. As it was, in three other big states—Massachusetts, Virginia, and New York—ratification succeeded by razor-thin margins. At Virginia's convention, Patrick Henry excoriated Wilson's opening words to the preamble, and the presumptuousness of the delegates in agreeing to them. "Who authorized them to speak the language of, *We the people*, instead of, *We the states?*" he demanded to know. "States are the characteristics and the soul of a confederation."

But Wilson's eloquence and confidence in parrying the Constitution's critics gave energy to his allies and created the framework that Federalists in every state would rely on over the coming months, ensuring the adoption of the national charter. In short, without Wilson's energy, clarity, and eloquence, there might not have been a United States of America after 1788.

And yet something had happened to Wilson during those three weeks in the State House. The central animating principle of his life had been put to the test, and he had prevailed—but it had not worked in practice the way it had in his theories. The people, as it turned out, had lots of different ideas about how to run a country, if only you asked them. Wilson could have celebrated this as the ideal expression of his worldview; instead, his "dictatorial" side came out.

Meanwhile, the resistance to the new government showed no sign of fading. As the months wore on, the critics grew only more persistent, and their criticisms more pointed. One of the most common was the fear of the power the framers were arrogating to themselves through their creation of the new government.

"These lawyers, and men of learning, and moneyed men, that talk so finely, and gloss over matters so smoothly," said Amos Singletary, a Massachusetts Anti-Federalist, would "get into Congress themselves" and would become "the managers of this Constitution, and get all the power and all the money into their own hands, and then they will swallow up all us little folks."

One of the most colorful denunciations came from Wilson's old antagonist Luther Martin, who pointed to the establishment of a standing army as one of the Constitution's greatest threats to state sovereignty. Using a metaphor he credited to Elbridge Gerry, Martin compared the Federalists' conduct toward the states to that of jockeys breaking in young colts. "They begin with the appearance of kindness, giving them a lock of hay, or a handful of oats, and stroking them while they eat," he said. Gradually, they add halters, bridles, saddles, and finally whips, until the horses "soon become as tame and passive as their masters could wish them."

Attacks on the Federalists also played out in the streets. The day after Christmas 1787, a group of Federalists gathered in the center of Carlisle, where Wilson had begun his legal career two decades earlier, to celebrate ratification with a parade. The parade was scheduled for five that afternoon in the town square. But armed Anti-Federalists swarmed the square, setting on the crowd and burning a copy of the new Constitution as the revelers scattered. As Centinel himself recounted, "it was laughable to see Lawyers, Doctors, Colonels, Captains etc. etc. leave the scene of their rejoicing in such haste."

The Federalists returned the following day, now armed with

bayonets and muskets, and completed their celebratory march. The Anti-Federalists waited for the parade to finish before dragging out two effigies, both dressed in robes and ruffled shirts, bearing the nameplates Thomas McKean and James de Caledonia, the latter a pejorative for Wilson. They carried the effigies aloft through the town square and, "with shouts and most dreadful execrations, committed them to the flames."

That's how "An Old Man," a pro-Federalist writer, told the story, anyway. On January 9, the *Gazette* published another letter, signed by "One of the People," an Anti-Federalist who had been among the crowd that confronted the Federalists and who railed against the "vein of misrepresentation and falsehood" that ran through "An Old Man's" account. He argued that the Federalists constituted "an unhallowed riotous mob," and when told their position "was contrary to the minds of three-fourths of the inhabitants, and must therefore produce bad consequences if they persisted," replied that they were going to fire their cannon anyway, "and if they would not clear the way, they would blow them up in the air."

The writer acknowledged that the Anti-Federalists had burned effigies of "two of the most distinguished characters in the state," McKean and Wilson. But instead of praising them, he called out Wilson with every epithet Wilson had earned over the past decade, including "his cowardice and timidity in the day of trial, for his opposition to the independence of America; and for inventing every possible scheme to destroy the liberty of her citizens."

The author of "One of the People" was William Petrikin, a local tailor. Like Wilson, he was a Scottish immigrant, but unlike Wilson, he firmly opposed the new Constitution and was insulted at the implication that he and other Anti-Federalists were uneducated simpletons. "Teach these domineering despots," Petrikin wrote, "that you perceive their designs, that you can both read and understand their constitution, and spurn it with contempt."

Petrikin then went directly after Wilson, referring to "the midnight mob headed by Jemey the Caledonian, who attacked the lodgings of the western members of Assembly and Council, on the night of the elections for convention men." The hard feelings had not abated. Indeed, Petrikin went on, "were it not for the mob the new constitution would not yet have been adopted in Pennsylvania."

News of the Carlisle attack spread up and down the Eastern Seaboard, evoking unpleasant memories of Shays's Rebellion. Within weeks, twenty-one of the Anti-Federalists involved in the riot were arrested and taken to the Cumberland County jail. When the judge offered to release them on bail, fourteen accepted, but seven, including William Petrikin, refused to leave on principle.

Over the coming days, a standoff developed as Anti-Federalists organized a militia in preparation for the "rescuing" of the remaining prisoners. At the last minute, a group of Carlisle citizens made up of Federalists and Anti-Federalists, desperate to keep the peace, joined together to sign a petition seeking the release of the remaining prisoners and dropping all charges against them. The petition was granted, after which the militia marched into town to retrieve the seven prisoners.

The Carlisle riot turned out to be among the most dramatic examples of the deep-seated anger felt by critics of the Constitution and the way it was ratified. It also illustrated a core contradiction in James Wilson's theory of government. He had devoted his life and work to the idea that regular people were the font of all political power and no less wise than the wealthiest elites, that the will of the majority of the people should "in all questions" prevail. And yet here were the people themselves—many, like Wilson, raised in poverty— telling him in the clearest possible terms that they knew what sort of government they wanted and that a majority of them agreed that the Constitution currently being rammed down their throats wasn't it. They saw the efforts of Wilson and the other Federalists not as a vindication of their supposed sovereignty but as a sign of contempt for it.

Did Wilson believe his own words? When confronted with the discrepancy between his theory and the reality on the ground, which would he choose? He had powerful things to say about the people being in charge, and yet when the people attempted to use that power, he balked. Was he, as Centinel had put it, just like all the other "wealthy and ambitious" elites who "think they have a right to lord it over their fellow creatures"? Did Wilson fear that there might be such a thing as too much democracy after all? To go by his public speeches, he did not.

On July 4, 1788, Wilson gave the keynote address at a celebration in Philadelphia marking the adoption of the Constitution, which had been made official a few weeks earlier, when New Hampshire became the ninth and decisive state to ratify it. Earlier that morning, Wilson had marched in a grand procession holding the Pennsylvania state flag, alongside representatives of the other states that had ratified the Constitution. In his speech, he refrained from reprising the point-by-point rebuttals of the Anti-Federalists that had occupied so much of his previous fall, focusing instead on the wisdom of the people.

"A people free and enlightened, establishing and ratifying a system of government which they have previously considered, examined and approved! This is the spectacle which we are assembled to celebrate," he began, following with a string of references to the great governments of the ancient world—Greece, Rome, Egypt—and contending that the American one bested them all.

He then described the ratification process, during which, he claimed, the Constitution "was laid before the people. It was discussed and scrutinized in the fullest, freest, and severest manner—by speaking, by writing, and by printing—by individuals and by public bodies—by its friends and by its enemies." Such a depiction would surely have come as news to any of the Anti-Federalists in the crowd, no less than his claim, during the ratification debates, that the people "can sit as calmly and deliberate as coolly, in order to change a constitution, as a legislature can sit and deliberate under the power of a constitution, in order to alter or amend a law."

But Wilson had won this one, and he did not waste the chance to revel in his victory. After emphasizing the importance of a virtuous citizenry, he wound up his remarks on his favorite topic, voting—a "momentous part" of the new system that "every citizen will frequently be called to act." This was the ultimate expression of the people's sovereignty, and it was as valuable as any king's edict. "Let no one say that he is but a single citizen, and that his ticket will be but one in the box. That one ticket may turn the election."

It was a stirring call, and yet the resistance to the new Constitution had not abated. That same day, a couple of hundred miles to the north, a band of about fifty Anti-Federalists gathered in a vacant lot on the outskirts of Albany, New York, where Fort Frederick had once stood. After firing thirteen guns, they produced a copy of the Constitution and set it on fire. A much larger group of Federalists heard what had happened and began their own march, brandishing a pine tree on top of which they had tied a copy of the Constitution and setting it at the spot where the Anti-Federalists had burned the Constitution.

When they reached Green Street, a narrow alley with a local tavern where the Anti-Federalists were getting drunk, the Federalists were warned to stop. A fight broke out. There were "swords, bayonets, clubs, stones, etc.," according to one account, and the fighting did not end until the more numerous Federalists chased their adversaries into a safe house, leaving dozens wounded.

The people were asserting their sovereignty in all sorts of ways, whether Wilson was listening or not.

15

The Supreme Court

"A SUBJECT OF MUCH IMPORTANCE TO ME"

By the beginning of 1789, James Wilson was sitting on top of a world he had played a central role in creating.

He had largely led the design and ratification of his country's Constitution, which was premised on his unique vision of popular rule. His convention colleague George Washington was in the process of being elected the United States' first president, cementing Federalist control of the new national government. Wilson's law practice was earning him large amounts of money, he was buying more land almost daily, and his six children—Mary, the oldest, was now sixteen—were healthy, growing, and beginning to venture out into the world.

No one would have begrudged him had he chosen to spend the rest of his life in a house in the country—a Mount Vernon, Montpelier, or Monticello—and lived out his years in relative calm and quiet. But Wilson could not conceive of that life. His frantic energy had brought him this far, and he wasn't going to slow down now. Already he was mapping out his next steps, looking for opportunities for the world to properly recognize his legal stature as well as his political acumen. The first could be satisfied by a top position in the new federal government—chief justice of the United States. The second would happen when he had the opportunity to redress his bitterest political defeat, the Pennsylvania constitution enacted in 1776, which he viewed as a lingering affront to his carefully worked-out principles of government.

For the Scottish immigrant who had enjoyed such success in his new home, both goals seemed eminently achievable. In the case of the court, it started with a letter that arrived on George Washington's desk in the days before he was due to be sworn in as the first president on April 30, 1789. Among the piles of well-wishes, offers of lodging, and job recommendations, the letter must have stood out to the punctilious general. Other than Wilson's beseeching love letters to Rachel, it may have been the most personally vulnerable thing the proud Scot ever wrote, conveying in the strained protocol of its few sentences a lifetime's worth of ambition and yearning.

"A delicacy arising from your situation and character as well as my own has hitherto prevented me from mentioning to your Excellency a subject of much importance to me," Wilson began. With "a regard to the dignity of the government over which you preside," he continued in his precise, flowing hand, "I . . . inform you that my aim rises to the important office of Chief Justice of the United States."

In fact, Washington did not yet preside over the government. It had been only two weeks since the first Congress had certified his election; it would be another nine days before he was inaugurated. But in Wilson's mind, there wasn't a moment to waste.

His urgency was understandable. Wilson was the best and wealthiest and most respected lawyer in America. He had had a central hand in designing the government he now sought to serve at the highest level, and he believed it was his due. He understood, perhaps better than anyone else, how that government should function. The job would also pay four thousand dollars per year, five hundred dollars more than the associate justices earned—a not insignificant difference to a man who was spending every penny.

But this was a uniquely delicate appeal to make, so Wilson had to mask his overwhelming sense of entitlement with a patina of false modesty. "But how shall I now proceed?" he wrote. "Shall I enumerate reasons in justification of my high pretensions? I have not yet employed my pen in my own praise. When I make those high pretensions, and offer them to so good a judge, can I say, that they are altogether without foundation? Your Excellency must relieve me from the Dilemma. You will think and act properly on the occasion without my saying anything on either side of the question."

Wilson was far from alone in presuming his appointment was a done deal. Weeks before he wrote to Washington, *The Federal Gazette* celebrated his imminent ascension to high office: "It is with singular pleasure we hear that James Wilson, esq. of this state, is destined by the voice of many thousand federalists, to fill the station of CHIEF JUSTICE of the UNITED STATES." A friend wrote prematurely to congratulate him on "an appointment, so generally acknowledged, due to your professional and other merits." The financier Robert Morris, who was believed to be as close as anyone to the incoming president, was working behind the scenes to ensure Wilson's appointment.

And Benjamin Rush, the doctor and Wilson's close friend, had written to the incoming vice president, John Adams, citing Wilson's commitment to the Federalist cause, "his abilities and knowledge in framing the Constitution, and his zeal in promoting its establishment." Rush then added, in a telling aside, "Much will be said of the deranged state of his affairs. But where will you find an American landholder free from embarrassments?"

Adams's reply was unenthusiastic. "If I had a vote, I could not promise to give it for him to be Chief Justice," he wrote. Wilson should be on the court, Adams agreed, but in his mind, John Jay was the best man for the top job. Adams took offense at what he considered Rush's implication that Wilson was owed support. "I am not obliged to vote for a man because he voted for me," he wrote.

Others were blunter in their distaste for a Chief Justice Wilson. "It is the opinion of *many thousands* of Federalists, throughout the United States, that he is not the proper person for that high and important office," an article in *The New-York Journal* read. "There are characters in the other states of the union, as well as in that of Pennsylvania, who are more deserving of it, on account of their abilities, and from their principles and manners being more republican than those of Mr. Wilson." Ten years after his defense of those accused of treason and the mob attack on his house, Wilson could not shake his reputation as a Tory sympathizer.

As it turned out, Adams's prickly reaction was a harbinger of Washington's response in the first week of May. The president's tone was always scrupulously formal, but his letter to Wilson carried something more—almost a scolding. "To you, my dear sir, and others who know me, I presume it will be unnecessary for me to say that I have entered upon my office without the constraint of a single *engagement*."

Wilson knew this was a pointed rebuke, made even more so because of the nature of his appeal—presumptuous to a degree one historian described as "generally done by law school graduates seeking positions with law firms," not by potential chief justices. The insult might have cut even deeper had Wilson seen the nearly identical letter Washington sent the same day to Thomas McKean, the Pennsylvania chief justice and Wilson's former ally in the ratification debates, who also asked the incoming president for an appointment to the court.

In the end, Washington picked the man who had declined his offer to be secretary of state—John Jay. Jay's qualifications were beyond doubt—in addition to serving as foreign affairs secretary, he had been chosen as president of the Second Continental Congress and an early chief justice of the New York high court. In the aftermath of the Constitution's signing, he coauthored *The Federalist Papers* with Alexander Hamilton and James Madison. In many respects, his life paralleled Wilson's—born three years apart, both began their legal studies, got married, and had six children around the same time. Both served in the Continental Congress and would play a key role in drafting their home state's constitution. But unlike Wilson, who had had a peasant upbringing, Jay was born into great wealth, his childhood spent in a large house in the enclave of Rye, New York, where he was taught by private tutors.

Jay was also no match for Wilson when it came to legal intellect—making the decision sting that much more—but for Washington, that was less important than other considerations, including political prominence, Federalist commitments, and personal character. Jay was the clear choice on that final count. His sense of propriety was so pervasive as to make him balk at offers of free lodging during the justices' frequent travels, for fear of the appearance of a conflict of interest.

In a letter to Jay following the nomination, Washington expressed his confidence that Jay had "the talents, knowledge and integrity which are so necessary to be exercised at the head of that department which must be considered as the Keystone of our political fabric." "Integrity"—a tacit swipe, perhaps, at Wilson and "the deranged state of his affairs."

Washington filled out the remaining seats on the first Supreme Court with an eye toward legal experience and geographic diversity. All the initial nominees, with the exception of Wilson, had previous judicial experience. William Cushing had been chief justice of Massachusetts; John Blair was chief justice of Virginia; John Rutledge had served on the chancery court of South Carolina; and Robert Hanson Harrison had been chief judge of the Maryland General Court. Harrison never took his seat, falling ill en route to the court's first term and dying soon after. In his place, Washington nominated James Iredell, who had immigrated to Edenton, North Carolina, from England in the years before the Revolution.

On October 5, 1789, ten years and a day after he escaped his house in the middle of the night following a mob attack, Wilson stood before Samuel Powel, the mayor of Philadelphia, and swore his oath to serve as associate justice on the first US Supreme Court. For Wilson, it was at once a moment of gratifying success and profound frustration.

The justices met for the first time on February 1, 1790, at the Exchange Building on Water Street, a block from the Hudson River at the southern tip of Manhattan. For the first two years, they heard almost no cases. But several high-profile matters soon reached the court, and Wilson would be, in one way or another, at the center of nearly all of them.

The first raised the most fundamental question of all: What powers did the Supreme Court possess? Did it have the authority to rule on the constitutionality of laws passed by Congress?

The law in question was called the Invalid Pensions Act, which Congress passed in March 1792 to ensure that injured Revolutionary War veterans would receive financial assistance. Under the law, a veteran who wished to claim benefits had to make his case to a circuit court. If the court determined that he was entitled to a pension, it had to submit his name and a recommendation of the amount of the pension to the secretary of war. The secretary then had the power to make a factual finding either accepting or reversing the circuit court's decision.

This did not sit right with the judges. Within weeks of its passage, the law came before two different circuit courts, in New York and Pennsylvania. In June, it arrived at the North Carolina circuit court as well. In each court, two of the circuit-riding justices, joined by a district judge, examined the law and agreed that it violated a basic principle of the separation of powers. Court decisions cannot be examined, much less overruled, by another branch of government.

This is what judicial review means: that the courts exist to pass judgment on the constitutionality of acts by the other branches, not to be judged by them. It was at the heart of Wilson's vision for a supreme national court. A government based on the separation of powers would be undermined without it.

Wilson had explicitly made this point at the Pennsylvania ratifying convention five years earlier. Because the Constitution is "paramount to the power of the legislature acting under that Constitution," he argued, Congress might "transgress the bounds assigned to it" by passing a law in conflict with the Constitution. If such a law were to come before the justices, and if they were to "consider its principles and find it to be incompatible with the superior power of the Constitution, it is their duty to pronounce it void."

Alexander Hamilton had echoed this in *Federalist* no. 78, arguing that courts were necessary to keep legislators "within the limits assigned to their authority."

A thornier issue was how to convey this message about the Invalid Pensions Act to Congress and the White House in a politically acceptable manner. Nothing was written down, and there was as yet no protocol for striking down a law of Congress. Out of respect for the dignity of the other branches, all three circuit courts chose to write directly to the president and explain their views. In New York and North Carolina, there was no petitioner involved, only the law itself, and the judges in both cases bent over backward to be polite. Even as they intimated that the law was unconstitutional, they did not use that word. Chief Justice Jay, sitting on the New York circuit, emphasized the court's respect for Congress and the sympathetic nature of the law's subjects ("exceedingly benevolent," as he put it). In Pennsylvania, it was a different story. There, Wilson and Blair were the justices sitting on circuit, and they had before them an actual person seeking federal money, a veteran named William Hayburn. On April 11, they announced their opinion from the bench. Going farther than their colleagues on the other circuits, they said they would not even hear Hayburn's petition.

"It is a principle important to freedom that in government, the judicial should be distinct from and independent of the legislative department," read the Pennsylvania court's letter to Washington, which was almost certainly written by Wilson. "To this important principle the people of the United States, in forming their Constitution, have manifested the highest regard. They have placed their judicial power not in Congress, but in 'courts.'"

Refusing to consider Hayburn's petition "was far from being pleasant," Wilson wrote in a minor concession to political expediency. "To be obliged to act contrary either to the obvious directions of Congress or to a constitutional principle, in our judgment equally obvious, excited feelings in us which we hope never to experience again."

Wilson's letter could be seen as a landmark in Supreme Court history—proof that the court in fact possessed the power to strike down acts of Congress. And that was the general understanding of what had happened at the time. *The General Advertiser* edition of April 12 described the judges' opinion as "the first instance in which a court of justice has declared a law of Congress to be unconstitutional."

In driving this outcome, Wilson effectively established the principle of judicial review, creating the Supreme Court largely as we know it today. And yet, because *Hayburn's Case* played out in the lower circuit courts and Wilson and the other judges issued no written opinions, it is missing from the history books. Another decade would pass before the court would invoke the principle plainly enough for it to endure. In *Marbury v. Madison*, decided in 1803, Chief Justice John Marshall stated that "it is emphatically the duty of the Judicial Department to say what the law is"—in other words, to strike down unconstitutional laws. In the centuries since, the decision in *Marbury* has stood as the most consequential of all the court's rulings. Few are aware that a decade earlier, James Wilson tried to do the same thing—once again anticipating where the country was headed well before it got there.

The early 1790s gave Wilson an opportunity to settle his political scores as well as his legal ones. As he took his seat on the Supreme Court, he was about to help rewrite the Pennsylvania constitution of 1776, which he despised as much as he had when it was drafted.

The radicals who had succeeded in getting that constitution passed genuinely believed that it represented the apex of popular sovereignty—the notion at the heart of the Declaration of Independence that had been signed earlier the same year. If the people were the source of all power, then what better way to instantiate that fact than to remove all obstacles to the exercise of that power? To Wilson, it was the reverse: The 1776 state constitution had subverted the essence of his most cherished principle by establishing a weak executive panel (not even a single person!) and a unicameral legislature with nearly unchecked power. This opened the door to precisely the sort of corruption and even tyranny that the framers had later worked so hard to avoid at the national level.

It was a fundamental debate over the nature of self-government, and Wilson was sure he had the better of it. The good news for him and other opponents of the 1776 charter was that it had never been popular. In fact the arguments over it had persisted almost without cease since the moment it became law. Wilson and his fellow republicans had attempted to replace the constitution multiple times through the 1780s, without success. Now, with a federal constitution in place, and with Pennsylvania enjoying the distinction of the first large state to ratify it, the pressure to bring the state into line increased.

In March 1789, a group of republicans in the state assembly proposed a resolution that amending and altering the state constitution was "immediately necessary." Their rationale for such a dramatic shift? "The people have at all times an inherent right to alter and amend the form of government, in such manner as they shall think proper; and also . . . they are not and cannot be limited to any certain rule or mode of accomplishing the same." It was a classic Wilsonian argument and one that no doubt rankled the radicals who had used it more than a decade earlier.

The proposal passed easily, and a convention to amend the state constitution was set for November; only weeks before that, the state held its annual elections, and republicans were swept into power. The Pennsylvania constitution would be rewritten, this time with the advocates of reform in charge and with the US Constitution as their model.

The result, which became final the following September, would incorporate most of the features of the US Constitution: a bicameral legislature with enumerated powers; a single executive with a veto to check lawmakers; and a judiciary with fixed salaries and life tenure—in other words, one that did not depend on the generosity of the legislature and could not be voted out, making it a more effective check on both the executive and the legislature. It would not, notably, be sent to the people for ratification. The sense was that the public was solidly in favor of constitutional reform, and indeed, there was no significant dissent over the final product.

Once again, Wilson would play a central role in the crafting of a constitution. Among the sixty-two signers, his name was at the top. But now he was not simply advocating for his preferred theoretical outcome; he was doing the work of a seasoned politician, negotiating with adversaries to achieve something that was, if not perfect, at least far closer to the ideal in his mind.

To do this, he had to walk a careful path. On the one hand, he insisted on checks and balances, which the radicals who crafted the 1776 constitution had rejected. On the other hand, he insisted on direct elections, the prospect of which unnerved many of his peers. They believed in barriers to popular participation in government, such as by interposing specially chosen electors between voters and state senators. Wilson's lifelong philosophy of trusting in the people recoiled at this approach.

He found an unlikely ally in William Findley, the radical who was one of his biggest nemeses from 1776. Both men believed that all power emanates from regular people; the issue was how to ensure that power would be exercised for the benefit of society.

The only way the people at large could be properly heard was through direct elections, Wilson said in a speech to the convention on December 31. That immediacy between voter and representative created a trust "of the most intimate and important kind." That trust would be "wholly destroyed" if the republicans got their way. "Can a trust subsist without some mutual agreement or consent? Can responsibility, resulting from an election, operate in behalf of those who do not choose?" he asked.

"Every degree of removal is attended with a corresponding degree of danger."

And for the people to be able to hold up their end of this trust, they had to be able to cast a ballot. Wilson then launched into one of the most vibrant defenses of the right to vote from the founding era. "In order to impart the true republican lustre to freemen, I know no means more efficacious, than to invite and admit them to the rights of suffrage, and to enhance, as much as possible, the value of that right," he said. To the extent the people failed to take full advantage of the right to vote, it was "owing neither to defect nor degeneracy in the minds and principles of our citizens," but to America's overly restrictive voting laws.

Direct elections, with proportional representation and broad access to voting, was a remarkably progressive and expansive approach to a subject that many if not most of Wilson's peers danced around. But to Wilson, it all fit together naturally, forming the base of the pyramid of representative government.

The December 31 speech was "ingenious, solid, sublime," according to William Bradford, the state's attorney general. But many of the republicans, who had considered Wilson one of their own, were furious. In taking such a strong position in favor of direct elections, "he has disobliged many of his old friends," Bradford wrote in a letter to his father-in-law, Elias Boudinot.

But Wilson withstood the vitriol, and on January 4, the convention agreed to let the people directly elect their senators. Critically, the apportionment of those senators would be based on population only.

He may have lost the republicans, but with the help of Findley, Wilson assembled a solid majority coalition comprising mostly the radicals, along with a few delegates whose allegiances were unclear but who tended to side with the republicans. Wilson was the only republican who consistently supported popular democracy.

The new charter also included something that the previous one had not, and which Wilson had resisted at the federal level—a bill of rights. In the debates over the US Constitution, Wilson had vehemently opposed enumerating individual rights on the grounds that such a list would be incomplete by definition and would thus allow the government to intrude on any rights not included. Whether he genuinely believed that argument or was using it only as an expedient to convince wary Americans that the Constitution was complete as written, he lost the fight. By 1790, a federal bill of rights was moving through the states for ratification, and Wilson offered no recorded opposition to Pennsylvania's version—maybe because it sounded so much like something he would write.

Section 1 of Pennsylvania's bill of rights declared, "That all men are born equally free and independent, and have certain inherent and indefeasible rights, among which are those of enjoying and defending life and liberty, of acquiring, possessing, and protecting property and reputation, and of pursuing their own happiness."

Section 2 declared, "That all power is inherent in the people, and all free governments are founded on their authority, and instituted for their peace, safety and happiness: For the advancement of those ends, they have, at all times, an unalienable and indefeasible right to alter, reform, or abolish their government, in such manner as they may think proper." Here was the essence of the Declaration of Independence and of popular sovereignty—Wilson's career in a nutshell, and all in two sentences.

Overall, Pennsylvania's bill of rights largely tracked the federal version. For example, it included the right to freedom of religion and of the press, to bear arms, to "free and equal" elections, and to the suite of protections for those accused of crimes—to see the evidence against them, to confront their accusers, to have a jury trial, and so on. But Pennsylvania's charter did contain one provision that was not in the US Constitution and that would become a model for states around the country: under Section 16, which was carried over from the 1776 version, debtors who give over their estate to their creditors could not be held in prison, at least "where there is not strong presumption of fraud."

Wilson didn't win every fight at the 1790 convention. The new state constitution would prohibit Pennsylvanians from holding federal and state office at the same time, a prohibition that he considered absurd and personally offensive, given that he had been appointed as an associate justice to the US Supreme Court the month before the convention began. What sense did it make to deny public office to highly qualified people like him?

Pennsylvania "is about to strip me of the most valuable rights of citizenship," Wilson complained on January 19. "And this is to be done without any offence or cause of forfeiture on my part; unless to have been highly honored by the president and senate of the United States is, in her consideration, now become a crime."

Wilson reminded his colleagues that in a few days' time he would have to leave them and head north to New York, where the US Supreme Court was about to open its first term. "On my way to the government of the United States," he said, "I might turn and look back from the opposite shore of the Delaware; and though Pennsylvania should reject my faithful services, she might permit me, with a fluttering heart and faultering tongue, to wish her well."

The prohibition on dual officeholding would survive despite his pleas. By then, Wilson had his finger in so many different pies, he didn't have time to linger on the defeat.

16

The Law Lectures

ON DECEMBER 4, 1790, three months after the new Pennsylvania constitution had taken effect, Vice President John Adams, settled into his official quarters at Bush Hill in Philadelphia, wrote to his son Charles in New York. The subject was the famous lawyer newly appointed to the US Supreme Court and the lectures he planned to give at the College of Philadelphia, soon to be known as the University of Pennsylvania.

"Judge Wilsons Lectures commence on Monday fortnight: and I wish you to apply to him as early as possible," Adams wrote. "He will be pleased to have you and your Brother, as Hearers. You must take minutes of what you may hear and Send them to John," referring to his eldest son, John Quincy. He added, "The great Judges and Masters of the Law are to be the Objects of your Admiration and Imitation. There is no Character more venerable on this side of Heaven than a wise and upright Judge."

Adams was right. For any educated young man in late eighteenth-century America who might be interested in a career in the law, the upcoming lectures were not to be missed. By 1790, Wilson was arguably the greatest legal mind in the country. In anticipation of teaching at the school, he planned to deliver twenty-four lectures covering an extraordinary range of topics—the design of the federal

Constitution and state constitutions, the history of the common law and its operation in America, civil and criminal law, maritime law, and international law. The lectures would encompass historical examples and modern practice. In all, Wilson said, they would "furnish a rational and a useful entertainment to gentlemen of all professions, but particularly to assist in forming the legislator, the magistrate, & the lawyer."

It was an enormous undertaking, and yet Wilson had leapt at the chance. Apparently, rewriting a state constitution in Pennsylvania while sitting on the first Supreme Court was not enough to occupy him, but his self-confidence was understandable. He had been immersed in the study and creation of law and legal systems for a quarter century by then, and he was unmatched in either learning or experience. As he organized the lectures, he considered himself the American version of William Blackstone, the renowned British jurist who had published the first systematic commentaries on English common law in 1765, the year Wilson landed in New York Harbor.

Blackstone's commentaries were required reading for all lawyers and judges in the English-speaking world. But no one had yet attempted something similar in America, where the law was still an inchoate mix of colonial practices and English common law.

Wilson took on the job with relish and brought to it the wide-ranging intellectual approach—encompassing natural and moral philosophy, psychology, and epistemology—that had characterized his own education in Scotland decades earlier. His goal was "nothing less than the presentation of a complete political theory . . . leading to a philosophy of American law."

The opening lecture fell on December 15, 1790, at the college's main hall, on Fourth Street. As the late-autumn sky faded from dull orange to dark blue, the expectant attendees who had gathered outside made their way into the hall, past trees bare of leaves. Everyone with any sort of rank in the nation's capital, it seemed, was there. Seated in the front row were President Washington and his wife, Martha; Vice President Adams; representatives of both chambers of Congress; and the president and both houses of the Pennsylvania legislature. "A most brilliant and respectable audience," in the words of *The Pennsylvania Packet*—even if many were there because Wilson had given them tickets. As the justice stepped to the podium, the crowd quieted.

"Though I am not unaccustomed to speak in public, yet on this occasion I rise with much diffidence to address you," he began in his distinctive brogue. After all, as he pointed out, there were ladies present. "I never before had the honor of addressing a *fair* audience."

He turned to the subject at hand, invoking the political genius of the ancient Greeks and offering a bold claim: America was still a young nation, he admitted, but before long "it will outshine the glory of Greece." This was for two reasons—Americans' love of liberty and their love of law. "Neither of them can exist without the other," Wilson explained. "Without liberty, law loses its nature and its name, and becomes oppression. Without law, liberty also loses its nature and its name and becomes licentiousness."

The lecture series was intended for law students, but on this first night, Wilson's audience was much grander—not only the president and vice president, but the American people and, he hoped, the nation's history books. "Law should be studied and taught as a historical science," Wilson told the crowd, reflecting his own educational training in the Scottish tradition, as opposed to the English one, which, as we recall, treated the law as more of a trade.

This science of law should "be the study of every free citizen, and of every free man," he said. But—and this key point he directed at those who were not lawyers or law students—the law's essence was accessible to all people, no matter their learning. "Though the elephant may swim, yet the lamb may wade in it," he said, borrowing an axiom from the study of religion. Some practitioners may "involve themselves in a thick mist of terms of art, and use a language unknown to all but those of the profession," but law ought not be a mystery that regular people are "blindly and implicitly to obey." Rather, "those rational principles on which the law is founded ought, especially in a free government, to be diffused over the whole community." Thomas Reid could not have said it better. And not surprisingly, it led straight to the heart of Wilson's worldview, that the people should (and can) understand the law because it belongs to them and no one else—they create it, they consent to it, they embody it.

"The dread and redoubtable sovereign, when traced to his ultimate and genuine source, has been found, as he ought to have been found, in the free and independent man. This truth, so simple and natural, and yet so neglected or despised, may be appreciated as the first and fundamental principle in the science of government."

The inevitable consequence was what Wilson called the "revolution principle"—the idea that because sovereignty resides in the people alone, "they may change their constitution and government whenever they please." That document, which Wilson had such a major hand in writing, "is as clay in the hands of the potter," and the people "have the right to mold, to preserve, to improve, to refine, and to finish it as they please."

To fellow founders in the audience, likely hesitating at sentiments like these, Wilson was quick to add that his was "not a principle of discord, rancor, or war: it is a principle of melioration, contentment, and peace." Whether that reassured President Washington, who had led one revolution and put down another, is not clear.

Wilson closed his talk that evening with an appeal to the women in attendance. "Methinks I hear one of the female part of my audience exclaim—What is all this to us?" he said. "We have heard much of societies, of states, of governments, of laws, and of a law education. Is everything made for your sex? Why should not we have a share? Is our sex less honest, or less virtuous, or less wise than yours?"

To the contrary, Wilson said, answering his own question, women are, if anything, men's betters in all those respects. Still, they are not built for "the management of public affairs." Rather they contribute the most to society through their domestic role, a place where "the lovely and accomplished woman shines with superior lustre."

It was not a surprising attitude from a man of that era, and yet it wasn't the first time that Wilson seemed to have a foot in multiple centuries at once. Perhaps sensing the shadow of the forward-looking, female-admiring Visitant lurking over his shoulder, Wilson explained that women—mothers, specifically—were responsible for shaping history's best orators. "In your sex, too, there is a natural, an easy, and, often, a pure flow of diction, which lays the best foundation for that eloquence, which, in a free country, is so important to ours," he said.

In a later lecture, the Visitant showed up. "'Know thou thyself,' is an inscription peculiarly proper for the porch of the temple of science," Wilson said. It was the same quote, from Alexander Pope, that he had used to open his introductory advice column more than two decades earlier.

Through the following winter, Wilson delivered fifty-eight lectures three days a week to fifteen young law students. They were almost exclusively focused on theory and covered the nature of law, the design of government, the demands of morality, and the obligations of citizens. Not until the next winter did Wilson get down to what he referred to, with a sniff, as the "retail business of law," the kind that actually paid the bills: corporate law, maritime law, criminal law, and the like.

In many ways, Wilson's law lectures served as a summary of the high points of his life to that moment. The focus on common sense theory ("all sound reasoning must rest ultimately on the principles of common sense") was a nod to his Scottish upbringing and his training under Thomas Reid. The emphasis on popular sovereignty and political equality reflected his efforts at the 1787 convention and during ratification. ("All elections ought to be equal. . . . Elections are equal, when a given number of citizens, in one part of the state, choose as many representatives, as are chosen by the same number of citizens, in any other part of the state.") His attention to the crucial democratic role played by juries, both grand and trial ("Is it not, then, of immense consequence . . . that jurors should possess the spirit of just discernment, to discriminate between the innocent and the guilty?") was a reminder of his own life-threatening experience arguing on behalf of men accused of treason in the late 1770s.

In the end, Wilson produced nearly 700 pages of material, or roughly 350,000 words—an astounding achievement and the most comprehensive treatise on American law that would be produced for generations. Like everything else about him, the lectures were a brilliant jumble, "a conglomerate of values and impulses drawn from widely variant worlds," in the words of Robert McCloskey, "reconciled only by his own incurable optimism that they *could* be reconciled in some apocalyptic day that never quite arrived."

The lectures also represented another strategy Wilson employed to pull in some extra cash. The university's trustees, acting on a request from Wilson himself, charged each student of the lectures ten guineas, a sizable amount for the service provided, which was "not one likely to throng the lecture hall with students."

Cash flow was an ever-present concern for Wilson as the 1790s progressed and his land dealings grew more complex and frenetic. Even as he was drafting a new state constitution, writing and delivering dozens of original lectures on law, and sitting on the Supreme Court, he was seeking out other avenues of income. In March 1791, he convinced the Pennsylvania House to appoint him to produce a revised digest of the laws of the state. Later that year, he wrote a lengthy letter to the Assembly, explaining that he had gathered together all statutes of the commonwealth "from its first settlement till the beginning of the last session of the legislature"—1,702 in all, by his count. He sought guidance on how best to organize them, but of course he had his own ideas. "Simplicity and plainness and precision should mark the texture of a law," he wrote. "It claims the obedience—it should be level to the *understandings* of all." It was an almost inconceivably massive undertaking, but it would pay eight hundred dollars—that is, it would have paid eight hundred dollars, except the state senate (the new house of the bicameral legislature Wilson had pushed so hard for in the 1790 constitution) rejected the funding for Wilson's assistants and materials that the House had approved.

Meanwhile, the Supreme Court, in its debut, was proving to be something of an anticlimax. It began with the court's accommodations, which fell far short of the solemn authority of its name. The Exchange Building, on Water Street in Manhattan, had been built as a European-style market hall, a two-story brick structure with an arched roof and stalls on the lower level. Over the years, it had functioned as a theater, an exhibition hall, a coffeehouse, and a home base for the

New York legislature. Outside was a dusty, noisy street filled with merchants and butchers, who had to be pushed back before the court's first session on February 1, 1790. The courtroom was "uncommonly crowded" with dignitaries and commoners that day, one newspaper reported, but they would be disappointed. The session could not get under way because, in an echo of the 1787 Constitutional Convention, the necessary players were slow to arrive. Only three justices—the northerners Jay, Wilson, and Cushing—showed up, not enough for a quorum, and the court had to adjourn. The court clerk, noting this in his first minutes, misspelled Wilson's name and referred to the court as "the Supreme Judicial Court of the United States."

John Blair arrived from Virginia later that night, and the quorum was met, so the next afternoon, the justices planned to get down to business. The problem was there was no business to get down to. No cases to be heard, no litigants waiting to address the justices. The Supreme Court was the most novel part of the new Constitution, and it was not yet clear what cases it would even be handling. In some matters, the court had original jurisdiction, meaning it could take a case directly, without waiting for it to move through the lower courts. Beyond that, it was supposed to hear appeals, but the country and its judicial system were young enough that there were few appeals from state or lower federal courts to be responded to.

Once again, as soon as the justices had taken their seats, they adjourned. On Wednesday, they officially appointed John Tucker as clerk and adopted an official seal, then adjourned, and on Friday they admitted a handful of attorneys to the court's bar. By the next week, it was clear that nothing more was going to happen, and the court ended its first term eight days after it began. It reconvened for its second term in August, but for only two days before closing up shop. Wilson must have been more than a bit frustrated. Not only had he been denied the title of chief justice but the court he had helped design was now twiddling its thumbs and waiting to be given a real job to do.

On the bright side, the absence of cases at the high court gave the justices a lot of extra time to focus on other aspects of the job. For

Wilson, the most alluring was the opportunity to deliver instructions to grand juries. Despite being the only justice among Washington's first batch of nominees with no prior judicial experience, Wilson had profound respect for the idea and institution of the jury. "Whoever were its inventors or improvers," he said in one of his earliest charges in April, "it is the most admirable method for the trial and investigation of the truth; and the best guardian both of public and private liberty, that has been hitherto discovered by the ingenuity of man."

This charge, versions of which Wilson would deliver around the country through 1790 and 1791, was for the benefit of the seventeen men comprising the first-ever grand jury seated in the circuit court of Pennsylvania, in the break between the court's February and August terms. By that time, Wilson had come to realize that he was playing on an open field. If the American people were going to be taught about their brand-new legal system—and the jury charges were widely reprinted in local newspapers—then no one was better prepared than Wilson to do the teaching.

Jury instructions also gave Wilson the chance to expound once more on his philosophy of popular sovereignty. The jury, after all, was a perfect microcosm of the people. "In a well constituted government, the great movements of the state receive their first force and direction immediately from the people, at elections," he said. And because all people everywhere have an equal, God-given ability to discern fundamental truths, each juror is as well situated as anyone to pass judgment on his fellow citizens.

As at the Philadelphia convention, Wilson was not shy about expressing a faith in regular citizens far beyond that evinced by his peers. "We now see the circle of government, beautiful and complete," he said in closing his charge. "By the people, its springs are put in motion originally. By the people, its administration is consummated: At first; at last; their power is predominant and supreme."

Another part of the job was much less to Wilson's taste, and that was riding circuit. Six months out of the year, the justices had to preside at the sittings of the three lower circuit courts—eastern, middle, and southern—established by the Judiciary Act of 1789. Each state had one three-judge circuit court, which conducted higher-level trials involving serious criminal and civil matters; and a one-judge district court, which handled admiralty, maritime, and other minor cases. There was a catch, though. To save money, Congress provided for no circuit judges, meaning that each circuit court sitting—there would be two per year—required two Supreme Court justices and one district judge.

Circuit riding was a good idea in theory. In addition to conveying the power and reach of the new government to all parts of the country, the justices' physical presence would keep them abreast of local political opinion and ensure that federal laws were uniform. The court would also be playing the role of "republican schoolmaster," educating regular Americans about the new judiciary. In practice, Wilson and his colleagues were miserable. The justices were forced to trudge along "execrable" roads, covering hundreds and even thousands of miles over ruts and bumps and mud, through bad weather and worse, amid outbreaks of yellow fever and smallpox, losing their luggage and finding themselves stuck in rooms with up to a dozen lodgers, and bundled up in bone-rattling carriages, if not seated directly on horseback. The ride from Baltimore to Savannah took three weeks. "I fear the journey, and am anxious for information," Justice Samuel Chase wrote to Iredell soon after joining the court.

It was no job for a young man, let alone those in their forties and fifties. They often missed court dates on account of illness or bad weather. And for this misery, the justices paid out of their own pockets—there was no extra salary or even reimbursement for riding circuit.

They came to despise it so much that they discussed proposing a five-hundred-dollar pay cut in return for being relieved of all circuit riding, with the saved money being used to hire new judges who would ride the circuits. They never proposed this to Congress, though, out of a concern that it would look bad. Despite their upset, the new justices took their duties seriously, even if they never stopped complaining to one another.

The southern circuit was by far the largest and occasioned the most griping. "I will venture to say no Judge can conscientiously undertake to ride the Southern Circuit constantly, and perform the other parts of his duty," Iredell wrote to his colleagues in February 1791. "Besides the danger his health must be exposed to, it is not conceivable that accidents will not often happen." He estimated he had ridden 1,900 miles on the last circuit. "Can any Man have a probable chance of going that distance twice a year, and attending at particular places punctually on particular days?"

Wilson had a comparatively easier job in the more compact middle circuit, but he was no happier with his conditions. In a letter to Thomas Johnson, who joined the court as a recess appointment in 1791 and was beset by health complications, Wilson commiserated and called circuit riding "one part of the judiciary system in which a change is, on many accounts, highly, I might say indispensably necessary." Johnson retired after just over a year on the court.

Each year, the justices were to make two trips to the Pennsylvania State House in Philadelphia, where the court had relocated to temporary headquarters; and two trips out into the wilds of America. By the summer of 1792, the justices had had enough. They sent two jointly signed letters—one to Congress and one to the president—pleading for an overhaul of the circuit-riding system.

"We really, Sir, find the burdens laid upon us so excessive that we cannot forbear representing them in strong and explicit terms," they wrote to Washington. "We cannot reconcile of ourselves to the idea of existing in exile from our families."

It was generally understood at the time that the circuit-riding arrangement was temporary, and yet it had now dragged on for more than two years with no end in sight, they said in the letter. "To require of the Judges to pass the greater part of their days on the road, and at Inns, and at a distance from their families" was too much, especially considering that several of them were not in the best of health—in early 1791, John Rutledge was struck with a case of gout, while John Blair came down with influenza severe enough to keep him bedridden for the term. Then there was the central design flaw of the system, which was to employ the same justices to rule at two different levels of the same judiciary—or, as they put it in the letter to Congress, to empower them "to correct in one capacity the errors which they themselves may have committed in another."

But no respite came from Congress or the White House. The most the justices got was an updated law, passed early in 1793, that required only one of them, not two, to sit on a circuit panel. Left to their own devices, the justices made do. They learned the benefits of trading circuit rides for convenience, although Wilson went a step further, often pawning off his duties on the other justices. And they each contributed one hundred dollars to the justice stuck with the southern circuit, to compensate for the extra travel costs. In the first decade of the court, four justices retired, in large part because of the burdens of riding circuit. It would be more than a century before the justices were relieved of their circuit-riding duties for good.

Meanwhile, Wilson's visions for the Supreme Court, and for himself as a member of it, were painfully slow in materializing. In the first two years, the justices heard a single case. It was 1792 before they heard a major case, *Chisholm v. Georgia*, which would be the most consequential ruling of the court's first decade. This was in part because it represented the first time the court issued a full interpretation of a constitutional provision, but it was mainly because the decision—a 4–1 ruling, with Wilson writing the longest and most significant majority opinion—triggered immediate and widespread outrage, leading to a constitutional amendment that overturned it. In the process, Wilson's theory of government by popular sovereignty would be simultaneously vindicated and rejected by the people themselves.

Chisholm was about whether the court had jurisdiction over a lawsuit between one state and citizens of another state. The court ruled that it did have that jurisdiction: States could be hauled into federal court by citizens of other states.

The dispute involved the state of Georgia's refusal to pay a South Carolina merchant named Robert Farquhar (represented after his death by his executor, Alexander Chisholm) the modern equivalent of nearly two million dollars for an order for Revolutionary War supplies. Agents for Georgia had apparently kept the money they were supposed to pay Farquhar. On the surface, the answer seemed straightforward: Article III of the Constitution gives federal courts jurisdiction over suits "between a State and Citizens of another State," and *Chisholm v. Georgia* obviously met that description.

Georgia disagreed. In replying to the lawsuit, its governor, Edward Telfair, argued that Georgia was "a free, sovereign and independent State," and that it "cannot be drawn or compelled" to answer before any court of law anywhere, federal or otherwise.

Sovereign states had long been considered immune from being sued by their own citizens without their consent. But the *Chisholm* case involved a state being sued by a citizen from another state—thus bringing the federal government into the picture. And this is where Wilson's elaborate theories of sovereignty would be put to the test. As he had said so many times, only the people are sovereign, and any sovereignty possessed by a state is derivative of, and subordinate to, theirs.

That was emphatically not the view of many of Wilson's contemporaries. To the Anti-Federalists, state sovereignty was akin to holy writ and more necessary than ever in the face of potentially crippling debts from the Revolutionary War. During the 1787 convention and throughout the ratification debates, they had fought off the slightest intimations that states would relinquish to the federal government any of the sweeping powers they possessed. Wilson and his allies sought to reassure the doubters, to little avail.

In the fall of 1791, Chisholm's lawsuit went before the circuit court of Georgia, which ruled in favor of the state, throwing out Chisholm's claim for the funds. Sitting on that court was Justice Iredell, who was riding the southern circuit that term. Chisholm then appealed to the Supreme Court. When the justices took up the case in August 1792, Georgia did not make an appearance, its absence based on the governor's assertion that the state was not subject to the jurisdiction of a federal court. The justices then ordered Georgia to appear, but it again refused to; the following term, the justices finally heard arguments in the case. Edmund Randolph, the attorney general, argued the case for Chisholm. Georgia remained absent.

Two weeks later, the justices delivered their opinions—five in all, one by each justice. Four justices sided with Chisholm and said he could sue Georgia in federal court, meaning that there was no such thing as state sovereignty. The darkest suspicions of the Anti-Federalists had been correct.

Only Justice Iredell dissented. As the junior justice, he announced his opinion first. He didn't take the position that the court *couldn't* have jurisdiction over cases like these, only that it was up to Congress to explicitly confer such jurisdiction, which it had not done. Chief Justice Jay and Justices Blair and Cushing sided with Chisholm, each for his own reasons.

Then came Wilson. While he also took Chisholm's side on the central legal question of suing Georgia, he sought to make a much larger point. Jurisdiction and state sovereignty were only the surface issues, he wrote. The true question "ultimately resolved into one, no less radical than this—'do the People of the United States form a nation?'"

It was a bracing and very Wilsonian way to put it: Had the framers created a nation or a league of sovereign states? This question was at the heart of the debate over the Constitution, and Wilson was aware that the *Chisholm* case was his first opportunity to weigh in on that question at length.

The litigants could be forgiven for growing impatient. Wilson felt he was being charged with defining the nature of the American union; Alexander Chisholm just wanted his money. But Wilson had the stage, and he wasn't going to surrender it, launching into a disquisition on the meaning of the term *sovereign* in which he pointed out that the word itself appears nowhere in the Constitution—and rightly so, because sovereigns generally have subjects, and under the Constitution, "there are citizens, but no subjects."

In Wilson's mind, there was no such thing as a sovereign state. "A state, like a merchant, makes a contract. A dishonest state, like a dishonest merchant, wilfully refuses to discharge it. The latter is amenable to a court of justice. Upon general principles of right, shall the former, when summoned to answer the fair demands of its creditor, be permitted, Proteus-like, to assume a new appearance, and to insult him and justice by declaring 'I am a Sovereign state?' Surely not."

Therefore, when the citizens of Georgia—a subset of the American people—agreed to sign on to the federal union, they "did not surrender the supreme or sovereign power to that state, but, as to the purposes of the Union, retained it to themselves. As to the purposes of the Union, therefore, Georgia is NOT a sovereign state."

At the end of his opinion, following a lengthy historical survey of governments and societies through history, Wilson finally turned to the actual text of the Constitution—odd, given that the textual evidence for Wilson's position was rock solid. First, though, he could not resist citing himself (a prerogative only a founding father could enjoy) by invoking the words that opened the nation's new charter. "Our national scene opens with the most magnificent object which the nation could present. 'The PEOPLE of the United states' are the first personages introduced." He was answering the question that had preoccupied him as long as he had thought about politics and government.

Wilson surely could have limited his analysis to this, as his colleagues in the majority did, if he had believed it was all that needed to be said. But he took seriously his job as republican schoolmaster, teaching the American people what they had just chosen of their own free will to become and how it was all supposed to work. With *Hayburn's Case* he had laid the groundwork for the court's power to strike down federal laws in the name of the people; now, in *Chisholm v. Georgia*, he had established the supremacy of those people over the states.

His contemporaries, and those who came after, took Wilson to task for this indulgence. In a letter to Iredell, William Davie wrote, "Perhaps, notwithstanding the tawdry ornament and poetical imagery with which it is loaded and bedizened, it may still be very 'profound.'"

"Pretentious and disorganized," wrote one Supreme Court historian. "A pile of verbiage."

"At its worst," wrote Robert McCloskey, the Harvard professor and

Wilson enthusiast, "his prose seems the result of a cross-fertilization between a pedant and a Fourth of July orator."

But Wilson wasn't simply writing for the sake of it. He understood the power and importance of language in communicating new ideas to the public—ideas like popular sovereignty. It was not by chance that he opened his opinion with a quote from one of his favorite Scottish instructors, Thomas Reid, on the necessity of precision in the usage of words, like *sovereign*. The influence of his education in Scotland and under Scots law was also clear in his focus on first principles, like the nature of sovereignty, rather than the close examination of legal precedent that is usually expected of appellate judges.

The good news for him was that the American people understood exactly what he was saying. The bad news was, to judge by the immediate public reaction to the decision in *Chisholm v. Georgia*, a large number of them did not agree with it. Hadn't the Federalists assured them during the ratification debates that this was not how they understood federal power?

On February 19, the day the ruling was publicly announced, a resolution was introduced in the House of Representatives to amend the Constitution to bar suits against states by citizens of other states. The following day, a similar proposal was introduced in the Senate.

The broad rebuke of *Chisholm v. Georgia* was not a surprise, given that Georgia was not the only state facing lawsuits, many of which, like *Chisholm*, involved Revolutionary War debts.

In February 1795, less than two years after the court's ruling in *Chisholm*, the amendment had won the required support of two-thirds of both houses of Congress and three-quarters of the states, making it the first amendment to be ratified following the Bill of Rights. In January 1798, President John Adams announced the Eleventh Amendment's ratification in Congress. The amendment had not been in effect before that time, so for the five years between the ruling and Adams's announcement, the Supreme Court continued to hear suits brought against states by citizens of other states. *Chisholm* remained the law of the land.

By the time it wasn't, Wilson was no longer present on the bench;

he had been on the run from the law for a year by that point and may never have learned of the Eleventh Amendment's adoption. Either way, that brief window of time when *Chisholm* was operational was a bittersweet coda for him. He had gone to pains to venerate the power of the people, the centrality of popular sovereignty to his theory of government—first writing it into the Constitution, then reinforcing it in his interpretation as a justice. And this was how the people repaid him: by taking some of that power away from themselves and giving it back to the states.

Meanwhile, litigation related to the initial *Chisholm* suit would drag on for decades, bouncing around the Georgia state legislature and Congress until it was finally resolved in 1847, seventy years after the case began and nearly half a century after Wilson died.

James Wilson, by Max Rosenthal, 1890. (*Collection of the Supreme Court of the United States*)

St. Salvator's College at the University of St. Andrews. Wilson was accepted here as a bursar in 1757. Sketch by John Oliphant, 1769. (*The University of St. Andrews Libraries and Museums*)

A ca. 1931 photograph of the farmhouse in Carskerdo, Scotland, where Wilson was born and raised. (Andrew Bennett, in Randolph G. Adams, "James Wilson and St. Andrews," *The General Magazine and Historical Chronicle* (October 1931): 20)

The first installment of the Visitant's column, written by Wilson and published on the front page of the *Pennsylvania Chronicle*, February 1, 1768. (*Pennsylvania Chronicle*)

For the PENNSYLVANIA CHRONICLE.

[No. 1.]   The VISITANT.

Know then thyself.   POPE.

THE motto, which I have prefixed to this paper, contains a precept of the greatest importance. Our happiness, which is the final end of our existence, and the mark at which we aim, though sometimes injudiciously, in all our conduct, cannot be obtained without being acquainted with those sentiments and affections, which are to enjoy that happiness. Before we can learn whether any particular passion can be gratified with any particular object, we must compare the passion with the object; and before we can compare them, we must know them; for it is impossible to discover the relation betwixt two things, while we are ignorant of the things themselves.

An inattention to this principle produces many of the inconsistent and unsatisfactory pursuits, in which we see mankind continually engaged. Without considering the passion that influences them, and without examining the propriety of what they pursue as the means of gratifying it, they run inconsiderately from project to project, till, at length, they are bewildered in the maze of their own absurdities; and, upon recollection, are at a loss to find out the principle, from which they have acted, or the end, which they have had in view. Those, who know themselves, follow a very opposite course of action. Before they permit any affection to have a general influence upon their conduct, they deliberate whether it is proper to indulge it. If they determine that it ought to be indulged, they next consider the object which is adapted to gratify it, the means of obtaining that object, and the probability of being furnished with those means. By using these precautions, they know their aims; they know, and are satisfied, when they have fulfilled them.

As the advantages resulting from the study of human nature are great; so is the study itself agreeable and interesting. Knowledge is delightful to the mind; and every new idea brings along with it a new pleasure: The pleasure is increased if the idea is important as well as new: Every thing becomes important in proportion as it is connected with us: Nothing has a stricter connexion with us than reflections on human nature: The study of human nature must therefore be interesting and agreeable.

The study of the different sciences is only the study of man in different views. Logic considers us as men of sense; ethics, as men of virtue; criticism, as men of taste; jurisprudence, as members of society. Mathematics and natural philosophy have not indeed such an intimate relation to us; but they derive all their value either from improving our judgments, from enlarging our conceptions, or from ministering to our conveniency.

Two methods, totally different, and neither sufficient, have been followed in studying human nature. One is from books; the other is from men. Both should be joined. He who observes only the first method, may perhaps be able to form a regular system; his general principles may be just; his application of them may be plausible; and his inferences may be drawn according to the strictest rules of reasoning. But, after all, the observation of the poet will be verified in his learned labours;

" They may be reason; but they are not man."

When he comes to examine his work, he will find, that, though the outlines may be justly taken, and some of the most obvious proportions accurately marked; yet many of the finer features are omitted; some aggravated, others distorted; the air and graces of the original lost; and that the picture, however, regular and exact it appeared, when viewed by itself, bears, when compared with what it was intended to represent, only the same dull and mortifying resemblance, which a skeleton has to a human body. There is a fineness, and a variety in our frame, that mocks the formal regularity of a systematic thinker.

He who gains his knowledge of men, only from being much in company, or *seeing the world*, as it is called, will not commit so many mistakes as the other; but for a very obvious reason—because he will confine himself wholly to what he sees and hears. He will remember facts, and tell stories; but he will deduce no consequences, nor make any observations on them. A few general remarks, perhaps, he may have, which he will apply indiscriminately on every occasion; and if they happen sometimes to be justly applied, chance, and not his ingenuity, should have the merit of them.

If we would study human nature with success, we must join the two methods above-mentioned. We must have experience in order to correct our reasoning; and we must employ reasoning in order to profit by our experience. The latter, taking advantage of every incident, will use it as a test of some refined deduction; the former, taking advantage of every incident likewise, will convert it into a subject of solid reflection.

Though the knowledge of books is necessary as well as that of men, yet I must own that I receive greater satisfaction from the latter, than the former. Formed for society, and fond of it, I experience, from my observation on the usual occurrences of life, not only the intellectual delight of having the number of my ideas increased, but the moral one of participating in the joys and distresses of those I converse with. When I hear a sentiment that can proceed only from a laudable principle in the person that utters it, my mind is transported with a pleasure superior to that, which can arise from the investigations of the most sublime truths, which the understanding alone is fitted to relish. In tracing the connexion that subsists between the conduct and the sentiments of a good man, my mind is satisfied with its reflections, and my heart rejoices in the discovery of virtue. Sometimes indeed unfavourable appearances obtrude themselves upon me; (I never search after them)—but in such cases I exert my ingenuity in putting favourable constructions on what I see, and in finding out excuses for it; and if after all, I am *unable* to reconcile it to virtue, I solace myself with the merit of being *willing* to do so.

These reasons will explain the propriety of my assuming the character of a VISITANT, and of living in such a manner as to render that character applicable to me. I propose to communicate to the Public my observations on the common incidents of life in a loose unconnected manner, as my humour shall prompt me, or as the subjects themselves shall direct. I hope they may be of use to convince the learned pedant that familiar occurrences are worth attending to; and the shallow coxcomb that they are worth observing.

My readers will judge of my remarks. If they are thought sensible or entertaining, I expect they will be received with applause; if they are thought to have the opposite qualities, I shall be obliged to the first pen that will give me a friendly admonition to discontinue them.

Before I conclude, it will not be improper to obviate some disagreeable impressions, which the gravity, perhaps severity, of this prefatory discourse may have a tendency to make. Though my reflections are sometimes abstracted, my disposition is easy. I am inclined to view every thing in the most agreeable light; and to create to myself imaginary pleasures, rather than imaginary uneasinesses. I conform myself to the temper of my company, as far as rules which I deem more sacred than those of complaisance will permit. With the chearful, I am gay; with the serious, I am grave; with the witty, I am smart. I talk of state affairs, with the politician; of commerce, with the merchant; of trifles, with the coquette; of divinity, with the parson. When I am pensive, I murmur not at the pleasantry of others; and when I am frolicksome, I do not think them bound to join with me in my impertinence. I am happiest in small companies; and those, I think, are best when they are composed of near an equal number of both sexes. The conversation has then an agreeable mixture of sense and delicacy. Nothing offends me so much as double *entendres*, especially when Ladies are present. I believe they really feel all the confusion that appears in their faces, and therefore cannot forbear looking upon those who occasion it as inhumanly sporting themselves at the expence of others. One particular more in my disposition I must mention, because it is a particular, on which I greatly value myself—I prefer the conversation of a fine woman to that of a philosopher.

C.

The Bird Mansion, home of the Bird family and site of the reception following the wedding of Wilson and his first wife, Rachel Bird, in 1771. (*Springfield College Archives and Special Collections*)

The front page of *Rivington's New-York Gazetteer*, October 20, 1774. The first installment of Wilson's groundbreaking essay on British parliament (mistakenly attributed to Benjamin Franklin) begins in the leftmost column. (*Rivington's New-York Gazetteer*)

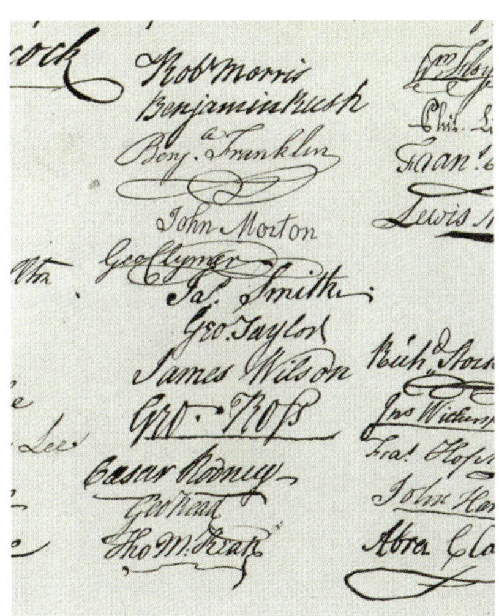

The vote on the Declaration of Independence. Wilson is standing in the center, facing left, opposite most of the other signers. By Robert Edge Pine, 1784–88. (*Bridgeman Images*)

Wilson's signature on the Declaration of Independence, August 2, 1776. The image is from the 1823 engraving by William Stone. (*The National Archives*)

The Wilson family home at the southwest corner of Walnut and Third Streets in Philadelphia, depicted as it would have looked at the time of the 1779 mob attack. By Benjamin Ridgway Evans, 1888. (*Historical Society of Pennsylvania*)

A map of central Philadelphia around 1776, three years before the Fort Wilson Riot. In 1779, Wilson's house was at the corner of Walnut and Third Streets. (*Library of Congress*)

The signing of the Constitution on September 17, 1787. By Howard Chandler Christy, 1940. (*Architect of the Capitol*)

The nation's leaders, including President George Washington and Vice President John Adams, arrive at the University of Pennsylvania for the opening night of Wilson's lectures on American law, December 15, 1790. This painting, by Simon Greco, was used in a 1948 magazine advertisement for whisky. (*The Illustrated Gallery*)

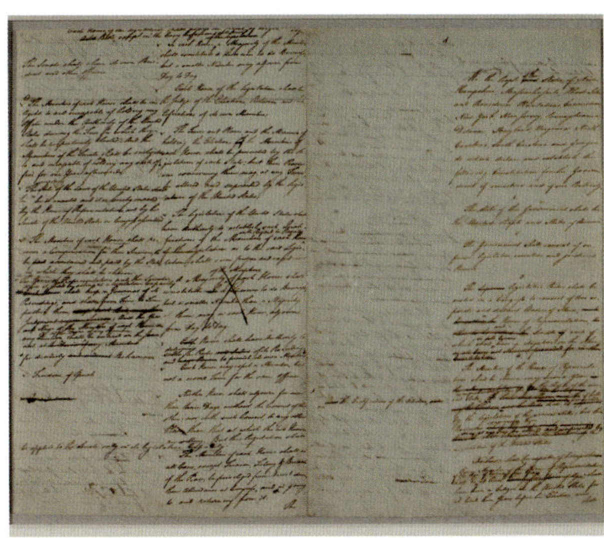

A page from Wilson's first handwritten draft of the Constitution. (*Historical Society of Pennsylvania*)

Hannah Gray Wilson, in a portrait done around 1805, after she had remarried and was known as Mrs. Thomas Bartlett. By Gilbert Stuart. (*Museum of Fine Arts, Boston*)

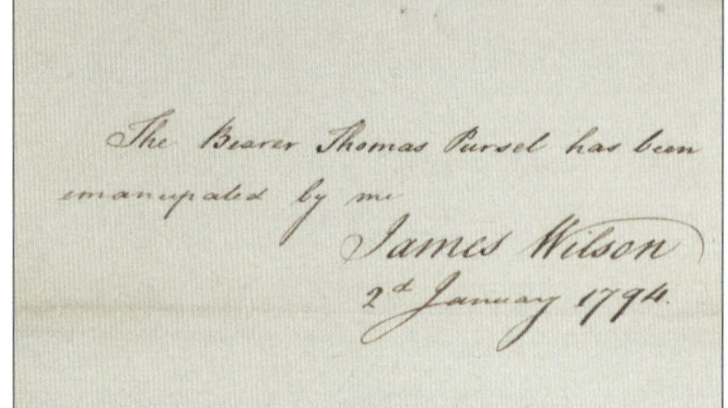

Wilson's manumission (or "emancipation," as he referred to it) of Thomas Pursel, his household servant, dated January 2, 1794. (*Historical Society of Pennsylvania*)

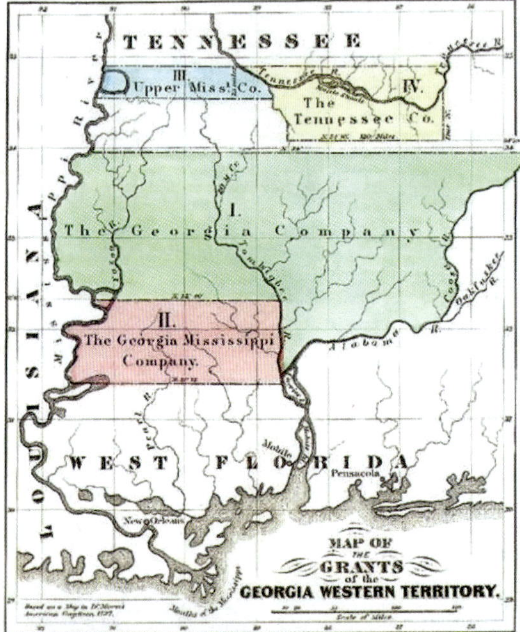

A 1797 map of a grant by Georgia, transferring 35 million acres of state land to four private companies for $500,000, a deal that became known as the Yazoo land fraud. Wilson was the largest shareholder of one of the companies, and was deeply implicated in the ensuing scandal. (*Digital Library of Georgia*)

John Horniblow's tavern in Edenton, North Carolina, where Wilson spent the last months of his life in hiding. (*North Carolina State Historic Sites*)

In September 1797, after Wilson was thrown in jail for unpaid debts, he wrote to his son Bird, asking for clothing and bail money. (*Historical Society of Pennsylvania*)

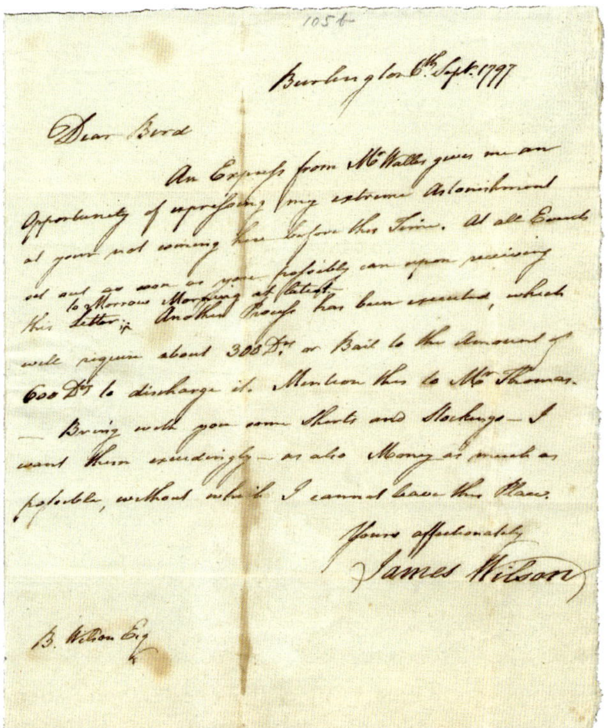

Sailors carry a coffin containing Wilson's remains, which had been exhumed in North Carolina, to the courtyard of Christ Church in Philadelphia, 1906. (*Library of Congress*)

A rare statue of Wilson, in the Signers' Hall at the National Constitution Center in Philadelphia. (*National Constitution Center*)

Wilson's official Supreme Court portrait, by Robert S. Susan, 1936. (*Collection of the Supreme Court of the United States*)

17

The Walls Close In

"PROPERTY IS NOT AN END, BUT A MEANS"

IT WAS INEVITABLE that Wilson's various personas—legal luminary, visionary democrat, and insatiable land speculator—would sooner or later collide. And as he spent less time on authoritative Supreme Court opinions and more on trying to build and protect his vast holdings in frontier property, that's exactly what happened.

Since 1779, he had served as chairman of the Illinois and Wabash Company, one of the bigger land investment ventures of the era, which for years had been purchasing huge tracts of western lands, much of them from Indian Nations. As the Revolutionary War dragged on and the mountain of debt facing states, especially, became clear, those purchases—and the sheer value of the lands involved—came under scrutiny, particularly from the states. A Virginia law, passed only weeks before Wilson assumed his chairmanship of the company, invalidated "all sales and deeds" of land by Indians to private buyers, past and future, on the ground that only Virginia had the right to purchase such lands or to permit someone else to.

Wilson had personal, political, and legal reasons to be deeply concerned about measures like these. His personal holdings in the Illinois-Wabash lands alone are estimated to have comprised up to one million acres..And that was only one of numerous companies in which he held shares.

The political concern was related. For decades, from his time in the Continental Congress to his opinion in the *Chisholm* case, Wilson had expressed his skepticism of state claims to sovereignty. Laying out the reasons for the failure of the Articles of Confederation, he warned that the state governments' "jealousy and ambition" had reduced the country "to the impotent condition in which it now stands."

Then there were the legal issues. Laws like Virginia's appeared to be in direct violation of the Constitution's ex post facto clauses. Latin for "after the fact," ex post facto laws apply retroactively—for example, by invalidating land sales that were legal when they occurred. The Constitution barred such laws, which the framers believed epitomized the arbitrary, vindictive power of tyrants. This was especially the case with criminal laws, where conviction can result in imprisonment. The delegates at the 1787 convention broadly agreed that ex post facto laws were unacceptable; the debate centered over whether or not to bar them explicitly. Wilson said no, arguing that such laws were so obviously invalid that to prohibit them would be to "proclaim that we are ignorant of the first principles of Legislation." Since then, Wilson had said little in public about the clauses, but available records suggest that he understood them to be applicable to all laws, whether criminal or, like the Virginia law, civil.

Conveniently for Wilson, all three of these concerns pointed to the same conclusion: that he and the company's other investors should be allowed to retain their title to the Virginia lands they had purchased. Over the course of the 1780s, he wrote no fewer than three memos to the Confederation Congress to this effect.

His landholdings had only increased by the time he joined the court, yet he did not appear to be chastened by his new position. Between 1790 and 1797, he wrote three additional memos to Congress, all making the case against ex post facto laws like Virginia's and in favor of ownership of the lands he had purchased. Even by the ethical standards of certain modern justices, it would be shocking if one of them lobbied Congress publicly on behalf of his or her personal business interests. But that's what Wilson did.

The memos surely mortified Wilson's colleagues on the court and were not well received by lawmakers, either. When Congress rejected the last of them, in February 1797, Wilson was furious. He wrote a final letter to the House and Senate committees that had considered the memo, making clear his conviction that the Constitution (including the Ex Post Facto Clause) represents "the permanent will of the people, and is the supreme law of the land." Legislatures, in contrast, are "creatures of the Constitution," and any law they may pass that conflicts with that Constitution is void.

While Wilson was drafting his letter to Congress, the Supreme Court agreed to hear *Calder v. Bull*, a case involving a Connecticut law that granted a new trial in probate court to a party that had been inadvertently disinherited by that court—in other words, a civil law that applied retroactively.

In early August 1798, the court ruled unanimously in the case that the Ex Post Facto Clause applied only to criminal laws, not to civil laws like the one at issue. Therefore, the Connecticut law stood. Justices Chase, Paterson, Iredell, and Cushing each wrote an opinion. Two justices did not take part in the case. One was Oliver Ellsworth, the chief justice, who was out sick. The other was Wilson. On the day of the *Calder v. Bull* ruling, he was hundreds of miles to the south of the court, hidden in a back room of John Horniblow's tavern in coastal North Carolina, fevered and delirious, days from death. It is likely he never learned of the court's rejection of his interpretation of the clause.

Perhaps that was for the best. Wilson had already endured his share of rejection by that point—the rejection by the states and then by Congress of his attempts to claim title to the lands he had purchased; the rejection by Congress and then by the people of his opinion in the *Chisholm* case on popular sovereignty; and now the rejection of his understanding of the Ex Post Facto Clause, a provision in a charter he had played the central role in drafting. For all his visions of American democracy, for all the prescience of his political theories and the precision of his legal thought, Wilson never fully grasped the way politics works.

Had Wilson not been consumed with propping up his financial house of cards, had he not been so distracted by its impending collapse, he might have been able to exert himself further in the service of his great passions: the law and the power of the people. He might have succeeded in establishing the Supreme Court as the truly co-equal branch of government he envisioned it to be. The accolades that now fall on John Marshall might have been directed at him.

But at this point in his life, Wilson had neither the time nor the focus to achieve such things. Even in the few opportunities he had to lay out his grand theories for American life and society, he was foiled. When confronted with actual cases and real-life litigants who merely wanted resolution of a dispute in their favor, Wilson found himself mired in the mundane practicalities of litigation, not to mention the indignity of having to share the stage with five other justices. For these reasons, and the fact that so much of the justices' time was taken up with riding circuit, Wilson developed no clear jurisprudence during his years on the bench. And yet his frustrations with the job weren't entirely within his control. His conviction that the Supreme Court was empowered to declare laws of Congress unconstitutional was right, but it remained a matter of great sensitivity for several years. The court was feeling its way to its proper role in the new constitutional system, and mutual forbearance was essential. Forbearance on a personal level, however, was not Wilson's strength. He was dogged by too much ambition and not enough money. Two more times over his remaining years on the court he would be reminded that, his legal luminosity notwithstanding, he had advanced as far as he could.

The first reminder came in the winter of 1792, when Wilson decided that being a Supreme Court justice, writing and delivering a multiyear series of law lectures, rewriting a state constitution, managing a massive land empire, and raising six children alone was not enough to keep him busy. On the last day of 1791, he drafted a long, ingratiating proposal to President Washington: He wanted to compile, by himself, a definitive digest of the laws of the United States. It was an inconceivably vast undertaking, and he went to lengths to assure the president that he was the man—the only man—for a job of such "immense importance." For starters, he was already at work on a similar project for the state of Pennsylvania. That assignment was supposed to pay him eight hundred dollars, and the prospect of more income was a key part of his desire to take on the larger project.

At the same time, his belief in the value of such a digest was genuine, and his understanding of its significance was, as usual, prescient. "The most intricate and the most delicate questions in our national jurisprudence will arise in running the line between the authority of the national government and that of the several states," he wrote, anticipating the key dispute in a civil war that was still half a century away. A digest, in his mind, would help the country navigate future conflicts.

Wilson had not forgotten Washington's rejection of his request to be named chief justice, and his request this time carried the same overly solicitous tone: "If you think that, at a proper time, it ought to be 'recommended' by you to the national legislature," he wrote, with a wink that he should have known would make the president uncomfortable, "I declare my willingness, nay, my desire to undertake it." Like his earlier appeal to be appointed chief justice, this false humility broadcast his insecurity in the face of the stolid Washington.

The reaction from the executive branch was skeptical. Edmund Randolph, the attorney general, wrote to Washington that he saw no need for such a digest "when no crisis demands it." Anyway, it was highly doubtful that a single person could manage such a "Herculean task." But Randolph's bigger concern was with Wilson himself—both his financial motivations for proposing the project and the risk that hiring a Supreme Court justice to undertake such a job would call his integrity into question. If Washington was not already of the same mind, Randolph's arguments convinced him. In a terse reply at the end of January, he shot Wilson down once again. "I question much whether the time is yet arrived, the necessity so generally apparent, or the temper of Congress so well framed for these things, as to render such a proposition acceptable," Washington wrote. In response to Wilson's nudge, he added, "I doubt still more whether at any time, its coming from the Executive would be the most auspicious mode of bringing it forward." In other words, members of Congress would take offense at the implication that they were not bright enough to see the need for a digest themselves.

Sitting in his office and reading Washington's latest rejection by candlelight, Wilson must have suppressed a rising panic. He desperately needed money, but there would be no more than his judge's salary coming to him from the federal government, nor any at all from Pennsylvania. He would not deliver any more law lectures at the University of Pennsylvania after the spring of 1792, even though he had made it only halfway through his prepared series. The insistent demands of being a justice, especially riding circuit, and the ever more chaotic nature of his business life, made it impossible. At times, he appeared to show some awareness of the predicament he was in. In his opening law lecture he had remarked, almost in passing, that "Property, highly deserving security, is, however, not an end, but a means. How miserable, and how contemptible is that man, who inverts the order of nature, and makes his property, not a means, but an end!"

A more pointed reminder that his reckless financial activity was generating increasing discomfort among his peers came when President Washington was faced with filling a vacancy in the chief justiceship in 1795. Chief Justice John Jay had been appointed a special envoy to England to negotiate a new treaty on trade that would help avert another military conflict. Ever the loyal servant, Jay took on the post while keeping his job on the court, but it soon became impossible to do both at once, and he chose to stay put in England, leaving the court shorthanded. That gave Washington the job of replacing the chief justice. The widely held expectation was that he would pick the most senior remaining justice—in this case, William Cushing. But Cushing's own poor health issues left him with little support. "Between ourselves," one court observer wrote another, "Cushing is superannuated and contemptible." Next in line was Wilson, and while his superiority as a legal thinker was without doubt, his land dealings were so sprawling and over-leveraged by this time that Washington wanted to keep as much distance as he could.

Instead, the president reached out to John Rutledge, the South Carolinian whom Washington had previously appointed to the court but who almost immediately resigned because, like Wilson, he believed he deserved to be chief. Eager to fill the post, Washington made Rutledge a recess appointment, which gave him about six months to convince Congress to confirm him as the permanent chief. But soon after, Rutledge destroyed his chances by giving an intemperate speech denouncing Jay's recently signed treaty. Rumors of Rutledge's declining mental health were already in circulation in Congress, and when the Senate met to consider his nomination in December, they rejected it.

Around the same time, Rutledge sent a letter to Washington resigning from the court due to his poor health. He neglected to mention that the day before he sent the letter, he had tried to kill himself by walking off the end of a wharf into Charleston Harbor. He was dragged from the water after an enslaved child saw him struggling and alerted a nearby boat.

By the beginning of 1796, with the new court term only weeks away, Washington was exasperated. "I am really at a loss to know what measures now to adopt," he wrote (and then crossed out) in a note to Henry Lee. Wilson was, of course, still available and eager for the post. But Washington did not need the headaches he knew would come with appointing someone so financially compromised. Almost anyone else would be preferable—even his old friend Patrick Henry, the famous Anti-Federalist, whom he turned to in desperation. Henry had in recent years become friendlier to the nationalist cause, but in no sense was he as committed as Wilson. Henry declined.

Days before the February term was to begin, and without any other good options, Washington turned back to Cushing, who thanked him profusely for the honor, then said he would prefer to remain an associate justice due to "my infirm and declining state of health." Strike three.

Wilson was waiting patiently to be called to the job he knew should be his by right. But few others felt that way. As Samuel Johnston, the former North Carolina senator, wrote to Justice Iredell, who was his brother-in-law, "I am sorry that Mr. Cushing refused the office of Chief Justice, as I don't know whether a less exceptionable character can be obtained without passing over Mr. Wilson, which would perhaps be a measure that could not be easily reconciled to strict propriety."

Washington cast about for a few more weeks before landing at last on Oliver Ellsworth, the Connecticut senator, state court judge, and devoted Federalist who had been a key player at the Philadelphia convention and had helped write the Judiciary Act. The president nominated Ellsworth on March 3. The Senate, as relieved as everyone else, confirmed him the next day, with a single no vote.

It had been a tortuous path for Washington. When it was all over, Vice President Adams explained to his wife, Abigail, that in contrast to Ellsworth's "courage constancy fortitude and capacity . . . Mr. Wilson's ardent speculations had given offence to some, and his too frequent affectation of popularity to others."

What was left for Wilson? "I think it not unlikely that Wilson will resign," Justice Iredell confided to his wife, Hannah.

Wilson did not resign, but within a little over a year, he was absent, consumed by his collapsing land ventures and on the run from the law. He would never return to the bench. Within a few years, most of Wilson's contributions to the Supreme Court were overwritten or erased entirely. John Marshall, who took over as chief justice in 1801, wrote more words in his opinion in *Marbury v. Madison* than Wilson did in his entire tenure.

18

New Love and Escape from Philadelphia

"NEVER TO BE IN WANT OF MONEY"

THERE IS NO record of precisely when, or if, James Wilson realized the world was closing in around him because of his obsessive spending and debt, but by early 1792 the signs were indisputable.

That spring, William Duer, a prominent Federalist who had recently served as assistant secretary of the treasury, was carted off to the New Gaol, New York City's main debtors' prison. Duer lived, like Wilson, at the tangled intersection of his public duties and his private compulsions. As a signer of the Articles of Confederation, a member of the Continental Congress, and a high-ranking Treasury official, he was a key player in the nation's early development. He was also, like Wilson, an inveterate speculator in both land and stocks. In a dangerous scheme he cooked up with an accomplice, Alexander Macomb, Duer tried to corner the market in government bonds, triggering the nation's first financial crisis, which required Alexander Hamilton to step in to save the economy.

"Act with fortitude and honor," Hamilton counseled Duer during the panic, urging him to pay back his many creditors. "If you cannot reasonably hope for a favorable extrication do not plunge deeper. Have the courage to make a full stop." It was advice Wilson, no less than Duer, needed to hear.

But it was for naught. Already hounded by creditors for the modern equivalent of millions of dollars, Duer was sued by the federal government for failing to report almost two hundred forty thousand dollars in loans he had taken several years earlier. Soon he found himself behind bars in New York.

By the middle of April, a mob, including many victims of Duer's scheme, gathered each night around the prison. Violent confrontations erupted as some in the crowd threw rocks at the New Gaol, shattering lamps and windows and drawing gunfire from constables and militiamen. Duer likely heard the ruckus outside from his cell, which for all its cold discomforts must have felt like the safest place to be.

The public anger at speculators would only grow in the months and years to come. "It is a remark in every person's mouth, that were they torn to pieces, or hung without undergoing any form of trial, it would be only a necessary example and a just punishment," Henry Remsen wrote in a letter to Thomas Jefferson describing the mob's sentiments toward Duer and his associates.

If Wilson, who had his own firsthand experience facing down a life-threatening mob, was shaken by the grim news out of New York, he didn't make note of it. To the contrary, even as Duer sat locked away in Manhattan, Wilson was forging ahead with his sprawling and debt-laden business operation. In 1792 he had become one of the nation's largest private landowners and arguably its most prodigious speculator.

Speculation was a common enterprise among the nation's elite at the time—in addition to Duer, George Washington, Thomas Jefferson, Alexander Hamilton, Benjamin Franklin, George Mason, Robert Morris, Patrick Henry, and many other founders engaged in the practice to some degree. But none approached it with the uncontrolled rapacity of Wilson. Through the 1780s and into the '90s, his holdings expanded to as much as four million acres of land, larger than the state of Connecticut.

It was an empire of massive scope and complexity. He was president and a major shareholder of the Illinois and Wabash Land Company, which had grown into one of the biggest and most influential corporations in the country at the time, powerful enough to influence the course of the debate over the Articles of Confederation. The company claimed title to about thirty million acres across modern-day Ohio, Indiana, and Illinois, and Wilson's share was between six hundred thousand and one million acres.

He also owned many shares in and provided legal services to the Indiana Company, whose land claims would end up in a dispute before the Supreme Court in 1798, while Wilson was still a sitting justice (though not present on the bench, for reasons we will shortly see). And he was the largest individual shareholder of the Georgia Company, which joined three other land companies in the purchase of roughly 35 million acres in what is now Alabama and Mississippi. Title to the valuable land, much of which bordered the Mississippi River, was claimed at various times by multiple jurisdictions, including Indian Nations, but it was sold to the companies by the cash-hungry Georgia state government for the sum of five hundred thousand dollars. Wilson himself had purchased 1,750,000 of those acres. As details emerged of the Great Yazoo Lands Sale, as it became known, it blew up into a national scandal, complete with political bribes and corrupt backroom deals. There were calls for Wilson's impeachment, and Georgia voters elected new leadership, which passed laws overturning the sale and burning nearly all legal documents that recorded it. The dispute would drag on for more than a decade until it finally reached the Supreme Court, which did not resolve it until 1810.

In full, Wilson personally owned (or claimed title to) a decent chunk of the country: from northern New York and western Pennsylvania to Kentucky and Virginia and as far south as North Carolina, South Carolina, and Georgia, including what would later become some of the most valuable land in America.

He could justify all this as being in harmony with his vision for the health and happiness of a rapidly growing young nation. He laid this vision out in an essay, "On the Improvement and Settlement of Lands in the United States." It proposed a vast program of immigration and development that would merge the unique advantages of

America and Europe—the former's "immense quantity" of "rich" and "well-situated" land, the latter's "abundance of labor and capital and stock." In Wilson's eyes, if Americans made it easy and appealing enough, Europeans would move to and develop these lands, and everyone would benefit by a virtuous circle. "As new settlements are made and encreased, new states will be formed and established," he wrote.

Wilson acknowledged that the plan was "uncommonly extensive" and laden with risks, not the least of which was the peril for immigrants of making the transatlantic voyage, followed by the struggles of settling a family in a foreign land. Not a problem, Wilson suggested: Just provide the best ships stocked with the healthiest food and steered by the most humane captains. Then build "a chain of houses and farms at convenient distances"—ten miles seemed like a reasonable number—where immigrant families could stop and rest for the night on their journey west. Then provide a stable of horses, oxen, cows, sheep, pigs, and poultry for the settlers to buy upon their arrival on their new land.

All this would cost a huge amount, Wilson knew. Thus the "first axiom" of his plan: "*never to be in want of money.*" That could be ensured by convincing capitalists in both America and Europe that his plan was the best way forward for modern society, and for their own pocketbooks. In the end, he believed the plan's success would be guaranteed by its sheer size: "The very *extent* may sometimes aid the *execution* of a system."

This certainty in the rightness of his view of the world seemed to ride, as it always did with Wilson, on little more than his own insistence. In his words, "Confidence must be the soul of a plan so enlarged and so interesting as this is."

For confidence to play a meaningful role, though, it had to exist in hearts and minds other than Wilson's. By the mid-1790s, there weren't many of those left. One was Arthur St. Clair, his fellow Scot. "You are as rich as a Jew already," St. Clair wrote to Wilson in 1793. "I wish you had ten times as much, because I think you are one of those folks money would not spoil."

A more common observation about Wilson appeared in a letter printed in the June 10, 1793, edition of the *Federal Gazette*, shortly after he had arrived in Boston on his circuit-riding duties. The writer was responding to a report of a jury charge Wilson had delivered to prospective Boston jurors, which was described as "replete with the happiness of equal government." "This idea comes with an ill grace from a man, who parades our streets with a coach and four horses, when it is known his exorbitant salary enables him to make this flashy parade, and the money is taken from the pockets of the industrious part of the community," the writer said. "Where is the 'equality' when an officer of government is enabled by his excessive salary, to live in a stile vastly superior to any member in the society that supports him?"

Wilson did manage to win over at least one heart and mind on that trip to Boston, during a Sunday church visit to Dr. Thatcher's meeting. There he met Hannah Gray, the nineteen-year-old second cousin of Boston lawyer Harrison Gray Otis, and was immediately taken with her. It was the first time he had dared approach romance since Rachel's death seven years earlier.

"My dear Hannah," he wrote to her from Rhode Island a few days after their meeting. "I mentioned that, at the conclusion of the court here, I would either see you in Boston, or write to you. . . . But why should I delay writing till the conclusion of the court? Why should not my pen sooner take up a theme so constantly present to my thoughts?" The Visitant had returned, with his ardor and persistence intact. "When I find it so difficult to delay writing; you may easily judge how much I long for an answer: Do let that answer be speedy and favorable: Let it authorize me to think and call you mine." It is the only known surviving letter from Wilson to Hannah.

Word of the middle-aged judge's interest in Hannah—who was three years younger than his eldest daughter—spread quickly around Boston. The commentary carried a tone of affectionate mockery that pierced the aloof public image Wilson had cultivated. "He came, he saw, and was overcome," John Quincy Adams wrote to his younger brother Thomas after Wilson's letter to Hannah. "The gentle Caledon was smitten at meeting with a first sight love. Unable to contain his amorous pain, he breathed his sighs about the Streets; and even when seated on the bench of Justice, he seemed as if teeming with some woful ballad to his mistress eyebrow."

Speculating on the likelihood of "a new edition of January and May," Adams wrote, "Cupid himself must laugh at his own absurdity, in producing such an union." On the same day, Henry Jackson, a Boston merchant, wrote to Henry Knox, "It will be highly flattering to see one of our Boston girls in her coach & four rolling the streets of Philadelphia." The gossips proved as prophetic as they were precipitous. Wilson and Hannah were married in September in Boston.

Just above the announcement of their wedding in *The Boston Gazette* was a dispatch from a Philadelphia newspaper describing a fever that "still rages in our city." "Philadelphia, the boast of America, has been deserted by near half its inhabitants!" The yellow fever epidemic that was tearing through the nation's capital was the worst in more than three decades, killing upward of one in ten people—most working class or poor. The disease would haunt the city nearly every summer through the rest of the decade.

Wilson's land sickness was not as acute or as lethal as yellow fever, but it was a sickness nevertheless. Benjamin Rush, Wilson's friend and fellow signer of the Declaration of Independence, characterized it most accurately in a satirical essay he published in the late 1780s. Rush, America's preeminent doctor just as Wilson was its lawyer, catalogued the twenty-six manias that he believed described the country at the time. Second on the list was "land mania"—"a frequent disease in every part of America. It broke out with peculiar violence in most of the states immediately after the peace, and has continued to be more or less the epidemic of our country ever since. A room in a gaol, instead of a cell in a hospital, is the usual cure of this species of madness."

Love and a new wife did nothing to diminish Wilson's primary passion. By 1794, he was purchasing land not so much to amass more of it as to pay off his earlier purchases, in the hope that at least some of the tracts would appreciate enough in value that he could flip them for the cash he so desperately needed. By this time, he had to buy nearly everything on credit—often hundreds of thousands of acres at a time. Purchases of this size usually involved land warrants, which allowed buyers to put a hold on land for a fraction of the purchase price and authorized them to conduct a survey and pay the balance after.

Many of the warrants were held by Revolutionary War veterans, who had received them in lieu of cash for their service. The state would give the soldier a certificate that could be redeemed for an unspecified plot of land. The problem was that most of the veterans were themselves in debt, and the land was their only negotiable property, so they were eager to make deals. Enter speculators like Wilson, who were ready to take advantage of the situation and scoop up warrants representing thousands of acres for pennies. The plan was to sell that land at a premium before the balance came due, reinvesting any profit into yet more land. It was a morally dubious, high-risk scheme that assumed land values were always rising. But when the streams of European immigrants Wilson envisioned never materialized, those lands, much of which he had never personally laid eyes on, were essentially worthless.

Another obstacle was an anti-speculator law passed by the Pennsylvania legislature, which limited the number of acres that could be sold in a private transaction. It was an attempt to protect small farmers from aggressive speculators like Wilson, but it wasn't hard to game the system. One historian believes Wilson got around this law by using fake names to purchase land warrants, then transferring the land to his own name on the deeds.

Not everyone was fooled. Wilson's debts had grown so big that the Bank of North America, which he had fought so hard to create and protect, rejected one of his loan applications for being too risky. As a Supreme Court justice holding a position of national trust, Wilson should have felt humbled by this rebuke; instead, it emboldened him. And thanks to his high standing and powerful post, there was always someone willing to lend him more money.

A prime example of this happened in the summer of 1794, when

Wilson saw a development opportunity in the wilds of northeastern Pennsylvania. The heavily wooded region around the Wallenpaupack River, several days' ride north of Philadelphia, had long been occupied by Native Nations. But by the 1770s, the tribes had mostly left or been pushed out by settlers, and Wilson was able to purchase from William Penn 12,500 acres in what was known as Wallenpaupack Manor, which came with several waterfalls that seemed ideal for powering hemp and flax mills. In June 1794, he ordered construction to begin on a 160-foot-long factory for making cloth and rope, at a cost of more than ten thousand dollars. Around the same time, he oversaw the building of housing—along with roads, bridges, and stores—for factory workers. The name of the complex: Wilsonville.

"The whole scene has the appearance of enchantment," the *Gazette of the United States* reported, marveling that the factory was expected to be up and running within six months. "The liberal, patriotic Judge Wilson certainly deserves the highest encomiums from his fellow citizens."

"Enchantment" was apt. Wilson moved Wilsonville forward at such a fast pace only by offering an exorbitant salary—six pounds a month, or twice the going rate—which lured laborers away from other jobs in the area and drew the ire of competing developers and speculators like Henry Drinker. A friend of Drinker's wrote him that Wilson could not possibly afford to pay such wages "unless he is backed by some almost inexhaustible fund, or his own purse is very deep, the expense is so enormously great."

There was no fund, although Wilson himself was inexhaustible. He was also aggressive, in some cases relying on minor legal technicalities to undercut his competitors. At one point, Drinker felt the need to remind him of the impropriety of such behavior from a Supreme Court justice, asking "how it would appear for a person in his exalted station, appointed to promote and distribute equal justice through the land, to come into the land office a long time after and search for some informality or supposed deficiency in the descriptive part of our Locations."

And yet Drinker fell into the same trap as so many others before him—trusting Wilson precisely because his vision was so big. "Notwithstanding J. Wilson's imprudent management and the extravagance of his agents in the wages they pay," Drinker wrote a friend in November 1794, "it appears to me he had made such large acquisitions of late in the land way that there will be safety in trusting to his sufficiency in any engagements made clearly by his directions." It was a striking echo of the philosophy Wilson offered in his essay on land development: "The very *extent* may sometimes aid the *execution* of a system."

19
The Tavern Hideout

"HUNTED LIKE A WILD BEAST"

THE YEAR 1796 started badly for Wilson, and then it got worse.

In March, George Washington denied him the chief justiceship for the second time. The position had been open for nine months by then, and Washington had multiple chances to offer Wilson the job. But Wilson's disastrous finances were now widely known, and the president had no desire to expose the leadership of a coordinate branch of government to chaos and imputations of corruption.

Meanwhile, Wilson's law students—who, like the president's nephew Bushrod, had paid dearly for the privilege of studying with the greatest lawyer in the nation—found him to be absent or distracted most of the time. As a teacher, he had grown "rare, distant and reserved . . . almost useless," according to the recollections of one former student, Samuel Sitgreaves.

By the summer, the American economy was in full-blown crisis after the bubble burst in land values, upending credit markets and causing a national panic. Wilson and other major speculators including Robert Morris, who had been the wealthiest man in America, began to default on their loans.

"Ruin is staring in ye faces of most of ye land speculators," Edward Burd, an elite Philadelphia lawyer, wrote to Jasper Yeates, a state supreme court justice and longtime associate of Wilson's. "The day of reckoning is at hand, and no prospect of disposing of their lands. There are a great number of judgments against your friend Wilson lately confessed by him. People speak very freely as to the situation he is likely to be in very shortly."

That August, Justice Iredell wrote to Wilson, "I never expect to hear in a letter from you how you or your Family are. But I assure you I shall always be solicitous to know, and shall feel real satisfaction in hearing favorable accounts."

What Wilson probably had not told Iredell by then was that in May, Hannah had given birth to a baby boy, Henry—their first child together and Wilson's seventh. Whether or not he shared the news, his concerns were not with his children any longer, but with his creditors. His friend Benjamin Rush wrote that Wilson was "deeply distressed; his resource was reading novels constantly." He skipped the entire fall term of the Supreme Court.

By December, the biggest speculators in Philadelphia were leaving town or getting locked up. "This place furnishes indication of great depravity; bankruptcies are frequently happening," Chauncey Goodrich, a Connecticut congressman, wrote to treasury secretary Oliver Wolcott about the financial panic of 1796. "Mr. Morris is greatly embarrassed. 'Tis said that Nicholson has fled to England; that Judge Wilson has been to gaol and is out on bail; but there are so many rumors I vouch for the credit of neither."

The rumor about Wilson, at least, was true, according to Morris. "Judge W-n was taken by the Sheriff last night," he wrote to Nicholson on December 8. "It will be my turn next." He added, "I am seriously uneasy for W-l-n's affair will make the Vultures more keen after me."

As 1797 dawned, Wilson's finances were becoming only more entangled. One of his biggest creditors, Pierce Butler, had begun pressing him for repayment of a debt that was approaching two hundred thousand dollars and growing by the day. In late winter, Butler's friend James Gibson reported back to him on Wilson's condition. "The prospect before him is very gloomy," Gibson wrote. "It is impossible at present to foretell the final issue." Wilson was present for the court's February 1797 term, but his attendance was no longer reliable. Many sittings of courts in his circuit could not be held because he never showed.

"There is such an immensity of business to do here that I cannot even conjecture when I can get away," James Iredell wrote to his Hannah in May. "For a great deal of it I am to thank Judge Wilson who suffered the court last Term to be entirely lost by his non-attendance."

Soon after, Wilson and Hannah left Philadelphia to evade his creditors, holing up at Morris Tavern in Bethlehem, fifty miles north of the city. Writing to Bird, Wilson asked him to bring "the newspapers and all the news," as well as "your papa's black cassimere coat that hangs up in my chamber closet." It was the first time he had been forced to flee his home since the Fort Wilson Riot in 1779. This time, he would not return.

When the August term of the Supreme Court opened, Wilson was not in his seat. "All the Judges are here but Wilson who unfortunately is in a manner absconding from his creditors, his Wife with him, the rest of the Family here!" Iredell wrote to his Hannah. "What a situation!"

Wilson didn't get far, and staying so close to the Philadelphia area made it easy for his creditors to find him. Samuel Wallis, a fellow speculator to whom Wilson owed $120,000, tracked him down in Burlington, New Jersey, and demanded repayment. Wilson said he did not have the full amount in cash but offered to either pay half or give Wallis lands equaling the total value. The men decided to leave matters as they were for the time being, planning to meet again and finalize a deal.

Weeks later, two of Wilson's other creditors, Simon Gratz and Isaac Hopper, found him still in Burlington, but they were not as conciliatory as Wallis. They had him thrown in debtors' prison. The news spread quickly.

"What shall we come to?" Thomas Shippen wrote in his diary. "One of the highest Court in the United States, one of the 6 Judges in a Jersey Gaol!"

George Washington, back home at Mount Vernon after leaving the White House, must have felt a sad sense of vindication. In a letter to Henry Lee, he mentioned as an aside, "I had declined receiving Wilson's notes when they were proposed, because I could not depend upon converting them into cash."

On September 6, Wilson sent another letter to Bird, this time from behind bars, and with less patience than before. He mentioned that Samuel Wallis had written to him seeking repayment, which led Wilson to express "my extreme astonishment at your not coming here before this time. At all events set out as soon as you possibly can upon receiving this letter; tomorrow morning at the latest," he wrote. He needed six hundred dollars for bail, he told Bird, as well as "some shirts and stockings. I want them exceedingly, as also money as much as possible, without which I cannot leave this place."

Bird came up with the funds somehow, because when circuit-riding assignments were handed out for the fall of 1797, Wilson was out of prison and explicitly requesting the southern route—the most arduous of the three and the one all the justices took pains to avoid. He had ridden it only once before, but now getting away from the North and his creditors was his best hope to avoid recapture and imprisonment. It also would give him an opportunity to canvass the lands he had purchased in the Carolinas and Georgia and to reorganize his finances. The last months of 1797 and into 1798 marked the frantic downward spiral of a man who had largely lost contact with reality.

In December, he wrote his lawyer, Joseph Thomas, from Raleigh, North Carolina, to report that even though he couldn't account for all the lands he had purchased there, the information he had been able to gather about them "has been favorable in a degree much exceeding my most sanguine hopes." Still, he told Thomas, he would need to stay the winter in the South, and he would need money. "You can have no conception of what importance it is to me to have some funds. Twenty thousand dollars would I believe secure every thing: Ten thousand would secure a great deal," he said, before saying it again for good measure. "I can only repeat you can have no conception of what importance it would be. Without funds much must be lost." On the same day, he wrote Bird to ask why he was not providing more updates about his debts and business situation.

"To this Day I have not heard a single Syllable from you," Wilson complained, a notable echo of the complaints his mother and relatives had made about him for years. He told Bird to meet him in Edenton, North Carolina, the home of James and Hannah Iredell, which offered a sanctuary of sorts. "I need not tell you to bring with you all the Money that shall be possible," he closed his letter to Bird. "I have many things to say to you, which cannot be communicated by letter."

A month later, Wilson was settled in Edenton, but Bird had sent no word. At home in Philadelphia, he had only recently passed the bar and was scrambling to build up a small legal practice while also dealing with his father's financial collapse and tending to the home Wilson had abandoned. Hannah, selling her needlework to help pay the mountain of bills, was deeply torn. Her children needed her in Philadelphia, but her husband on the lam needed her even more. One day in February, she was shopping on Market Street when she ran into Iredell, who was in town for the Supreme Court's winter term. When he told her that Wilson was not coming back, she broke down in sobs and asked him if she could travel with him when he returned to Edenton.

They set out by carriage on February 18. Days earlier, Robert Morris had been sent to debtors' prison, where he would remain for three years. Meanwhile in Edenton, Wilson was frantically trying to stave off Pierce Butler's demands for repayment and his threats to sue him and have him taken into custody for the $197,000 he owed. But Butler was still trying to give Wilson a way out, offering him two to three years to make the payments, as long as Wilson put up his property in Pennsylvania as security.

The few people who would still consider doing business with Wilson consulted with each other about what to do. "I beseech you not to be his security," Thomas Blount, a North Carolina lawmaker and landowner, wrote to his brother John. "He has no real estate anywhere that is not encumbered with at least one mortgage, & if you rely on his honor, or trust him in any thing, he will certainly deceive you. Let him go to gaol." Another Blount brother, Jacob, was skeptical that

Butler's threats would do any good. "In my opinion it is bad policy to sue him, he having no property that can be got hold of," Jacob wrote to John Gray. Jacob thought Wilson would be so upset by any legal action that he would double down and refuse to pay. "If he is sued[,] not being able to procure security will probably make a finish of him and the debt finally lost."

But on April 10, a writ of debt was issued against Wilson, ordering him to pay Butler, with a court date set for October 6. Writing to Bird again to inform him of Butler's lawsuit, Wilson said it would force him to remain in North Carolina until it was resolved.

By May, Wilson had made no progress in satisfying the debt and was full of self-pity. "I have been hunted—I may be hunted—like a wild beast," he wrote to Thomas, his lawyer. His creditors were after him "with an avidity cruel, treacherous and insatiable." Still, he insisted he would satisfy all debts and refused to relinquish his optimism. "I think there is reason to believe that the season is approaching when such exertions may be crowned with the most abundant success." In closing, he wrote, "My life has not been a life of idleness or indolence. But there are times, when nothing, not ruinous, can be done. Such times I have unfortunately experienced."

Butler, for his part, was out of patience. In late May, he wrote to his lawyer to say he had given Wilson and Bird every chance to repay and that they had not come through. He held on to a reed of sympathy for his former colleague. "I have no wish to possess his lands nor the most distant inclination to Speculate on his ruin." But he was prepared to "let the law have its operation"—that is, to have Wilson arrested and thrown into debtors' prison again.

Butler believed that this led to Wilson's being locked up, although the surviving records suggest he was mistaken and that Wilson managed to stay out of prison in Edenton by promising to remain in town until the matter was resolved. By then, it didn't matter much. Wilson was in a prison of his own choosing—stashed away with Hannah in a back room of Horniblow's tavern, a few blocks from the Iredells in one direction and the waterfront in the other.

Hannah passed the days doing her needlework and sending letters to Bird back in Philadelphia. "I begin to feel quite home sick, but when we shall leave Edenton I do not know," she wrote in late June. "We are at a very great expense here, and if your pap does not attend the Supreme Court, I feel afraid of the consequence." In confidence, she wrote, "I still think it would be but justice for your papa to give up everything, if he can not settle any other way, I am sure he would feel much happier, but it is a subject that he never wishes to hear mentioned."

Those who knew of the situation believed the best outcome would be for Wilson to resign from the Supreme Court, if only to avoid the disgrace of being convicted or impeached. But Wilson refused and insisted on being outfitted to ride the court's fall circuit, even though he and Hannah didn't have enough money to pay their room and board, let alone to buy new clothing or rent a horse and carriage.

As the brutal North Carolina summer sank in, the mysterious pestilence arrived on mosquitoes' wings. In late July, Hannah wrote Bird to tell him that Wilson had come down with "an intermiting fever"—malaria. He was bedridden and getting weaker by the day. "Write me what people say to our not coming home," Hannah wrote. "You need not be afraid of distressing me, as I can hear nothing worse than I expect."

Wilson himself reached out to Bird once more, in early August—upbraiding him again for being a poor correspondent. But what concerned him more was that he had not heard anything from his lawyer. That silence would be explained a few days later. Writing from Philadelphia, James Iredell reported that Joseph Thomas had left his pregnant wife and run off with more than sixty thousand dollars of his clients' funds, including the last of the Wilsons' money. There was now nothing standing between Wilson and total ruin.

The Supreme Court's August term began the same day, but it was cut short two days later, due to another outbreak of yellow fever in Philadelphia, "nursed by a bad air & dirty narrow streets," in the words of Justice William Cushing. At Horniblow's, Wilson's fever was getting worse with each passing hour; Hannah tended to him, but it was of little use. He spent most of the middle weeks of August in a delirious haze, refusing to take the medicinal bark that was the only known treatment for malaria.

On August 17, James Iredell's brother Thomas, a lawyer in Edenton, wrote to inform the justice that Wilson "is by no means well." Iredell himself was already on his way back home from Philadelphia, escaping one plague in the North for another in the South. He arrived home four days later and rushed over to Horniblow's, a few blocks away. Wilson was no longer conscious. Hannah had been by his side but was too distraught to remain; she left when Iredell arrived. A few hours later, with Iredell standing watch, Wilson drew his last breath. He was buried the following day, August 22, under a small grove of trees at the edge of a field on the estate of Samuel Johnston, the state's governor and Iredell's brother-in-law. There was no ceremony or official recognition, just the simple burial of a complicated man across the creek from where he had hidden himself for the past year.

The task of informing Wilson's family of his death fell to Billy White, his best friend from his college days—now known as Bishop William White, the presiding bishop of the Episcopal Church. Iredell and Hannah Wilson both wrote letters to Bird and mailed them to White to deliver personally. The yellow fever was still rampant in Philadelphia, and the Wilson home was closed to outsiders. But White managed to get word to Wilson's daughters and to Bird.

Hannah's letter recounted what Bird already knew: that Wilson's "mind had been in such a state for the last six months, harassed and perplexed, that it was more than he could possibly bear, and brought on a violent nervous fever." Bird knew this, of course, because Hannah had kept him informed—a courtesy he did not always reciprocate. "I never knew of his arrest till since his death, and now can account for many things he said in his delirium," she wrote.

Iredell's letter, which was mailed together with Hannah's, told Bird of what his stepmother had endured. "What she underwent for some days previous to the unfortunate event of anxiety . . . and distress, I believe no language could paint." He then turned to business, proposing that Bird was best situated to administer what he delicately referred to as "the complicated concerns" of his father's estate. He also sent Bird the bill for the Wilsons' months at Horniblow's, which totaled $845, and for funeral costs, which amounted to another $42.

The newspapers that took notice of Wilson's passing over the next several weeks did so only briefly, and not always accurately. *J. Russell's Gazette* in Boston included a notice that got both Wilson's name and the date of his death wrong. It reported that he had spent the previous eight months in Edenton "in a very private manner."

Wilson's peers and colleagues seemed relieved. "These are perilous times; a man may be well today and dead tomorrow. . . . Our friend Judge Wilson is good poor fellow and there is an end to his troubles in this world," Robert Morris wrote from behind bars.

Pierce Butler, learning that he had been mistaken about Wilson's incarceration, wrote, "I feel a degree of satisfaction that I prohibited his being put in gaol." But Butler would never get his money. Wilson died before the scheduled court date, and there was no cash to be had.

George Washington wrote to his nephew Bushrod, whom President John Adams was about to appoint to the Supreme Court seat of his mentor Wilson. (Adams had initially asked John Marshall to accept the nomination, but Marshall declined because he was running for office at the time.) "I only regret that Judge Wilson had it not in his power to have postponed his [exit] (which I am persuaded he was not indisposed to do) to a later period," Washington wrote.

At the Iredells' insistence, Hannah stayed on at their home in Edenton through the winter. She and James Iredell spent much of the time in correspondence with Bird, who was struggling to untangle the mess of his father's failed business. When Iredell traveled back to Philadelphia for the court's February term in 1799, she accompanied him.

Even in death, Wilson's legal and financial troubles dogged him and his family. In mid-September, Samuel Wallis finally reached Edenton, intent on getting his money back. On discovering that Wilson had died a month before, he headed back north, stopping for a night in an inn where he caught yellow fever. He soon succumbed. Robert Morris wrote to a friend that Wallis was "dead of the fever so that his land fever is cured."

Bird was never able to free himself from the disaster his father had left behind. All over the country, landholdings that Wilson had not already defaulted on were sold to pay off costs, bringing in $35,000 here, 10,000 pounds there. His personal effects were auctioned—scores of volumes from his library, a set of English trout flies, his Supreme Court robe (bought by Justice Samuel Chase for $17), copies of the Pennsylvania constitution of 1790, and, in a nod to his childhood, a pile of books on farming.

In 1804, Bird published a three-volume set of Wilson's law lectures, speeches, essays, and other remarks—a natural undertaking by the son whom Wilson had always trusted with his legal work. And yet Bird would ultimately follow the opposite path of his father. After being trained in the law and working as a lawyer and then a judge, he was faced with sentencing a convicted murderer to death. Unable to square capital punishment with his conscience, he resigned from the bench and entered the ministry, where he studied with the Reverend William White, his father's dear friend.

Meanwhile, Wilson's debts turned out to be as persistent as the man who incurred them. More than half a century after Wilson's death, Bird—by then Reverend Wilson—was still dealing with legal matters relating to his father's land and other transactions.

In 1926, the Pennsylvania Power and Light Company flooded the valley around Wilsonville to create the reservoir known as Lake Wallenpaupack. For the past century, the only place in America named for the man who was instrumental in creating it has been underwater.

Epilogue

AT DAWN ON Sunday, November 18, 1906, the USS *Dubuque* steamed out of Philadelphia Harbor carrying a stripped-down crew, a handful of guests, and an empty casket draped in an American flag. The ship was headed to Norfolk, Virginia, and then to North Carolina, where its guests met up with a delegation of state lawmakers and dignitaries underneath a small grove of trees at the edge of a field in Edenton.

A crew of gravediggers went to work on a site in the shadow of the trees, at last exhuming a dirt-crusted coffin. When the coffin was opened, the assembled group of about thirty somber men could see that the skull's "heavy hair, tied in the fashion of the day, was of a slightly sandy color."

One of the main architects of the American nation had been thoroughly forgotten, "hustled offstage as quickly as possible" after his tawdry death, as one historian of the founding era put it. Now, more than a century later, James Wilson was going home to Philadelphia.

Burton Alva Konkle, a history professor at Swarthmore College and biographer of famous Pennsylvanians, stood among the Philadelphia contingent that November day. He was one of a small group of men who had decided that Wilson deserved a more dignified send-off than he had received at his death and that it was their job to right this historical wrong.

Konkle had employed Wilsonian persistence to convince authorities in Pennsylvania and North Carolina that this forgotten founder needed to be moved to the city where he had spent nearly his entire adult life. He would be reinterred at Christ Church, the resting place of Benjamin Franklin, Robert Morris, Benjamin Rush, and many other Revolutionary-era luminaries—as well as Rachel Wilson, whose grave lay in the churchyard adjacent to the church, the result of a direct appeal from her granddaughter.

The James Wilson reburial project was part of a colonial revival playing out at the turn of the twentieth century, as Americans disoriented by the changes wrought over decades of rapid industrialization sought solace and stability in a supposedly uncomplicated honoring of the founders.

But Wilson wasn't an easy man to befriend in life, and he would be no easier to beatify in death. On the journey back north, Konkle got seasick, fog delayed the *Dubuque* for three hours outside the port of Philadelphia, and the ship nearly ran into a ferryboat as it entered the harbor. A New York newspaper commented on the day's events with the headline "Beatification of a Briber," describing Wilson as a "corruptionist and bribe-giver, the leader of the 'land sharks' of 1795." The justice would at last be getting a proper burial, but it would not magically restore his reputation.

Still, they tried. On November 22, amid lowered flags and gun salutes, soldiers from the *Dubuque* hoisted Wilson's casket—a gift from Andrew Carnegie, the Scottish-born steel magnate who had grown up in Dunfermline, not far from Carskerdo—and carried it from the Chestnut Street wharf ten blocks to Independence Hall, setting it down on a pedestal in the same room where Wilson had signed the Declaration of Independence and the Constitution more than a century before. For two and a half hours, the casket was overseen by an honor guard as members of the public filed past in silence.

The casket was then carried aloft another four blocks to Christ Church, escorted by Philadelphia's City Light Horse Cavalry (the same one that had ridden to Wilson's rescue during the Fort Wilson Riot). Following close behind, in top hats and canes, were three

Supreme Court justices—Chief Justice Melville Fuller and two associate justices, Edward Douglass White and Oliver Wendell Holmes Jr. The justices took their seats in the front row of the church as a capacity crowd squeezed in behind them.

It was a fitting show of pomp and circumstance, and yet the moment the speeches began, any illusion that Wilson's legacy was secure disappeared. The first speaker, a conservative Democrat representing the Philadelphia bar, went to lengths to deny that Wilson had advocated for a powerful central government. This was contradicted immediately by the next speaker, the dean of the University of Pennsylvania law school, who described Wilson as "the most democratic among the fathers of our country."

Pennsylvania's attorney general, William Henry Moody (who was about to become a Supreme Court justice himself), called it "one of the mysteries of history" that Wilson's "fame has not kept pace with his service."

No one could see with clarity the man lying before them, not even Burton Konkle, who had been the driving force behind the day's ceremonies. As the person in charge of the text on the massive headstone that was placed over Wilson's casket in the churchyard, Konkle had inserted a significant error—Wilson's date of death is chiseled in stone as August 28, 1798, one week after he died.

Wilson now lies under that erroneous headstone, next to Rachel, in a line of graves along the southern wall of the church that includes his fellow speculator and prisoner Robert Morris, his former colleague and creditor Pierce Butler, and his best friend, Billy (the Rev. William) White.

Wilson's 1906 reinterment marked the high point of public acknowledgment of his centrality to the nation's creation.

Through much of the nineteenth century, his life, to the degree it was remembered at all, was still defined by the financial calamity that marked its end. History books marginalized him when they didn't omit him entirely. Works of art consigned him to the background, like John Trumbull's massive depiction of the signing of the Declaration of Independence, which hangs today in the Rotunda of the US

Capitol and includes Wilson only at the edge of the scene, his face contorted into a scowl.

Politicians ignored Wilson, even those who had good reason not to. Abraham Lincoln—whose own vision of national supremacy and political equality aligned with Wilson's worldview better than any president's—never mentioned his name in public. Even the Supreme Court seemed inclined to forget one of its founding members and greatest legal minds. As late as the 1870s, Wilson's name appeared in the court's rulings at least as often in his capacity as a party to land dispute lawsuits as in his tenure as a justice.

Perhaps tellingly, the only people who made public use of Wilson's ideas were abolitionists, many of whom believed, as he had, that the Constitution was not a barrier to ending slavery. In their arguments, they quoted liberally from Wilson's speech in the ratifying convention, where he insisted that the Constitution was "laying the foundation for banishing slavery out of this country." It was the first time, but not the last, that Americans seeking to force the nation's practices to be more in line with its founding principles would turn to Wilson for support.

Decades would go by before Wilson's name would be invoked in another public forum. As the twentieth century dawned, the expanding nation was being knitted together, physically and legally, to a degree no one living had witnessed—raising new and contested questions about the nature of American federalism. In 1901, *The New York Times* ran an article asking whether the country's name should be rendered in the plural ("these united States") or the singular ("the United States"). The newspaper came down on the side of singular, citing Wilson as its authority. He was "probably the one member of the convention of 1787 who best comprehended the significance of the work of that body," the *Times* wrote. It quoted Wilson saying that "by adopting this Constitution we shall become a Nation."

Five years later and only weeks before Wilson's remains were exhumed in North Carolina, President Theodore Roosevelt invoked Wilson at length during a speech in Harrisburg, Pennsylvania, commemorating the state's new capitol building. Roosevelt's reliance on

Wilson is easy to understand: Both men saw a powerful national government as essential to the success of the American experiment.

The Industrial Revolution had led to "new evils," Roosevelt said—corporate monopolies that consolidated massive amounts of power in the hands of a few oligarchs, generating an unsustainable wealth gap and undermining the president's "full and complete power to work on behalf of the people." To accomplish that work, Roosevelt argued, the federal government has inherent powers that extend beyond those enumerated in the Constitution. These powers are the only way to "enable the people in effective form to assert their sovereignty over the immense corporations of the day."

Roosevelt then attacked the Supreme Court's "narrow construction" of the government's powers, saying that the court's rulings had "left blanks between the limits of actual national jurisdiction over the control of the great business corporations." This happened, the president said, because the justices had failed to approach these profound questions in "the spirit of your great Pennsylvanian, Justice Wilson."

This speech could have been written and delivered almost verbatim today, and yet Roosevelt appears to be the only president in American history to have invoked James Wilson's name, for any reason.

Over the last century, Wilson's stature has grown, but only among scholars and historians of the founding era. The leading chroniclers of the 1787 convention, starting with Max Farrand in 1911, came to appreciate Wilson's legal and intellectual brilliance and the significance of his role that summer and in the ratification debates that fall. Still, there was no sustained effort to cement Wilson's standing. Burton Konkle died in 1944, with twenty-one biographies to his name. The only one he failed to publish was about Wilson. In 1954, a Harvard graduate student named Charles Page Smith converted his doctoral dissertation into the first full-length Wilson biography, now long out of print.

Then, in the 1960s, the Supreme Court at last gave Wilson his due in a series of landmark decisions—the so-called one-person, one-vote cases, which required that all state and federal legislative seats represent equal numbers of people. It was a vindication of one of Wilson's central ideas, nearly two hundred years after he had expressed it.

By the end of the decade, leading historians like Robert McCloskey and Gordon Wood were releasing new editions of Wilson's writings and speeches and making the case that he was among the most important of the founders.

Still, while any schoolchild could identify Washington, Jefferson, Madison, Hamilton, and the rest, few Americans could have picked Wilson out of a lineup of one. His only appearance in mainstream culture came as a minor character in the hit Broadway musical *1776*, which portrayed him as a coward who voted in favor of independence not out of principle but out of a fear of calling too much attention to himself if he voted no. "I'm different from you, John," the Wilson character says to his mentor John Dickinson. "I'm different from most of the men here. I don't want to be remembered. I just don't want the—responsibility."

It was unflattering and misleading, and yet there was no one to object. Two hundred years later, Wilson's legacy was still essentially unrecorded, open to the misperceptions and distortions that had dogged it from the start.

In the twenty-first century, Wilson is the province of a coterie of dedicated scholars toiling at universities around the country. Their work on him has been comprehensive and illuminating. For most Americans, however, Wilson remains the nonentity he has been since his death, when he was driven out of our history.

So why does James Wilson's story matter to us today? Because, above all, he was right.

He was right in two distinct but related senses. First, he was prescient about the United States. Wilson anticipated the nation's democratic, egalitarian arc more accurately than any other founder. Indeed, his ideas about government and society were so far ahead of their time as to be timeless. Like all prescient thinkers, Wilson put together concepts and ways of thinking that survived on their own unique energy, allowing them to endure through the generations that followed.

But prescience and endurance alone do not guarantee moral clarity; plenty of bad ideas have survived the centuries. Which is why it is important that Wilson was right not only on the facts but on the values he held dear. Most Americans today agree that it is morally right to treat all people as equal, to recognize their ultimate political authority, and to give them a more direct role in shaping their government and choosing their leaders than many of Wilson's peers desired. For those of us alive in the twenty-first century, this is the essence of representative democracy—and Wilson was there from the start.

At the same time, the process of democracy carries inherent risks, as we are seeing today in both the United States and around the world. It is no longer the unaccountable monarch who threatens democracy, but the elected leader who, once empowered by voters, works to erode democracy from within.

The founders anticipated this risk and designed the Constitution largely as a safeguard against it. But even that safeguard can be twisted and undermined when political actors of the present seek to redefine our past.

This is the importance of understanding both Wilson's ideas and his story. For better or worse (I think the stronger case is for worse), the dominant form of constitutional interpretation in the judiciary today is known as originalism. According to originalists, the Constitution means what it was understood to mean at the time of its adoption. If Wilson's role in that critical period is erased, the originalist meaning of the Constitution is distorted.

"We're a republic, not a democracy," is a common refrain among those who seek to deny the right of voters to have the ultimate say—and a free and fair one—over our government. But once Wilson is restored to his proper place in our history, an honest inclusion of his ideas in our founding story renders false that six-word rallying cry.

A proper originalist view, accounting for the central role Wilson played, must acknowledge the centrality of his most important idea to our constitutional story: popular sovereignty—that is, the idea that the only true and legitimate source of authority rests with the people themselves. Their will, as expressed by a majority, must be honored by mechanisms like direct elections and proportional representation. And if those do not lead to a desired outcome, as Wilson put it in his opening law lecture, the people "may change their constitution and government whenever they please."

That is the central message of the Declaration of Independence, which Wilson insisted was the foundation of the American experiment, predating and thus supreme over the Constitution itself. Had he lived longer, or had his people-centered vision of government taken root more deeply in the nation's early years, America might have charted a very different course. Instead, for more than two centuries, he has been almost entirely absent from the prevailing narrative about the founding, warping and diminishing the conversation we are able to have about ourselves, our past, and our future.

That conversation usually centers on the boldface names: Thomas Jefferson and his local, agrarian ideal; James Madison and his counterbalancing factions; Alexander Hamilton and his general distrust of the common people.

Those founders were essential to the nation's birth, of course, and yet many of them came around to agree with Wilson in time. In 1821, Madison, preparing his notes on the 1787 convention for eventual publication, wrote that his comments on voting rights during that summer did not convey his "more full and matured view of the subject." He continued, "The right of suffrage is a fundamental article in republican constitutions." More than a decade later, Madison wrote that "the will of the majority" is "the vital principle of republican Government."

Jefferson, writing in 1816 to his friend Samuel Kercheval, referred to what he called "the mother-principle, that 'governments are republican only in proportion as they embody the will of their people, and execute it.'" He proposed a set of amendments to the Virginia constitution, including "general suffrage," "equal representation in the legislature," and "an executive chosen by the people." He was echoing what Wilson had sought to establish in the United States Constitution nearly thirty years before.

What would America look like if we could see ourselves as Wilson saw us? Take the recent debate over what ties this country together in the first place.

Is it "a group of people with a shared history and a common future," as Vice President J. D. Vance has said? Or is it, as Wilson and other founders understood, a creed? A living, unexpiring promise of freedom and self-determination that can be adopted by anyone who believes in it, even a poor farmer's son from the Scottish Lowlands. Vance has argued that this creedal definition is "way overinclusive," as it would open America's doors to all who agree with our foundational values.

Abraham Lincoln, on the other hand, understood things in a more Wilsonian spirit. In 1858, Lincoln described the essential lines of the Declaration of Independence, the ones Wilson himself helped inspire—"We hold these truths to be self-evident, that all men are created equal"—as an "electric cord" that "links the hearts of patriotic and liberty-loving men together." Lincoln understood how the "moral sentiment" of those words has the power to unite people from disparate parts of the earth, giving them "a right to claim it as though they were blood of the blood, and flesh of the flesh of the men who wrote that Declaration, and so they are." Lincoln was expressing the essence of Wilson's worldview, whether he knew it or not.

Today, 250 years after America's birth, Wilson continues to challenge us to live up to his vision, and to use its light to chart our way forward. Were he alive now, he would look at a Senate increasingly skewed in favor of smaller states and an Electoral College that has turned popular-vote losers into presidents twice already in this century and say, *I told you so.* He would be grimly amused that the greatest obstacles to majority rule in the twenty-first century reside in the Constitution itself.

This is not to say Wilson was infallible. It is difficult, for example, to look favorably at his insistence on a powerful chief executive in our moment, when President Trump has arrogated to himself near-monarchical powers. (Previous presidents have sought to expand their power in their own ways, of course, but none with a comparable speed or tenacity.) Many of Wilson's contemporaries foresaw this risk and were rightly desperate to avoid it, but Wilson's expansive vision for Article II of the Constitution won out. He might respond that the other branches were designed to serve as reliable checks on executive overreach: through judicial review in the courts and the Necessary and Proper Clause in Congress.

That is cold comfort in 2026, when the Supreme Court has green-lighted most of this overreach and Congress has ceded many of its core constitutional powers to the executive (at least when both branches are controlled by the same party).

In the big picture, however, resurrecting James Wilson reminds us how the insistence on democracy in America was there from the start, and from one of the nation's foremost architects. At the same time, his story serves as a warning that democracy has always been an elusive thing. Now our democracy's future—the future Wilson saw more clearly than anyone else—is in real doubt. The question we face today is whether we can reimagine it. Whether we can reimagine a Constitution, and a country, shaped by his vision. Wilson cannot answer that question, but we have no choice. As he said in his speech in the State House Yard, "The seeds of reformation are sown in the work itself."

Acknowledgments

The idea for this book came to me at an inopportune time. It was late 2018 and I was sitting at a desk in the back corner of the subbasement of the law library at New York University, working on a tight deadline to finish my previous book, *Let the People Pick the President,* about the history and dysfunction of the Electoral College. As I scoured James Madison's notes of the Constitutional Convention of 1787, trying to locate the moment of the College's creation, I found myself repeatedly distracted by the remarks of one delegate in particular—a long-winded Pennsylvanian named Wilson. He kept advocating ideas that stopped me in my tracks, ideas about democracy and self-government and the political power of regular people, ideas that sounded shockingly prescient coming from a man 250 years ago.

A man, by the way, whose name I barely recognized. This mortified me. I am not a scholar, but I graduated from college and law school, I worked in the federal courts, and for more than a decade I wrote daily for a national audience about the Supreme Court and constitutional law. I considered myself fairly conversant in American legal and political history, familiar with all the major players and concepts of the nation's founding. And yet here I was, transfixed by a cipher. Who *was* this guy? This socially awkward pedant, as physically imposing as George Washington but without the charisma, his glasses always threatening to slip off the end of his nose, insisting in his heavy Scottish brogue that the American people should vote directly for their president?

Thus began weeks of intensive reading and research that sent me deep into the world of James Wilson. I became so immersed in his majestic, pathetic, ultimately devastating life story that I started sending my editor regular updates with lengthy quotes and obscure biographical details. Unfailingly wise and patient, my editor finally had enough, and picked up the phone. "You need to move on," he told me gently. "This book isn't about James Wilson." *No*, I thought, *but the next one will be.*

That's how I, and now you, ended up here. In the years that followed I never stopped thinking and reading about Wilson and his radically democratic vision for this brand-new country he had adopted. Along the way, my embarrassment at not knowing more about him was assuaged; as it turned out, I was in good company. It didn't matter whom I spoke to—top newspaper editors, law firm partners, politicians, well-read Americans of all sorts—whenever I mentioned Wilson's name, the response was a blank stare. The experience was the opposite of the one I had when I engaged people in conversation about the Electoral College, a subject about which everyone has a strong opinion.

The most memorable of my Wilson encounters involved a justice of the Supreme Court, whom I bumped into at an event and then cornered in the hope that here, at last, was someone who would understand. The justice knew who Wilson was, of course. But within half a minute, it was clear that I knew more. Our conversation was brief and before it was over I knew I was going to write this book.

The good news for me was that, while very few people have heard of James Wilson, those who have are as excited about him as I am, if not more. Most have spent years studying him, and they are forever on the lookout for fellow travelers. In a piece for the *Times* editorial page in 2021, I mentioned in passing that I was working on a biography of Wilson. I didn't realize it at the time, but I had sent up a bat signal. Within hours, my inbox was filled with emails from people who were already on the case and thrilled to find they had someone else to talk to.

My deepest gratitude goes to these people—the community of

Wilson aficionados scattered around the country, studying deeply and writing with grace about this singularly underappreciated figure in American history. Foremost among this group is William Ewald, professor of law and philosophy at the University of Pennsylvania, where Wilson delivered his famous law lectures in the early 1790s. Ewald is arguably the world authority on Wilson, which is why I am so grateful that for the past seven years he has responded to every email and phone call of mine with a remarkable level of care, generosity, and thoughtfulness. We have spent hours on the phone and in person exploring Wilson and his ideas, even driving into the wilds of northeastern Pennsylvania in search of the lost city of Wilsonville. Ewald's own work on the topic goes back almost two decades and has resulted in several groundbreaking law review articles, all of which informed this book; his efforts will culminate in the definitive intellectual treatment of this most compelling founder.

The other members of this small but mighty community have also shown me enormous generosity, of both their time and their wisdom: Akhil Reed Amar at Yale University, the unmatched scholar and inconceivably prolific (and my favorite) writer on the history and ideas of America and its Constitution, including what I consider the *Born to Run* of law review articles (see "The Consent of the Governed" in the bibliography); John Mikhail and William Treanor at Georgetown; John Gienapp at Stanford; Stephen Conrad; and Martin Clagett, who has spent more time than anyone in the world reconstructing Wilson's crucial early years and education in Scotland, tracking down the teachers he studied with and the books he borrowed.

A word of posthumous gratitude, as well, to two people: first, Burton Alva Konkle, the early twentieth-century historian of Pennsylvania luminaries who wrote a six-hundred-page Wilson biography, complete with hundreds of transcribed letters, but died before he was able to publish it. That manuscript, and Konkle's efforts to bring Wilson back into public consciousness, has been invaluable to those of us in the resurrection business. Second, Walter Dellinger, the delightful scholar and constitutional litigator whose affection for America's founding documents, and the ideas at their heart, knew no bounds. I asked Walter to accompany me on a road trip to Edenton, North Carolina, the town where Wilson spent his ghastly last months and where he was buried for a century. To my surprise, Walter accepted with enthusiasm. He passed away a few weeks before we were scheduled to head out.

I gained countless insights from other scholars of the Constitution and the founding era: Jack Balkin at Yale, who urged me to take up this project in the first place; Michael Klarman at Harvard, whose account of the 1787 convention is as comprehensive as it is indispensable; Jeffrey Rosen at the National Constitution Center, who wandered the streets of Philadelphia with me on an impromptu tour of Wilson's grave site and the scene of the Fort Wilson Riot, even though he surely had more pressing matters to attend to; Jed Purdy; Kate Shaw; Garrett Epps; Danielle Allen; Mary Sarah Bilder; and Sandy Levinson.

A very special thanks to Nick Pedersen, who was still a law student when he published his outstanding 2010 law review article on Wilson's erasure from the story of America's founding. I borrowed the title for this book from that article, but Nick's generosity didn't end there. His excitement for and encouragement of the project boosted me at crucial points along the way.

To research Wilson's life in the outside world as opposed to the world inside his head, I traveled to Scotland, Pennsylvania, and North Carolina, and found in each place a wonderful cast of people ready and willing to help. At St. Andrews, Anthony Lang and Andrew Edwards provided depth and new perspectives; Paula Martin, who wrote the book on the history of Cupar, drove me through that town and out to the rolling fields of Carskerdo, where Wilson was born and raised. Carskerdo remains a four-hundred-cow dairy operation, owned today by a welcoming farmer named James Wilson, who insists there is no relation.

In Edenton, Sam Dixon took me out to Hayes Plantation and the small plot where Wilson was buried immediately after his death; Lexie Tobias-Jacavone and Joy Thames Harvill at the Edenton Historical Commission connected me to everyone I needed to talk to, including

Charles Boyette and the Honorable Terrence W. Boyle, who sits in the Eastern District of North Carolina and shared my enthusiasm for Wilson from a judge's eye view.

In Philadelphia, where Wilson spent most of his adult life, I depended on the assistance of Anthony DiGiovanni and the staff of the Historical Society of Pennsylvania, where the majority of Wilson's papers reside; Heather Hendrickson at the Philadelphia Historical Commission; the Library Company of Philadelphia; and the Free Library of Philadelphia. At Dickinson College in Carlisle, Pennsylvania, Jim Gerencser retrieved obscure correspondence between Wilson and other frontiersmen, and at Swarthmore College, Celia Caust-Ellenbogen gave me access to Burt Konkle's massive typewritten (and hand-corrected) manuscript. In northeast Pennsylvania, Kristen Brown of the Wallenpaupack Historical Society, Jon Tandy, and Peter Becker of the *Tri-County Independent* gave me and Bill Ewald an illuminating tour and history of the region where Wilson's land ventures began to collapse. Karie Diethorn and Renee Albertoli at Independence National Historic Park provided me with copious records of the Pennsylvania State House, the State House Yard, and day-to-day life in the city during the consequential summer of 1787.

I benefited from the vast knowledge and kindness of people with critical storehouses of specific knowledge, including Maeva Marcus, lead editor of the magisterial *Documentary History of the Supreme Court* and possessor of the most remarkable memory for details I have ever seen; Natalie Wexler, who wrote a semi-fictional novel imagining an intense romantic backstory involving Wilson, his fellow justice James Iredell, and their wives; Knox Peden; Alexis Coe; and Michael Waldman of the Brennan Center for Justice, who somehow writes both faster and better than I do, but who still finds the time to counsel me on projects like this.

My team of researchers, fact-checkers, and readers was unparalleled in quality and commitment: Walker Schulte Schneider, Charles Randall, Owen Keenan, Jack Haney, Jack Malamud, Luke Pittman, Terrell Seabrooks, Joe Liberman, Ian Bassin, Lee Drutman, Mike Sacks, Mark Yessian, and Rhiannon O'Neil, who transcribed inscrutable correspondence between Wilson and his family members in Scotland (at least one of whom was near illiterate) with astonishing speed and accuracy.

Writing a book like this while holding down a full-time job is not something I would recommend, but given that is how it happened, I feel immense gratitude to my bosses, editors, and colleagues at *The New York Times* for helping make this book a reality. To A. G. Sulzberger, the best steward of the best daily newspaper in the world; Katie Kingsbury, who has always had my back when I needed it; Patrick Healy; Mara Gay; Brent Staples; Jeneen Interlandi; Farah Stockman; Binyamin Appelbaum; Michelle Cottle; Serge Schmemann; Nick Fox; Julie Ho; Anna Marks; Elfie Engl; Aaron Retica; Adam Liptak; and, most of all, David Firestone.

Finally, thank you to the people and organizations who literally made this book happen:

To the National Endowment for the Humanities and the Eugene C. Pulliam Fellowship of the Society of Professional Journalists Foundation, whose financial support pulled me through.

To my indefatigable agent, David Kuhn, and the rest of the wonderful folks at Aevitas Creative Management, especially Nate Muscato and Rachel Anne Cantor.

To the superb team at Celadon, including Margaux Kanamori, Molly Bloom, Jenna Dolan, and above all to my editor, Bill Hamilton, whose excitement for this book carried me along from the start, and who always knew exactly when to push me and when to back off. His clarity, vision, and editorial judgment were essential in making *The Lost Founder* what it is.

To my friends, who have read some or all of this book, offered excellent feedback, and sustained me with conversation and food and drink over the last several years: Alex Podulke, Jei Olson, Micah Kelber, Tracy Perrizo, Zachary Thacher, Adam Davidson, Jen Banbury, Mehrsa Baradaran, Jack Fairweather, Christina Asquith, Justin Samuel, Erin Bleichfeld, and Brie and Justin Gelinas.

And, most important, to my family: Kyra, my love and my life, who has supported me in every way imaginable; Natalya, at nine already a better, funnier, and more thoughtful writer than I was when I was a good deal older; Sami, who awes me with the passion and precision of her dancing, moving with a grace and power that I can only achieve in dreams; David Wegman; Carolyn Mugar; Marya Wegman; Diane and Frank Himmelbaum; Ruth Nelson and Lynda Josse; Mark Nelson and Margaret Van Houten; and to the memory of my uncle Steve Nelson, a wonderful songwriter who always heard the music in my own writing. He knew this book was underway and I wish he, and my mother, was here to see the final product.

Notes

See the Selected Bibliography on page 347 for full bibliographic information.

Prologue

1   observed in 1788: Schoepf, *Travels in the Confederation 1783–1784*, 114.

1   "in the autumn a hospital": Schoepf, *Travels in the Confederation 1783–1784*, 172–73.

2   drink their own urine: Anuraag Bukkuri, "The History of Malaria in the United States: How It Spread, How It Was Treated, and Public Responses," *MOJ Applied Psychology* 2, no. 3 (April 2016), MedCrave Online, https://medcraveonline.com/MOJAP/MOJAP-02-00048.pdf.

2   gawking at women: Parramore, *Cradle of the Colony*, 44–45.

3   John Horniblow's tavern: Charles Page Smith, *James Wilson: Founding Father, 1742–1798* (University of North Carolina Press, 1956), 386.

3   "I have been hunted": James Wilson to Joseph Thomas, May 12, 1798, in Marcus et al., *The Documentary History of the Supreme Court of the United States, 1789–1800*, 3:265–67.

3   "from my face and hands": Hannah Wilson to Bird Wilson, July 28, 1798, in Marcus et al., *The Documentary History of the Supreme Court of the United States, 1789–1800*, 3:281.

4   "I can hear nothing worse than I expect": Hannah Wilson to Bird Wilson, July 28, 1798, in Marcus et al., *The Documentary History of the Supreme Court of the United States, 1789–1800*, 3:282.

4   camphire, sweet mercury: "Advertisement by Alexander Gaston concerning the sale of medicines [as printed in the *North-Carolina Gazette*]," *Colonial and State Records of North Carolina*, vol. 13 (May 22, 1778), 421, *Documenting the American South*, University Library, University of North Carolina at Chapel Hill, https://docsouth.unc.edu/csr/index.html/document/csr13-0485.

4   "The illness of which he died": James Iredell to [Sarah?] Gray, August 25,

1798, in Marcus et al., *The Documentary History of the Supreme Court of the United States, 1789–1800*, 1(2):861.

4   "They told me he died easy": Hannah Wilson to Bird Wilson, September 1, 1798, in Marcus et al., *The Documentary History of the Supreme Court of the United States, 1789–1800*, 3:288–89.

4   "What a dark cloud overcast": Jacob Rush to Benjamin Rush, September 8, 1798, in Marcus et al., *The Documentary History of the Supreme Court of the United States, 1789–1800*, 1(2):862.

5   "James Wilson, dec.": *State Gazette of North Carolina*, August 29 and October 31, 1798.

Introduction

7   "I know of no other living source": Robert Waln Jr. to Samuel Sitgreaves, May 24, 1824, letter in Dickinson College Archives and Special Collections, https://archives.dickinson.edu/document-descriptions/letter-robert-waln-jr-samuel-sitgreaves.

8   "major shapers of the United States": Founders Online, National Archives, https://founders.archives.gov/.

9   a delegate from Georgia: William Pierce, "Character Sketches of Delegates to the Federal Convention," in Max Farrand, ed., *The Records of the Federal Convention of 1787*, vol. 3 (Yale University Press, 1911) (hereafter cited as "Character Sketches of Delegates"), 91–92.

9   completed their work: George Washington to David Stuart, October 17, 1787, Founders Online, National Archives, https://founders.archives.gov/documents/Washington/04-05-02-0346. Original source: *The Papers of George Washington*, Confederation Series, vol. 5, *1 February 1787–31 December 1787*, ed. W. W. Abbot (University of Virginia Press, 1997), 379–80.

9   "one blaze of light": Commager and Morris, *The Spirit of '76*, 276.

10   Wilson was as central: See, e.g., Schwartz and Mikhail, "The Other Madison Problem," 2040–42, 2063; Ewald, "The Committee of Detail"; Warren, *The Making of the Constitution*, 686–88; Amar, "The Consent of the Governed."

10   "remains with the people": James Wilson at Pennsylvania ratifying convention, December 4, 1787, in *The Documentary History of the Ratification of the Constitution*, vol. 2, *Ratification of the Constitution by the States: Pennsylvania*, ed. Merrill Jensen (State Historical Society of Wisconsin, 1976), 471–72.

12   "most dramatic riot of the revolutionary period": Witt, *Patriots and Cosmopolitans*, 17.

12   "whenever and however they please": Wilson, *The Collected Works of James Wilson*, ed. Hall and Hall, 1:191.

12   "the excess of democracy": Elbridge Gerry at Philadelphia convention, May 31, in Max Farrand, *The Records of the Federal Convention of 1787*, vol. 1 (Yale University Press, 1911), 48.

12   "as may be about the government": Roger Sherman at Philadelphia convention, May 31, in Farrand, *The Records of the Federal Convention of 1787*, 1:48.

12   "the devil's own government": Benjamin Rush to John Adams, July 21, 1789, in Philip B. Kurland and Ralph Lerner, eds., *The Founders' Constitution* (University of Chicago Press, 1987), vol. 1, chap. 4, doc. 30, https://press-pubs.uchicago.edu/founders/documents/v1ch4s30.html.

13   **"The majority of people wherever found"**: James Wilson, July 13, 1787, in Farrand, *The Records of the Federal Convention of 1787*, 1:605.

13   **"an equal right with forty thousand"**: Thomas Jefferson's notes on congressional debates of July 30, 31, and August 1, 1776. "U.S. Constitution: Article I, Section 2, Clause 3," in Kurland and Lerner, *The Founders' Constitution*. Originally in Jefferson, *Autobiography* (1821), in *The Works of Thomas Jefferson*, ed. Paul Leicester Ford, vol. 1 (G. P. Putnam's Sons, 1904), 43–57.

13   **"level to the *understanding* of all"**: James Wilson to the Speaker of the Pennsylvania House of Representatives, August 24, 1791, in Bird Wilson, ed., *The Works of the Honourable James Wilson, L.L.D.*, vol. 1 (Bronson and Chauncey, 1804), ix.

14   **"not a lawyer's contract"**: Franklin D. Roosevelt, "Address on Constitution Day, Washington, D.C.," September 17, 1937, *American Presidency Project*, https://www.presidency.ucsb.edu/documents/address-constitution-day-washington-dc

14   **the justices cited Wilson**: Wesberry v. Sanders, 376 U.S. 1, 17 (1964); Reynolds v. Sims, 377 U.S. 533, 564n41 (1964).

14   **"will remain invariably the same"**: Wilson, *The Collected Works of James Wilson*, ed. Hall and Hall, 2:837.

15   **"his time was limited"**: Wilson, *The Works of James Wilson*, ed. McCloskey, 1:29.

15   **"deranged state of his affairs"**: Benjamin Rush to John Adams, April 22, 1789, in Marcus et al., *The Documentary History of the Supreme Court of the United States, 1789–1800*, 1(2):613.

15   **"very ordinary indeed"**: Wood, *The Radicalism of the American Revolution*, 266.

15   **his most meticulous scholar**: Ewald, "James Wilson and the American Founding," 17.

15   **original drafts of the Constitution**: Ewald, "James Wilson and the American Founding," 2.

15   **"have Nothing to say"**: James Wilson to John Montgomery, May 22, 1775, in Konkle, "The Life and Writings of James Wilson," 2:51; Pedersen, "The Lost Founder," 285–86.

16   **"his unsungness is sung"**: Miller, *The Business of May Next*, 62.

1: A Scottish Childhood

18   **to keep out the wind**: Randolph G. Adams, "James Wilson and St. Andrews," *The General Magazine and Historical Chronicle*, University of Pennsylvania (October 1931), photo of Wilson Homestead at Carskerdo, Scotland, reproduced in Clagett, "James Wilson Before America," cover.

18   **eat down the house**: Handley, *Scottish Farming in the Eighteenth Century*, 76–77.

18   **sackcloth pillows filled with chaff**: Handley, *Scottish Farming in the Eighteenth Century*, 77.

19   **mixed with water and cabbage**: Graham, *The Social Life of Scotland in the Eighteenth Century*, 9; Plant, *The Domestic Life of Scotland in the Eighteenth Century*, 97–98.

19   **"half-starved flies"**: Charles Churchill, "The Prophecy of Famine: A Scots

Pastoral," 1763, in Eighteenth-Century Poetry Archive, https://www
.eighteenthcenturypoetry.org/works/04110-w0010.shtml.

19   seasons of bad weather away: Plant, *The Domestic Life of Scotland in the
      Eighteenth Century*, ix–xi.

19   "in Scotland supports the people": Quoted in Ewald, "James Wilson and the
      Scottish Enlightenment," 1087.

19   that would change world history: McCloskey in Wilson, *The Works of James
      Wilson*, ed. McCloskey, 1:14–16.

19   five miles north of Carskerdo: Robert Annan to Bird Wilson, May 16, 1805,
      Rush Family Papers, vol. 43, 133, Library Company of Philadelphia.

20   a life in law or business: Martin, *Cupar*, 127–28.

20   housework and younger siblings: Martin, *Cupar*, 129–30.

20   highest in the Western world: Ewald, "James Wilson and the Scottish En-
      lightenment," 1082.

20   burgh schools in the region: Clagett, "James Wilson Before America," 30;
      Martin, *Cupar*, 129; Clagett, "James Wilson—His Scottish Background," 159.

20   sunlight or coal fires: Clagett, "James Wilson Before America," 28.

20   used him at the farm: Robert Annan to Bird Wilson, May 16, 1805.

20   human equality in practice: Clagett, "James Wilson Before America," 30.

21   could not afford tuition: "Upon the usual trials the following four [includ-
      ing Wilson] were found most deserving, who were called and allowed to
      take their seats at the Bursar's table and appointed to pay each of them £10
      Scots to the Tailor" (Clagett, "James Wilson Before America," plate I).

21   the Latin version of James: J. M. Anderson, *The Matriculation Roll of the Uni-
      versity of St. Andrews, 1747–1897* (William Blackwood and Sons, 1905), 10.

21   accompanied by private tutors: Clagett, "James Wilson Before America," 39.

21   logic, and natural philosophy: Clagett, "James Wilson Before America," 40–
      41; Ewald, "James Wilson and the Scottish Enlightenment," 1114.

21   aristocratic finishing schools: Between 1750 and 1850, Scotland trained
      ten thousand doctors; in the same period, England trained five hundred.
      Ewald, "James Wilson and the Scottish Enlightenment," 1083.

21   their own inborn senses: Robertson, *The Enlightenment*, xvii–xviii.

22   to adapt to the modern world: Howe, "Why the Scottish Enlightenment
      Was Useful to the Framers of the American Constitution," 575–76; Ewald,
      "James Wilson and the Scottish Enlightenment," 1082–85; Diestelow, "The
      Republic of Happiness," 17.

22   egalitarian societies of the West: Ewald, "James Wilson and the Scottish
      Enlightenment," 1082, 1105; Howe, "Why the Scottish Enlightenment Was
      Useful to the Framers of the American Constitution," 576.

22   their public, political ones: Quoted in Witt, *Patriots and Cosmopolitans*, 32.

22   our public and private passions: Quoted in Witt, *Patriots and Cosmopolitans*, 33.

22   "very nearly the same": Smith, *The Theory of Moral Sentiments*, book I, part
      III, chap. 3, §6.

23   a copy of his latest book: Benjamin Franklin, Degree of Doctor of Laws
      (LL.D.), University of St. Andrews, 12 February 1759, in Founders Online,
      National Archives, https://founders.archives.gov/documents/Franklin
      /01-08-02-0072.

23   "the Remainder of my Days in": Benjamin Franklin to Lord Kames, London, January 3, 1760, in Benjamin Franklin, *The Works of Benjamin Franklin*, vol. 3: *Letters and Miscellaneous Writings, 1753–1763*, ed. Jared Sparks et al. (Little, Brown, 1856), 179.

24   "a subverter of his own rights and ours": Quoted in Ewald, "James Wilson and the Scottish Enlightenment," 1072.

25   its agricultural practices: Handley, *Scottish Farming in the Eighteenth Century*, 117–43.

25   cities like Edinburgh and Glasgow: Devine, *The Scottish Clearances*, 1–14.

25   to enter the ministry: In his letter to Bird Wilson of May 16, 1805, Annan wrote that James Wilson's father was a "ruling Elder in the Church of Scotland," although there is no independent record of this.

25   with equal votes: See, e.g., Thomas M. Devine, *The Scottish Nation: 1700–2000* (Viking, 1999), 84.

25   as his parents wished: Ewald, "James Wilson and the Scottish Enlightenment," 1063–65.

26   at the age of sixty-nine: Clagett, "James Wilson Before America," 47–76.

26   to earn money for the family: "After going regularly through the different stages, which then commonly occupied four years, he applied to the study of Divinity for some time. But to the best of my recollection, his Father died about that time, and the Widow having a numerous family to attend to, he became for some time a tutor in a Gentleman's family." Robert Annan to Bird Wilson, May 16, 1805.

26   the town clerk of Cupar: Clagett, "James Wilson—His Scottish Background," 163, 167. Wilson's signature appears in the Cupar record books multiple times through the spring of 1764.

26   political, and philosophical development: Ewald, "James Wilson and the Scottish Enlightenment," 1091–94.

26   by appeal to first principles: Ewald, "James Wilson and the Scottish Enlightenment," 1092–93, 1097.

26   its own reasoning and argumentation: "Scottish Enlightenment: Influences," *Encyclopaedia Britannica*, https://www.britannica.com/event/Scottish-Enlightenment/Influences. (The *Encyclopedia Britannica* is a product of the Scottish Enlightenment.)

26   a modern, commercializing society: Ewald, "James Wilson and the Scottish Enlightenment," 1102.

27   and regional violence: Howe, "Why the Scottish Enlightenment Was Useful to the Framers of the American Constitution," 581.

27   more traditional forms of Christianity: Howe, "Why the Scottish Enlightenment Was Useful to the Framers of the American Constitution," 582–83; Ewald, "James Wilson and the Scottish Enlightenment," 1090–91.

27   "it remain a friendly state": Quoted in Ewald, "James Wilson and the Scottish Enlightenment," 1107.

27   none was as steeped: Ewald, "James Wilson and the Scottish Enlightenment," 1108.

27   an auspicious place and time: Clagett, "James Wilson—His Scottish Background," 164.

27   in *The Wealth of Nations*: Clagett, "James Wilson—His Scottish Background," 171.

28   he studied directly with Reid: Clagett, "James Wilson—His Scottish Background," 167.

28   and reactions to, the world: Reid, *Systems of Morals*, in *Essays on the Active Powers of Man*, chap. 2, sec. 5, 13.

28   "some mistaken religious principle": Reid, *Essays on the Intellectual Powers of Man* (1785), in Hamilton, *The Works of Thomas Reid*, 438.

28   approach to human problems: Arthur Herman, *How the Scots Invented the Modern World: The True Story of How Western Europe's Poorest Nation Created Our World and Everything in It* (Crown, 2001), 222.

28   rules that came out of it: Hume, *A Treatise of Human Nature*, book 1, pt. II, sec. 6, 66.

28   a "profoundly democratic" conception: Stimson, "A Jury of the Country," 195.

28   "all science and common sense" Thomas Reid, *An Inquiry into the Human Mind on the Principles of Common Sense* (Bell and Bradfute, 1810), ch. V, sec. 8, 150.

29   "a fortuitous meeting of man and idea": McCloskey in Wilson, *The Works of James Wilson*, ed. McCloskey, 15.

29   "Let my soul dwell": Reid, *An Inquiry into the Human Mind on the Principles of Common Sense*, ch. 1, sec. III, 20; Wilson, "Of Man, as an Individual," in *The Collected Works of James Wilson*, ed. Hall and Hall, 1:603; Peters, "James Wilson's Reidian Democratic Political Theory," 89–90.

29   sociability and sense of justice: Peters, "James Wilson's Reidian Democratic Political Theory," 92.

30   "the one most people approve": McCloskey in Wilson, *The Works of James Wilson*, ed. McCloskey, 16.

30   "His genius being too sublime": Robert Annan to Bird Wilson, May 16, 1805.

30   and never returned: Thomas Young to James Wilson, January 24, 1785, in Konkle, "The Life and Writings of James Wilson," 2:295.

2: New Life in America

31   their own family members: Fischer, *Albion's Seed*, 612; Bailyn, *Voyagers to the West*, 582–83.

31   "this epidemical fury of emigration": Fischer, *Albion's Seed*, 608n6.

31   the one they were leaving: Fischer, *Albion's Seed*, 609–11.

32   "bad wether": John Balfour to James Wilson, April 4, 1773, in Konkle, "The Life and Writings of James Wilson," 2:27.

32   he had wanted something bigger: McCloskey in Wilson, *The Works of James Wilson*, ed. McCloskey, 8.

32   "if not by birth": Robert Waln Jr., biography of James Wilson, in *Biography of the Signers to the Declaration of Independence*, vol. 6, ed. John Sanderson and Robert Waln Jr. (R. W. Pomeroy, 1823), 117.

32   "the best classical scholar": Waln, biography of James Wilson, 114–15; Ewald, "James Wilson and the Scottish Enlightenment," 1112n116.

32   **the best-educated people in the colonies:** McCloskey in Wilson, *The Works of James Wilson*, ed. McCloskey, 9.

33   **support himself during his apprenticeship:** Robert Annan to Bird Wilson, May 16, 1805.

33   **"by assurances made good in Scotland":** Waln, biography of James Wilson, 115; Konkle, "The Life and Writings of James Wilson," 1:30.

33   **large tracts of unclaimed land:** Witt, *Patriots and Cosmopolitans*, 30; Konkle, "The Life and Writings of James Wilson," 1:32 and note 45; Louis Richards, "Hon. James Wilson at Reading, Penna.," *The Pennsylvania Magazine of History and Biography* 31, no. 1 (1907): 48.

34   **"a sound and nothing else":** John Dickinson, Letter II, in *Empire and Nation: Letters from a Farmer in Pennsylvania and Letters from the Federal Farmer*, ed. Forrest McDonald (Liberty Fund, 1999), 21.

34   **and in England and France:** Amar, *The Words That Made Us*, 66.

34   **did not appear on the *Chronicle*'s front page:** Konkle, "The Life and Writings of James Wilson," 1:38–39, 2: note 6.

34   **"is the final end of our existence":** *Pennsylvania Chronicle*, February 1, 1768, 1.

35   **Wilson writing the odd-numbered installments:** Konkle, "The Life and Writings of James Wilson," 1:39n36.

35   **"humble servant of the ladies":** *Pennsylvania Chronicle*, February 15, 1768, 1.

35   **distillation of the common sense philosophy:** Diestelow, "The Republic of Happiness," 20–28.

36   **Silence Dogood:** Benjamin Franklin to the *New-England Courant*, April 2, 1722, Founders Online, n.d., National Archives, https://founders.archives .gov/documents/Franklin/01-01-02-0008; Benjamin Franklin, "Silence Dogood," No. 13, September 24, 1722, Founders Online, National Archives, n.d., https://founders.archives.gov/documents/Franklin/01-01-02-0020. Original source: Benjamin Franklin, *The Papers of Benjamin Franklin*, vol. 1, January 6, 1706, through December 31, 1734, ed. Leonard W. Labaree (Yale University Press, 1959), 41–42.

36   **equated with morality and virtue:** Diestelow, "The Republic of Happiness," 26.

37   **"I judge he don't want it printed":** William White to James Wilson, November 27, 1768, Konkle, "The Life and Writings of James Wilson," 2:5–6.

37   **a native Scot could feel at home:** Konkle, "The Life and Writings of James Wilson," 1:48, 52–53n45.

38   **were beginning to pay off:** Konkle, "The Life and Writings of James Wilson," 1:50–51.

38   **more than 40 percent:** Edward W. Biddle, *James Wilson, James Smith, and George Ross, Three Signers of the Declaration of Independence Who Were Members of the Cumberland County Bar. Historical Address* (Historical Committee of the Carlisle Civic Club, 1902), 8.

38   **hired him to handle their future cases:** Waln, biography of James Wilson, 116; Konkle, "The Life and Writings of James Wilson," 1:70–71.

38   **that would eventually infect him:** Among the forty-eight citizens called that April day for jury duty was a man named Abraham Lincoln. On a list of prospective jurors Wallis drew up for the purpose of lodging challenges,

someone wrote next to Lincoln's name, "illiterate and apt to be influenced by the pleadings of lawyers." The man appears to have been the grandfather and namesake of the nation's sixteenth president. See Meginness, *History of Lycoming County, Pennsylvania*, 65.

39   **an area known as Birdsboro:** Richards, "Hon. James Wilson at Reading, Penna.," 48; Konkle, "The Life and Writings of James Wilson," 2: note 14.

39   **"in the phrase of us lawyers, one person":** James Wilson to William White, October 2, 1770, in Konkle, "The Life and Writings of James Wilson," 2:14.

39   **"she did not purpose ever to marry":** James Wilson to William White, c. December 2, 1770, in Konkle, "The Life and Writings of James Wilson," 2:16–21.

39   **stunned and uncomprehending:** James Wilson to William White, c. December 2, 1770, in Konkle, "The Life and Writings of James Wilson," 2:18.

39   **the longest letter of a personal nature:** Konkle refers to at least two other letters from Wilson to Rachel in 1769, although he expresses discomfort with making personal romantic correspondence public, an unfortunate inclination in a biographer. Neither letter has been located. See Konkle, "The Life and Writings of James Wilson," vol. 2, note 14.

40   **"a very agreeable young lady":** *Pennsylvania Gazette*, November 21, 1771, 2.

40   **173 acres for two hundred pounds:** Biddle, *James Wilson, James Smith, and George Ross . . .*, 7.

40   **"three horses and a cow":** Biddle, *James Wilson, James Smith, and George Ross . . .*, 7.

41   **more than six times what they had paid:** Biddle, *James Wilson, James Smith, and George Ross . . .*, 7, 8.

41   **netting barely one hundred pounds:** William Wilson to James Wilson, March 19, 1771, in Konkle, "The Life and Writings of James Wilson," 2:22.

41   **"it is not for want of writing":** William Wilson and Alison Landales to James Wilson, July 6, 1770, in Konkle, "The Life and Writings of James Wilson," 2:12–13.

41   **"monied individuals and companies":** Alexander Hamilton, "Report on Vacant Lands," July 20, 1790, in Alexander Hamilton, *The Papers of Alexander Hamilton*, vol. 6, ed. Harold C. Syrett (Columbia University Press, 1962), 502.

42   **the country they were creating:** Blaakman, *Speculation Nation*, 32.

42   **He was intoxicated most of all:** McCloskey in Wilson, *The Works of James Wilson*, ed. McCloskey, 17.

42   **more often through extortion or fraud:** Blaakman, *Speculation Nation*, 31–33.

42   **King George III prohibited colonists:** George R [George III], "By the King. A Proclamation," Royal Proclamation of 1763, October 7, 1763, reprinted in the Avalon Project, Yale Law School, https://avalon.law.yale.edu/18th _century/proc1763.asp; Blaakman, *Speculation Nation*, 37.

42   **That's what Wilson did:** Witt, *Patriots and Cosmopolitans*, 30n24.

43   **"I can give any security for the money":** James Wilson to Jasper Yeates, December 3, 1773, in Konkle, "The Life and Writings of James Wilson," 2:32 and note 23.

43   "an engine of civilizing progress": See Witt, *Patriots and Cosmopolitans*, 31–32.

43   could go hand in hand: Blaakman, *Speculation Nation*, 178; Friedenberg, "James Wilson: A Morality Tale."

43   beyond where others were prepared to go: McCloskey in Wilson, *The Works of James Wilson*, ed. McCloskey, 18.

44   "I am a good deal indisposed": John Dickinson to James Wilson, August 11, 1774, in Konkle, "The Life and Writings of James Wilson," 2:42 and note 36.

44   "under the protection of which they live": John Dickinson, Letter XII, in McDonald, *Empire and Nation*, 59–63.

3: The "Considerations" Essay

46   a daunting question: *Rivington's New-York Gazetteer*, October 20, 1774, 1.

47   "the *first* law of every government": *Rivington's New-York Gazetteer*, October 20, 1774, 1; Wilson, "Considerations on the Nature and Extent of the Legislative Authority of the British Parliament" (1774), in *The Collected Works of James Wilson*, ed. Hall and Hall, 1:4–5.

48   had reserved such thoughts: Robert Edward Ziegler, *The Evolution of Benjamin Franklin's Thought in Relation to the Role and Authority of the British Parliament over the North American Colonies, 1763–1775* (master's thesis, Sam Houston State Teachers College, 1965), 23–41.

49   nearly double the 72 million pounds: That is the equivalent of more than $18 billion today. Morgan and Morgan, *The Stamp Act Crisis*, 21.

49   living under a distracted empire: Taylor, *American Colonies*, 25.

49   by sympathetic local juries: Morgan and Morgan, *The Stamp Act Crisis*, 23–24.

49   more new taxes were around the corner: Amar, *The Words That Made Us*, 46.

50   "the miserable state of tributary slaves": Morgan and Morgan, *The Stamp Act Crisis*, 35.

50   "in person, or by representation": James Otis, "The Rights of the British Colonies Asserted and Proved," in *The American Republic: Primary Sources*, ed. Bruce Frohnen (Liberty Fund, 2002), 183.

50   "she must assist our revenue": "Debate, House of Commons. Committee of Ways and Means: Resolutions for Colonial Stamp Duties, February 6, 1765," *America in Class*, National Humanities Center, https://americainclass.org/sources/makingrevolution/crisis/text3/parliamentarydebate1765.pdf.

50   "that burden which we lie under": "Debate, House of Commons. Committee of Ways and Means: Resolutions for Colonial Stamp Duties, February 6, 1765."

51   "supreme, irresistible, absolute, uncontrolled": William Blackstone, "Introduction," in his *Commentaries on the Laws of England*, Avalon Project, Yale Law School, https://avalon.law.yale.edu/18th_century/blackstone_intro.asp#2; William Blackstone, *Commentaries on the Laws of England: A Facsimile of the First Edition of 1765–1769* (University of Chicago Press, 1979), 156–57.

51   "and we must obey": Otis, "The Rights of the British Colonies Asserted and Proved," 185.

51   began his quest to answer it: John Balfour to James Wilson, April 4, 1773, in Konkle, "The Life and Writings of James Wilson," 2:27.

51   "would never be disputed": Morgan and Morgan, *The Stamp Act Crisis*, 55.

52   "the Americans in their place": Morgan and Morgan, *The Stamp Act Crisis*, 65.

52   openly defied the law: Amar, *The Words That Made Us*, 64, 718n52, 720.

52   the same rights as British citizens: "Resolutions of the Stamp Act Congress," October 19, 1765, *Teaching American History*, Ashbrook Center, https://teachingamericanhistory.org/document/resolutions-of-the-stamp-act-congress-2/.

53   stealing money, clothing, and silverware: Morgan and Morgan, *The Stamp Act Crisis*, 129–33.

53   "in all cases whatsoever": Declaratory Act, 1766, Avalon Project, Yale Law School, https://avalon.law.yale.edu/18th_century/declaratory_act_1766.asp.

53   "We are but parts of a whole": John Dickinson, Letter II, in McDonald, *Empire and Nation*, 21.

54   the most punishing set of laws yet: "The Coercive (Intolerable) Acts of 1774," *Mount Vernon Digital Encyclopedia*, Mount Vernon Ladies' Association, https://www.mountvernon.org/library/digitalhistory/digital-encyclopedia/article/the-coercive-intolerable-acts-of-1774/.

54   "Scarcely have our minds": Thomas Jefferson, *A Summary View of the Rights of British America*, 1774, Avalon Project, Yale Law School, https://avalon.law.yale.edu/18th_century/jeffsumm.asp.

55   "Thought too bold": Thomas Jefferson, *Autobiography* (1821), in *Thomas Jefferson: Writings*, ed. Merrill D. Peterson (Library of America, 1984), 10.

55   the world's most famous legal authority: See Hedges, "Telling Off the King," 166–74.

57   response to the Intolerable Acts: Neither Jefferson nor Wilson was a member of the First Continental Congress, to the frustration of his allies, but both were elected to the Second Continental Congress in 1775. See Thomson, "Early Days of the Revolution in Philadelphia," 418.

57   "Nobody will be argued into slavery": Edmund Burke, *The Works of Edmund Burke*, vol. 1 (Harper & Brothers, 1860), 215.

58   sovereignty is, after all, indivisible: Amar, *The Words That Made Us*, 52.

58   they couldn't explain why: Jezierski, "Parliament or People," 99–105.

58   "the most sophisticated legal analysis": Ewald, "James Wilson and the American Founding," 19.

58   *then it's nothing*: Amar, *The Words That Made Us*, 89–90.

59   "Upon the Principles of Law": Thomas Smith to James Wilson to Robert Morris, January 2, 1775, in Konkle, "The Life and Writings of James Wilson," 2:45-a.

59   "greatly outshine his Master's": John Adams to Abigail Adams, July 23, 1775, in *Letters of Delegates to Congress, 1774–1789*, vol. 1, ed. Paul H. Smith, with Gerard W. Gawalt, Rosemary Fry Plakas, and Eugene R. Sheridan (Library of Congress, 1976), 649. Adams is referring to John Dickinson, whose fame Adams resented.

59   pasted them into his commonplace book: Ewald, "James Wilson and the American Founding," 10–12.

59   have come to that conclusion: See, e.g., Ewald, "James Wilson and the American Founding," 10–11; Ewald, "James Wilson and the Drafting of the Constitution," 905; Chinard, *Thomas Jefferson*, 73; Wills, *Inventing America*, 251;

James Hart, review of *The Commonplace Book of Thomas Jefferson, Review of Politics* 3, no. 4 (Autumn 1927). ("Curiously enough, Jefferson, in making his excerpt, quoted the paragraphs which immediately precede, and the one which immediately follows, but omitted the two paragraphs which contain ideas and phrases so strikingly similar to some in the Declaration. . . . It becomes quite possible that Jefferson remembered not only Locke, but also Wilson, who quoted Burlamaqui, who drew his inspiration from Locke.")

60   **"earnest wish and desire"**: *Proceedings of the Convention for the Province of Pennsylvania: Held at Philadelphia, January 23, 1775, and Continued by Adjournments to the 28th* (William and Thomas Bradford, 1775), 5.

60   **"the invidious and ill-grounded clamor"**: Wilson, "Speech Delivered in the Convention for the Province of Pennsylvania, Held at Philadelphia, in January, 1775" (1775), in *The Collected Works of James Wilson*, ed. Hall and Hall, 1:32.

61   **"the spirit of our constitutions"**: Wilson, "Speech Delivered in the Convention for the Province of Pennsylvania, Held at Philadelphia, in January, 1775," in *The Collected Works of James Wilson*, ed. Hall and Hall, 1:37.

61   **you did it first**: Wilson, "Speech Delivered in the Convention for the Province of Pennsylvania, Held at Philadelphia, in January, 1775," in *The Collected Works of James Wilson*, ed. Hall and Hall, 1:37.

61   **"the fate of millions yet unborn"**: Wilson, "Speech Delivered in the Convention for the Province of Pennsylvania, Held at Philadelphia, in January, 1775," in *The Collected Works of James Wilson*, ed. Hall and Hall, 1:38.

61   **"he has sunk to theirs"**: Wilson, "Speech Delivered in the Convention for the Province of Pennsylvania, Held at Philadelphia, in January, 1775," in *The Collected Works of James Wilson*, ed. Hall and Hall, 1:45.

62   **he was made a colonel**: Smith, *James Wilson*, 61.

62   **a seemingly endless string of them**: See *Journals of the Continental Congress, 1774–1789*, 2:79, 93, 183.

62   **relations with the Indian nations**: Smith, *James Wilson*, 72.

62   **"the Belts are getting ready"**: *Letters of Delegates to Congress, 1774–1789*, 1:629–30, 706.

63   **"A certain eminent Gentleman"**: Cited in Mikhail, "James Wilson, Early American Land Companies, and the Original Meaning of Ex Post Facto Law," 99–100.

63   **"very triffling" debts**: *Journals of the Continental Congress, 1774–1789*, 3:417, 460.

63   **debts under thirty-five dollars**: *Journals of the Continental Congress, 1774–1789*, 3:460.

4: The Declaration

65   **"we are *determined* to continue freemen"**: Wilson, "An Address to the Inhabitants of the Colonies (1776)," in *The Collected Works of James Wilson*, ed. Hall and Hall, 1:58.

65   **"*sacred Authority of the People*"**: Wilson, "An Address to the Inhabitants of the Colonies (1776)," in *The Collected Works of James Wilson*, ed. Hall and Hall, 1:53.

65   **"to lead the public mind"**: *Journals of the Continental Congress, 1774–1789*, 4:146.

65   **"in possession of the key":** Thomas Paine, *Common Sense* (1776), Online Library of Liberty, https://oll.libertyfund.org/pages/1776-paine-common-sense-pamphlet. Originally published in Thomas Paine, *The Writings of Thomas Paine*, ed. Moncure Daniel Conway, vol. 1 (G. P. Putnam's Sons, 1894).

65   **the fetters of empire:** See Beeman, *Our Lives, Our Fortunes, and Our Sacred Honor*, 316–17.

65   **"pulling down than building":** John Adams to Abigail Adams, March 19, 1776, Founders Online, National Archives, https://founders.archives.gov/documents/Adams/04-01-02-0235. Originally published in *The Adams Papers: Adams Family Correspondence*, vol. 1, December 1761–May 1776, ed. Lyman H. Butterfield (Harvard University Press, 1963), 362–64.

66   **"the happiness and Safety of their Constituents":** John Adams, *Autobiography*, [Friday, May 10, 1776], in *The Adams Papers: Diary and Autobiography of John Adams*, vol. 2, ed. L. H. Butterfield (Belknap Press of Harvard University Press, 1961), 240.

66   **some sort of government was needed:** Beeman, *Our Lives, Our Fortunes, and Our Sacred Honor*, 347.

66   **"cruel depredations of their enemies":** John Adams, *Autobiography*, entry for May 15, 1776, in *Diary and Autobiography of John Adams*, ed. L. H. Butterfield, vol. 3 (Belknap Press of Harvard University Press, 1961), 386.

67   **"the most important Resolution":** Selsam, *The Pennsylvania Constitution of 1776*, 113n71; John Adams to James Warren, May 15, 1776, Founders Online, National Archives, https://founders.archives.gov/documents/Adams/06-04-02-0079. Original source: *The Adams Papers: Papers of John Adams*, vol. 4, February–August 1776, ed. Robert J. Taylor (Harvard University Press, 1979), 186–87.

67   **"all the inclemencies of the season":** John Adams, *Autobiography*, [Friday, May 10, 1776], in Butterfield, *The Adams Papers: Diary and Autobiography of John Adams*, 2:240.

67   **the most ardent Loyalists:** Selsam, *The Pennsylvania Constitution of 1776*, 113.

67   **"the general voice of America":** *Letters of Delegates to Congress, 1774–1789*, vol. 4 (Library of Congress, 1976), 160.

68   **its prohibition on its congressional delegates:** "The Pennsylvania Assembly: Instructions to Its Delegates in Congress, 9 November 1775," Founders Online, National Archives, https://founders.archives.gov/documents/Franklin/01-22-02-0149. Originally published in Benjamin Franklin, *The Papers of Benjamin Franklin*, vol. 22, March 23, 1775, through October 27, 1776, ed. William B. Willcox (Yale University Press, 1982; hereafter cited as Willcox, *Papers of Benjamin Franklin*), 251–52.

68   **"approaching to a Crisis":** *Letters of Delegates to Congress, 1774–1789*, 4:302.

68   **"what the heart is to the human body":** Robert Morris to John Hancock, February 4, 1777, quoted in Anne Bezanson, *Prices and Inflation During the American Revolution: Pennsylvania, 1770–1790* (University of Pennsylvania Press, 1951), 17–18.

69   **Dickinson and Morris stayed "behind the bar":** Beeman, *Our Lives, Our Fortunes, and Our Sacred Honor*, 378.

69   **Pennsylvania was on board:** *Letters of Delegates to Congress, 1774–1789,* 4:364–65; Ewald, "James Wilson and the Drafting of the Constitution," 906n11; Smith, *James Wilson,* 78–89.

69   **paraded through the streets and burned:** Abigail Adams to John Adams, July 21–22, 1776, Adams Family Papers: An Electronic Archive, Massachusetts Historical Society, https://www.masshist.org/digitaladams/archive /doc?id=L17760721aa; Ryerson, *The Revolution Is Now Begun,* 239.

70   **"the harmonizing sentiments of the day":** Thomas Jefferson to Henry Lee, May 8, 1825, in *The Life and Selected Writings of Thomas Jefferson,* ed. Adrienne Koch and William Peden (Random House, 1944), 719.

70   **"concise and nervous style":** John Adams to Abigail Adams, March 19, 1776, Founders Online, National Archives, https://founders.archives.gov /documents/Adams/04-01-02-0235. Originally published in Butterfield, *The Adams Papers: Adams Family Correspondence,* 1:362–64.

70   **the Virginia Declaration of Rights:** *Virginia Declaration of Rights,* June 12, 1776, Avalon Project, Yale Law School, https://avalon.law.yale.edu/18th _century/virginia.asp.

70   **the structure outlined by Mason:** Ewald, "The Committee of Detail," 222–23.

70   **both Mason and Jefferson had clearly read it:** William Ewald, personal communication, November 10, 2023.

70   **"the most soaring line of all":** Amar, *The Words That Made Us,* 123.

71   **They almost never did:** Ewald, "James Wilson and the American Founding," 12–15.

71   **both spoken on the same day:** Ewald, "James Wilson and the American Founding," 15–16; John P. Kaminski and Gaspare J. Saladino, eds., *The Documentary History of the Ratification of the Constitution* (State Historical Society of Wisconsin, 1993); James Wilson, speech of December 4, 1787, in Jensen, *The Documentary History of the Ratification of the Constitution,* 2:472– 73. Ewald also credits the historian Pauline Maier, author of the definitive narrative history of the ratification period. See Maier, *Ratification.*

71   **"on the same certain and solid foundation":** Ewald, "James Wilson and the American Founding," 16.

72   **that should come as no surprise:** Allen and Sneff, "Golden Letters," 211.

72   **complete with golden lettering:** Allen and Sneff, "Golden Letters," 196, 200.

72   **"*these United Colonies*":** Wilson, "Considerations on the Bank of North America," in *The Collected Works of James Wilson,* ed. Hall and Hall, 1:66; see also Mikhail, "The Necessary and Proper Clauses," 1126n357.

72   **"not *Individually* but *Unitedly*":** James Wilson, June 19, 1787, in Farrand, *The Records of the Federal Convention of 1787,* 1:324.

72   **the only reference to the Declaration:** Ewald, "James Wilson and the American Founding," 16; see also Allen and Sneff, "Golden Letters," 195 ("Wilson did more than any other founder to activate the Declaration of Independence as foundational to the ideological origins of the new nation."); 201 ("He had internalized the text of the Declaration," Allen wrote, "and made it simply a part of his ordinary vocabulary and cadences").

73   **"that all men are created equal":** Abraham Lincoln, "Gettysburg Address," November 19, 1863, Library of Congress, https://www.loc.gov/item/rbpe .24404500/.

73   **practice's moral profanity:** See Wood, *The Radicalism of the American Revolution*, 186.

73   **"the loudest yelps for liberty":** Samuel Johnson, *Taxation No Tyranny: An Answer to the Resolutions and Address of the American Congress* (T. Cadell, 1775), 89.

73   **the first anti-slavery society in the world:** Amar, *The Words That Made Us*, 146; Wood, *The Radicalism of the American Revolution*, 186.

73   **"our black brethren":** Quoted in Ewald, "James Wilson and the American Founding," 13.

5: The Pennsylvania Constitution of 1776

74   **both his friends and his foes:** See McCloskey in Wilson, *The Works of James Wilson*, ed. McCloskey, 11–13.

74   **the halting path he took:** McCloskey in Wilson, *The Works of James Wilson*, ed. McCloskey, 11.

74   **he would pay dearly for it:** The persistence of this stain is why Wilson's foremost historian has referred to the story of his involvement in the Declaration of Independence as a "painful" one. Ewald, "James Wilson and the American Founding," 7.

75   **twenty-two of his fellow delegates:** *Letters of Delegates to Congress, 1774–1789*, 4:271–73.

75   **Lawmakers were not in the habit:** Hampton L. Carson, "Oration," *American Law Register* 55, no. 1, new ser. vol. 46 (January 1907): 39.

75   **Wilson's "danger":** *Letters of Delegates to Congress, 1774–1789*, 4:273.

75   **"I will never trust a Scotchman again":** *Letters of Delegates to Congress, 1774–1789*, 4:274.

75   **he had sought to postpone the matter:** Smith, *James Wilson*, 78. ("We strictly enjoined you, that you, in behalf of this Colony, dissent from and utterly reject any propositions, should such be made, that may cause or lead to a separation from our Mother Country, or a change in the form of this Government.")

75   **until legislators could vote:** *Letters of Delegates to Congress, 1774–1789*, 4:271–76.

75   **he took particular offense:** *Letters of Delegates to Congress, 1774–1789*, 4:422.

76   **a Congress left severely short-staffed:** Smith, *James Wilson*, 92–93.

76   **pacifist Quakers and landed aristocrats:** Selsam, *The Pennsylvania Constitution of 1776*, 2, 7.

76   **"elected oligarchy":** Ryerson, *The Revolution Is Now Begun*, 5.

76   **devalued their voices and their votes:** Williams, "The Influences of Pennsylvania's 1776 Constitution on American Constitutionalism During the Founding Decade," 29, 35 ("Pennsylvania was one of the few states where the radicals successfully formed a coalition of urban working people and interior small farmers"); Janet Wilson, "The Bank of North America and Pennsylvania Politics: 1781–1787," *Pennsylvania Magazine of History and Biography* 66, no. 1 (January 1942): 5, 28.

76   **and they were listening:** Selsam, *The Pennsylvania Constitution of 1776*, 169, 173.

76   **the radicals were not politically experienced:** Selsam, *The Pennsylvania Constitution of 1776*, 208–9.

76   "**They seem hardly equal to the Task**": Selsam, *The Pennsylvania Constitution of 1776*, 148–49.

76   "**Numsculs**": Selsam, *The Pennsylvania Constitution of 1776*, 149.

77   "**Education perverts the understanding**": Thomas Smith to Arthur St. Clair, August 22, 1776, in *The St. Clair Papers*, vol. 1, ed. William Henry Smith (Robert Clarke 1882), 373.

77   "**we despise you**": Thomas Smith to General Arthur St. Clair, August 22, 1776, in William Henry Smith, *The St. Clair Papers*, 1:374.

77   **couldn't even get a quorum**: The history of the Assembly's 1776 collapse told here is drawn primarily from Ryerson, *The Revolution Is Now Begun*; Selsam, *The Pennsylvania Constitution of 1776*; and David Freeman Hawke, *In the Midst of a Revolution* (University of Pennsylvania Press, 1961).

77   **dominated by the backcountry Germans and Scots-Irish**: Janet Wilson, "The Bank of North America and Pennsylvania Politics: 1781–1787," 28; Ryerson, *The Revolution Is Now Begun*, 229.

77   **who had long been excluded**: Williams, "The Influences of Pennsylvania's 1776 Constitution on American Constitutionalism During the Founding Decade," 29.

77   "***on the authority of the people only***": Ryerson, *The Revolution Is Now Begun*, 230; Selsam, *The Pennsylvania Constitution of 1776*, 136–38.

78   **denying allegiance to the Crown**: Ryerson, *The Revolution Is Now Begun*, 234.

78   **profess their faith in Jesus Christ**: Selsam, *The Pennsylvania Constitution of 1776*, 138–40; John B. Linn and Wm. H. Egle, eds., *Pennsylvania Archives*, ser. 2, vol. 3 (State Printer of Pennsylvania, 1896), 641.

78   **rooted like none before it**: See Selsam, *The Pennsylvania Constitution of 1776*, 146–52.

78   **a Declaration of Rights**: The Pennsylvania Constitution of 1776, Avalon Project, Yale Law School, https://avalon.law.yale.edu/18th_century/pa08.asp.

78   **stayed faithful to the constitution**: See Brown, "The Pennsylvania Council of Censors and the Debate on the Guardian of the Constitution in the Early United States," 1–26; Williams, "The Influences of Pennsylvania's 1776 Constitution on American Constitutionalism During the Founding Decade," 25–48.

78   "**the most vital participatory democracy**": Ryerson, *The Revolution Is Now Begun*, 5.

79   "**seem to think it is their right**": A Citizen of New Jersey, *Pennsylvania Evening Post*, July 30, 1776, "Document 19: Pennsylvania Constitution of 1776," in Kurland and Lerner, *The Founders' Constitution*.

79   **it was cut**: "Revisions of the Pennsylvania Declaration of Rights, [Between 29 July 1776 and 15 August 1776]," Founders Online, National Archives, https://founders.archives.gov/documents/Franklin/01-22-02-0314. Original source: Willcox, ed., *The Papers of Benjamin Franklin*, 529–33.

79   **published in the *Evening Post***: Selsam, *The Pennsylvania Constitution of 1776*, 162.

79   **especially recent immigrants**: "It is a fact," Benjamin Franklin (who did not oppose the new constitution) said, "that the Irish emigrants and their

children are now in possession of the government of Pennsylvania, by their majority in the Assembly, as well as of a great part of the territory; and I remember well the first ship that brought any of them over." Quoted in Selsam, *The Pennsylvania Constitution of 1776*, 208.

79   **the "leveling spirit":** During an early debate in the 1787 convention about the election of national legislators, Elbridge Gerry warned that "the evils we experience flow from the excess of democracy," and that "he had been taught by experience the danger of the levilling spirit." Elbridge Gerry, May 31, 1787, in Farrand, *The Records of the Federal Convention of 1787*, 1:48. In another debate about the importance of a bicameral Congress, Gouverneur Morris said, "Ask any man if he confides in Congress if he confides in the state of Pennsylvania if he will lend his money or enter into contract? He will tell you no. He sees no stability. He can repose no confidence." Gouverneur Morris, July 2, 1787, in Farrand, *The Records of the Federal Convention of 1787*, 1:513. Benjamin Rush, who had at one time supported the 1776 constitution, wrote in the closing weeks of the convention to Timothy Pickering, "The new federal government like a new Continental waggon will overset our State dung cart, with all its dirty contents . . . and thereby restore order and happiness to Pennsylvania." *Supplement to Max Farrand's "The Records of the Federal Convention of 1787,"* ed. James H. Hutson (Yale University Press, 1987), 250.

79   **"fall upon their knees":** Quoted in Williams, "The Influences of Pennsylvania's 1776 Constitution on American Constitutionalism During the Founding Decade," 32, 33.

79   **the "democratical order":** Benjamin Rush, quoted in Selsam, *The Pennsylvania Constitution of 1776*, 209.

80   **"to avoid a like calamity":** Williams, "The Influences of Pennsylvania's 1776 Constitution on American Constitutionalism During the Founding Decade," 34, 35.

80   **the essence of Wilson's Reidian political vision:** Pennsylvania Constitution of 1776, Avalon Project, Yale Law School, https://avalon.law.yale.edu/18th_century/pa08.asp. (Section 17: "Representation in proportion to the number of taxable inhabitants is the only principle which can at all times secure liberty, and make the voice of a majority of the people the law of the land.")

80   **"the effect of magic, not of reason":** Thomas Jefferson's notes on congressional debates of July 30, 31, and August 1, 1776. "U.S. Constitution: Article I, Section 2, Clause 3," in Kurland and Lerner, *The Founders' Constitution*. Originally in Jefferson, *Autobiography* (1821), in *The Works of Thomas Jefferson*, ed. Paul Leicester Ford, vol. 1 (G. P. Putnam's Sons, 1904), 43–57.

80   **the "revolution principle":** See Amar, "The Consent of the Governed," 471n43 (citing Wilson's use of "revolution principle" to refer to the "legal right of popular sovereignty").

81   **"should rouse themselves":** James Wilson to William Atlee and Jasper Yeates, March 13, 1777, in *Letters of Delegates to Congress, 1774–1789*, vol. 6, ed. Paul H. Smith (Library of Congress, 1980), 502n1.

81   **the evils the constitution had introduced:** *Pennsylvania Gazette*, March 24, 1779. The group initially dubbed itself the anti-constitutionalists. Wilson

had expressed himself on the constitution at least once before. In a letter to Anthony Wayne in 1778, he referred to the constitution as "the most detestable that ever was formed." Cited in Larson, *The Trials of Allegiance*, 118.

81   **there was no mistaking:** "From the style and manner of them," Timothy Matlack, a leading member of the 1776 Pennsylvania convention, wrote in the following week's paper, they "appear to be performances of James Wilson, Esquire." *Pennsylvania Gazette*, March 31, 1779. Matlack was a lapsed Quaker, a former brewer, and a hothead who had spent time in debtors' prison, but whose penmanship was good enough that he had been chosen to handwrite the official, signed copy of the Declaration of Independence. Matlack had defended the Pennsylvania constitution in the newspapers for the past three years, usually under the pseudonym Tiberius Gracchus. In Wilson, he faced his most daunting opponent.

82   **"scenes of weakness and distraction":** Perhaps he was recalling the letter from Col. Thomas Hartley in York in December 1776: "There are no Justices—no Law—every one seems to do what he listeth—I am surprized that there are not more Murders & Robberies committed for these ever flourish in anarchy and Confusion" (Selsam, *The Pennsylvania Constitution of 1776*, 239).

83   **in the name of emergency:** See Selsam, *The Pennsylvania Constitution of 1776*, 136, 165.

83   **"internal violence":** Ryerson, *The Revolution Is Now Begun*, 237.

83   **the "excess of democracy":** Elbridge Gerry, May 31, 1787, in Farrand, *The Records of the Federal Convention of 1787*, 1:48.

83   **missing from Pennsylvania's:** At the start of the 1787 convention, Pennsylvania was the only dissenting vote against a bicameral Congress, though not out of principle. See Madison's notes, May 31, in Farrand, *The Records of the Federal Convention of 1787*, 1:48. "(The 3d. Resolution) 'that the national Legislature ought to consist of two branches' was agreed to without debate or dissent, (except that of Pennsylvania, given probably from complaisance to Docr. Franklin who was understood to be partial to a single House of Legislation)."

83   **"trust no body of men":** *Pennsylvania Gazette*, March 24, 1779.

6: The Fort Wilson Riot

84   **crossed him off the list:** Smith, *James Wilson*, 99.

85   **"having done my Duty":** James Wilson to Arthur St. Clair, February 19, 1777, in *Letters of Delegates to Congress, 1774–1789*, 6:326.

85   **as his cash flow allowed:** Smith, *James Wilson*, 128.

85   **"I find myself incapable":** James Wilson to Arthur St. Clair, January 14, 1777, in Konkle, "The Life and Writings of James Wilson," 2:99.

85   **"I am undetermined how to act":** James Wilson to Robert Morris, February 28, 1777, in Konkle, "The Life and Writings of James Wilson," 2:112.

85   **"Pennsylvania is in the greatest confusion":** James Wilson to Arthur St. Clair, March 27, 1777, in Konkle, "The Life and Writings of James Wilson," 2:114.

85 **Wilson was again removed:** *Journals of the Continental Congress, 1774–1789,* 8:746.

86 **They returned to a city in ruins:** Jackson, *With the British in Philadelphia,* 265–73.

86 **"your treachery to this country":** Cited in Larson, "The Revolutionary American Jury," 1453.

87 **state supreme court was in no position:** Larson, "The Revolutionary American Jury," 1451; see also Maxey, "Treason on Trial in Revolutionary Pennsylvania," 17, 31–32.

87 **"There is every reason to suppose":** Larson, "The Revolutionary American Jury," 1454.

87 **"dreadful engines of tyranny":** *Pennsylvania Gazette,* October 18, 1780, cited in Larson, *The Trials of Allegiance,* 200.

87 **The twenty-three trials held that fall:** Larson, "The Revolutionary American Jury," 1443.

88 **good reason to fear for his life:** Larson, "The Revolutionary American Jury," 1443n11.

88 **one of Philadelphia's more prominent citizens:** Larson, "The Revolutionary American Jury," 1481, 1492.

88 **rode south into the city:** Maxey, "Treason on Trial in Revolutionary Pennsylvania," 20.

88 **Wilson, along with another lawyer:** Larson, "The Revolutionary American Jury," 1485.

88 **seen in the company of British forces:** Larson, "The Revolutionary American Jury," 1487.

88 **Roberts's trial began:** Maxey, "Treason on Trial in Revolutionary Pennsylvania," 44.

88 **"no persuasion to inlist":** Maxey, "Treason on Trial in Revolutionary Pennsylvania," 43.

89 **witnesses were not reliable:** Larson, "The Revolutionary American Jury," 1487, 1492.

89 **sentenced to death:** Maxey, "Treason on Trial in Revolutionary Pennsylvania," 32, 71; Larson, "The Revolutionary American Jury," 1492.

89 **a cart carrying their coffins:** Maxey, "Treason on Trial in Revolutionary Pennsylvania," 1, 2, 90–91.

89 **"his sacred honor":** Larson, "The Revolutionary American Jury," 1443, 1479, 1488.

89 **an astonishing record of success:** Larson, "The Revolutionary American Jury," 1443.

89 **The trials raised profound questions:** Maxey, "Treason on Trial in Revolutionary Pennsylvania," 6.

89 **meet a far higher standard:** Ewald, "James Wilson and the Drafting of the Constitution," 907; Larson, *The Trials of Allegiance,* 230–33. Larson agrees with the compelling evidence that Wilson was the driving force behind the Constitution's inclusion of a treason clause, even as he notes that some of the clause's details appear to have been drafted by others. At the Pennsylvania ratifying convention in the fall of 1787, Wilson praised the final

product as containing a "current running strong in favor of humanity," and observed that "history informs us, that more wrong may be done on this subject than on any other whatsoever." In his list of seventeen reasons to defend the Constitution, he included the treason clause as a critical bulwark against tyrannical government. See Jensen, *The Documentary History of the Ratification of the Constitution*, 2:483, 493.

90   **"open to the public eye"**: Larson, "The Revolutionary American Jury," 1456, 1501–3, citing *Pennsylvania Packet*, April 29, 1779, 3.

90   **the skyrocketing costs of bread**: Bezanson, "Inflation and Controls, Pennsylvania, 1774–1779," 15.

90   **"not a bit to be bought"**: John Alexander, "The Fort Wilson Incident of 1779," 593, 595.

90   **"no longer be trampled upon"**: John Alexander, "The Fort Wilson Incident of 1779," 598–99.

91   **tried and acquitted of treason**: Rosswurm, *Arms, Country, and Class*, 210–12.

91   **as many as thirty men**: Rosswurm, *Arms, Country, and Class*, 214–15; Rappleye, *Robert Morris*, 191–92.

91   **to wait out the storm**: Smith, *James Wilson*, 133.

91   **"determined to defend himself"**: Letter of James Gibson, in Konkle, "The Life and Writings of James Wilson," 2:136–38, note 107.

92   **the leaders denied it**: Allen McLane, *Journal*, in Commager and Morris, *The Spirit of '76*, 813.

92   **he was struck immediately**: Rosswurm, *Arms, Country, and Class*, 215–16; Benjamin Rush to John Adams, October 12, 1779, Founders Online, National Archives, https://founders.archives.gov/documents/Adams/06-08 -02-0138. Original source: *The Papers of John Adams*, vol. 8, *March 1779–February 1780*, ed. Gregg L. Lint, Robert J. Taylor, Richard Alan Reyerson, Celeste Walker, and Joanna M. Revelas (Harvard University Press, 1989), 199–201.

92   **The wound was fatal**: McLane, *Journal*, in Commager and Morris, *The Spirit of '76*, 814; Charles Willson Peale, *Statement*, in Commager and Morris, *The Spirit of '76*, 812.

92   **"armed with bars of iron"**: McLane, *Journal*, in Commager and Morris, *The Spirit of '76*, 814.

92   **others dragged Wilson's defender**: Philip Hagner's Narrative, in Reed, *Life and Correspondence of Joseph Reed*, 427.

92   **a cannon was being hauled over**: Philip Hagner's Narrative, in Reed, *Life and Correspondence of Joseph Reed*, 427; Rosswurm, *Arms, Country, and Class*, 216; Rappleye, *Robert Morris*, 193.

92   **Peale and, ironically, Timothy Matlack**: Commager and Morris, *The Spirit of '76*, 812.

92   **at least seventeen were wounded**: Charles Willson Peale, *Statement*, in Commager and Morris, *The Spirit of '76*, 812; John Alexander, "The Fort Wilson Incident of 1779," 589.

92   **hide out at the Hills**: Rappleye, *Robert Morris*, 194; "The Hills," *History of Early American Landscape Design*, National Gallery of Art, https://heald.nga .gov/mediawiki/index.php/The_Hills.

93   "as a kind of retaliation": Philip Hagner's Narrative, in Reed, *Life and Correspondence of Joseph Reed*, 427.

93   "As the ferment is particularly high": Robert Morris to James Wilson, October 5, 1779, in Konkle, "The Life and Writings of James Wilson," 2:141.

93   "we called upon them": James Wilson to Robert Morris, October 6, 1779, in Konkle, "The Life and Writings of James Wilson," 2:144.

93   "don't come in tomorrow": Robert Morris to James Wilson, October 6, 1779, in Konkle, "The Life and Writings of James Wilson," 2:146.

93   "tolerable Degree of Quiet": James Wilson to Robert Morris, October 7, 1779, in Konkle, "The Life and Writings of James Wilson," 2:148.

94   "a convulsion among the people": Cited in John Alexander, "The Fort Wilson Incident of 1779," 589.

94   "stained with fraternal blood": Benjamin Rush to John Adams, October 12, 1779, Founders Online, National Archives, https://founders.archives.gov/documents/Adams/06-08-02-0138.

94   "a consequence of that liberty": Konkle, "The Life and Writings of James Wilson," 2:151.

94   "the exceeding lenity": Cited in Larson, "The Revolutionary American Jury," 1444.

94   "gave weight to their conduct": Cited in Larson, "The Revolutionary American Jury," 1507.

94   a ten-thousand-dollar bond: *Colonial Records of Pennsylvania*, vol. 12 (Theophilus Fenn, 1853), 121–22, 137.

95   even toward sympathetic ends: Diestelow, "The Fort Wilson Riot and Pennsylvania's Republican Formation," paragraph ending with n28.

95   the virtual disappearance: Larson, "The Revolutionary American Jury," 1508.

95   members of the merchant class: Foner, *Tom Paine and Revolutionary America*, 184.

95   "being considered as an enemy": *Pennsylvania Packet*, October 16, 1779.

95   former would often lose: Foner, *Tom Paine and Revolutionary America*, 146–47; Diestelow, "The Fort Wilson Riot and Pennsylvania's Republican Formation."

96   at the center of both: Diestelow, "The Fort Wilson Riot and Pennsylvania's Republican Formation."

96   foreclosing any criminal action: Rosswurm, *Arms, Country, and Class*, 221.

96   "you live opposed that damned Wilson": Quoted in Rosswurm, *Arms, Country, and Class*, 222.

96   "the fears of popular rapacity": McCloskey in Wilson, *The Works of James Wilson*, ed. McCloskey, 24.

96   "the Panglossian excesses": Witt, *Patriots and Cosmopolitans*, 71.

97   "extravagant and daring business schemes": McCloskey in Wilson, *The Works of James Wilson*, ed. McCloskey, 18.

97   triggered congressional investigations: See Mikhail, "James Wilson, Early American Land Companies, and the Original Meaning of Ex Post Facto Law," 79–146.

97   Wilson sent word to John Adams: James Wilson to John Adams, April 20, 1780, in *The Adams Papers Digital Edition*, Massachusetts Historical Society,

https://www.masshist.org/publications/adams-papers/index.php/view
/ADMS-06-09-02-0117#PJA09d128n1. Originally published in *The Adams
Papers: Papers of John Adams*, vol. 9, ed. Gregg L. Lint et al. (Harvard University Press, 1996), 128–32.

97   **ten thousand livres:** Waln biography of James Wilson, 121–27.

7: Prosperity, Speculation, and Crisis

98   **She joined Polly:** Smith, *James Wilson*, 210–11.

98   **and to accompany him:** Bronson, *A Memorial of the Rev. Bird Wilson*, 211.

99   **be dutiful to God:** Alison Landales to James Wilson, October 6, 1783, in Konkle, "The Life and Writings of James Wilson," 2:272.

99   **she was going door-to-door:** Reed, *Life and Correspondence of Joseph Reed*, 429; Rappleye, *Robert Morris*, 215.

99   ***ubi libertas ibi patria:*** Smith, *James Wilson*, 203–5; T. I. Wharton, *A Memoir of William Rawle, LL.D., President of the Historical Society, &c.* (Philadelphia, 1840), 57; Robert B. Beath, *Historical Catalogue of the St. Andrew's Society of Philadelphia, with Biographical Sketches of Deceased Members*, vol. 2, 1749–1913 (J. B. Lippincott, 1913), 15, 20 (the catalog records Wilson's proposal as being rejected, but provides no explanation).

100   **"making a fortune rapidly":** Marquis de Chastellux, *Travels in North America in the Years 1780, 1781, and 1782*, trans. and annotated by an English gentleman, vol. 1 (S. G. J. and J. Robinson, 1787), 224.

100   **George Washington agreed to underwrite the cost:** Carson, *An Historical Sketch of the Law Department of the University of Pennsylvania*, 16; George Washington to James Wilson, 22 March 1782, *Papers of Bushrod Washington*, University of Virginia, http://bushrod.washingtonpapers.org/node/2049. In a letter to Bird Wilson in 1822, Bushrod wrote, "Altho' your father required from his students a much higher fee than was usually paid to the other gentlemen of the law, the General unhesitatingly overrule[d] the intention I expressed to him of entering some other office on account of that difference, by arguments strongly indicating the high opinion he entertained of your father" (Bushrod Washington to Bird Wilson, October 26, 1822, *Papers of Bushrod Washington*, University of Virginia, http://bushrod.washingtonpapers.org /node/1762).

100   **up to one hundred thousand pounds of capital:** James Wilson to William Bingham, May 27, 1783, in Konkle, "The Life and Writings of James Wilson," 2:252-b.

100   **"still larger sums":** James Wilson to Certain Dutch Capitalists, January 16, 1785, in Konkle, "The Life and Writings of James Wilson," 2:289; James Wilson to William Bingham, May 27, 1783, in Konkle, "The Life and Writings of James Wilson," 2:252-a (for amount of loan).

101   **"We have nothing":** Rappleye, *Robert Morris*, 394–96.

101   **"insatiable leeches":** Janet Wilson, "The Bank of North America and Pennsylvania Politics: 1781–1787," 5, 6.

101   **loaned him close to one hundred thousand dollars:** Rappleye, *Robert Morris*, 400; Terry Bouton, *Taming Democracy: "The People," the Founders, and the Troubled Ending of the American Revolution* (Oxford University Press, 2007), 134–35,

293n16; Smith, *James Wilson*, 210; Janet Wilson, "The Bank of North America and Pennsylvania Politics: 1781–1787," 11.

101   **increasingly intertwined**: Robert G. McCloskey, "James Wilson," in *The Justices of the United States Supreme Court: Their Lives and Major Opinions*, vol. 1, ed. Leon Friedman and Fred L. Israel (Infobase, 2013), 43.

102   **"The act of independence"**: Wilson, "Considerations on the Bank of North America," in *The Collected Works of James Wilson*, ed. Hall and Hall, 1:64.

102   **the Assembly revoked the bank's state charter**: Janet Wilson, "The Bank of North America and Pennsylvania Politics: 1781–1787," 13.

103   **"yet most of us were ignorant"**: Benjamin Rush, "Address to the People of the United States," *The American Museum* (January 1787), in John P. Kaminski and Gaspare J. Saladino, eds., *The Documentary History of the Ratification of the Constitution*, vol. 13 (The State Historical Society of Wisconsin, 1981). Originally published in *Commentaries on the Constitution*, vol. 1, February 21–November 7, 1787, 46.

104   **it had no enforcement mechanism**: Amar, *The Words That Made Us*, 173; Farrand, *The Framing of the Constitution of the United States*, 3–4.

104   **one sixtieth of the country's population**: Klarman, *The Framers' Coup*, 25–26.

105   **"government should be small"**: Beeman, *Plain, Honest Men*, 7.

105   **"eternally counteracting each other"**: Klarman, *The Framers' Coup*, 112.

105   **strengthen the powers of the union**: "Notes on Debates, 1 April 1783," n9, Founders Online, National Archives, https://founders.archives.gov /documents/Madison/01-06-02-0145. Originally published in *The Papers of James Madison*, 6:424–27.

105   **many ended up in debtors' prison**: Klarman, *The Framers' Coup*, 76, 77–81.

106   **"help the feeble against the mighty"**: Klarman, *The Framers' Coup*, 77, 81.

106   **"lazy, lounging, lubberly"**: Klarman, *The Framers' Coup*, 83.

106   **"Nothing but evil"**: Klarman, *The Framers' Coup*, 86.

106   **a private militia**: Klarman, *The Framers' Coup*, 91–92.

106   **"indeed wretched"**: Quoted in Maier, *Ratification*, 12.

107   **"the exigencies of the Union"**: Beeman, *Plain, Honest Men*, 18–20.

108   **"unfit for their own government"**: Beeman, *Plain, Honest Men*, 17, 19–20.

8: Philadelphia 1787

109   **would be added in March**: Farrand, *The Records of the Federal Convention of 1787*, 565–67.

109   **just 35 of 63 votes**: Smith, *James Wilson*, 217; Beeman, *Plain, Honest Men*, 49; Jacob Hiltzheimer, *Extracts from the Diary of Jacob Hiltzheimer, 1765–1798*, ed. Jacob Cox Parsons (W. F. Fell, 1893), 111–12.

110   **"for the sole and express purpose"**: Klarman, *The Framers' Coup*, 119, 133.

110   **a civic church**: The steeple, originally made of wood, was removed due to rot in 1781; it was reassembled in 1828. See "Independence Hall: Architecture—Change over Time," National Park Service, https://www.nps .gov/inde/learn/historyculture/places-independencehall-architecture -changeovertime.htm.

110   **"The number as yet assembled"**: James Madison to Thomas Jefferson, May 15, 1787, Founders Online, National Archives, https://founders.archives

.gov/documents/Madison/01-09-02-0229. Originally published in *The Papers of James Madison*, vol. 9, April 9, 1786–May 24, 1787, and supplement 1781–1784, ed. Robert A. Rutland and William M. E. Rachal (University of Chicago Press, 1975), 415.

111   same lack of urgency: See, e.g., Beeman, *Plain, Honest Men*, 22–23.

111   "the best porter they had ever tasted": "Fringe Meetings at the U.S. Constitutional Convention: Letter on a Dinner Held at Franklin's House—16 May 1787," Quill Project, https://www.quillproject.net/resources/resource_item/38/3080; Beeman, *Plain, Honest Men*, 53.

112   "fatal to the object": Beeman, *Plain, Honest Men*, 22; James Madison, "Vices of the Political System of the United States, April 1787," Founders Online, National Archives, https://founders.archives.gov/documents/Madison/01-09-02-0187. Originally published in Rutland and Rachal, *The Papers of James Madison*, 9:345–58.

112   "positive and complete authority": James Madison to George Washington, April 16, 1787, Founders Online, National Archives, https://founders.archives.gov/documents/Madison/01-09-02-0208. Originally published in Rutland and Rachal, *The Papers of James Madison*, 9:382–87.

112   "a total alteration": Quoted in Farrand, *The Records of the Federal Convention of 1787*, 3:23.

112   "a violation of that equality": Farrand, *The Records of the Federal Convention of 1787*, 1:10–11n*.

113   "to disarm themselves": Farrand, *The Records of the Federal Convention of 1787*, 1:10–11n*.

113   "you will be speedy": George Read to John Dickinson, May 21, 1787, in Farrand, *The Records of the Federal Convention of 1787*, 3:24–26.

113   "I am mortified": Rufus King to Jeremiah Wadsworth, May 24, 1787, in Farrand, *The Records of the Federal Convention of 1787*, 3:26.

114   On Friday, May 25: Klarman, *The Framers' Coup*, 134.

114   "clear, copious, and comprehensive": Pierce, "Character Sketches of Delegates," 91–92.

115   any errors he might make: Farrand, *The Records of the Federal Convention of 1787*, 1:3–4.

115   the Delawareans had been expressly prohibited: Farrand, *The Records of the Federal Convention of 1787*, 1:6.

115   Wilson foremost among them: Larson and Winship, *The Constitutional Convention*, 3–4, 9; Beeman, *Plain, Honest Men*, 65.

116   Some delegates grumbled: Beeman, *Plain, Honest Men*, 83–84; Luther Martin to the Maryland legislature, December 28, 1787–February 8, 1788, in Farrand, *The Records of the Federal Convention of 1787*, 3:173–74.

116   honored it in the breach: See Farrand, *The Records of the Federal Convention of 1787*, 1:15n2, for examples of delegates' discussion of secrecy; see also Kaminski, *Secrecy and the Constitutional Convention*.

116   "the jealousy of the states": Edmund Randolph, May 29, 1787, in Farrand, *The Records of the Federal Convention of 1787*, 1:18–19.

117   three resolutions: Edmund Randolph, May 30, 1787, in Farrand, *The Records of the Federal Convention of 1787*, 1:33.

117　"meant to abolish the state governments": Charles Pinckney, May 30, 1787, in Farrand, *The Records of the Federal Convention of 1787*, 1:34.

117　the "Pinckney Plan": Beeman, *Plain, Honest Men*, 93–98.

117　"their business was at an end": Charles Cotesworth Pinckney, May 30, 1787, in Farrand, *The Records of the Federal Convention of 1787*, 1:34, 39.

118　having served in that Congress: Klarman, *The Framers' Coup*, 101.

118　The motion failed: Farrand, *The Records of the Federal Convention of 1787*, 1:35.

118　"retire from the convention": George Read, May 30, 1787, in Farrand, *The Records of the Federal Convention of 1787*, 1:37.

118　flatly refused to attend: Klarman, *The Framers' Coup*, 134.

118　"whatever reason might have existed": James Madison, May 30, 1787, in Farrand, *The Records of the Federal Convention of 1787*, 1:37.

119　"The people of America": William Grayson to James Monroe, May 29, 1787, in Farrand, *The Records of the Federal Convention of 1787*, 3:30.

119　"confusion will inevitably ensue": George Washington to Thomas Jefferson, May 30, 1787, in Farrand, *The Records of the Federal Convention of 1787*, 3:31.

119　a single substantive word: Wilson did speak up briefly, on May 25, to nominate Benjamin Franklin's grandson as the convention's secretary. The nomination failed. Farrand, *The Records of the Federal Convention of 1787*, 1:4.

120　"liable to be misled": Roger Sherman, May 31, 1787, in Farrand, *The Records of the Federal Convention of 1787*, 1:48.

120　memory of Shays's Rebellion: Quoted in Pierce, "Character Sketches of Delegates," 88; Beeman, *Plain, Honest Men*, 112.

120　"excess of democracy": Elbridge Gerry, May 31, 1787, in Farrand, *The Records of the Federal Convention of 1787*, 1:48.

120　"every part of the community": George Mason, May 31, 1787, in Farrand, *The Records of the Federal Convention of 1787*, 1:48–49.

120　"raising the federal pyramid": James Wilson, May 31, 1787, in Farrand, *The Records of the Federal Convention of 1787*, 1:49.

121　meddling in the relationship: James Wilson, May 31, 1787, in Farrand, *The Records of the Federal Convention of 1787*, 1:49.

121　who spoke 173 times: Merrill Jensen, *The Documentary History of the Ratification of the Constitution*, vol. 13, *Commentaries on the Constitution, Public and Private* (State Historical Society of Wisconsin, 1976), 337.

122　"lost sight of altogether": James Madison, May 31, 1787, in Farrand, *The Records of the Federal Convention of 1787*, 1:49–50.

122　"ought to be chosen by the people": James Wilson, May 31, 1787, in Farrand, *The Records of the Federal Convention of 1787*, 1:52.

122　a thickset, easygoing Boston merchant: Pierce, "Character Sketches of Delegates," 87–88; Farrand, *The Records of the Federal Convention of 1787*, 1:62–63.

123　"a considerable pause": Farrand, *The Records of the Federal Convention of 1787*, 1:65. James Madison's notes of the convention are far and away the most comprehensive and illuminating single source of what happened in the Pennsylvania statehouse in the summer of 1787. At the same time, Madison's notes have serious limitations. First, they are incomplete, including no record of various committee negotiations or other extracurricular conversations that may have been important to the debates. See, e.g., Ewald, "The

Committee of Detail," 197–201. Second, Madison altered some of his notes years after the fact. For an in-depth analysis of these changes, see Bilder, *Madison's Hand*.

123   "a point of great importance": Farrand, *The Records of the Federal Convention of 1787*, 1:65.

123   In his rapid-fire cadence: Pierce, "Character Sketches of Delegates," 96.

124   "no Man has a better Heart": Pierce, "Character Sketches of Delegates," 88–89.

124   a replica of "the royal brute": Thomas Paine, *Common Sense* (1776), Online Library of Liberty, https://oll.libertyfund.org/pages/1776-paine-common -sense-pamphlet. Originally published in *The Writings of Thomas Paine*, vol. 1.

124   "as our prototype": Edmund Randolph, June 1, 1787, in Farrand, *The Records of the Federal Convention of 1787*, 1:66.

125   "a corrupt multitude": James Wilson, June 1, 1787, in Farrand, *The Records of the Federal Convention of 1787*, 1:71.

125   and had chosen well: James Wilson, June 1, 1787, in Farrand, *The Records of the Federal Convention of 1787*, 1:68.

125   "as independent as possible": James Wilson, June 1, 1787, in Farrand, *The Records of the Federal Convention of 1787*, 1:69.

126   "shall be vested": James Wilson, June 2, 1787, in Farrand, *The Records of the Federal Convention of 1787*, 1:77, 80.

126   8 to 2: Farrand, *The Records of the Federal Convention of 1787*, 1:81.

126   "the greatest blot": Charles Pinckney, June 2, 1787, in Farrand, *The Records of the Federal Convention of 1787*, 1:132; Charles Pinckney to Rufus King, January 26, 1789; Charles Pinckney to James Madison, March 28, 1789, in Farrand, *The Records of the Federal Convention of 1787*, 3:355.

126   "men of indigence": Elbridge Gerry, June 6, 1787, in Farrand, *The Records of the Federal Convention of 1787*, 1:132.

127   "The people had already parted": James Wilson, June 6, 1787, in Farrand, *The Records of the Federal Convention of 1787*, 1:141.

127   "unless it is abused": Rush, "Address to the People of the United States," 1.

128   he did not trust the people: John Dickinson, June 7, 1787, in Farrand, *The Records of the Federal Convention of 1787*, 1:150.

128   "dissensions will naturally arise": James Wilson, June 7, 1787, in Farrand, *The Records of the Federal Convention of 1787*, 1:150–51.

128   "Our manners, our laws": James Wilson, June 7, 1787, in Farrand, *The Records of the Federal Convention of 1787*, 1:153–54.

129   "very fine haymaking weather": "Thomas Morris: Diary, 1787," in Weather Reports During the U.S. Constitutional Convention, Quill Project, https:// www.quillproject.net/resources/resource_item/57/3148.

129   "a formidable phalanx": David Brearley, June 9, 1787, in Farrand, *The Records of the Federal Convention of 1787*, 1:176–77.

129   "We have no power": William Paterson, June 9, 1787, in Farrand, *The Records of the Federal Convention of 1787*, 1:177–78; Beeman, *Plain, Honest Men*, 148.

130   "must be abolished": William Paterson, June 9, 1787, in Farrand, *The Records of the Federal Convention of 1787*, 1:178.

130   "New Jersey will never confederate": William Paterson, June 9, 1787, in Farrand, *The Records of the Federal Convention of 1787*, 1:179.

130   "equal numbers of people": James Wilson, June 9, 1787, in Farrand, *The Records of the Federal Convention of 1787*, 1:179.

131   "I never will confederate": James Wilson, June 9, 1787, in Farrand, *The Records of the Federal Convention of 1787*, 1:183; Madison casts this part of the speech somewhat differently, at 180: "We have been told that each State being sovereign, all are equal. So each man is naturally a sovereign over himself, and all men are therefore naturally equal. Can he retain this equality when he becomes a member of civil Government? He can not. As little can a Sovereign State, when it becomes a member of a federal Governt."

131   Given the high stakes involved: William Paterson, June 9, 1787, in Farrand, *The Records of the Federal Convention of 1787*, 1:180.

131   The New Jersey Plan: Farrand, *The Records of the Federal Convention of 1787*, 1:242–45.

132   "Has it less dignity?": James Wilson, June 16, 1787, in Farrand, *The Records of the Federal Convention of 1787*, 1:250–53.

132   "the most corrupt": James Wilson, June 16, 1787, in Farrand, *The Records of the Federal Convention of 1787*, 1:254.

132   The convention rejected: Farrand, *The Records of the Federal Convention of 1787*, 1:313.

133   "ought to be represented in it": James Wilson, June 25, 1787, in Farrand, *The Records of the Federal Convention of 1787*, 1:406.

133   "lost in the magnitude of the object": James Wilson, June 25, 1787, in Farrand, *The Records of the Federal Convention of 1787*, 1:405.

133   "we may injure the superstructure": James Wilson, June 25, 1787, in Farrand, *The Records of the Federal Convention of 1787*, 1:413.

133   Maybe God could help?: Benjamin Franklin, June 28, 1787, in Farrand, *The Records of the Federal Convention of 1787*, 1:451–52.

133   "the very heavens obey": Pierce, "Character Sketches of Delegates," 91.

134   the anniversary of independence: Farrand, *The Records of the Federal Convention of 1787*, 1:452.

134   to a more earthly power: Farrand, *The Records of the Federal Convention of 1787*, 1:481.

134   "Seven states will control six": James Wilson, June 30, 1787, in Farrand, *The Records of the Federal Convention of 1787*, 1:482–83.

134   "the imaginary beings called *states*": James Wilson, June 30, 1787, in Farrand, *The Records of the Federal Convention of 1787*, 1:483.

134   "a mere illusion of names": James Wilson, June 30, 1787, in Farrand, *The Records of the Federal Convention of 1787*, 1:483.

135   "do them justice": Gunning Bedford, June 30, 1787, in Farrand, *The Records of the Federal Convention of 1787*, 1:490–92.

135   "grieved that such a thought": Rufus King, June 30, 1787, in Farrand, *The Records of the Federal Convention of 1787*, 1:493.

135   "Something must be done": Roger Sherman, Hugh Williamson, July 2, 1787, in Farrand, *The Records of the Federal Convention of 1787*, 1:511; Elbridge Gerry, July 2, 1787, in Farrand, *The Records of the Federal Convention of 1787*, 1:515.

135   tending to various business matters: Brookhiser, *Gentleman Revolutionary*, 81.

136   "the work of the sword": Gouverneur Morris, July 5, 1787, in Farrand, *The Records of the Federal Convention of 1787*, 1:530.

136   Morris did not apologize: Gunning Bedford, July 5, 1787, in Farrand, *The Records of the Federal Convention of 1787*, 1:531.

137   state equality in the Senate: James Wilson, July 13, 1787, in Farrand, *The Records of the Federal Convention of 1787*, 1:605.

137   "the natural and precise measure": James Wilson, July 13, 1787, in Farrand, *The Records of the Federal Convention of 1787*, 1:605 (emphasis in original).

137   "a point of such critical importance": James Wilson, July 14, 1787, in Farrand, *The Records of the Federal Convention of 1787*, 2:4.

138   "taxes and troops": Luther Martin and James Wilson, July 14, 1787, in Farrand, *The Records of the Federal Convention of 1787*, 2:4–5.

138   "and finally death itself": James Wilson, July 14, 1787, in Farrand, *The Records of the Federal Convention of 1787*, 2:10.

138   "all the weakness of the former government": James Wilson, July 14, 1787, in Farrand, *The Records of the Federal Convention of 1787*, 2:10–11.

138   "decided by a bare majority": James Madison's notes, July 17, 1787, in Farrand, *The Records of the Federal Convention of 1787*, 2:20.

139   the people themselves: James Wilson, June 5, 1787, in Farrand, *The Records of the Federal Convention of 1787*, 1:127; see also James Wilson, June 5, 1787, in Farrand, *The Records of the Federal Convention of 1787*, 1:123: "Mr. Wilson took this occasion to lead the Committee by a train of observations to the idea of not suffering a disposition in the plurality of States to confederate anew on better principles, to be defeated by the inconsiderate or selfish opposition of a few (States). He hoped the provision for ratifying would be put on such a footing as to admit of such a partial union, with a door open for the accession of the rest." In a footnote to this remark, Farrand added: "This hint was probably meant *in terrorem* to the smaller States of N. Jersey & Delaware. Nothing was said in reply to it."

9: The Real Work Begins

141   that ten-day period: Ewald, "The Committee of Detail," 201. Ewald has written the definitive account of the committee's work. As he points out, the job was complicated by the remarkable lack of similar past efforts. For this reason, my account of this period of the convention relies heavily on his research and conclusions. For my recounting of the Necessary and Proper Clause, I am indebted to the work of John Mikhail. See Mikhail, "The Necessary and Proper Clauses," 1045–1132.

141   final product: Ewald, "The Committee of Detail," 209.

141   "the main event": Ewald, "The Committee of Detail," 201.

142   edits and comments: Ewald, "The Committee of Detail," 246–47.

142   "altered the course": Ewald, "The Committee of Detail," 208.

142   "the very core of American federalism": Ewald, "The Committee of Detail," 210.

143   the circumstantial evidence suggests: See, e.g., Mikhail, "The Necessary and Proper Clauses," 1074–78, 1096–1103; Ewald, "The Committee of

Detail," 271 (Wilson is "the likeliest candidate" to have initiated the Necessary and Proper Clause), 274 (Wilson is again "the likeliest suspect" for the Supremacy Clause). Ewald also leans toward Wilson as the primary author of "We the People," the Treason Clause, and much of the shape of what became Article II, on the executive branch. See 282–83. Still, he is careful to note that "full proof is impossible," 276.

143 would not exist: Ewald, "The Committee of Detail," 211.

143 "we are one large state": James Wilson in Congress, August 1, 1776, cited in Mikhail, "The Necessary and Proper Clauses," 1126n358.

143 the "first constitution": Mikhail, "The Necessary and Proper Clauses," 1126 and n357.

144 the people don't care: James Wilson, June 6, 1787, in Farrand, *The Records of the Federal Convention of 1787*, 1:132–33.

144 "The people are more happy": Roger Sherman, June 6, 1787, in Farrand, *The Records of the Federal Convention of 1787*, 1:133.

144 "fair sense of the people": Roger Sherman, July 7, 1787, in Farrand, *The Records of the Federal Convention of 1787*, 1:550.

144 "the worst governed": Oliver Ellsworth, June 25, 1787, in Farrand, *The Records of the Federal Convention of 1787*, 1:406.

144 "swallow all of them up": George Read, June 6, 1787, in Farrand, *The Records of the Federal Convention of 1787*, 1:136.

144 "the parts composing it": James Wilson, June 6, 1787, in Farrand, *The Records of the Federal Convention of 1787*, 1:137.

145 "Within their proper orbits": John Dickinson and James Wilson, June 7, 1787, in Farrand, *The Records of the Federal Convention of 1787*, 1:152–54.

145 "to the impotent condition": James Wilson, June 8, 1787, in Farrand, *The Records of the Federal Convention of 1787*, 1:166.

145 "local habits and attachments": James Wilson, June 25, 1787, in Farrand, *The Records of the Federal Convention of 1787*, 1:413.

146 "the teeth of the serpents": Gouverneur Morris, July 5, 1787, in Farrand, *The Records of the Federal Convention of 1787*, 1:529–30 (note that Madison crossed out "the states").

146 "not individually but unitedly": James Wilson, June 19, 1787, in Farrand, *The Records of the Federal Convention of 1787*, 1:324.

146 the essence of American federalism: Ewald, "The Committee of Detail," 259.

146 the Necessary and Proper Clause: Mikhail, "The Necessary and Proper Clauses," 1096n218; Ewald, "The Committee of Detail," 271, 281. Ewald believes Wilson was the main actor behind the Necessary and Proper and Supremacy Clauses. Ewald, "The Committee of Detail," 276.

147 as much power as it needed: Mikhail, "The Necessary and Proper Clauses," 1048–49; Wilson's land speculation also convinced him of the importance of a strong federal government.

147 "ought to have": James Wilson, May 30, 1787, in Farrand, *The Records of the Federal Convention of 1787*, 1:60.

147 the scope of Congress's power: Mikhail, "The Necessary and Proper Clauses," 1077–78.

147   *in all cases*: Mikhail, "The Necessary and Proper Clauses," 1078.

147   to establish lower federal courts: Mikhail, "The Necessary and Proper Clauses," 1087.

147   "make all laws necessary": Mikhail, "The Necessary and Proper Clauses," 1088.

147   prepared to go: For example, Robert Yates of New York, a committed Anti-Federalist, acknowledged that in any grant of general powers, "the powers to execute are implied." *The Documentary History of the Ratification of the Constitution*, vol. 23, *Ratification of the Constitution by the States: New York*, ed. John P. Kaminski and Gaspare J. Saladino (State Historical Society of Wisconsin, 2008), 2248. Yates abandoned the convention on July 10, weeks before the Committee of Detail met and more than two months before the Constitution was completed, and thus he could not object to the broad grant of federal power in the moment.

148   "a dead letter": Quoted in Mikhail, "The Necessary and Proper Clauses," 1091.

148   defense and general welfare: Mikhail, "The Original Federalist Theory of Implied Powers," 62.

148   across from the State House: Mikhail, "The Necessary and Proper Clauses," 1096; Ewald, "The Committee of Detail," 281.

148   "any department or officer thereof": "Draft of the United States Constitution," Historical Society of Pennsylvania, https://digitallibrary.hsp.org/index.php/Detail/objects/1663 (emphasis added); see also Ewald and Toler, "Early Drafts of the U.S. Constitution," 227–59.

148   "circumstances of the moment": Mikhail, "The Necessary and Proper Clauses," 1121; Farrand, *The Records of the Federal Convention of 1787*, 2:125.

149   Wilson's sweeping clause: Mikhail, "The Necessary and Proper Clauses," 1051.

149   "any laws they please": Farrand, *The Records of the Federal Convention of 1787*, 2:635.

149   Benjamin Franklin implicitly referred to it: "Petition from the Pennsylvania Society for the Abolition of Slavery to the First Congress (1790)," National Constitution Center, https://constitutioncenter.org/the-constitution/historic-document-library/detail/petition-from-the-pennsylvania-society-for-the-abolition-of-slavery-to-the-first-congress-1790.

149   to establish a national bank: Mikhail, "The Original Federalist Theory of Implied Powers," 63.

149   "of the said United States": For an analysis of the drafting process, see Ewald, "The Committee of Detail," 246–48.

150   the last folio in his draft: Ewald, "The Committee of Detail," 248.

150   the document as a whole: Mikhail, "The Original Federalist Theory of Implied Powers," 61–62.

150   "in the great article of government": James Wilson, speech of November 28, 1787, in Jensen, *The Documentary History of the Ratification of the Constitution*, 2:383–84.

150   It was a small but significant change: Ewald, "The Committee of Detail," 249.

150   put the people first: Ewald, "The Committee of Detail," 249 and note 139.

151   **one brick too many:** Committee of Detail, IX, in Farrand, *The Records of the Federal Convention of 1787*, 2:163.

151   **The convention would take up:** Farrand, *The Records of the Federal Convention of 1787*, 2:175; Ewald, "The Committee of Detail," 278.

151   **would be accountable to the people:** DiClerico, "James Wilson's Presidency," 314.

152   **clearest and most consistent vision:** See, e.g., McConnell, "James Wilson's Contributions to the Construction of Article II," 24; Yoo, "James Wilson as the Architect of the American Presidency," 52–53; Calabresi and Prakash, "The President's Power to Execute the Laws," 608.

152   **"ought to be clothed":** James Madison to George Washington, April 16, 1787, Founders Online, National Archives, https://founders.archives.gov/documents/Madison/01-09-02-0208. Originally published in Rutland and Rachal, *The Papers of James Madison*, 9:382–87.

152   **who would replace him:** This question would not be formally resolved for nearly two hundred years, with the passage of the Twenty-Fifth Amendment in the wake of John F. Kennedy's assassination.

152   **"what sort may come afterwards":** Benjamin Franklin, June 4, 1787, in Farrand, *The Records of the Federal Convention of 1787*, 1:103.

152   **"fetus of monarchy":** Edmund Randolph, June 1, 1787, in Farrand, *The Records of the Federal Convention of 1787*, 1:66.

152   **"in a limited monarchy":** John Dickinson, June 2, 1787, in Farrand, *The Records of the Federal Convention of 1787*, 1:86.

152   **"a single magistrate is not a King":** James Wilson, June 4, 1787, in Farrand, *The Records of the Federal Convention of 1787*, 1:96.

153   **traced back to the seventeenth-century:** Immediately after the beheading of King Charles I in 1649, England's Rump Parliament passed an act abolishing the monarchy.

153   **"in a single person":** John Adams, *A Defence of the Constitutions of Government of the United States of America*, vol. 1 (C. Dilly, 1787), quoted in Nelson, *The Royalist Revolution*, 185–86.

153   **echoes of his own words:** Nelson, *The Royalist Revolution*, 185–86.

153   **"unfit to be the ruler":** Declaration of Independence, July 4, 1776, https://www.archives.gov/founding-docs/declaration-transcript.

153   **a king got things done:** Nelson, *The Royalist Revolution*, 178–83.

153   **"passions of a multitude":** *Connecticut Courant* (Hartford), November 20, 1786.

154   **"we never once thought of a king":** Jensen, *The Documentary History of the Ratification of the Constitution*, 13:174.

154   **Mercer laughed:** James McHenry's notes, August 6, 1787, in Farrand, *The Records of the Federal Convention of 1787*, 2:191–92; Daniel Carroll: Notes and Correspondence, in Farrand, *The Records of the Federal Convention of 1787*, 3:319–24.

154   **his "tavern harangues":** Daniel Carroll to James Madison, May 28, 1788, in Farrand, *The Records of the Federal Convention of 1787*, 3:305–6.

154   **his tendency to show up to court:** Beeman, *Plain, Honest Men*, 174.

155   **"domestic vigor and stability":** James Wilson at the Pennsylvania ratifying

convention, November 24, 1787, in Jensen, *The Documentary History of the Ratification of the Constitution*, 2:360.

155 the sheer exhaustion of late summer: DiClerico, "James Wilson's Presidency," 310–11; McConnell, "James Wilson's Contributions to the Construction of Article II," 40; Ewald, "The Committee of Detail," 277.

155 "architect": Yoo, "James Wilson as the Architect of the American Presidency," 51–73.

155 "intellectual father": Calabresi and Prakash, "The President's Power to Execute the Laws," 608.

155 following a few steps behind: DiClerico, "James Wilson's Presidency," 303; Ewald, "The Committee of Detail"; see also McConnell, "James Wilson's Contributions to the Construction of Article II"; McCarthy, "James Wilson and the Creation of the Presidency."

156 "paternal care and affection": James Wilson at the Pennsylvania ratifying convention, December 1, 1787, in Jensen, *The Documentary History of the Ratification of the Constitution*, 2:452.

156 "to exalt the mind": Wilson, Pennsylvania constitutional convention of 1789–1790, December 31, 1789, in *The Collected Works of James Wilson*, ed. Hall and Hall, 1:300–301.

156 "by the people at large": Gouverneur Morris, July 17, 1787, in Farrand, *The Records of the Federal Convention of 1787*, 2:29.

157 "the best chance for the appointment": Roger Sherman, July 17, 1787, in Farrand, *The Records of the Federal Convention of 1787*, 2:29.

157 "The concurrence of a majority": James Wilson, July 17, 1787, in Farrand, *The Records of the Federal Convention of 1787*, 2:30.

157 "great and illustrious characters": Gouverneur Morris, July 17, 1787, in Farrand, *The Records of the Federal Convention of 1787*, 2:30–31.

157 "a trial of colors to a blind man": George Mason, July 17, 1787, in Farrand, *The Records of the Federal Convention of 1787*, 2:31.

158 "Her slaves will have no suffrage": Hugh Williamson, July 17, 1787, in Farrand, *The Records of the Federal Convention of 1787*, 2:32.

158 to every slaveholding state: See, e.g., Klarman, *The Framers' Coup*, 228.

158 it passed unanimously: Farrand, *The Records of the Federal Convention of 1787*, 2:32.

158 "let him be appointed by the people": Gouverneur Morris, July 19, 1787, in Farrand, *The Records of the Federal Convention of 1787*, 2:52–53.

158 "within a narrow sphere": Gouverneur Morris, July 19, 1787, in Farrand, *The Records of the Federal Convention of 1787*, 2:54.

159 "liable to fewest objections": Rufus King, July 19, 1787, in Farrand, *The Records of the Federal Convention of 1787*, 2:55–56.

159 "perceived with pleasure": James Wilson, July 19, 1787, in Farrand, *The Records of the Federal Convention of 1787*, 2:56.

159 "on the score of the Negroes": James Madison, July 19, 1787, in Farrand, *The Records of the Federal Convention of 1787*, 2:56–57.

159 "when they can rather increase it": George Mason, July 11, 1787, in Farrand, *The Records of the Federal Convention of 1787*, 1:578.

159 "the substitution of electors": James Madison, July 19, 1787, in Farrand, *The Records of the Federal Convention of 1787*, 2:57.

160 "almost any length of time": James Wilson, July 24, 1787, in Farrand, *The Records of the Federal Convention of 1787*, 2:102.

160 "entirely at a loss": Elbridge Gerry, July 24, 1787, in Farrand, *The Records of the Federal Convention of 1787*, 2:103.

160 "a digested idea": James Wilson, July 24, 1787, in Farrand, *The Records of the Federal Convention of 1787*, 2:103.

160 "not by chance": Rufus King, July 24, 1787, in Farrand, *The Records of the Federal Convention of 1787*, 2:105–6.

160 "willing to make the sacrifice": James Madison, July 25, 1787, in Farrand, *The Records of the Federal Convention of 1787*, 2:111.

161 to state governors, and to others: Farrand, *The Records of the Federal Convention of 1787*, 1:176.

161 seemed to be gaining: Farrand, *The Records of the Federal Convention of 1787*, 2:401–4.

161 the Committee on Postponed Parts: Farrand, *The Records of the Federal Convention of 1787*, 2:481.

161 among the top five finishers: Farrand, *The Records of the Federal Convention of 1787*, 2:493–94.

161 "the most difficult of all": James Wilson, September 4, 1787, in Farrand, *The Records of the Federal Convention of 1787*, 2:501.

162 "nineteen times in twenty": George Mason, September 4, 1787, in Farrand, *The Records of the Federal Convention of 1787*, 2:500.

162 "not a favorite of mine": James Wilson in the Pennsylvania ratifying convention, December 4, 1787, in Farrand, *The Records of the Federal Convention of 1787*, 3:161–62.

162 He also proposed limiting the choice: James Wilson, September 4, 1787, in Farrand, *The Records of the Federal Convention of 1787*, 2:501–2.

162 a single vote in the House: Farrand, *The Records of the Federal Convention of 1787*, 2:527.

163 "the second-most democratic idea": McConnell, "James Wilson's Contributions to the Construction of Article II," 50.

163 "but against his parliament": Quoted in Nelson, *The Royalist Revolution*, 1–2.

163 "not against an unity": James Wilson, June 1, 1787, in Farrand, *The Records of the Federal Convention of 1787*, 1:71.

163 Wilson held a consistent vision: Nelson, *The Royalist Revolution*, 187.

164 the distinction between reigning over: Nelson, *The Royalist Revolution*, 232 ("While the king reigns, this man seems to rule").

164 "no leading principles in them": Thomas Jefferson to "Henry Tompkinson" [Samuel Kercheval], July 12, 1816, Founders Online, National Archives, https:// founders.archives.gov/documents/Jefferson/03-10-02-0128-0002. Original source: *The Papers of Thomas Jefferson*, Retirement Series, vol. 10, *May 1816 to 18 January 1817*, ed. J. Jefferson Looney (Princeton University Press, 2013), 222–28.

165 "possesses a constitutional dignity": John Adams to Roger Sherman, July 18, 1789, Founders Online, National Archives, https://founders.archives .gov/documents/Adams/06-20-02-0055. Original source: *The Adams Papers: Papers of John Adams*, vol. 20, *June 1789–February 1791*, ed. Sara Georgini et al. (Harvard University Press, 2020), 81–83.

165 "under a different name": Quoted in Wood, *The Idea of America*, 240.

10: The Signing

166   **in the history of democracy:** In 1781, the State House also served as the site of the formal adoption of the Articles of Confederation, when Maryland became the last state to sign the document.

166   **was an afterthought:** Maier, *American Scripture*, 167; Allen and Sneff, "Golden Letters," 197–200.

167   **through the end of the eighteenth century:** The Declaration's Preamble was cited briefly by Massachusetts's and Vermont's decisions to abolish slavery. Allen and Sneff, "Golden Letters," 199.

167   **The exception was Wilson:** Allen and Sneff, "Golden Letters," 196; Ewald, "James Wilson and the American Founding," 12–16.

167   **"not *Individually* but *Unitedly*":** James Wilson, June 19, 1787, in Farrand, *The Records of the Federal Convention of 1787*, 1:324.

167   **The Declaration came first:** Wilson, "Considerations on the Bank of North America," in *The Collected Works of James Wilson*, ed. Hall and Hall, 1:66; Allen and Sneff, "Golden Letters," 211.

167   **"On the same certain and solid foundation":** Ewald, "James Wilson and the American Founding," 16.

168   **decades after the convention:** See, e.g., Gouverneur Morris to Timothy Pickering, December 22, 1814, in Farrand, *The Records of the Federal Convention of 1787*, 3:420 ("That instrument was written by the fingers, which write this letter. Having rejected redundant and equivocal terms, I believed it to be as clear as our language would permit."); James Madison to Jared Sparks, April 8, 1831, in Farrand, *The Records of the Federal Convention of 1787*, 3:499 (italics in original). ("The *finish* given to the style and arrangement of the Constitution fairly belongs to the pen of Mr Morris; the task having, probably, been handed over to him by the chairman of the Committee, himself a highly respectable member, and with the ready concurrence of the others. A better choice could not have been made, as the performance of the task proved.")

168   **placed Wilson at the center:** "Ezra Stiles: Diary, Dec. 21, 1787," in Farrand, *The Records of the Federal Convention of 1787*, 3:170 ("Morris and Wilson had the chief hand in the last arrangement and composition," according to Abraham Baldwin, a Georgia delegate); Warren, *The Making of the Constitution*, 688. ("Timothy Pickering, writing in 1828, said that Wilson told him that 'its final revision in regard to correctness of style was committed to him', and again that 'James Wilson once told me that after the Constitution had been finally settled, it was committed to him to be critically examined respecting its style, in order that the instrument might appear with the most perfect precision and accuracy of language.'")

168   **"equally, if not more, entitled":** Warren, *The Making of the Constitution*, 687–88.

169   **exaggerates Madison's influence:** Schwartz and Mikhail, "The Other Madison Problem," 2034–103.

169   **what Wilson envisioned in 1787:** Amar, *The Words That Made Us*, 211.

169   **"spiritual adviser":** Amar, *The Words That Made Us*, 211.

170   **he was doing that again:** Farrand, *The Records of the Federal Convention of 1787*, 2:641–43.

171   **"put his name to this instrument":** Benjamin Franklin, September 17, 1787, in Farrand, *The Records of the Federal Convention of 1787*, 2:641–43.

171 "chop off his right hand": Quoted in Maier, *Ratification*, 43.

171 "take this or nothing": Edmund Randolph and George Mason, September 15, 1787, in Farrand, *The Records of the Federal Convention of 1787*, 2:631–32.

172 Not a single delegation: Maier, *Ratification*, 45.

172 "Notwithstanding the vast majority": Edmund Randolph, September 17, 1787, in Farrand, *The Records of the Federal Convention of 1787*, 2:644–45.

172 "the most awful of his life": Edmund Randolph, September 17, 1787, in Farrand, *The Records of the Federal Convention of 1787*, 2:646.

172 "Entre nous": Quoted in Beeman, *Plain, Honest Men*, 291.

172 he would not go public: Elbridge Gerry, September 17, 1787, in Farrand, *The Records of the Federal Convention of 1787*, 2:647.

173 "not a setting sun": Benjamin Franklin, September 17, 1787, in Farrand, *The Records of the Federal Convention of 1787*, 2:648.

173 "large crowd of citizens": Maier, *Ratification*, 59–69; *The Documentary History of the Ratification of the Constitution, Ratification of the Constitution by the States: Pennsylvania. Microform Supplement* (State Historical Society of Wisconsin, 1976), 357.

173 "Reports and conjectures": James Madison to Thomas Jefferson, September 6, 1787, Founders Online, National Archives, https://founders.archives.gov/documents/Madison/01-10-02-0115. Original source: *The Papers of James Madison*, vol. 10, *27 May 1787–3 March 1788*, ed. Robert A. Rutland, Charles F. Hobson, William M. E. Rachal, and Frederika J. Teute (University of Chicago Press, 1977), 163–65.

174 "lest you should be hanged": Quoted in Farrand, *The Records of the Federal Convention of 1787*, 3:85; "Papers of Dr. James McHenry on the Federal Convention of 1787," *American Historical Review* 11, no. 3 (April 1906): 618.

174 left to take part in a duel: Maier, *Ratification*, 52.

174 "which everywhere *excite disgusts*": James Madison to Thomas Jefferson, September 6, 1787, Founders Online, National Archives, https://founders.archives.gov/documents/Madison/01-10-02-0115. Original source: Rutland et al., *The Papers of James Madison*, 10:163–65. Madison encrypted the italicized words in case the letter was intercepted.

174 far more power to the executive: Farrand, *The Records of the Federal Convention of 1787*, 2:645–46.

11: Slavery and the Three-Fifths Clause

177 "repugnant to reason": Blackstone, *Commentaries on the Laws of England*, Book 1, Chapter 14, 411.

177 not being sufficiently protective: Patrick Henry at the Virginia ratifying convention, June 24, 1788, in Kaminski et al., *The Documentary History of the Ratification of the Constitution*, 10:1476.

177 "destructive to Liberty": Cited in Beeman, *Plain, Honest Men*, 312–13.

177 "we are daily robbing and plundering": Cited in Klarman, *The Framers' Coup*, 259.

177 "the judgment of heaven": George Mason, August 22, 1787, in Farrand, *The Records of the Federal Convention of 1787*, 2:370.

177 "dishonorable to the American character": Luther Martin, August 21, 1787, in Farrand, *The Records of the Federal Convention of 1787*, 2:364.

177 the Maryland Society for the Abolition of Slavery: Beeman, *Plain, Honest Men*, 320.

178 "the political creed of America": "Petition from the Pennsylvania Society for the Abolition of Slavery," Benjamin Franklin Historical Society, http://www.benjamin-franklin-history.org/petition-from-the-pennsylvania-society-for-the-abolition-of-slavery/.

178 Twenty-five of the fifty-five men: Klarman, *The Framers' Coup*, 263.

178 enslaved more than one hundred Black people himself: Madison was the convention's primary notetaker, and there is a risk in relying too heavily on his account of these debates, especially about a charged topic like slavery. Madison, who lived fifty years past the convention, is well known to have altered sections of his notes later in his life, in some cases to update views that may have been accepted at the time but no longer were. See Bilder, *Madison's Hand*. Bilder's research suggests, however, that the most likely alterations occurred in the entry for August 25, when Madison attributed to himself anti-slavery comments that it is likely he did not make at the time, if ever.

178 "the size of the States": James Madison, June 29, 1787, in Farrand, *The Records of the Federal Convention of 1787*, 1:476.

178 "between the Northern and Southern": James Madison, June 30, 1787, in Farrand, *The Records of the Federal Convention of 1787*, 1:486.

179 in general agreement: James Madison, July 14, 1787, in Farrand, *The Records of the Federal Convention of 1787*, 2:9–10. ("It seemed now to be pretty well understood that the real difference of interests lay, not between the large & small but between the northern and southern states," Madison said late in the debate over the design of Congress. "The institution of slavery and its consequences formed the line of discrimination.")

179 with full credit for their slaves: Klarman, *The Framers' Coup*, 266–70.

179 "three-fifths of all other persons": James Wilson, June 11, 1787, in Farrand, *The Records of the Federal Convention of 1787*, 1:201.

179 He hadn't invented the ratio: Klarman, *The Framers' Coup*, 269–70.

180 Wilson had seen Pinckney's plan: Beeman, *Plain, Honest Men*, 154.

180 slaves had no interest in their labor: Klarman, *The Framers' Coup*, 270.

180 "Are they admitted as property?": James Wilson, July 11, 1787, in Farrand, *The Records of the Federal Convention of 1787*, 1:587.

180 with 6 voting against: Beeman, *Plain, Honest Men*, 210.

180 "at least as three-fifths": William Davie, July 12, 1787, in Farrand, *The Records of the Federal Convention of 1787*, 1:593.

180 Nine states voted in favor: Farrand, *The Records of the Federal Convention of 1787*, 1:606.

181 the protection of property: Beeman, *Plain, Honest Men*, 214; Rakove, *Original Meanings*, 73–74, 92–93; Van Cleve, *A Slaveholders' Union*, 11; Klarman, *The Framers' Coup*, 264–65, 286–87.

181 an economic threat first and foremost: Klarman, *The Framers' Coup*, 259, 262.

181 "All men wherever placed": James Wilson, July 13, 1787, in Farrand, *The Records of the Federal Convention of 1787*, 1:605.

182 **to undermine the slave trade:** Klarman, *The Framers' Coup*, 283–84; Beeman, *Plain, Honest Men*, 315–19; Ewald, "The Committee of Detail," 231–32; Van Cleve, *A Slaveholders' Union*, 130.

182 **Wilson was not the author:** Ewald, "The Committee of Detail," 244–45, 253–54.

182 **"bound by duty to his state":** Charles Cotesworth Pinckney, July 23, 1787, in Farrand, *The Records of the Federal Convention of 1787*, 2:95.

182 **"a most grating circumstance":** Rufus King, August 8, 1787, in Farrand, *The Records of the Federal Convention of 1787*, 2:220.

182 **"monument to Southern craft and gall":** Cited in Van Cleve, *A Slaveholders' Union*, 130.

182 **"so much inequality and unreasonableness":** Rufus King, August 8, 1787, in Farrand, *The Records of the Federal Convention of 1787*, 2:220.

182 **"sacrifice of every principle of right":** Gouverneur Morris, August 8, 1787, in Farrand, *The Records of the Federal Convention of 1787*, 2:221–22.

183 **"sooner submit himself to a tax":** Gouverneur Morris, August 8, 1787, in Farrand, *The Records of the Federal Convention of 1787*, 2:221–23.

183 **"nefarious institution":** Gouverneur Morris, August 8, 1787, in Farrand, *The Records of the Federal Convention of 1787*, 2:221.

183 **"will never be such fools":** John Rutledge, August 22, 1787, in Farrand, *The Records of the Federal Convention of 1787*, 2:373.

184 **"liberal conduct toward the views":** Charles Cotesworth Pinckney, August 29, 1787, in Farrand, *The Records of the Federal Convention of 1787*, 2:449–50.

184 **"An understanding on the two subjects":** James Madison, in Farrand, *The Records of the Federal Convention of 1787*, 2:449 at *; Klarman, *The Framers' Coup*, 289–90.

184 **"at the public expense":** James Wilson, August 28, 1787, in Farrand, *The Records of the Federal Convention of 1787*, 2:443.

184 **no recorded debate or dissent:** Farrand, *The Records of the Federal Convention of 1787*, 2:443.

184 **an insult to the northerners:** Beeman, *Plain, Honest Men*, 330.

185 **in his 1956 biography of Wilson:** Smith, *James Wilson*, 367n14. Smith uses the spelling "Purcell" despite citing to the manumission note, in which Wilson himself used the spelling "Pursel."

185 **no slaves in the Wilson household:** Heads of Families at the First Census of the United States Taken in the Year 1790: Pennsylvania, Bureau of the Census, https://babel.hathitrust.org/cgi/pt?id=uc2.ark:/13960/t09wors6v&seq=239&q1=wilson (Government Printing Office, 1908), 227. Credit for the unearthing of this detail goes to user JEQuidam at Thirty-Thousand.org, who used Gemini, Google's AI assistant, to produce a report on slave ownership by delegates to the Constitutional Convention. See "Gemini Report: The 1787 Constitutional Convention: A Comprehensive Analysis of Delegate Slave Ownership (6/13/2025)," https://thirty-thousand.org/forum/viewtopic.php?p=1281#p1281.

186 **"it will be prohibited altogether":** James Wilson at the Pennsylvania ratifying convention, December 3, 1787, in Jensen, *The Documentary History of the Ratification of the Constitution*, 2:463.

186   more than two hundred thousand enslaved Africans: Beeman, *Plain, Honest Men*, 333.

186   at least eighteen extra representatives: Wiecek, "The Witch at the Christening," 180.

186   "Negro electors": Jefferson initially ended up in an electoral vote tie with Aaron Burr, which was resolved only after a chaotic, thirty-six-ballot marathon in Congress. The Twelfth Amendment was passed soon after to ensure such a scenario could not be repeated.

186   "their masters for them choose 15 Electors!": Quoted in Wills, *"Negro President,"* 2; Richards, *The Slave Power*, 42.

187   Eighteen of the first justices: Richards, *The Slave Power*, 9.

187   "if they made that a sine qua non": Roger Sherman, August 22, 1787, in Farrand, *The Records of the Federal Convention of 1787*, 2:374.

187   "which might be odious in the ears": Beeman, *Plain, Honest Men*, 327.

187   "a principle of which we are ashamed": Klarman, *The Framers' Coup*, 265; Max Farrand, *The Records of the Federal Convention of 1787: Supplement* (Yale University Press, 1937), 158.

188   more enlightened generations: Michael Klarman suggests this perspective. Klarman, *The Framers' Coup*, 265.

188   the price of a union: Wilson, "Of the Natural Rights of Individuals," in *The Collected Works of James Wilson*, ed. Hall and Hall, 2:1077; Klarman, *The Framers' Coup*, 303.

12: The Speech in the State House Yard

189   The Massachusetts constitution of 1780: "Massachusetts Constitution (1780)," National Constitution Center, https://constitutioncenter.org/the-constitution/historic-document-library/detail/massachusetts-constitution; Amar, *The Words That Made Us*, 158–59; Wood, *The Creation of the American Republic, 1776–1787*, 339–42 (quoting a 1776 message from the town of Boston that because the proposed form of government "effects every Individual, every Individual therefore ought to be consulting, aiding and assisting"). Wood notes that New Hampshire also took the popular-ratification approach, passing its state constitution in 1783.

190   "one abundant fountain": James Wilson at Pennsylvania ratifying convention, November 24, 1787, in Jensen, *The Documentary History of the Ratification of the Constitution*, 2:363.

190   its lack of a bill of rights: Maier, *Ratification*, 47.

190   by force if necessary: See, e.g., Smith, *James Wilson*, 279.

191   dragged them through the streets: The extended, and often humorous, version of this story, complete with theatrical dialogue, can be found in Jensen, *The Documentary History of the Ratification of the Constitution*, 2:95–110.

191   "their lodgings were violently broken open": Jensen, *The Documentary History of the Ratification of the Constitution*, 2:114.

191   "The Federal Mania": *The Documentary History of the Ratification of the Constitution, Ratification of the Constitution by the States: Pennsylvania. Microform Supplement*, 531.

191 **The purpose of the gathering:** *The Documentary History of the Ratification of the Constitution*, vol. 13, ed. Kaminski and Saladino. Originally published in *Commentaries on the Constitution*, vol. 1, 337.

192 **Centinel's broadside:** Centinel I, *Independent Gazetteer*, October 5, 1787; for circulation, *The Documentary History of the Ratification of the Constitution* vol. 13, ed. Kaminski and Saladino. Originally published in *Commentaries on the Constitution*, vol. 1, 327–37.

192 **so as to answer them in turn:** Maier, *Ratification*, 78.

192 **"I confess that I am unprepared":** "James Wilson, Speech in the State House Yard, October 6, 1787," in Jensen, *The Documentary History of the Ratification of the Constitution*, 2:167–72.

193 **no power to withhold it:** Klarman, *The Framers' Coup*, 551; Maier, *Ratification*, 108.

194 **"schemes of wealth and consequence":** *The Documentary History of the Ratification of the Constitution*, vol. 13, ed. Kaminski and Saladino. Originally published in *Commentaries on the Constitution*, vol. 1, 343.

194 **Wilson's habit of keeping lists:** Maier, *Ratification*, 78.

195 **"raised to that system":** *The Documentary History of the Ratification of the Constitution*, vol. 13, ed. Kaminski and Saladino. Originally published in *Commentaries on the Constitution*, vol. 1, 337.

195 **taking place in every state:** Ian C. Bartrum, "James Wilson in the State House Yard: Ratifying the Structures of Popular Sovereignty," *Buffalo Law Review* 64, no. 2 (2016): 256–57; Bailyn, *The Ideological Origins of the American Revolution*, 328; Maier, *Ratification*, 77, 80–81.

195 **"as able, candid, & honest a member":** *The Documentary History of the Ratification of the Constitution*, vol. 13, ed. Kaminski and Saladino. Originally published in *Commentaries on the Constitution*, vol. 1, 385.

195 **Yet, for all their insight:** Maier, *Ratification*, 84; Bailyn, *The Ideological Origins of the American Revolution*, 238.

195 **"a temptation too great":** *The Documentary History of the Ratification of the Constitution*, vol. 13, ed. Kaminski and Saladino. Originally published in *Commentaries on the Constitution*, vol. 1, 401.

195 **"in support of so bad a cause":** *The Documentary History of the Ratification of the Constitution*, vol. 13, ed. Kaminski and Saladino. Originally published in *Commentaries on the Constitution*, vol. 1, 387.

196 **at Wilson personally:** *The Documentary History of the Ratification of the Constitution*, vol. 13, ed. Kaminski and Saladino. Originally published in *Commentaries on the Constitution*, vol. 1, 338, for a full list.

196 **"the spirit of *high aristocracy*":** James Wilson at Pennsylvania ratifying convention, December 4, 1787, in Jensen, *The Documentary History of the Ratification of the Constitution*, 2:213, 216.

196 **the "transcendent merit" of "Revelation":** *The Documentary History of the Ratification of the Constitution*, , vol. 13, ed. Kaminski and Saladino. Originally published in *Commentaries on the Constitution*, vol. 1, 459.

196 **"driving it down our throats":** Robert Whitehill, Pennsylvania Assembly debate, September 28, 1787, in Jensen, *The Documentary History of the Ratification of the Constitution*, 2:72.

196   "the terror of *your mob*": *The Documentary History of the Ratification of the Constitution*, vol. 13, ed. Kaminski and Saladino. Originally published in *Commentaries on the Constitution*, vol. 1, 531.

196   "the quaintness of a conundrum": *The Documentary History of the Ratification of the Constitution*, vol. 13, ed. Kaminski and Saladino. Originally published in *Commentaries on the Constitution*, vol. 1, 531.

197   "repair your shattered fortunes": Cincinnatus VI, December 6, 1787, in *The Documentary History of the Ratification of the Constitution*, vol. 14, *Commentaries on the Constitution: Public and Private*, vol. 2, *8 November to 17 December 1787*, ed. John P. Kaminski, Gaspare J. Saladino, Richard Leffler, and Charles D. Hagermann (State Historical Society of Wisconsin, 1983), 362–63.

13: Ratification

198   It was the most extreme position: James Madison appeared to be open to a seven-state minimum for ratification, but he did not advocate for it. See Farrand, *The Records of the Federal Convention of 1787*, 2:469.

198   "The House on fire": James Wilson, August 30, 1787, in Farrand, *The Records of the Federal Convention of 1787*, 2:469.

198   which could at least be justified: Klarman, *The Framers' Coup*, 41.

199   "public discussion of the subject": *The Documentary History of the Ratification of the Constitution*, vol. 13, ed. Kaminski and Saladino. Originally published in *Commentaries on the Constitution*, vol. 1, 421.

199   "the wildest ideas of government": Elbridge Gerry, June 5, 1787, in Farrand, *The Records of the Federal Convention of 1787*, 1:123.

199   "forced upon them": Quoted in Maier, *Ratification*, 89.

200   throw their excrement: Klarman, *The Framers' Coup*, 399–400.

200   there was essentially no opposition: Klarman, *The Framers' Coup*, 408.

200   "devoted to the cause of despotism": Klarman, *The Framers' Coup*, 409.

200   risk being tarred and feathered: Jensen, *The Documentary History of the Ratification of the Constitution*, 2:148–49.

201   the more remote western counties: Klarman, *The Framers' Coup*, 406–7.

201   "I dread the cold and sour temper": Gouverneur Morris to George Washington, October 30, 1787, in Jensen, *The Documentary History of the Ratification of the Constitution*, 2:206.

201   victory would be narrow: Klarman, *The Framers' Coup*, 428.

201   supporters were still in shock: Klarman, *The Framers' Coup*, 429 at *.

201   tracked down the dissenting assemblymen: Jensen, *The Documentary History of the Ratification of the Constitution*, 2:225.

201   "Does not this give us a foretaste": William Shippen to Thomas Lee Shippen, November 7, 1787, in Jensen, *The Documentary History of the Ratification of the Constitution*, 2:235.

201   punishment of the rioters: Jensen, *The Documentary History of the Ratification of the Constitution*, 2:237.

201   "the midnight mob": Jensen, *The Documentary History of the Ratification of the Constitution*, 2:293, 689.

202   who never stopped pushing: Klarman, *The Framers' Coup*, 428–29.

203   "arguing with ghosts": Maier, *Ratification*, 101.

203 **couldn't leave anything to chance**: The convention had been set by law to start the previous day, November 20, but only thirty-eight of the sixty-nine delegates were in attendance. In an echo of the federal convention, many of the delegates from the western parts of the state were taking longer to arrive than expected, and a quorum was not attained until the following day.

203 **"the business would have been lost"**: *Independent Gazetteer*, December 21, 1787, in Jensen, *The Documentary History of the Ratification of the Constitution*, 2:609.

203 **the absence of a bill of rights**: Klarman, *The Framers' Coup*, 429.

203 **"bind themselves and their posterity"**: James Wilson at Pennsylvania ratifying convention, November 24, 1787, in Jensen, *The Documentary History of the Ratification of the Constitution*, 2:342.

204 **"can ever deprive them"**: James Wilson at Pennsylvania ratifying convention, November 24, 1787, in Jensen, *The Documentary History of the Ratification of the Constitution*, 2:361–62.

204 **"we shall never be able to understand"**: James Wilson at Pennsylvania ratifying convention, December 4, 1787, in Jensen, *The Documentary History of the Ratification of the Constitution*, 2:472.

204 **"Demosthenes and Cicero"**: Francis Hopkinson to Thomas Jefferson, December 14, 1787, *The Documentary History of the Ratification of the Constitution, Ratification of the Constitution by the States: Pennsylvania. Microform Supplement*, 1186.

204 **"in his own fertile imagination"**: Centinel V, December 4, 1787, in *The Documentary History of the Ratification of the Constitution*, vol. 14, *Commentaries on the Constitution: Public and Private*, vol. 2, *8 November to 17 December 1787*, ed. John P. Kaminski, Gaspare J. Saladino, Richard Leffler, and Charles D. Hagermann (State Historical Society of Wisconsin, 1983), 346.

204 **"Shall we not employ a few days"**: John Smilie at Pennsylvania ratifying convention, November 24, 1787, in Jensen, *The Documentary History of the Ratification of the Constitution*, 2:336.

205 **The proposal was shot down**: Maier, *Ratification*, 105.

205 **they had the right to do**: Maier, *Ratification*, 106.

206 **could never take those rights away**: James Wilson at Pennsylvania ratifying convention, November 28, 1787, in Jensen, *The Documentary History of the Ratification of the Constitution*, 2:382–83.

206 **"the first six words of the Preamble"**: Quoted in Maier, *Ratification*, 107.

206 **"like clay in the hands of the potter"**: James Wilson at Pennsylvania ratifying convention, November 28, 1787, in Jensen, The Documentary History of the Ratification of the Constitution, 2:383.

206 **"where will be the harm"**: Jensen, *The Documentary History of the Ratification of the Constitution*, 2:304.

206 **"The secret is now disclosed"**: James Wilson at Pennsylvania ratifying convention, December 1, 1787, in Jensen, *The Documentary History of the Ratification of the Constitution*, 2:448.

207 **stop worrying**: Maier, *Ratification*, 109–10.

207 **"this system is erected"**: "James Wilson at Pennsylvania ratifying convention, December 4, 1787," in Jensen, *The Documentary History of the Ratification of the Constitution*, 2:472–73.

207   unmatched by any of his peers: Allen and Sneff, "Golden Letters," 196;
      Ewald, "James Wilson and the American Founding," 12–16.

207   a "natural aristocracy": Quoted in Cornell, "Aristocracy Assailed," 1158.

207   "Is there any danger": James Wilson at Pennsylvania ratifying convention,
      December 4, 1787, in Jensen, *The Documentary History of the Ratification of the
      Constitution*, 2:488.

208   "on the principle of descent": James Wilson at Pennsylvania ratifying con-
      vention, December 4, 1787, in Jensen, *The Documentary History of the Ratifica-
      tion of the Constitution*, 2:489.

208   a fitting epitaph: James Wilson at Pennsylvania ratifying convention, De-
      cember 4, 1787, in Jensen, *The Documentary History of the Ratification of the
      Constitution*, 2:489.

208   its allowance of slavery: James Wilson at Pennsylvania ratifying convention,
      December 3, 1787, in Jensen, *The Documentary History of the Ratification of the
      Constitution*, 2:463.

208   "The Convention, sir, were perplexed": James Wilson at Pennsylvania ratify-
      ing convention, December 11, 1787, in Jensen, *The Documentary History of the
      Ratification of the Constitution*, 2:566–67.

209   "What a stroke to the pride": William Shippen to Thomas Lee Shippen,
      December 18, 1787, in Jensen, *The Documentary History of the Ratification of
      the Constitution*, 2:549.

209   "I do not pretend to remember": James Wilson at Pennsylvania ratifying
      convention, December 11, 1787, in Jensen, *The Documentary History of the
      Ratification of the Constitution*, 2:551.

209   "we shall also form a national character": James Wilson at Pennsylvania
      ratifying convention, December 11, 1787, in Jensen, *The Documentary History
      of the Ratification of the Constitution*, 2:581–82.

209   "I feel myself lost": James Wilson at Pennsylvania ratifying convention,
      December 11, 1787, in Jensen, *The Documentary History of the Ratification of
      the Constitution*, 2:584.

209   It passed 46 to 23: Jensen, *The Documentary History of the Ratification of the
      Constitution*, 2:590–91.

14: Aftermath

210   "the characteristics and the soul": Patrick Henry at Virginia ratifying
      convention, June 4, 1788, in *The Documentary History of the Ratification of
      the Constitution*, vol. 9, *Ratification of the Constitution by the States: Pennsyl-
      vania*, ed. Merrill Jensen (State Historical Society of Wisconsin, 1990),
      930.

211   his "dictatorial" side: William Shippen Jr. to Thomas Lee Shippen, Decem-
      ber 18, 1787, in Jensen, *The Documentary History of the Ratification of the Con-
      stitution*, 2:549.

211   "all us little folks": Quoted in Cornell, "Aristocracy Assailed," 1167.

211   "as their masters could wish them": Luther Martin, *Maryland Journal*,
      January 18, 1788, in *The Documentary History of the Ratification of the Constitu-
      tion*, vol. 11, *Ratification of the Constitution by the States: Maryland*, ed. Merrill
      Jensen (Wisconsin Historical Society Press, 2015), 193–94.

211   **burning a copy of the new Constitution:** An Old Man, *Carlisle Gazette*, January 2, 1788, in Jensen, *The Documentary History of the Ratification of the Constitution*, 2:670–71.

211   **"it was laughable":** Quoted in Cornell, "Aristocracy Assailed," 1154.

212   **"committed them to the flames":** An Old Man, *Carlisle Gazette*, January 2, 1788, in Jensen, *The Documentary History of the Ratification of the Constitution*, 2:672.

212   **"blow them up in the air":** One of the People, *Carlisle Gazette*, January 9, 1788, in Jensen, *The Documentary History of the Ratification of the Constitution*, 2:675.

212   **"his cowardice and timidity":** One of the People, *Carlisle Gazette*, January 9, 1788, in Jensen, *The Documentary History of the Ratification of the Constitution*, 2:678.

212   **"spurn it with contempt":** This appeared in a separate letter, published under the name "The Scourge." The Scourge, *Carlisle Gazette*, January 23, 1788, in Jensen, *The Documentary History of the Ratification of the Constitution*, 2:688.

213   **"were it not for the mob":** The Scourge, *Carlisle Gazette*, January 23, 1788, in Jensen, *The Documentary History of the Ratification of the Constitution*, 2:689, 690.

213   **dropping all charges against them:** Petition to the Council, *Independent Gazetteer*, March 14, 1788, in Jensen, *The Documentary History of the Ratification of the Constitution*, 2:708.

213   **the militia marched into town:** The Release of the Prisoners, 1 March, *Carlisle Gazette*, March 5, 1788, in Jensen, *The Documentary History of the Ratification of the Constitution*, 2:701; John Montgomery to James Wilson, March 2, 1788, in Jensen, *The Documentary History of the Ratification of the Constitution*, 2:703.

213   **should "in all questions" prevail:** James Wilson, July 13, 1787, in Farrand, *The Records of the Federal Convention of 1787*, 1:605.

213   **their supposed sovereignty:** Cornell, "Aristocracy Assailed," 1153.

214   **holding the Pennsylvania state flag:** *Philadelphia, Pa. Order of Procession, in Honor of the Establishment of the Constitution of the United States. To Parade Precisely at Eight O'Clock in the Morning, of Friday, the 4th of July* . . . (Philadelphia, 1788), Library of Congress, https://www.loc.gov/item/rbpe.14700600a/.

214   **"A people free and enlightened":** Wilson, "Oration Delivered on the Fourth of July 1788, at the Procession Formed at Philadelphia to Celebrate the Adoption of the Constitution of the United States," in *The Collected Works of James Wilson*, ed. Hall and Hall, 1:285.

214   **"can sit as calmly":** James Wilson at Pennsylvania ratifying convention, December 4, 1787, in Jensen, *The Documentary History of the Ratification of the Constitution*, 2:473.

215   **"may turn the election":** Wilson, "Oration Delivered on the Fourth of July 1788, at the Procession Formed at Philadelphia to Celebrate the Adoption of the Constitution of the United States," in *The Collected Works of James Wilson*, ed. Hall and Hall, 1:292.

215   **"swords, bayonets, clubs, stones, etc.":** Fourth of July Celebrations, in Jensen, *The Documentary History of the Ratification of the Constitution*, 21:1264–75.

15: The Supreme Court

217 **"a subject of much importance"**: James Wilson to George Washington, April 21, 1789, in Marcus et al., *The Documentary History of the Supreme Court of the United States, 1789–1800*, 1(2):612.

217 **spending every penny**: Marcus, "Wilson as a Justice," 147; "Judicial Salaries: Supreme Court Justices," Federal Judicial Center, https://www.fjc.gov/history/judges/judicial-salaries-supreme-court-justices.

218 **"It is with singular pleasure"**: *Federal Gazette*, March 9, 1789, in Marcus et al., *The Documentary History of the Supreme Court of the United States, 1789–1800*, 1(2):609.

218 **"your professional and other merits"**: Anthony Wayne to James Wilson, May 20, 1789, in Marcus et al., *The Documentary History of the Supreme Court of the United States, 1789–1800*, 1(2):619–20.

218 **to ensure Wilson's appointment**: Arthur Lee to [Francis Lightfoot Lee], May 9, 1789, in Marcus et al., *The Documentary History of the Supreme Court of the United States, 1789–1800*, 1(2):617.

218 **"the deranged state of his affairs"**: Benjamin Rush to John Adams, April 22, 1789, in Marcus et al., *The Documentary History of the Supreme Court of the United States, 1789–1800*, 1(2):613.

218 **"If I had a vote"**: John Adams to Benjamin Rush, May 17, 1789, in Marcus et al., *The Documentary History of the Supreme Court of the United States, 1789–1800*, 1(2):619.

218 **"he is not the proper person"**: *New-York Journal*, April 16, 1789, in Marcus et al., *The Documentary History of the Supreme Court of the United States, 1789–1800*, 1(2):611 (emphasis in original).

219 **"a single *engagement*"**: George Washington to James Wilson, May 9, 1789, in Marcus et al., *The Documentary History of the Supreme Court of the United States, 1789–1800*, 1(2):618–19.

219 **"positions with law firms"**: Leo Pfeffer, *This Honorable Court: A History of the United States Supreme Court* (Beacon Press, 1965), 39.

219 **The insult might have cut even deeper**: Thomas McKean to George Washington, April 27, 1789, in Marcus et al., *The Documentary History of the Supreme Court of the United States, 1789–1800*, 1(2):614–16; George Washington to Thomas McKean, May 9, 1789, in Marcus et al., *The Documentary History of the Supreme Court of the United States, 1789–1800*, 1(2):618.

219 **their home state's constitution**: Wilson was not involved in the drafting of the first Pennsylvania constitution in 1776, but he was a leader at the convention to revise it in 1790.

220 **balk at offers of free lodging**: See, e.g., John Jay to Edward Rutledge, November 16, 1789, rejecting Rutledge's offer to stay with him for reasons that "will occur to you without details. I am inclined to think some general rule on this subject would be prudent—as yet I have not considered it maturely." In Marcus et al., *The Documentary History of the Supreme Court of the United States, 1789–1800*, 2:10.

220 **"our political fabric"**: George Washington to John Jay, October 5, 1789, in Marcus et al., *The Documentary History of the Supreme Court of the United States, 1789–1800*, 1(1):11.

220 **swore his oath to serve:** Record of Oath, October 5, 1789, in Marcus et al., *The Documentary History of the Supreme Court of the United States, 1789–1800,* 1(1):51.

222 **"within the limits assigned":** Alexander Hamilton, *Federalist* No. 78, in *The Federalist Papers,* https://avalon.law.yale.edu/18th_century/fed78.asp.

222 **they did not use that word:** Hayburn's Case, 2 U.S. (2 Dall.) 409, 414 (1792).

222 **"we hope never to experience again":** Hayburn's Case, 2 U.S. (2 Dall.) 409, 411–12 (1792).

223 **"the first instance":** Proceedings of the United States House of Representatives, *General Advertiser,* April 13, 1792, in Marcus et al., *The Documentary History of the Supreme Court of the United States, 1789–1800,* 6:48. See also Edmund Randolph to George Washington, April 5, 1792, cited in Maeva Marcus and Robert Teir, "Hayburn's Case: A Misinterpretation of Precedent," *Wisconsin Law Review* (1988): 527, 531n25. ("Some days ago I met Mr. Wilson in Sixth Street, and he stopped to ask me" about the pensioners' act, Randolph recalled. Wilson offered "a strong remark against its constitutionality [but by the way I suspect that in this the judges, if they persist, will be found wrong].")

223 **"to say what the law is":** Marbury v. Madison, 5 U.S. (1 Cranch) 137, 177 (1803).

224 **"accomplishing the same":** Minutes of the Convention That Formed the Present Constitution of Pennsylvania, *The Proceedings Relative to Calling the Conventions of 1776 and 1790* (John S. Wiestling, 1825), 129–30.

225 **recoiled at this approach:** Wilson, Pennsylvania constitutional convention of 1789–1790, December 31, 1789, in *The Collected Works of James Wilson,* ed. Hall and Hall, 1:299. ("The pyramid of government," Wilson said, using his familiar metaphor, "should be raised to a dignified altitude: but its foundations must, of consequence, be broad, and strong, and deep. The authority, the interests, and the affections of the people at large are the only basis, on which a superstructure, proposed to be at once durable and magnificent, can be rationally erected.")

225 **"Can a trust subsist":** Wilson, Pennsylvania constitutional convention of 1789–1790, December 31, 1789, in *The Collected Works of James Wilson,* ed. Hall and Hall, 1:296–97.

225 **"corresponding degree of danger":** Wilson, Pennsylvania constitutional convention of 1789–1790, December 31, 1789, in *The Collected Works of James Wilson,* ed. Hall and Hall, 1:307.

225 **"the true republican lustre":** Wilson, Pennsylvania constitutional convention of 1789–1790, December 31, 1789, in *The Collected Works of James Wilson,* ed. Hall and Hall, 1:300–301.

226 **"ingenious, solid, sublime":** William Bradford Jr. to Elias Boudinot, January 10, 1790, cited in Brunhouse, *The Counter-Revolution in Pennsylvania, 1776–1790,* 298n113.

226 **Pennsylvania's version:** The Pennsylvania Constitution of 1790, Pennsylvania Constitution Web Project, https://www.paconstitution.org/texts-of-the-constitution/1790-2/.

227 **"now become a crime":** Wilson, "Speech Delivered, on 19th January, 1790, in the Convention of Pennsylvania, Assembled for the Purpose of Reviewing,

Altering, and Amending the Constitution of the State," in *The Works of James Wilson*, ed. Hall and Hall, 1:309.

228   "to wish her well": Wilson, "Speech Delivered, on 19th January, 1790, in the Convention of Pennsylvania, Assembled for the Purpose of Reviewing, Altering, and Amending the Constitution of the State," in *The Works of James Wilson*, ed. Hall and Hall, 1:318.

16: The Law Lectures

229   "a wise and upright Judge": John Adams to Charles Adams, December 4, 1790, in *Adams Papers Digital Edition*, Massachusetts Historical Society, https://www.masshist.org/publications/adams-papers/index.php/view/ADMS-04-09-02-0079. Original source: *The Adams Papers: Adams Family Correspondence*, vol. 9, *January 1788–February 1789*, ed. Hobson Woodward (Harvard University Press, 1999), 163–65.

230   "a rational and a useful entertainment": Quoted in Wilson, *The Collected Works of James Wilson*, ed. Hall and Hall, 1:402–3.

230   an inchoate mix of colonial practices: Peters, "James Wilson's Reidian Democratic Political Theory," 14, 207–9; Ewald, "James Wilson and the Scottish Enlightenment," 1108.

230   in Scotland decades earlier: McCloskey in Wilson, *The Works of James Wilson*, ed. McCloskey, 37.

230   "a philosophy of American law": McCloskey in Wilson, *The Works of James Wilson*, ed. McCloskey, 37.

231   "A most brilliant and respectable audience": *Pennsylvania Packet*, December 25, 1790; Carson, *An Historical Sketch of the Law Department of the University of Pennsylvania*, 14.

231   "addressing a *fair* audience": Wilson, law lecture, December 15, 1790, in *The Collected Works of James Wilson*, ed. Hall and Hall, 1:431.

231   "the glory of Greece": Wilson, law lecture, December 15, 1790, in *The Collected Works of James Wilson*, ed. Hall and Hall, 1:432.

231   "and becomes licentiousness": Wilson, law lecture, December 15, 1790, in *The Collected Works of James Wilson*, ed. Hall and Hall, 1:435.

231   "the study of every free citizen": Wilson, law lecture, December 15, 1790, in *The Collected Works of James Wilson*, ed. Hall and Hall, 1:435.

231   "diffused over the whole community": Wilson, law lecture, December 15, 1790, in *The Collected Works of James Wilson*, ed. Hall and Hall, 1:435–36.

232   "the first and fundamental principle": Wilson, law lecture, December 15, 1790, in *The Collected Works of James Wilson*, ed. Hall and Hall, 1:445–46.

232   "they may change their constitution": Wilson, law lecture, December 15, 1790, in *The Collected Works of James Wilson*, ed. Hall and Hall, 1:443.

232   "to mold, to preserve, to improve": Wilson, law lecture, December 15, 1790, in *The Collected Works of James Wilson*, ed. Hall and Hall, 1:712.

232   "a principle of melioration": Wilson, law lecture, December 15, 1790, in *The Collected Works of James Wilson*, ed. Hall and Hall, 1:443; Gordon Wood argues that with this notion of popular sovereignty, Americans had created "the great panacea of human politics." Revolutions did not have to be violent. Wood, *The Creation of the American Republic*, 614.

232   "Why should not we have a share?": Wilson, law lecture, December 15, 1790, in *The Collected Works of James Wilson*, ed. Hall and Hall, 1:451.

232   "shines with superior lustre": Wilson, law lecture, December 15, 1790, in *The Collected Works of James Wilson*, ed. Hall and Hall, 1:452.

233   "a pure flow of diction": Wilson, law lecture, December 15, 1790, in *The Collected Works of James Wilson*, ed. Hall and Hall, 1:454.

233   "'Know thou thyself'": Wilson, *The Collected Works of James Wilson*, ed. Hall and Hall, 1:585.

233   fifteen young law students: Carson, *An Historical Sketch of the Law Department of the University of Pennsylvania*, 15; Hall, "James Wilson's Law Lectures," 75n38.

233   almost exclusively focused on theory: Hall, "James Wilson's Law Lectures," 64–65; Carson, *An Historical Sketch of the Law Department of the University of Pennsylvania*, 15; Wilson, *The Collected Works of James Wilson*, ed. Hall and Hall, 1:xx.

233   criminal law, and the like: Wilson, *The Collected Works of James Wilson*, ed. Hall and Hall, 2:825.

233   "all sound reasoning must rest": Wilson, *The Collected Works of James Wilson*, ed. Hall and Hall, 1:603–4.

233   "All elections ought to be equal": Wilson, *The Collected Works of James Wilson*, ed. Hall and Hall, 2:837. In Wilson's mind, equal elections led naturally to majority rule. "It is most reasonable; because it is not so probable, that a greater number, as that a smaller number, concurring in judgment, should be mistaken. It is most equitable; because the greater number are presumed to have an interest in the society proportioned to that number" (Wilson, *The Collected Works of James Wilson*, ed. Hall and Hall, 1:639).

233   "between the innocent and the guilty": Wilson, *The Collected Works of James Wilson*, ed. Hall and Hall, 1:437.

233   in the late 1770s: See Larson, "The Revolutionary American Jury," 1442–44; Larson, *Trials of Allegiance*, 133; Stimson, "A Jury of the Country."

234   "by his own incurable optimism": McCloskey in Wilson, *The Works of James Wilson*, ed. McCloskey, 41.

234   "the lecture hall with students": Carson, *An Historical Sketch of the Law Department of the University of Pennsylvania*, 15–16.

234   the state senate . . . rejected the funding: James Wilson, *The Works of the Honourable James Wilson, L.L.D.*, ed. Bird Wilson, vol. 1 (Bronson and Chauncey, 1804), xii; James Wilson to William Bingham, August 24, 1791, Founders Online, National Archives, https://founders.archives.gov/documents/Washington/05-09-02-0223-0003. Original source: *The Papers of George Washington*, Presidential Series, vol. 9, *23 September 1791–29 February 1792*, ed. Mark A. Mastromarino (University of Virginia Press, 2000), 351–56; Smith, *James Wilson*, 344.

235   a dusty, noisy street: Warren, "The First Decade of the Supreme Court of the United States," 635.

235   they would be disappointed: Marcus et al., *The Documentary History of the Supreme Court of the United States, 1789–1800*, 1(2):687.

235   it would even be handling: Marcus, "Wilson as a Justice," 149.

236   "the most admirable method": Charge to the Grand Jury of the Circuit Court for the District of Pennsylvania, *Pennsylvania Gazette*, April 12, 1790,

in Marcus et al., *The Documentary History of the Supreme Court of the United States, 1789–1800*, 2:39–40.

236 **"receive their first force and direction"**: Charge to the Grand Jury of the Circuit Court for the District of Pennsylvania, *Pennsylvania Gazette*, April 12, 1790, in Marcus et al., *The Documentary History of the Supreme Court of the United States, 1789–1800*, 2:33.

236 **"predominant and supreme"**: Charge to the Grand Jury of the Circuit Court for the District of Pennsylvania, *Pennsylvania Gazette*, April 12, 1790, in Marcus et al., *The Documentary History of the Supreme Court of the United States, 1789–1800*, 2:40.

237 **There was a catch**: Federal Judiciary Act (1789), National Archives: Milestone Documents, https://www.archives.gov/milestone-documents/federal-judiciary-act; Marcus, "Wilson as a Justice," 149.

237 **"republican schoolmaster"**: Marcus, "Wilson as a Justice," 150, 159; Lerner, "The Supreme Court as Republican Schoolmaster," 127–80; Glick, "On the Road," 1753.

237 **in bone-rattling carriages**: Marcus et al., *The Documentary History of the Supreme Court of the United States, 1789–1800*, 2:212, 295, 297.

237 **"I fear the journey"**: Marcus et al., *The Documentary History of the Supreme Court of the United States, 1789–1800*, 3:154–55.

237 **it would look bad**: Marcus et al., *The Documentary History of the Supreme Court of the United States, 1789–1800*, 2:235, 244.

238 **"I will venture to say"**: Marcus et al., *The Documentary History of the Supreme Court of the United States, 1789–1800*, 2:132.

238 **"indispensably necessary"**: Marcus et al., *The Documentary History of the Supreme Court of the United States, 1789–1800*, 2:245.

238 **"in exile from our families"**: Marcus et al., *The Documentary History of the Supreme Court of the United States, 1789–1800*, 2:288.

238 **bedridden for the term**: Marcus et al., *The Documentary History of the Supreme Court of the United States, 1789–1800*, 2:126, 132.

239 **"to correct in one capacity"**: Marcus et al., *The Documentary History of the Supreme Court of the United States, 1789–1800*, 2:290.

239 **pawning off his duties**: E.g., James Wilson to William Cushing, May 7, 1793, in Marcus et al., *The Documentary History of the Supreme Court of the United States, 1789–1800*, 2:372.

239 **for the extra travel costs**: Marcus et al., *The Documentary History of the Supreme Court of the United States, 1789–1800*, 2:497 (letter from James Iredell to James Wilson confirming the arrangement).

239 **the most consequential ruling**: Chisholm v. Georgia, 2 U.S. (2 Dall.) 419 (1793).

239 ***Chisholm* was about**: Technically, the case was not concluded with the February 1793 ruling. Because Georgia had refused to represent itself, the court ordered it to send someone to represent it or to show cause why it should not be required to do so by the following term. If it did neither of these things, the court would enter a default judgment in Chisholm's favor. The case dragged on at the court for the next several years, until the passage and announcement of the Eleventh Amendment.

240 **they were supposed to pay:** "The Trezevant Family in American History," Trezevant Family Project, Fall 2016, 13–17, https://www.trezevantfamilyproject .com/wp-content/uploads/2016/10/Fall-2016-p13-17.pdf.

240 **"cannot be drawn or compelled":** Mathis, "Chisholm v. Georgia," 22.

240 **Georgia remained absent:** In the nation's early years, the attorney general often represented private clients in addition to his work for the federal government. Marcus et al., *The Documentary History of the Supreme Court of the United States, 1789–1800*, 5:132–36.

241 **one by each justice:** Justice Thomas Johnson had resigned a month before and had not yet been replaced.

241 **he announced his opinion first:** Iredell had been assigned to the circuit court panel that originally heard and rejected Chisholm's claim in 1791. While the Judiciary Act of 1789 barred district court judges who sat on a circuit court from voting in cases that they had previously decided at the district level, it included no such prohibition for Supreme Court justices who had ruled on cases at the circuit level. Still, the inherent conflict of such a scenario was clear enough that at least once it was addressed in an opinion. See, e.g., Ware v. Hylton, 3 U.S. (3 Dall.) 199, 256 footnote.

241 **very Wilsonian way to put it:** McCloskey in Wilson, *The Works of James Wilson*, ed. McCloskey, 33.

241 **"there are citizens, but no subjects":** Chisholm v. Georgia, 2 U.S. (2 Dall.) 419, 456 (1793).

242 **"Surely not":** Chisholm v. Georgia, 2 U.S. (2 Dall.) 419, 456 (1793).

242 **"Georgia is NOT a sovereign state":** Chisholm v. Georgia, 2 U.S. (2 Dall.) 419, 457 (1793).

242 **"the first personages introduced":** Chisholm v. Georgia, 2 U.S. (2 Dall.) 419, 463 (1793).

242 **"notwithstanding the tawdry ornament":** Cited in Goebel, *History of the Supreme Court of the United States*, 731n30.

242 **"A pile of verbiage":** Currie, *The Constitution in the Supreme Court*, 58.

243 **"a Fourth of July orator":** McCloskey in Wilson, *The Works of James Wilson*, ed. McCloskey, 36.

243 **one of his favorite Scottish instructors:** Hall, "James Wilson: Democratic Theorist and Supreme Court Justice," 139.

243 **his focus on first principles:** Ewald, "James Wilson and the Scottish Enlightenment," 1098.

243 **was introduced in the Senate:** Mathis, "Chisholm v. Georgia," 25–26.

243 **involved Revolutionary War debts:** While Georgia and other states refused to recognize federal courts' jurisdiction, or did so only partially and grudgingly, others, like New York and Maryland, complied with subpoenas; New York even paid up when a trial jury ruled in favor of the plaintiff. See Marcus and Wexler, "Suits Against States," 73.

243 **the Eleventh Amendment's ratification:** The amendment was not officially included in the Constitution for almost three years after its ratification because several of the ratifying states failed to inform Congress of what they had done (suggesting that the outrage over the *Chisholm* ruling may not have burned as hot as generally believed). When ratification by the requi-

site number of states was finally known, the amendment could be adopted. See Marcus and Wexler, "Suits Against States," 86.

244   **half a century after Wilson died:** Mathis, "Chisholm v. Georgia," 29.

17: The Walls Close In

245   **or to permit someone else to:** Mikhail, "James Wilson, Early American Land Companies, and the Original Meaning of Ex Post Facto Law," 108–9.

245   **comprised up to one million acres:** Mikhail, "James Wilson, Early American Land Companies, and the Original Meaning of Ex Post Facto Law," 92, 94–95.

246   **"in which it now stands":** James Wilson, June 8, 1787, in Farrand, *The Records of the Federal Convention of 1787*, 1:166.

246   **"proclaim that we are ignorant":** James Wilson, August 22, 1787, in Farrand, *The Records of the Federal Convention of 1787*, 2:376.

246   **he understood them to be applicable:** Mikhail, "James Wilson, Early American Land Companies, and the Original Meaning of Ex Post Facto Law," 115–16.

246   **But that's what Wilson did:** Mikhail, "James Wilson, Early American Land Companies, and the Original Meaning of Ex Post Facto Law," 107–14.

247   **surely mortified Wilson's colleagues:** Mikhail, "James Wilson, Early American Land Companies, and the Original Meaning of Ex Post Facto Law," 116.

247   **"creatures of the Constitution":** Mikhail, "James Wilson, Early American Land Companies, and the Original Meaning of Ex Post Facto Law," 134.

247   **a civil law that applied retroactively:** Calder v. Bull, 3 U.S. (3 Dall.) 386 (1798).

247   **It is likely he never learned:** Mikhail, "James Wilson, Early American Land Companies, and the Original Meaning of Ex Post Facto Law," 80.

247   **played the central role in drafting:** Mikhail, "James Wilson, Early American Land Companies, and the Original Meaning of Ex Post Facto Law," 136.

247   **the way politics works:** See, e.g., McCloskey in Wilson, *The Works of James Wilson*, ed. McCloskey, 16.

248   **Wilson developed no clear jurisprudence:** See Marcus, "Wilson as a Justice," 148.

248   **a job of such "immense importance":** Marcus et al., *The Documentary History of the Supreme Court of the United States, 1789–1800*, 4:571–76.

249   **"I declare my willingness":** Marcus et al., *The Documentary History of the Supreme Court of the United States, 1789–1800*, 4:573.

249   **"I doubt still more":** Marcus et al., *The Documentary History of the Supreme Court of the United States, 1789–1800*, 4:576–77.

250   **"not a means, but an end!":** Wilson, *The Collected Works of James Wilson*, ed. Hall and Hall, 1:449.

250   **Cushing's own poor health:** Wexler, "In the Beginning," 1384.

250   **"superannuated and contemptible":** Marcus et al., *The Documentary History of the Supreme Court of the United States, 1789–1800*, 1:753.

251   **Rutledge destroyed his chances:** Wexler, "In the Beginning," 1385n56.

251   **Rutledge sent a letter to Washington:** Marcus et al., *The Documentary History of the Supreme Court of the United States, 1789–1800*, 1:100.

251   **he had tried to kill himself:** Marcus et al., *The Documentary History of the Supreme Court of the United States, 1789–1800*, 1:820–21.

251   **as committed as Wilson:** Wexler, "In the Beginning," 1386.

251   **"my infirm and declining state of health":** Marcus et al., *The Documentary History of the Supreme Court of the United States, 1789–1800*, 1:103.

252   **"reconciled to strict propriety":** Samuel Johnston to James Iredell, February 27, 1796, in Marcus et al., *The Documentary History of the Supreme Court of the United States, 1789–1800*, 1:840.

252   **with a single no vote:** Wexler, "In the Beginning," 1390.

252   **"Mr. Wilson's ardent speculations":** Marcus et al., *The Documentary History of the Supreme Court of the United States, 1789–1800*, 1:842.

252   **"I think it not unlikely":** Marcus et al., *The Documentary History of the Supreme Court of the United States, 1789–1800*, 1:841–42.

252   **than Wilson did in his entire tenure:** McCloskey in Wilson, *The Works of James Wilson*, ed. McCloskey, 30.

18: New Love and Escape from Philadelphia

253   **triggering the nation's first financial crisis:** See, e.g., Abram Brown, "The High Crimes and Misadventures of William Duer, the Founding Father Who Swindled America," *Forbes*, July 4, 2019, https://www.forbes.com/sites/abrambrown/2019/07/04/the-high-crimes-and-misadventures-of-william-duer-the-founding-father-who-swindled-america/.

253   **"Have the courage to make a full stop":** Alexander Hamilton to William Duer, March 14, 1792, Founders Online, National Archives, https://founders.archives.gov/documents/Hamilton/01-11-02-0108. Original source: Alexander Hamilton, *The Papers of Alexander Hamilton*, vol. 11, *February 1792–June 1792*, ed. Harold C. Syrett (Columbia University Press, 1966), 131–32.

254   **behind bars in New York:** Mann, *Republic of Debtors*, 114.

254   **"were they torn to pieces":** Henry Remsen Jr. to Thomas Jefferson, April 23, 1792, Image 9, manuscript/mixed material, Library of Congress, https://www.loc.gov/item/mtjbib006129/.

254   **engaged in the practice to some degree:** See, e.g., Marcus et al., *The Documentary History of the Supreme Court of the United States, 1789–1800*, 4:7n20; Smith, *James Wilson*, 159–68.

255   **Wilson's share:** Mikhail, "The Necessary and Proper Clauses," 1110–12; Smith, *James Wilson*, 160.

255   **it exploded into a national scandal:** "Wilson and Pendleton the fedl. Judges, tho' not named in the law are known adventurers. . . . The former is reprobated here by all parties" (James Madison to James Monroe, cited in Mikhail, "James Wilson, Early American Land Companies, and the Original Meaning of Ex Post Facto Law," 128); Marcus et al., *The Documentary History of the Supreme Court of the United States, 1789–1800*, 5:505–6.

255   **calls for Wilson's impeachment:** Marcus et al., *The Documentary History of the Supreme Court of the United States, 1789–1800*, 5:506.

255   **did not resolve it until 1810:** Mikhail, "The Necessary and Proper Clauses," 1110–12; Mikhail, "James Wilson, Early American Land Companies, and the Original Meaning of Ex Post Facto Law," 127–29; Marcus et al., *The Documentary History of the Supreme Court of the United States, 1789–1800*, 5:505–14;

for a contrary view that attempts to exonerate Wilson of wrongdoing, see Klingelsmith, "James Wilson and the So-Called Yazoo Frauds," 1–27.

255   the most valuable land in America: Witt, *Patriots and Cosmopolitans*, 30; Mikhail, "James Wilson, Early American Land Companies, and the Original Meaning of Ex Post Facto Law," 95; Smith, *James Wilson*, 159–68, 402.

255   "On the Improvement and Settlement of Lands . . .": Wilson, *The Collected Works of James Wilson*, ed. Hall and Hall, 1:372–86.

256   benefit by a virtuous circle: Wilson, *The Collected Works of James Wilson*, ed. Hall and Hall, 1:372; Witt, *Patriots and Cosmopolitans*, 36–37.

256   "As new settlements are made": Wilson, *The Collected Works of James Wilson*, ed. Hall and Hall, 1:373.

256   "a chain of houses and farms": Wilson, *The Collected Works of James Wilson*, ed. Hall and Hall, 1:379, 383–84.

256   *"never to be in want of money"*: Wilson, *The Collected Works of James Wilson*, ed. Hall and Hall, 1:378.

256   "the *execution* of a system": Wilson, *The Collected Works of James Wilson*, ed. Hall and Hall, 1:383.

256   "Confidence must be the soul": Wilson, *The Collected Works of James Wilson*, ed. Hall and Hall, 1:380.

256   "I wish you had ten times as much": Arthur St. Clair to James Wilson, August 10, 1793, cited in Smith, *James Wilson*, 366.

257   "a man, who parades our streets": Marcus et al., *The Documentary History of the Supreme Court of the United States, 1789–1800*, 2:406.

257   "Do let that answer be speedy": Marcus et al., *The Documentary History of the Supreme Court of the United States, 1789–1800*, 2:408.

257   It is the only known surviving letter: Wexler, "The Case for Love," 88.

257   "The gentle Caledon was smitten": John Quincy Adams to Thomas Boylston Adams, June 23, 1793, in Marcus et al., *The Documentary History of the Supreme Court of the United States, 1789–1800*, 2:408–10.

258   "It will be highly flattering": Henry Jackson to Henry Knox, June 23, 1793, in Marcus et al., *The Documentary History of the Supreme Court of the United States, 1789–1800*, 2:410–12.

258   Wilson and Hannah were married: *Boston Gazette*, September 23, 1793, 3.

258   most working class or poor: Marcus et al., *The Documentary History of the Supreme Court of the United States, 1789–1800*, 2:341; Powell, *Bring Out Your Dead*, 57.

258   "this species of madness": Dagobert D. Runes, *The Selected Writings of Benjamin Rush* (Philosophical Library, 1947), 213.

259   It was a morally dubious, high-risk scheme: McCloskey in Wilson, *The Works of James Wilson*, ed. McCloskey, 19; John Kloss, *James Wilson: Fallen Founding Father* (senior thesis, Gwynedd Mercy University, 2015), 17–18; Smith, *James Wilson*, 162–63; Blaakman, *Speculation Nation*, 139.

259   his own name on the deeds: Elizabeth K. Henderson, "The Northwestern Lands of Pennsylvania, 1790–1812," *Pennsylvania Magazine of History and Biography* 60, no. 2 (April 1936): 139.

260   "the appearance of enchantment": *Gazette of the United States*, September 17, 1794.

260 **"the expense is so enormously great"**: John Kinsey to Henry Drinker, September 24, 1794, cited in Maxey, "Of Castles in Stockport and Other Strictures," 431.

260 **"how it would appear for a person"**: Quoted in Maxey, "Of Castles in Stockport and Other Strictures," 431–32.

261 **"he had made such large acquisitions"**: Henry Drinker to Samuel Preston, November 1, 1794, quoted in Maxey, "Of Castles in Stockport and Other Strictures," 432.

261 **a striking echo of the philosophy**: Wilson, *The Collected Works of James Wilson*, ed. Hall and Hall, 1:383.

19: The Tavern Hideout

262 **"rare, distant and reserved"**: Waln biography of James Wilson, 171–72.

263 **"The day of reckoning is at hand"**: Edward Burd to Jasper Yeates, August 4, 1796, in *The Burd Papers: Selections from Letters Written by Edward Burd, 1763–1828*, ed. Lewis Burd Walker (1899), 191–92.

263 **"I never expect to hear"**: Marcus et al., *The Documentary History of the Supreme Court of the United States, 1789–1800*, 3:133.

263 **Hannah had given birth to a baby boy**: Marcus et al., *The Documentary History of the Supreme Court of the United States, 1789–1800*, 3:134n4. Citing Smith, *James Wilson*, 59, 97, 140, 210–11, 380; Harry C. Green and Mary W. Green, *The Pioneer Mothers of America*, 3 vols. (G. P. Putnam's Sons, 1912), 3:206.

263 **"his resource was reading novels constantly"**: Wilkinson, "Land Policy and Speculation in Pennsylvania, 1779–1800," 316, citing Benjamin Rush, *The Autobiography of Benjamin Rush*, ed. George W. Corner (Princeton University Press, 1948), 237.

263 **He skipped the entire fall term**: Marcus et al., *The Documentary History of the Supreme Court of the United States, 1789–1800*, 3:185.

263 **"Judge Wilson has been to gaol"**: Chauncey Goodrich to Oliver Wolcott, December 13, 1796, in George Gibbs, *Memoirs of the Administrations of Washington and John Adams, edited from the Papers of Oliver Wolcott, Secretary of the Treasury* (W. Van Norden, 1846), 1:410; Marcus et al., *The Documentary History of the Supreme Court of the United States, 1789–1800*, 3:152n20.

263 **"It will be my turn next"**: Robert Morris to John Nicholson, December 8, 1796, cited in Robert Morris, "Land Fever: The Downfall of Robert Morris," *Missouri Review* 15, no. 3 (1992): 133. Other personal letters from the period repeat the rumor that Wilson was jailed around this time, but I have found no independent record of his incarceration.

265 **"The prospect before him is very gloomy"**: Quoted in Marcus et al., *The Documentary History of the Supreme Court of the United States, 1789–1800*, 3:152.

264 **"entirely lost by his non-attendance"**: James Iredell to Hannah Iredell, May 25, 1797, in Marcus et al., *The Documentary History of the Supreme Court of the United States, 1789–1800*, 3:182.

264 **"hangs up in my chamber closet"**: James Wilson to Bird Wilson, June 9, 1797, cited in Smith, *James Wilson*, 383.

264   "What a situation!": James Iredell to Hannah Iredell, August 11, 1797, in
       Marcus et al., *The Documentary History of the Supreme Court of the United States,
       1789–1800*, 1(2):856.

264   to meet again and finalize a deal: Meginness, *History of Lycoming County,
       Pennsylvania*, 75–76, 80; Wilkinson, "Land Policy and Speculation in Penn-
       sylvania, 1779–1800," 313.

264   "one of the 6 Judges in a Jersey Gaol!": Thomas Shippen's diary, September
       3, 1797, in Marcus et al., *The Documentary History of the Supreme Court of the
       United States, 1789–1800*, 3:152.

265   "I could not depend upon converting them": George Washington to Henry
       Lee, September 8, 1797, in *The Writings of George Washington from the Original
       Manuscript Sources, 1745–1799*, vol. 36, *August 1797–October 1798*, ed. John C.
       Fitzpatrick (U.S. Government Printing Office, 1941), 29.

265   "I want them exceedingly": James Wilson to Bird Wilson, September 6,
       1797, Marcus et al., *The Documentary History of the Supreme Court of the United
       States, 1789–1800*, 3:223.

265   to avoid recapture and imprisonment: Marcus et al., *The Documentary History
       of the Supreme Court of the United States, 1789–1800*, 3:238.

265   to reorganize his finances: Marcus et al., *The Documentary History of the Su-
       preme Court of the United States, 1789–1800*, 3:225, 227.

265   "my most sanguine hopes": James Wilson to Joseph Thomas, December 17,
       1797, in Marcus et al., *The Documentary History of the Supreme Court of the
       United States, 1789–1800*, 3:231–32.

265   "Without funds much must be lost": James Wilson to Joseph Thomas, De-
       cember 17, 1797, in Marcus et al., *The Documentary History of the Supreme
       Court of the United States, 1789–1800*, 3:231–32.

266   "bring with you all the Money": James Wilson to Bird Wilson, December
       17, 1797, in Marcus et al., *The Documentary History of the Supreme Court of the
       United States, 1789–1800*, 3:230–31.

266   Bird had sent no word: James Wilson to Bird Wilson, January 17, 1798, in
       Konkle, "The Life and Writings of James Wilson," 2:520.

266   she broke down in sobs: James Iredell to Hannah Iredell, February 5 and
       8, 1798, in Marcus et al., *The Documentary History of the Supreme Court of the
       United States, 1789–1800*, 3:242; John Rutledge Jr. to Edward Rutledge, Feb-
       ruary 25, 1798, in Marcus et al., *The Documentary History of the Supreme Court
       of the United States, 1789–1800*, 1(2):858–59.

266   They set out by carriage: Marcus et al., *The Documentary History of the Supreme
       Court of the United States, 1789–1800*, 1(2):858.

266   as long as Wilson put up his property: Thomas Blount to John Gray Blount,
       February 16, 1798, in Marcus et al., *The Documentary History of the Supreme
       Court of the United States, 1789–1800*, 3:242.

266   "Let him go to gaol": Thomas Blount to John Gray Blount, February 26,
       1798, in Marcus et al., *The Documentary History of the Supreme Court of the
       United States, 1789–1800*, 3:243n6.

267   "the debt finally lost": Jacob Blount to John Gray Blount, March 8, 1798, in
       Marcus et al., *The Documentary History of the Supreme Court of the United States,
       1789–1800*, 3:243n4.

267 **a writ of debt was issued:** Marcus et al., *The Documentary History of the Supreme Court of the United States, 1789–1800*, 3:255n2.

267 **it would force him to remain:** Marcus et al., *The Documentary History of the Supreme Court of the United States, 1789–1800*, 3:254.

267 **"I have been hunted":** James Wilson to Joseph Thomas, May 12, 1798, in Marcus et al., *The Documentary History of the Supreme Court of the United States, 1789–1800*, 3:265–67.

267 **"let the law have its operation":** Pierce Butler to William Slade, May 24, 1798, in Marcus et al., *The Documentary History of the Supreme Court of the United States, 1789–1800*, 3:267n3.

267 **until the matter was resolved:** Pierce Butler to Samuel Wallis, June 14, 1798, in Marcus et al., *The Documentary History of the Supreme Court of the United States, 1789–1800*, 3:276–77n3.

268 **"he never wishes to hear mentioned":** Hannah Wilson to Bird Wilson, June 23, 1798, in Marcus et al., *The Documentary History of the Supreme Court of the United States, 1789–1800*, 3:279.

268 **convicted or impeached:** Samuel Johnston to James Iredell, July 28, 1798, in Marcus et al., *The Documentary History of the Supreme Court of the United States, 1789–1800*, 1(2):859.

268 **"nothing worse than I expect":** Hannah Wilson to Bird Wilson, July 28, 1798, in Marcus et al., *The Documentary History of the Supreme Court of the United States, 1789–1800*, 3:281.

268 **what concerned him more:** James Wilson to Bird Wilson, August 4, 1798, in Marcus et al., *The Documentary History of the Supreme Court of the United States, 1789–1800*, 3:282.

268 **the last of the Wilsons' money:** James Iredell to Hannah Iredell, August 6, 1798, in Marcus et al., *The Documentary History of the Supreme Court of the United States, 1789–1800*, 3:283.

268 **"a bad air & dirty narrow streets":** William Cushing to Charles Cushing, August 15, 1798, in Marcus et al., *The Documentary History of the Supreme Court of the United States, 1789–1800*, 1(2):860.

269 **in a delirious haze:** James Iredell to Sarah Gray, August 25, 1798, in Marcus et al., *The Documentary History of the Supreme Court of the United States, 1789–1800*, 1(2):861.

269 **"is by no means well":** Thomas Iredell to James Iredell, August 17, 1798, in Marcus et al., *The Documentary History of the Supreme Court of the United States, 1789–1800*, 1(2):860.

269 **Wilson drew his last breath:** James Iredell to William Cushing, October 28, 1798, in Marcus et al., *The Documentary History of the Supreme Court of the United States, 1789–1800*, 3:301.

269 **White managed to get word:** Marcus et al., *The Documentary History of the Supreme Court of the United States, 1789–1800*, 3:288n1.

269 **"I never knew of his arrest":** Hannah Wilson to Bird Wilson, September 1, 1798, in Marcus et al., *The Documentary History of the Supreme Court of the United States, 1789–1800*, 3:288–89.

270 **which amounted to another $42:** James Iredell to Bird Wilson, September 1, 1798, in Marcus et al., *The Documentary History of the Supreme Court of the United States, 1789–1800*, 3:287.

270   "in a very private manner": *Russell's Gazette* (Boston), September 10, 1798. ("At Edenton, on the 22d ult. the Honorable JAMES WILLSON, one of the Associate Judges of the Federal Court of the United States . . .")

270   "there is an end to his troubles": Robert Morris to John Nicholson, letter from debtors' prison in Philadelphia, September 12, 1798.

270   "I feel a degree of satisfaction": Marcus et al., *The Documentary History of the Supreme Court of the United States, 1789–1800*, 3:277n3.

270   "I only regret that Judge Wilson": Marcus et al., *The Documentary History of the Supreme Court of the United States, 1789–1800*, 3:300.

270   she accompanied him: Marcus et al., *The Documentary History of the Supreme Court of the United States, 1789–1800*, 3:288n3.

270   "his land fever is cured": Maxey, *Treason on Trial in Revolutionary Pennsylvania*, 131; Robert Morris to John Nicholson, October 17, 1798, quoted in Maxey, "A Cunning Man's Legacy," 435; Meginness, *History of Lycoming County, Pennsylvania*, 73.

271   a pile of books on farming: Smith, *James Wilson*, 390.

271   his father's dear friend: Bronson, *A Memorial of the Rev. Bird Wilson . . .* , 43–44, 48–50.

271   More than half a century after: Wilkinson, "Land Policy and Speculation in Pennsylvania, 1779–1800," 320.

271   flooded the valley around Wilsonville: Peter Becker, "Local History: Sonar Traces 'Town Under the Lake,'" *Tri-County Independent*, July 19, 2012, https://www.tricountyindependent.com/story/lifestyle/2012/07/19/local-history-sonar-traces-town/63635832007/.

Epilogue

272   a field in Edenton: Maxey, "The Translation of James Wilson," 36.

272   "a slightly sandy color": Maxey, "The Translation of James Wilson," 37.

272   "hustled offstage": Collier and Collier, *Decision in Philadelphia*, 288.

273   He would be reinterred: *Pennsylvania Gazette*, April 19, 1786; Maxey, "The Translation of James Wilson," 33–34.

273   uncomplicated honoring of the founders: Maxey, "The Translation of James Wilson," 32.

273   Konkle got seasick: Maxey, "The Translation of James Wilson," 37–38.

273   "corruptionist and bribe-giver": *The Independent* (New York), December 16, 1906.

273   The casket was then carried aloft: *An Historical Catalogue of the St. Andrew's Society of Philadelphia, with Biographical Sketches of Deceased Members, 1749–1907* (Loughead, 1907), 66.

274   "the most democratic among the fathers": Maxey, "The Translation of James Wilson," 39.

274   Wilson now lies: At least he made it to his new resting place in one piece. Thomas Paine's remains were exhumed from a grave at his farm, but his bones were later misplaced; if they are still intact, they may be in the possession of multiple people scattered across continents. See Robert Strauss, "Rehabilitating Thomas Paine, Bit by Bony Bit," *New York Times*, March 30, 2001, https://www.nytimes.com/2001/03/30/nyregion/rehabilitating-thomas-paine-bit-by-bony-bit.html.

275   contorted into a scowl: Pedersen, "The Lost Founder," 290–91.

275   never mentioned his name in public: Pedersen, "The Lost Founder," 297.

275   Wilson's name appeared: Pedersen, "The Lost Founder," 301n207.

275   they quoted liberally from Wilson's speech: Pedersen, "The Lost Founder," 292–95.

275   In 1901, *The New York Times*: Pedersen, "The Lost Founder," 302–3n223.

276   "the spirit of your great Pennsylvanian": Theodore Roosevelt, *Address at the New State Capitol Building at Harrisburg, Pennsylvania*, Theodore Roosevelt Collection, MS Am 1454.50 (151a), Houghton Library, Harvard College Library.

276   the only president in American history: Pedersen, "The Lost Founder," 306.

276   The only one he failed to publish: Konkle, "The Life and Writings of James Wilson."

276   the first full-length Wilson biography: Smith, *James Wilson*.

277   the most important of the founders: McCloskey in Wilson, *The Works of James Wilson*, ed. McCloskey; Wood, *The Creation of the American Republic, 1776–1787*.

277   "I'm different from you, John": Stone, *1776*.

277   a coterie of dedicated scholars: Notably, William Ewald at the University of Pennsylvania, Akhil Reed Amar at Yale University, Jonathan Gienapp at Stanford University, John Mikhail and William Treanor at Georgetown University, and Martin Clagett, a researcher and historian who has devoted considerable time and effort to digging up the details of Wilson's early years and education in Scotland.

277   He was right: For this analysis, I am indebted to the superb work of Nick Pedersen, especially pages 332–36.

278   the stronger case is for worse: Gienapp, *Against Constitutional Originalism*, 1–16.

279   warping and diminishing the conversation: McCloskey in Wilson, *The Works of James Wilson*, ed. McCloskey, 47–48.

279   "more full and matured view": Dahl, *How Democratic Is the American Constitution?*, 34–35.

279   "the vital principle": Dahl, *How Democratic Is the American Constitution?*, 37.

279   a set of amendments: Thomas Jefferson to "Henry Tompkinson" (Samuel Kercheval), July 12, 1816, Founders Online, National Archives, https://founders.archives.gov/documents/Jefferson/03-10-02-0128-0002. Original source: *The Papers of Thomas Jefferson*, Retirement Series, vol. 10, *May 1816 to 18 January 1817*, ed. J. Jefferson Looney (Princeton University Press, 2013), 222–28.

280   "a group of people": J. D. Vance, "Address Accepting the Vice Presidential Nomination at the Republican National Convention in Milwaukee, Wisconsin," The American Presidency Project / University of California, Santa Barbara, July 17, 2024, https://www.presidency.ucsb.edu/documents/address-accepting -the-vice-presidential-nomination-the-republican-national-convention-2.

280   an "electric cord": Abraham Lincoln, "Speech at Chicago, Illinois," debate, July 10, 1858. From Teaching American History, https://teachingamerican history.org/document/speech-at-chicago-illinois/.

Selected Bibliography

Alexander, John K. "The Fort Wilson Incident of 1779: A Case Study of the Revolutionary Crowd." *William and Mary Quarterly* 31, no. 4 (October 1974): 589–612.

Alexander, Lucien Hugh. "James Wilson, Nation Builder." *Green Bag* 19 (1907): 65–79.

Alexander, Lucien Hugh. "James Wilson, Patriot, and the Wilson Doctrine." *North American Review* 183, no. 603 (1906): 971–89.

Allen, Danielle. *Our Declaration: A Reading of the Declaration of Independence in Defense of Equality*. Liveright, 2014.

Allen, Danielle, and Emily Sneff. "Golden Letters: James Wilson, the Declaration of Independence, and the Sussex Declaration." *Georgetown Journal of Law and Public Policy* 17 (2019): 193–230.

Amar, Akhil Reed. *America's Constitution: A Biography*. Random House, 2005.

Amar, Akhil Reed. "The Consent of the Governed: Constitutional Amendment Outside Article V." *Columbia Law Review* 94, no. 2 (March 1994): 457–508.

Amar, Akhil Reed. *The Words That Made Us: America's Constitutional Conversation, 1760–1840*. Basic Books, 2021.

Ashcraft, Richard, and M. M. Goldsmith. "Locke, Revolution Principles, and the Formation of Whig Ideology." *Historical Journal* 26, no. 4 (1983): 773–800.

Bailey, Mark Warren. "Early Legal Education in the United States: Natural Law Theory and Law as a Moral Science." *Journal of Legal Education* 48, no. 3 (1998): 311–28.

Bailyn, Bernard. *The Ideological Origins of the American Revolution*. 50th anniversary ed. Belknap Press of Harvard University Press, 2017.

Bailyn, Bernard. *The Ordeal of Thomas Hutchinson*. Belknap Press of Harvard University Press, 1974.

Bailyn, Bernard. *To Begin the World Anew: The Genius and Ambiguities of the American Founders*. Alfred A. Knopf, 2003.

Bailyn, Bernard. *Voyagers to the West: A Passage in the Peopling of America on the Eve of the Revolution*. Alfred A. Knopf, 1986.

Balkin, Jack M. "Race and the Cycles of Constitutional Time." *Missouri Law Review* 86 (2021): 443–82.

Barber, M. A. "The History of Malaria in the United States." *Public Health Reports* 44, no. 43 (1929): 2575–87.

Beeman, Richard. *Our Lives, Our Fortunes, and Our Sacred Honor: The Forging of American Independence, 1774–1776*. Basic Books, 2013.

Beeman, Richard. *Plain, Honest Men: The Making of the American Constitution*. Random House, 2009.

Beitzinger, Alfonz. "The Philosophy of Law of Four American Founding Fathers." *American Journal of Jurisprudence* 21 (1976): 1–19.

Berkhofer, Robert F., Jr. "Americans Versus Indians: The Northwest Ordinance, Territory Making, and Native Americans." *Indiana Magazine of History* 84, no. 1 (1988): 90–108.

Bezanson, Anne. "Inflation and Controls, Pennsylvania, 1774–1779." *Journal of Economic History* 8, suppl. *The Tasks of Economic History* (1948): 15–28.

Bilder, Mary Sarah. *Madison's Hand: Revising the Constitutional Convention*. Harvard University Press, 2015.

Blaakman, Michael. *Speculation Nation: Land Mania in the Revolutionary American Republic*. University of Pennsylvania Press, 2023.

Bowen, Catherine Drinker. *Miracle at Philadelphia: The Story of the Constitutional Convention, May to September 1787*. Atlantic Monthly Press, 1966.

Bronson, W. White. *A Memorial of the Rev. Bird Wilson, Late Emeritus Professor of Systematic Divinity in the General Theological Seminary of the Protestant Episcopal Church in the United States of America*. J. B. Lippincott, 1864.

Brookhiser, Richard. *Gentleman Revolutionary: Gouverneur Morris, the Rake Who Wrote the Constitution*. Free Press, 2003.

Brown, Angus Harwood. "The Pennsylvania Council of Censors and the Debate on the Guardian of the Constitution in the Early United States." *American Journal of Legal History* 64 (2024): 1–26.

Brunhouse, Robert L. *The Counter-Revolution in Pennsylvania, 1776–1790*. Pennsylvania Historical Commission, 1942.

Burton, David H. "Theodore Roosevelt's Harrisburg Speech, a Progressive Appeal to James Wilson." *Pennsylvania Magazine of History and Biography* 93, no. 4 (1969): 527–42.

Calabresi, Steven G., and Saikrishna B. Prakash. "The President's Power to Execute the Laws." *Yale Law Journal* 104, no. 3 (1994): 541–665.

Carson, Hampton L. *An Historical Sketch of the Law Department of the University of Pennsylvania*. University of Pennsylvania, 1882.

Carson, Hampton L. "James Wilson and James Iredell: A Parallel and a Contrast." *Pennsylvania Magazine of History and Biography* 45, no. 1 (1921): 1–33.

Casto, William R. *The Supreme Court in the Early Republic: The Chief Justiceships of John Jay and Oliver Ellsworth*. University of South Carolina Press, 1995.

Chinard, Gilbert. *Thomas Jefferson: The Apostle of Americanism*. Little, Brown, 1929.

Clagett, Martin. "James Wilson Before America." Unpublished manuscript, 2008.

Clagett, Martin. "James Wilson—His Scottish Background: Corrections and Additions." *Pennsylvania History: A Journal of Mid-Atlantic Studies* 79, no. 2 (2012): 154–76.

Coby, John Patrick. "The Proportional Representation Debate at the Constitutional Convention: Why the Nationalists Lost." *Government: Faculty Publications*, Smith College, Northampton, MA (2018): 216–42.

Collier, James Lincoln, and Christopher Collier. *Decision in Philadelphia: The Constitutional Convention of 1787.* Ballantine Books, 1986.

Commager, Henry Steele, and Richard B. Morris, eds. *The Spirit of '76: The Story of the American Revolution as Told by Its Participants.* Harper and Row, 1958.

Conrad, Stephen A. "James Wilson's 'Assimilation of the Common-Law Mind.'" *Northwestern University Law Review* 84 (1989): 186–219.

Conrad, Stephen A. "Metaphor and Imagination in James Wilson's Theory of Federal Union." *Law and Social Inquiry* 13 (1988): 1–70.

Conrad, Stephen A. "Polite Foundation: Citizenship and Common Sense in James Wilson's Republican Theory." *Supreme Court Review* 1984 (1984): 359–86.

Conrad, Stephen A. "The Rhetorical Constitution of 'Civil Society' at the Founding: One Lawyer's Anxious Vision." *Indiana Law Journal* 72 (1997): 335–73.

Cornell, Saul. "Aristocracy Assailed: The Ideology of Backcountry Anti-Federalism." *Journal of American History* 76, no. 4 (March 1990): 1148–47.

Cornell, Saul. "The People's Constitution vs. the Lawyer's Constitution: Popular Constitutionalism and the Original Debate over Originalism." *Yale Journal of Law and the Humanities* 23 (2011): 295–337.

Crary, Catherine Snell. "The Tory and the Spy: The Double Life of James Rivington." *William and Mary Quarterly* 16, no. 1 (1959): 61–72.

Currie, David P. *The Constitution in the Supreme Court: The First Hundred Years, 1789–1888.* University of Chicago Press, 1985.

Dahl, Robert A. *How Democratic Is the American Constitution?* 2nd ed. Yale University Press, 2003.

Dennison, George M. "The 'Revolution Principle': Ideology and Constitutionalism in the Thought of James Wilson." *Review of Politics* 39, no. 2 (1977): 157–91.

Devine, T. M. *The Scottish Clearances: A History of the Dispossessed, 1600–1900.* Allen Lane, 2018.

DiClerico, Robert E. "James Wilson's Presidency." *Presidential Studies Quarterly* 17, no. 2 (1987): 301–17.

Diestelow, Kevin. "The Fort Wilson Riot and Pennsylvania's Republican Formation." *Journal of the American Revolution*, February 28, 2019. https://allthingsliberty.com/2019/02/the-fort-wilson-riot-and-pennsylvanias-republican-formation/.

Diestelow, Kevin. "The Republic of Happiness: James Wilson, Political Thought, and the American Revolution." Undergraduate honors thesis, College of William and Mary, 2021.

Ewald, William. "The Committee of Detail." *Constitutional Commentary* 28 (2012): 197–285.

Ewald, William. "James Wilson and the American Founding." *Georgetown Journal of Law and Public Policy* 17, no. 1 (2019): 1–21.

Ewald, William. "James Wilson and the Drafting of the Constitution." *University of Pennsylvania Journal of Constitutional Law* 10, no. 5 (2008): 901–1009.

Ewald, William. "James Wilson and the Scottish Enlightenment." *University of Pennsylvania Journal of Constitutional Law* 12, no. 4 (2010): 1053–114.

Ewald, William, and Lorianne Updike Toler. "Early Drafts of the U.S. Constitution." *Pennsylvania Magazine of History and Biography* 135, no. 3 (2011): 227–59.

Farrand, Max. *The Framing of the Constitution of the United States.* Yale University Press, 1913.

Farrand, Max, ed. *The Records of the Federal Convention of 1787.* 4 vols. Yale University Press, 1911.

Feldman, Noah. *The Three Lives of James Madison: Genius, Partisan, President.* Random House, 2017.

Finkelman, Paul. "The Founders and Slavery: Little Ventured, Little Gained." *Yale Journal of Law and the Humanities* 13 (2001): 413–49.

Fischer, David Hackett. *Albion's Seed: Four British Folkways in America.* Oxford University Press, 1989.

Foner, Eric. *Tom Paine and Revolutionary America.* Oxford University Press, 1976.

Foster, Joseph S. "The Politics of Ideology: The Pennsylvania Constitutional Convention of 1789–90." *Pennsylvania History: A Journal of Mid-Atlantic Studies* 59, no. 2 (1992): 122–43.

Frantz, John B., and William Pencak, eds. *Beyond Philadelphia: The American Revolution in the Pennsylvania Hinterland.* Pennsylvania State University Press, 1998.

Fried, Stephen. *Rush: Revolution, Madness, and the Visionary Doctor Who Became a Founding Father.* Crown, 2018.

Friedenberg, Daniel M. "James Wilson, a Morality Tale." In *Life, Liberty, and the Pursuit of Land: The Plunder of Early America.* Prometheus Books, 1992.

Fritz, Christian G. "Alternative Visions of American Constitutionalism: Popular Sovereignty and the Early American Constitutional Debate." *Hastings Constitutional Law Quarterly* 24 (1997): 287–357.

Gienapp, Jonathan. *Against Constitutional Originalism: A Historical Critique.* Yale University Press, 2024.

Gilberg, Benjamin, "Wilsonian Doctrine and Separation of Powers: A Comparative Reflection of the Ratification Debate." *University of Pennsylvania Journal of Constitutional Law* 23 (2021): 691–712.

Glick, Joshua. "On the Road: The Supreme Court and the History of Circuit Riding." *Cardozo Law Review* 24 (2003): 1753–844.

Goebel, Julius, Jr. *History of the Supreme Court of the United States.* Vol. 1: *Antecedents and Beginnings to 1801.* Macmillan, 1971.

Goodall, Katherine I. "The Burroughs Wreck: A Key to Eighteenth Century Ship Construction Techniques and the Life and Death of the Port of Edenton." Thesis, East Carolina University, 2003.

Graham, Henry Grey. *The Social Life of Scotland in the Eighteenth Century.* A. & C. Black, 1901. (Original work published 1871.)

Hall, Mark David. "James Wilson: Democratic Theorist and Supreme Court Justice." In *Seriatim: The Supreme Court Before John Marshall,* edited by Scott Douglas Gerber. New York University Press, 1998.

Hall, Mark David. "James Wilson's Law Lectures." *Pennsylvania Magazine of History and Biography* 128, no. 1 (2004): 63–76.

Hall, Mark David. *The Political and Legal Philosophy of James Wilson, 1742–1798.* University of Missouri Press, 1997.

Handley, James E. *Scottish Farming in the Eighteenth Century.* Faber and Faber, 1953.

Harlan, John Marshall. "James Wilson and the Formation of the Constitution." *American Law Review* 34 (1900): 544–55.

Hedges, William L. "Telling Off the King: Jefferson's 'Summary View' as American Fantasy." *Early American Literature* 22, no. 2 (1987): 166–74.

Herman, Arthur. *How the Scots Invented the Modern World: The True Story of How Western Europe's Poorest Nation Created Our World and Everything in It.* Crown, 2001.

Heyburn, Jack. "Gouverneur Morris and James Wilson at the Constitutional Convention." *University of Pennsylvania Journal of Constitutional Law* 20 (2017): 169–97.

Hills, Roderick M., Jr. "The Reconciliation of Law and Liberty in James Wilson." *Harvard Journal of Law and Public Policy* 12 (1989): 889–940.

Holton, Woody. *Unruly Americans and the Origins of the Constitution.* Hill and Wang, 2007.

Howe, Daniel Walker. "Why the Scottish Enlightenment Was Useful to the Framers of the American Constitution." *Comparative Studies in Society and History* 31, no. 3 (1989): 572–87.

Hume, David. *A Treatise of Human Nature.* Edited by L. A. Selby-Bigge. 2nd ed. rev. by P. H. Nidditch. Clarendon Press, 1978.

Innes, George. *Historical Notes and Reminiscences of Cupar.* Fife Herald Office, 1874.

Jackson, John W. *With the British in Philadelphia: Being the Diary of Lieutenant John Enys, 1777–1778.* Old Philadelphia Society, 1979.

Jacobs, Harriet. *Incidents in the Life of a Slave Girl.* Dover Publications, 2001. (Original work published 1861.)

Jensen, Merrill, John P. Kaminski, Gaspare J. Saladino, Richard Leffler, Charles H. Schoenleber, and Margaret A. Hogan, eds. *The Documentary History of the Ratification of the Constitution.* 34 vols. to date. Madison: State Historical Society of Wisconsin, 1976–.

Jezierski, John V. "Parliament or People: James Wilson and Blackstone on the Nature and Location of Sovereignty." *Journal of the History of Ideas* 32, no. 1 (January–March 1971): 95–106.

Journals of the Continental Congress, 1774–1789. Worthington Chauncey Ford et al., eds. 34 vols. Government Printing Office, 1904–37.

Kades, Eric. "The Dark Side of Efficiency: Johnson v. M'Intosh and the Expropriation of Amerindian Lands." *University of Pennsylvania Law Review* 148 (2000): 1065–190.

Kaminski, John P. *Secrecy and the Constitutional Convention.* Center for the Study of the American Constitution, University of Wisconsin–Madison, 2005.

Klarman, Michael J. *The Framers' Coup: The Making of the United States Constitution.* Oxford University Press, 2016.

Klingelsmith, M. C. "James Wilson and the So-Called Yazoo Frauds." *University of Pennsylvania Law Review* 56, no. 1 (1908): 1–27.

Knapp, Aaron T. "Law's Revolutionary: James Wilson and the Birth of American Jurisprudence." *Journal of Law and Politics* 29 (2013): 189–307.

Konkle, Burton Alva. "The Life and Writings of James Wilson, 1742–1798." 2 vols. Unpublished manuscript.

Larson, Carlton F. W. "The Revolutionary American Jury: A Case Study of the 1778–1779 Philadelphia Treason Trials." *SMU Law Review* 61 (2008): 1441–524.

Larson, Carlton F. W. *The Trials of Allegiance: Treason, Juries, and the American Revolution.* Oxford University Press, 2019.

Larson, Edward J., and Michael P. Winship. *The Constitutional Convention: A Narrative History from the Notes of James Madison.* Modern Library, 2005.

Leavelle, Arnaud B. "James Wilson and the Relation of the Scottish Metaphysics to American Political Thought." *Political Science Quarterly* 57, no. 3 (1942): 394–410.

Lerner, Ralph. "The Supreme Court as Republican Schoolmaster." *Supreme Court Review* (1967): 127–80.

Letters of Delegates to Congress, 1774–1789. Paul H. Smith et al., eds. 26 vols. Library of Congress, 1976–2000.

Letters of Members of the Continental Congress. Edmund C. Burnett, ed. 8 vols. Carnegie Institution of Washington, 1921–36.

Lewis, Jan. "'Of Every Age Sex and Condition': The Representation of Women in the Constitution." *Journal of the Early Republic* 15, no. 3 (1995): 359–87.

Lutz, Donald S. "The Relative Influence of European Writers on Late Eighteenth-Century American Political Thought." *American Political Science Review* 78, no. 1 (1984): 189–97.

Magliocca, Gerard N. *Washington's Heir: The Life of Justice Bushrod Washington.* University Press of Kansas, 2022.

Maier, Pauline. *American Scripture: Making the Declaration of Independence.* Alfred A. Knopf, 1997.

Maier, Pauline. *Ratification: The People Debate the Constitution, 1787–1788.* Simon and Schuster, 2010.

Mann, Bruce H. *Republic of Debtors: Bankruptcy in the Age of American Independence.* Harvard University Press, 2002.

Marcus, Maeva. "Wilson as a Justice." *Georgetown Journal of Law and Public Policy* 17, no. 1 (2019): 147–66.

Marcus, Maeva, James R. Perry, Charles F. Hobson, Richard Labunski, and Herbert A. Johnson, eds. *The Documentary History of the Supreme Court of the United States, 1789–1800.* 8 vols. Columbia University Press, 1985–2007.

Marcus, Maeva, and Natalie Wexler. "Suits Against States: The Evolution of Sovereign Immunity." *Journal of Supreme Court History* 18 (1993): 73–102.

Martin, Paula. *Cupar: A History.* Birlinn, 2006.

Mathis, Doyle. "Chisholm v. Georgia: Background and Settlement." *Journal of American History* 54, no. 1 (June 1967): 19–29.

Maxey, David W. "A Cunning Man's Legacy: The Papers of Samuel Wallis (1736–1798)." *Pennsylvania Magazine of History and Biography* 136, no. 4 (October 2012): 435–56.

Maxey, David W. "Of Castles in Stockport and Other Strictures: Samuel Preston's Contentious Agency for Henry Drinker." *Pennsylvania Magazine of History and Biography* 110, no. 3 (1986): 413–46.

Maxey, David W. "The Translation of James Wilson." *Pennsylvania Magazine of History and Biography* 114, no. 1 (1990): 3–38.

Maxey, David W. "Treason on Trial in Revolutionary Pennsylvania: The Case of John Roberts." *Transactions of the American Philosophical Society* 101, pt. 2 (2011).

McCarthy, Daniel J. "James Wilson and the Creation of the Presidency." *Presidential Studies Quarterly* 17, no. 4 (1987): 689–96.

McConnell, Michael W. "James Wilson's Contributions to the Construction of Article II." *Georgetown Journal of Law and Public Policy* 17 (2019): 23–50.

Meginness, John F. *History of Lycoming County, Pennsylvania.* Brown, Runk, 1892.

Mikhail, John. "James Wilson, Early American Land Companies, and the Original Meaning of Ex Post Facto Law." *Georgetown Journal of Law and Public Policy* 17 (2019): 79–146.

Mikhail, John. "The Necessary and Proper Clauses." *Georgetown Law Journal* 102, no. 4 (April 2014): 1045–132.

Mikhail, John. "The Original Federalist Theory of Implied Powers." *Harvard Journal of Law and Public Policy* 46, no. 1 (2023): 57–68.

Miller, Robert J. "American Indian Influence on the United States Constitution and Its Framers." *American Indian Law Review* 18, no. 1 (1993): 133–60.

Miller, William Lee. *The Business of May Next: James Madison and the Founding.* University of Virginia Press, 1992.

Monea, Nino C. "A Constitutional History of Debtors' Prisons." *Drexel Law Review* 14 (2022): 1–67.

Morgan, Edmund S., and Helen M. Morgan. *The Stamp Act Crisis: Prologue to Revolution.* University of North Carolina Press, 1953.

Nedelsky, Jennifer. *Private Property and the Limits of American Constitutionalism: The Madisonian Framework and Its Legacy.* University of Chicago Press, 1990.

Nelson, Eric. "James Wilson and the Ancient Constitution." *Georgetown Journal of Law and Public Policy* 17 (Winter 2019): 167–92.

Nelson, Eric. *The Royalist Revolution: Monarchy and the American Founding.* Belknap Press of Harvard University Press, 2014.

Nix, Robert N. C., Jr., and Mary M. Schweitzer. "Pennsylvania's Contributions to the Writing and the Ratification of the Constitution." *Pennsylvania Magazine of History and Biography* 112, no. 1 (1988): 3–24.

Parramore, Thomas C. *Cradle of the Colony: The History of Chowan County and Edenton, North Carolina.* Edenton Chamber of Commerce, 1967.

Pedersen, Nicholas. "The Lost Founder: James Wilson in American Memory." *Georgetown Law Journal* 98, no. 1 (2009): 293–352.

Peters, David Harrison. "James Wilson's Reidian Democratic Political Theory: One Founder's Contributions to the US Constitution." PhD diss., University of Glasgow, 2022.

Plant, Marjorie. *The Domestic Life of Scotland in the Eighteenth Century.* Edinburgh University Press, 1952.

Powell, J. H. *Bring Out Your Dead: The Great Plague of Yellow Fever in Philadelphia in 1793.* University of Pennsylvania Press, 1949.

Rakove, Jack N. "The Great Compromise: Ideas, Interests, and the Politics of Constitution Making." *William and Mary Quarterly* 44, no. 3 (1987): 424–57.

Rakove, Jack N. *Original Meanings: Politics and Ideas in the Making of the Constitution.* Alfred A. Knopf, 1996.

Rappleye, Charles. *Robert Morris: Financier of the American Revolution.* Simon and Schuster, 2010.

Rapport, Leonard. "Printing the Constitution: The Convention and Newspaper Imprints, August–November 1787." *Prologue: The Journal of the National Archives* 2, no. 2 (1970): 69–89.

Rasmussen, Dennis C. *Fears of a Setting Sun: The Disillusionment of America's Founders.* Princeton University Press, 2021.

Reed, William B. *Life and Correspondence of Joseph Reed.* Vol. 2. Lindsay and Blakiston, 1847.

Reid, Thomas. *Essays on the Intellectual Powers of Man* (1785). In *The Works of Thomas Reid,* edited by Sir William Hamilton, 8th ed., vol. 1. MacLachlan and Stewart, 1895.

Reid, Thomas. *An Inquiry into the Human Mind on the Principles of Common Sense.* Andrew Millar; Alexander Kincaid and J. Bell, 1764.

Reid, Thomas. *Systems of Morals, in Essays on the Active Powers of Man.* 1788; repr. Edinburgh University Press, 1997.

Richards, Leonard L. *The Slave Power: The Free North and Southern Domination, 1780–1860.* Louisiana State University Press, 2000.

Robertson, Ritchie. *The Enlightenment: The Pursuit of Happiness, 1680–1790.* Harper, 2021.

Rosswurm, Steven. *Arms, Country, and Class: The Philadelphia Militia and the "Lower Sort" During the American Revolution.* Rutgers University Press, 1987.

Ryerson, Richard Alan. *The Revolution Is Now Begun: The Radical Committees of Philadelphia, 1765–1776.* University of Pennsylvania Press, 1978.

Schlesinger, Arthur M. *Prelude to Independence: The Newspaper War on Britain, 1764–1776.* Alfred A. Knopf, 1958.

Schoepf, Johann David. *Travels in the Confederation 1783–1784.* Trans. Alfred J. Morrison. William J. Campbell, 1911.

Schwartz, David S., and John Mikhail. "The Other Madison Problem." *Fordham Law Review* 89, no. 5 (2021): 2033–83.

Selsam, J. Paul. *The Pennsylvania Constitution of 1776: A Study in Revolutionary Democracy.* University of Pennsylvania Press, 1936.

Shaw, John Stuart. *The Political History of Eighteenth-Century Scotland.* St. Martin's Press, 1999.

Simpson, Eve Blantyre. *Folk Lore in Lowland Scotland.* William Blackwood and Sons, 1908.

Smith, Adam. *The Theory of Moral Sentiments.* Andrew Millar; Alexander Kincaid and J. Bell, 1759.

Smith, Billy G. *The "Lower Sort": Philadelphia's Laboring People, 1750–1800.* Cornell University Press, 1990.

Smith, Charles Page. *James Wilson: Founding Father, 1742–1798.* University of North Carolina Press, 1956.

Stimson, Shannon C. "A Jury of the Country: Common Sense Philosophy and the Jurisprudence of James Wilson." In J. Smitten and R. Sher, eds. *Scotland and America in the Age of Enlightenment.* Edinburgh University Press, 1990.

Stone, Peter. *1776: A Musical Play.* Viking Press, 1970.

Tarbuck, Derya. "Sociability and Newtonianism in Scotland." *Academia Letters,* Article 802 (2021). https://doi.org/10.20935/AL802.

Taylor, Alan. *American Colonies: The Settling of North America.* Rev. ed. Penguin Books, 2016.

Thomson, Charles. "Early Days of the Revolution in Philadelphia." *Pennsylvania Magazine of History and Biography* 2, no. 4 (1878): 411–23.

Treanor, William M. "The Case of the Dishonest Scrivener: Gouverneur Morris and the Creation of the Federalist Constitution." *Michigan Law Review* 120 (2021): 1–124.

Van Cleve, George William. *A Slaveholders' Union: Slavery, Politics, and the Constitution in the Early American Republic.* University of Chicago Press, 2010.

Velásquez, Eduardo. "Rethinking America's Modernity: Natural Law, Natural Rights and the Character of James Wilson's Liberal Republicanism." *Polity* 29, no. 2 (1996): 193–220.

Waldstreicher, David. *Slavery's Constitution: From Revolution to Ratification.* Hill and Wang, 2009.

Waln, Robert, Jr. "James Wilson." In John Sanderson and Robert Waln Jr., eds. *Biography of the Signers to the Declaration of Independence.* Vol. 6. R. W. Pomeroy, 1823.

Warren, Charles. "The First Decade of the Supreme Court of the United States." *University of Chicago Law Review* 7, no. 4 (1940): 631–54.

Warren, Charles. *The Making of the Constitution.* Little, Brown, 1928.

Watson, Alan D. *Society in Colonial North Carolina.* North Carolina Department of Cultural Resources, Division of Archives and History, 1989.

Welch, John W., and James A. Heilpern. "Recovering Our Forgotten Preamble." *Southern California Law Review* 91, no. 6 (2018): 1021–138.

Wexler, Natalie. "The Case for Love." *American Scholar* 75, no. 3 (Summer 2006): 80–92.

Wexler, Natalie. "In the Beginning: The First Three Chief Justices." *University of Pennsylvania Law Review* 154, no. 6 (2006): 1373–419.

Wexler, Natalie. *A More Obedient Wife: A Novel of the Early Supreme Court.* Sourcebooks, 2006.

Wiecek, William W. "The Witch at the Christening: Slavery and the Constitution's Origins." In Leonard W. Levy and Dennis J. Mahoney, eds. *The Framing and Ratification of the Constitution.* Macmillan, 1987.

Wilkinson, Norman B. "Land Policy and Speculation in Pennsylvania, 1779–1800." PhD diss., University of Pennsylvania, 1958.

Williams, Robert F. "The Influences of Pennsylvania's 1776 Constitution on American Constitutionalism During the Founding Decade." *Pennsylvania History* 55, no. 1 (1988): 7–29.

Wills, Garry. *Inventing America: Jefferson's Declaration of Independence.* Doubleday, 1978.

Wills, Garry. *"Negro President": Jefferson and the Slave Power.* Houghton Mifflin, 2003.

Wilmarth, Arthur E., Jr. "Elusive Foundation: John Marshall, James Wilson, and the Problem of Reconciling Popular Sovereignty and Natural Law Jurisprudence in the New Federal Republic." *George Washington Law Review* 72, no. 1–2 (2003): 113–96.

Wilson, James. *The Collected Works of James Wilson.* Ed. Kermit L. Hall and Mark David Hall. 2 vols. Liberty Fund, 2007.

Wilson, James. *The Works of James Wilson.* Ed. Robert McCloskey. 2 vols. Belknap Press of Harvard University Press, 1967.

Wilson, Janet. "The Bank of North America and Pennsylvania Politics: 1781–1787." *Pennsylvania Magazine of History and Biography* 66, no. 1 (1942): 3–28.

Witt, John Fabian. *Patriots and Cosmopolitans: Hidden Histories of American Law.* Harvard University Press, 2007.

Wood, Gordon S. *The Creation of the American Republic, 1776–1787.* University of North Carolina Press, 1969.

Wood, Gordon S. *The Idea of America: Reflections on the Birth of the United States.* Penguin Press, 2011.

Wood, Gordon S. *The Radicalism of the American Revolution.* Alfred A. Knopf, 1992.

Yoo, Christopher S. "James Wilson as the Architect of the American Presidency." *Georgetown Journal of Law and Public Policy* 17 (2019): 51–77.

Young, Alfred F., Gary B. Nash, and Ray Raphael, eds. *Revolutionary Founders: Rebels, Radicals, and Reformers in the Making of the Nation.* Alfred A. Knopf, 2011.

Zink, James R. "James Wilson v. the Bill of Rights: Progress, Popular Sovereignty and the Idea of the U.S. Constitution." *Political Research Quarterly* 67, no. 2 (June 2014): 253–65.

Zink, James R., and Michelle Schwarze. "James Wilson's Science of Politics and the Moral Psychology of American Constitutionalism." *American Political Thought* 7, no. 4 (2018): 588–613.

Index

abolitionists, 177–78, 187, 275

Act of Free and General Pardon and Indemnity (Pennsylvania, 1779), 96

Adams, Abigail, 59, 65, 70, 177, 252

Adams, Charles, 229

Adams, John, 8, 59, 62, 65–67, 70–71, 75–77, 79, 87, 93–94, 97, 153, 164–66, 177, 187, 218–19, 229, 230, 243, 252, 270

Adams, John Quincy, 229, 257–58

Adams, Samuel, 62, 74–75

Adams, Thomas, 257

Addison, Joseph, 36

Address to the King (1775), 99

Affordable Care Act (2010), 13

Alabama, 255

Alison, Francis, 37, 76

Allen, Danielle, 72

"all men are created equal," 47, 59, 70–73, 166, 181, 227

Amar, Akhil Reed, 71, 169

amendments, 104, 194

American colonies, 27, 34, 46–54
Parliament's authority over, 36–37, 46–49, 56, 61, 64

American Philosophical Society, 37, 99

American Revolution, 10, 48, 65, 101

Anglican Church, 25

Annan, Robert (cousin), 19–20, 30, 33, 42

Annapolis petition for Constitutional Convention, 107–8, 110

Anti-Federalists, 190, 193–94, 196, 199–215, 240, 241, 251

anti-slavery movement, 73, 185

anti-speculator laws, 259

Appalachian mountains, 42

Article I, 187

Article III, 240

Articles of Association (1774), 57–58

Articles of Confederation (1781–89), 72, 80, 97, 102–7, 110, 112, 116–18, 129–30, 147–49, 155, 167, 171, 179, 198, 203, 246, 253, 255

Bache, Sarah, 90

Balfour, John (brother-in-law), 32, 41

Bank of North America, 72, 100–102, 109, 119, 147, 259

Banneker, Benjamin, 73

Bedford, Gunning, 135–36

Benton, Thomas Hart, 163

Bible, 19–20

bicameral vs. unicameral legislatures, 83

Bill of Rights, 150, 171, 190, 193, 196–97, 203, 205–6, 226, 243

Bingham, William, 100

Bird, Mark (brother-in-law), 39, 100

Bird, William, 38–39

About the Author

Jesse Wegman is a senior fellow at the Brennan Center for Justice, where he writes about Supreme Court reform and constitutional amendments. From 2013 to 2025, he was a member of the *New York Times* editorial board, covering law and politics, the Supreme Court, democracy, and electoral reforms. His first book, *Let the People Pick the President: The Case for Abolishing the Electoral College*, was published in 2020.

Founded in 2017, Celadon Books, a division of Macmillan
Publishers, publishes a highly curated list of twenty to
twenty-five new titles a year. The list of both fiction
and nonfiction is eclectic and focuses on publishing
commercial and literary books and discovering
and nurturing talent.